KV-191-022

CONTENTS

Foreword

Terrorism – in whatever form – is the ultimate foe of justice and human rights. It is a violation of the most fundamental principles of humanity, a defiance of the moral codes of all cultures and a sin in the eyes of all world religions. Terrorism is an attack on democracy, human rights and the rule of law – the values which the Council of Europe was set up to protect.

The aftermath of 11 September 2001 did not mark the beginning of the Council of Europe's involvement in international action against terrorism. Some of our key legal instruments – such as the 1977 European Convention on the Suppression of Terrorism – have been in force for decades. However, faced by the rapidly and dramatically changing character and level of the terrorist threat in recent years, the Council of Europe has responded by reviewing its existing anti-terrorist measures and by reinforcing them with new instruments and activities.

This publication contains relevant legal and political texts adopted by the Council of Europe, including the recently revised version of the 1977 European Convention on the Suppression of Terrorism; the two new Council of Europe conventions: the 2005 Council of Europe Convention on the Prevention of Terrorism and the 2005 Council of Europe Convention on Laundering, Search, Seizure and Confiscation of the Proceeds from Crime and on the Financing of Terrorism; and the 2005 Guidelines on the Protection of victims of terrorist acts. It should serve as a helpful reference for all governmental agencies, international institutions, non-governmental organisations, political parties, media or individuals, who are professionally involved or interested in the effort against terrorism.

The added value of the Council of Europe's contribution to the international fight against terrorism is its focus on human rights. The underlying message is that in the fight against terrorism the respect for the most fundamental values of our societies is not only possible, but necessary. Our best chance for a lasting victory against the terrorist threat is to stand firm in the defence of the very values which terrorists seek to destroy.

Terry DAVIS
Secretary General of the
Council of Europe

European Conventions

Consolidated text of the
European Convention on the Suppression of Terrorism (ETS No. 90)
as amended by its Protocol (ETS No. 190)

The member States of the Council of Europe, signatory hereto,

Considering that the aim of the Council of Europe is to achieve a greater unity between its members;

Aware of the growing concern caused by the increase in acts of terrorism;

Wishing to take effective measures to ensure that the perpetrators of such acts do not escape prosecution and punishment;

Convinced that extradition is a particularly effective measure for achieving this result,

Have agreed as follows:

Article 1

1   For the purposes of extradition between Contracting States, none of the following offences shall be regarded as a political offence or as an offence connected with a political offence or as an offence inspired by political motives:

a   an offence within the scope of the Convention for the Suppression of Unlawful Seizure of Aircraft, signed at The Hague on 16 December 1970;

b   an offence within the scope of the Convention for the Suppression of Unlawful Acts Against the Safety of Civil Aviation, concluded at Montreal on 23 September 1971;

c   an offence within the scope of the Convention on the Prevention and Punishment of Crimes Against Internationally Protected Persons, Including Diplomatic Agents, adopted at New York on 14 December 1973;

d   an offence within the scope of the International Convention Against the Taking of Hostages, adopted at New York on 17 December 1979;

e   an offence within the scope of the Convention on the Physical Protection of Nuclear Material, adopted at Vienna on 3 March 1980;

f	an offence within the scope of the Protocol for the Suppression of Unlawful Acts of Violence at Airports Serving International Civil Aviation, done at Montreal on 24 February 1988;

g	an offence within the scope of the Convention for the Suppression of Unlawful Acts Against the Safety of Maritime Navigation, done at Rome on 10 March 1988;

h	an offence within the scope of the Protocol for the Suppression of Unlawful Acts Against the Safety of Fixed Platforms Located on the Continental Shelf, done at Rome on 10 March 1988;

i	an offence within the scope of the International Convention for the Suppression of Terrorist Bombings, adopted at New York on 15 December 1997;

j	an offence within the scope of the International Convention for the Suppression of the Financing of Terrorism, adopted at New York on 9 December 1999.

2	In so far as they are not covered by the conventions listed under paragraph 1, the same shall apply, for the purpose of extradition between Contracting States, not only to the commission of those principal offences as a perpetrator but also to:

a	the attempt to commit any of these principal offences;

b	the participation as an accomplice in the perpetration of any of these principal offences or in an attempt to commit any of them;

c	organising the perpetration of, or directing others to commit or attempt to commit, any of these principal offences.

Article 2

1	For the purpose of extradition between Contracting States, a Contracting State may decide not to regard as a political offence or as an offence connected with a political offence or as an offence inspired by political motives a serious offence involving an act of violence, other than one covered by Article 1, against the life, physical integrity or liberty of a person.

2	The same shall apply to a serious offence involving an act against property, other than one covered by Article 1, if the act created a collective danger for persons.

3	The same shall apply to:

a	the attempt to commit any of the foregoing offences;

b the participation as an accomplice in any of the foregoing offences or in an attempt to commit any such offence;

c organising the perpetration of, or directing others to commit or attempt to commit, any of the foregoing offences.

Article 3

The provisions of all extradition treaties and arrangements applicable between Contracting States, including the European Convention on Extradition, are modified as between Contracting States to the extent that they are incompatible with this Convention.

Article 4

1 For the purpose of this Convention and to the extent that any offence mentioned in Article 1 or 2 is not listed as an extraditable offence in any extradition convention or treaty existing between Contracting States, it shall be deemed to be included as such therein. Contracting States undertake to consider such offences as extraditable offences in every extradition treaty subsequently concluded between them.

2 When a Contracting State which makes extradition conditional on the existence of a treaty receives a request for extradition from another Contracting State with which it has no extradition treaty, the requested Contracting State may, at its discretion, consider this Convention as a legal basis for extradition in relation to any of the offences mentioned in Articles 1 or 2.

Article 5

1 Nothing in this Convention shall be interpreted as imposing an obligation to extradite if the requested State has substantial grounds for believing that the request for extradition for an offence mentioned in Article 1 or 2 has been made for the purpose of prosecuting or punishing a person on account of his race, religion, nationality or political opinion, or that that person's position may be prejudiced for any of these reasons.

2 Nothing in this Convention shall be interpreted as imposing an obligation to extradite if the person subject of the extradition request risks being exposed to torture.

3 Nothing in this Convention shall be interpreted either as imposing an obligation to extradite if the person subject of the extradition request risks being exposed to the death penalty or, where the law of the requested State does not allow for life imprisonment, to life imprisonment without the possibility of parole, unless under applicable

extradition treaties the requested State is under the obligation to extradite if the requesting State gives such assurance as the requested State considers sufficient that the death penalty will not be imposed or, where imposed, will not be carried out, or that the person concerned will not be subject to life imprisonment without the possibility of parole.

Article 6

1   Each Contracting State shall take such measures as may be necessary to establish its jurisdiction over an offence mentioned in Article 1 in the case where the suspected offender is present in its territory and it does not extradite him after receiving a request for extradition from a Contracting State whose jurisdiction is based on a rule of jurisdiction existing equally in the law of the requested State.

2   This Convention does not exclude any criminal jurisdiction exercised in accordance with national law.

Article 7

A Contracting State in whose territory a person suspected to have committed an offence mentioned in Article 1 is found and which has received a request for extradition under the conditions mentioned in Article 6, paragraph 1, shall, if it does not extradite that person, submit the case, without exception whatsoever and without undue delay, to its competent authorities for the purpose of prosecution. Those authorities shall take their decision in the same manner as in the case of any offence of a serious nature under the law of that State.

Article 8

1   Contracting States shall afford one another the widest measure of mutual assistance in criminal matters in connection with proceedings brought in respect of the offences mentioned in Article 1 or 2. The law of the requested State concerning mutual assistance in criminal matters shall apply in all cases. Nevertheless this assistance may not be refused on the sole ground that it concerns a political offence or an offence connected with a political offence or an offence inspired by political motives.

2   Nothing in this Convention shall be interpreted as imposing an obligation to afford mutual assistance if the requested State has substantial grounds for believing that the request for mutual assistance in respect of an offence mentioned in Article 1 or 2 has been made for the purpose of prosecuting or punishing a person on account of his race, religion, nationality or political opinion or that that person's position may be prejudiced for any of these reasons.

3   The provisions of all treaties and arrangements concerning mutual assistance in criminal matters applicable between Contracting States, including the European Convention on Mutual Assistance in Criminal Matters, are modified as between Contracting States to the extent that they are incompatible with this Convention.

Article 9

The Contracting States may conclude between themselves bilateral or multilateral agreements in order to supplement the provisions of this Convention or to facilitate the application of the principles contained therein.

Article 10

The European Committee on Crime Problems (CDPC) is responsible for following the application of the Convention. The CDPC:

a   shall be kept informed regarding the application of the Convention;

b   shall make proposals with a view to facilitating or improving the application of the Convention;

c   shall make recommendations to the Committee of Ministers concerning the proposals for amendments to the Convention, and shall give its opinion on any proposals for amendments to the Convention submitted by a Contracting State in accordance with Articles 12 and 13;

d   shall, at the request of a Contracting State, express an opinion on any question concerning the application of the Convention;

e   shall do whatever is necessary to facilitate a friendly settlement of any difficulty which may arise out of the execution of the Convention;

f   shall make recommendations to the Committee of Ministers concerning non-member States of the Council of Europe to be invited to accede to the Convention in accordance with Article 14, paragraph 3;

g   shall submit every year to the Committee of Ministers of the Council of Europe a report on the follow-up given to this article in the application of the Convention.

Article 11

1   Any dispute between Contracting States concerning the interpretation or application of this Convention, which has not been settled either in the framework of Article 10.e or by negotiation, shall, at the request of any

Party to the dispute, be referred to arbitration. Each Party shall nominate an arbitrator and the arbitrators shall nominate a referee.

2   In the case of disputes involving Parties which are member States of the Council of Europe, where a Party fails to nominate its arbitrator in pursuance of paragraph 1 of this article within three months following the request for arbitration, an arbitrator shall be nominated by the President of the European Court of Human Rights at the request of the other Party.

3   In the case of disputes involving any Party which is not a member of the Council of Europe, where a Party fails to nominate its arbitrator in pursuance of paragraph 1 of this article within three months following the request for arbitration, an arbitrator shall be nominated by the President of the International Court of Justice at the request of the other Party.

4   In the cases covered by paragraphs 2 and 3 of this article, where the President of the Court concerned is a national of one of the Parties to the dispute, this duty shall be carried out by the Vice-President of the Court, or if the Vice-President is a national of one of the Parties to the dispute, by the most senior judge of the Court who is not a national of one of the Parties to the dispute.

5   The procedures referred to in paragraphs 2 or 3 and 4 above apply, *mutatis mutandis,* where the arbitrators fail to agree on the nomination of a referee in accordance with paragraph 1 of this article.

6   The arbitration tribunal shall lay down its own procedure. Its decisions shall be taken by majority vote. Where a majority cannot be reached, the referee shall have a casting vote. The tribunal's judgment shall be final.

Article 12

1   Amendments to this Convention may be proposed by any Contracting State, or by the Committee of Ministers. Proposals for amendment shall be communicated by the Secretary General of the Council of Europe to the Contracting States.

2   After having consulted the non-member Contracting States and, if necessary, the CDPC, the Committee of Ministers may adopt the amendment in accordance with the majority provided for in Article 20.d of the Statute of the Council of Europe. The Secretary General of the Council of Europe shall submit any amendments adopted to the Contracting States for acceptance.

3   Any amendment adopted in accordance with the above paragraph shall enter into force on the thirtieth day following notification by all the Parties to the Secretary General of their acceptance thereof.

Article 13

1   In order to update the list of treaties in Article 1, paragraph 1, amendments may be proposed by any Contracting State or by the Committee of Ministers. These proposals for amendment shall only concern treaties concluded within the United Nations Organisation dealing specifically with international terrorism and having entered into force. They shall be communicated by the Secretary General of the Council of Europe to the Contracting States.

2   After having consulted the non-member Contracting States and, if necessary the CDPC, the Committee of Ministers may adopt a proposed amendment by the majority provided for in Article 20.d of the Statute of the Council of Europe. The amendment shall enter into force following the expiry of a period of one year after the date on which it has been forwarded to the Contracting States. During this period, any Contracting State may notify the Secretary General of any objection to the entry into force of the amendment in its respect.

3   If one-third of the Contracting States notifies the Secretary General of an objection to the entry into force of the amendment, the amendment shall not enter into force.

4   If less than one-third of the Contracting States notifies an objection, the amendment shall enter into force for those Contracting States which have not notified an objection.

5   Once an amendment has entered into force in accordance with paragraph 2 of this article and a Contracting State has notified an objection to it, this amendment shall come into force in respect of the Contracting State concerned on the first day of the month following the date on which it has notified the Secretary General of the Council of Europe of its acceptance.

Article 14

1   This Convention shall be open to signature by the member States of and Observer States to the Council of Europe. It shall be subject to ratification, acceptance, approval or accession. Instruments of ratification, acceptance, approval or accession shall be deposited with the Secretary General of the Council of Europe.

2   The Convention shall enter into force three months after the date of the deposit of the third instrument of ratification, acceptance or approval.

3   The Committee of Ministers of the Council of Europe, after consulting the CDPC, may invite any State not a member of the Council of Europe, other than those referred to under paragraph 1 of this article, to accede to the Convention. The decision shall be taken by the majority provided

for in Article 20.*d* of the Statute of the Council of Europe and by the unanimous vote of the representatives of the Contracting States entitled to sit on the Committee of Ministers.

4   In respect of a signatory State ratifying, accepting, approving or acceding subsequently, the Convention shall come into force three months after the date of the deposit of its instrument of ratification, acceptance, approval or accession.

Article 15

1   Any State may, at the time of signature or when depositing its instrument of ratification, acceptance, approval or accession, specify the territory or territories to which this Convention shall or shall not apply.

2   Any State may, when depositing its instrument of ratification, acceptance, approval or accession or at any later date, by declaration addressed to the Secretary General of the Council of Europe, extend this Convention to any other territory or territories specified in the declaration and for whose international relations it is responsible or on whose behalf it is authorised to give undertakings.

3   Any declaration made in pursuance of the preceding paragraph may, in respect of any territory mentioned in such declaration, be withdrawn by means of a notification addressed to the Secretary General of the Council of Europe. Such withdrawal shall take effect immediately or at such later date as may be specified in the notification.

Article 16

1   Any State Party to the Convention on 15 May 2003 may, at the time of signature or when depositing its instrument of ratification, acceptance or approval of the Protocol amending the Convention, declare that it reserves the right to refuse extradition in respect of any offence mentioned in Article 1 which it considers to be a political offence, an offence connected with a political offence or an offence inspired by political motives. The Contracting State undertakes to apply this reservation on a case-by-case basis, through a duly reasoned decision and taking into due consideration, when evaluating the character of the offence, any particularly serious aspects of the offence, including:

a   that it created a collective danger to the life, physical integrity or liberty of persons; or

b   that it affected persons foreign to the motives behind it; or

c   that cruel or vicious means have been used in the commission of the offence.

2   When applying paragraph 1 of this article, a Contracting State shall indicate the offences to which its reservation applies.

3   Any Contracting State may wholly or partly withdraw a reservation it has made in accordance with paragraph 1 by means of a declaration addressed to the Secretary General of the Council of Europe which shall become effective as from the date of its receipt.

4   A Contracting State which has made a reservation in accordance with paragraph 1 of this article may not claim the application of Article 1 by any other State; it may, however, if its reservation is partial or conditional, claim the application of that article in so far as it has itself accepted it.

5   The reservations referred to in paragraph 1 of this article shall be valid for a period of three years from the day of the entry into force of this Convention in respect of the State concerned. However, such reservations may be renewed for periods of the same duration.

6   Twelve months before the date of expiry of the reservation, the Secretariat General of the Council of Europe shall give notice of that expiry to the Contracting State concerned. No later than three months before expiry, the Contracting State shall notify the Secretary General of the Council of Europe that it is upholding, amending or withdrawing its reservation. Where a Contracting State notifies the Secretary General of the Council of Europe that it is upholding its reservation, it shall provide an explanation of the grounds justifying its continuance. In the absence of notification by the Contracting State concerned, the Secretary General of the Council of Europe shall inform that Contracting State that its reservation is considered to have been extended automatically for a period of six months. Failure by the Contracting State concerned to notify its intention to uphold or modify its reservation before the expiry of that period shall cause the reservation to lapse.

7   Where a Contracting State does not extradite a person, in application of a reservation made in accordance with paragraph 1 of this article, after receiving a request for extradition from another Contracting State, it shall submit the case, without exception whatsoever and without undue delay, to its competent authorities for the purpose of prosecution, unless the requesting State and the requested State otherwise agree. The competent authorities, for the purpose of prosecution in the requested State, shall take their decision in the same manner as in the case of any offence of a grave nature under the law of that State. The requested State shall communicate, without undue delay, the final outcome of the proceedings to the requesting State and to the Secretary General of the Council of Europe, who shall forward it to the follow-up committee.

8   The decision to refuse the extradition request, on the basis of paragraph 1 of this article, shall be forwarded promptly to the requesting

State. If within a reasonable time no judicial decision on the merits has been taken in the requested State according to paragraph 7, the requesting State may communicate this fact to the Secretary General of the Council of Europe, who shall submit the matter to the Conference provided for in Article 17. This Conference shall consider the matter and issue an opinion on the conformity of the refusal with the Convention and shall submit it to the Committee of Ministers for the purpose of issuing a declaration thereon. When performing its functions under this paragraph, the Committee of Ministers shall meet in its composition restricted to the Contracting States.

Article 17

1   Without prejudice to the application of Article 10, there shall be a Conference of States Parties against Terrorism (hereinafter referred to as the "COSTER") responsible for ensuring:

   a   the effective use and operation of this Convention including the identification of any problems therein, in close contact with the CDPC;

   b   the examination of reservations made in accordance with Article 16 and in particular the procedure provided in Article 16, paragraph 8;

   c   the exchange of information on significant legal and policy developments pertaining to the fight against terrorism;

   d   the examination, at the request of the Committee of Ministers, of measures adopted within the Council of Europe in the field of the fight against terrorism and, where appropriate, the elaboration of proposals for additional measures necessary to improve international co-operation in the area of the fight against terrorism and, where co-operation in criminal matters is concerned, in consultation with the CDPC;

   e   the preparation of opinions in the area of the fight against terrorism and the execution of the terms of reference given by the Committee of Ministers.

2   The COSTER shall be composed of one expert appointed by each of the Contracting States. It will meet once a year on a regular basis, and on an extraordinary basis at the request of the Secretary General of the Council of Europe or of at least one-third of the Contracting States.

3   The COSTER will adopt its own Rules of Procedure. The expenses for the participation of Contracting States which are member States of the Council of Europe shall be borne by the Council of Europe. The Secretariat of the Council of Europe will assist the COSTER in carrying out its functions pursuant to this article.

4   The CDPC shall be kept periodically informed about the work of the COSTER.

Article 18

Any Contracting State may denounce this Convention by means of a written notification addressed to the Secretary General of the Council of Europe. Any such denunciation shall take effect immediately or at such later date as may be specified in the notification.

Article 19

The Secretary General of the Council of Europe shall notify the Contracting States of:

a   any signature;

b   any deposit of an instrument of ratification, acceptance, approval or accession;

c   any date of entry into force of this Convention in accordance with Article 14 thereof;

d   any declaration or notification received in pursuance of the provisions of Article 15;

e   any notification received in pursuance of Article 18 and the date on which denunciation takes effect.

In witness whereof, the undersigned, being duly authorised thereto, have signed this Convention.

Done at Strasbourg, this 27th day of February 1977, in English and in French, both texts being equally authoritative, in a single copy which shall remain deposited in the archives of the Council of Europe. The Secretary General of the Council of Europe shall transmit certified copies to each of the signatory States.

European Convention on Extradition (ETS No. 24)

The governments signatory hereto, being members of the Council of Europe,

Considering that the aim of the Council of Europe is to achieve a greater unity between its members;

Considering that this purpose can be attained by the conclusion of agreements and by common action in legal matters;

Considering that the acceptance of uniform rules with regard to extradition is likely to assist this work of unification,

Have agreed as follows:

Article 1 – Obligation to extradite

The Contracting Parties undertake to surrender to each other, subject to the provisions and conditions laid down in this Convention, all persons against whom the competent authorities of the requesting Party are proceeding for an offence or who are wanted by the said authorities for the carrying out of a sentence or detention order.

Article 2 – Extraditable offences

1   Extradition shall be granted in respect of offences punishable under the laws of the requesting Party and of the requested Party by deprivation of liberty or under a detention order for a maximum period of at least one year or by a more severe penalty. Where a conviction and prison sentence have occurred or a detention order has been made in the territory of the requesting Party, the punishment awarded must have been for a period of at least four months.

2   If the request for extradition includes several separate offences each of which is punishable under the laws of the requesting Party and the requested Party by deprivation of liberty or under a detention order, but of which some do not fulfil the condition with regard to the amount of punishment which may be awarded, the requested Party shall also have the right to grant extradition for the latter offences.

3   Any Contracting Party whose law does not allow extradition for certain of the offences referred to in paragraph 1 of this article may, in so far as it is concerned, exclude such offences from the application of this Convention.

4   Any Contracting Party which wishes to avail itself of the right provided for in paragraph 3 of this article shall, at the time of deposit of its instrument of ratification or accession, transmit to the Secretary General of the

Council of Europe either a list of the offences for which extradition is allowed or a list of those for which it is excluded and shall at the same time indicate the legal provisions which allow or exclude extradition. The Secretary General of the Council shall forward these lists to the other signatories.

5   If extradition is subsequently excluded in respect of other offences by the law of a Contracting Party, that Party shall notify the Secretary General. The Secretary General shall inform the other signatories. Such notification shall not take effect until three months from the date of its receipt by the Secretary General.

6   Any Party which avails itself of the right provided for in paragraphs 4 or 5 of this article may at any time apply this Convention to offences which have been excluded from it. It shall inform the Secretary General of the Council of such changes, and the Secretary General shall inform the other signatories.

7   Any Party may apply reciprocity in respect of any offences excluded from the application of the Convention under this article.

Article 3 – Political offences

1   Extradition shall not be granted if the offence in respect of which it is requested is regarded by the requested Party as a political offence or as an offence connected with a political offence.

2   The same rule shall apply if the requested Party has substantial grounds for believing that a request for extradition for an ordinary criminal offence has been made for the purpose of prosecuting or punishing a person on account of his race, religion, nationality or political opinion, or that that person's position may be prejudiced for any of these reasons.

3   The taking or attempted taking of the life of a Head of State or a member of his family shall not be deemed to be a political offence for the purposes of this Convention.

4   This article shall not affect any obligations which the Contracting Parties may have undertaken or may undertake under any other international convention of a multilateral character.

Article 4 – Military offences

Extradition for offences under military law which are not offences under ordinary criminal law is excluded from the application of this Convention.

Article 5 – Fiscal offences

Extradition shall be granted, in accordance with the provisions of this Convention, for offences in connection with taxes, duties, customs and exchange only if the Contracting Parties have so decided in respect of any such offence or category of offences.

Article 6 – Extradition of nationals

1 a A Contracting Party shall have the right to refuse extradition of its nationals.

   b Each Contracting Party may, by a declaration made at the time of signature or of deposit of its instrument of ratification or accession, define as far as it is concerned the term "nationals" within the meaning of this Convention.

   c Nationality shall be determined as at the time of the decision concerning extradition. If, however, the person claimed is first recognised as a national of the requested Party during the period between the time of the decision and the time contemplated for the surrender, the requested Party may avail itself of the provision contained in sub-paragraph a of this article.

2 If the requested Party does not extradite its national, it shall at the request of the requesting Party submit the case to its competent authorities in order that proceedings may be taken if they are considered appropriate. For this purpose, the files, information and exhibits relating to the offence shall be transmitted without charge by the means provided for in Article 12, paragraph 1. The requesting Party shall be informed of the result of its request.

Article 7 – Place of commission

1 The requested Party may refuse to extradite a person claimed for an offence which is regarded by its law as having been committed in whole or in part in its territory or in a place treated as its territory.

2 When the offence for which extradition is requested has been committed outside the territory of the requesting Party, extradition may only be refused if the law of the requested Party does not allow prosecution for the same category of offence when committed outside the latter Party's territory or does not allow extradition for the offence concerned.

Article 8 – Pending proceedings for the same offences

The requested Party may refuse to extradite the person claimed if the competent authorities of such Party are proceeding against him in respect of the offence or offences for which extradition is requested.

Article 9 – *Non bis in idem*

Extradition shall not be granted if final judgment has been passed by the competent authorities of the requested Party upon the person claimed in respect of the offence or offences for which extradition is requested. Extradition may be refused if the competent authorities of the requested Party have decided either not to institute or to terminate proceedings in respect of the same offence or offences.

Article 10 – Lapse of time

Extradition shall not be granted when the person claimed has, according to the law of either the requesting or the requested Party, become immune by reason of lapse of time from prosecution or punishment.

Article 11 – Capital punishment

If the offence for which extradition is requested is punishable by death under the law of the requesting Party, and if in respect of such offence the death-penalty is not provided for by the law of the requested Party or is not normally carried out, extradition may be refused unless the requesting Party gives such assurance as the requested Party considers sufficient that the death-penalty will not be carried out.

Article 12 – The request and supporting documents

1   The request shall be in writing and shall be communicated through the diplomatic channel. Other means of communication may be arranged by direct agreement between two or more Parties.

2   The request shall be supported by:

   a   the original or an authenticated copy of the conviction and sentence or detention order immediately enforceable or of the warrant of arrest or other order having the same effect and issued in accordance with the procedure laid down in the law of the requesting Party;

   b   a statement of the offences for which extradition is requested. The time and place of their commission, their legal descriptions and a reference to the relevant legal provisions shall be set out as accurately as possible; and

   c   a copy of the relevant enactments or, where this is not possible, a statement of the relevant law and as accurate a description as possible of the person claimed, together with any other information which will help to establish his identity and nationality.

Article 13 – Supplementary information

If the information communicated by the requesting Party is found to be insufficient to allow the requested Party to make a decision in pursuance of this Convention, the latter Party shall request the necessary supplementary information and may fix a time-limit for the receipt thereof.

Article 14 – Rule of speciality

1 A person who has been extradited shall not be proceeded against, sentenced or detained with a view to the carrying out of a sentence or detention order for any offence committed prior to his surrender other than that for which he was extradited, nor shall he be for any other reason restricted in his personal freedom, except in the following cases:

   a   when the Party which surrendered him consents. A request for consent shall be submitted, accompanied by the documents mentioned in Article 12 and a legal record of any statement made by the extradited person in respect of the offence concerned. Consent shall be given when the offence for which it is requested is itself subject to extradition in accordance with the provisions of this Convention;

   b   when that person, having had an opportunity to leave the territory of the Party to which he has been surrendered, has not done so within 45 days of his final discharge, or has returned to that territory after leaving it.

2 The requesting Party may, however, take any measures necessary to remove the person from its territory, or any measures necessary under its law, including proceedings by default, to prevent any legal effects of lapse of time.

3 When the description of the offence charged is altered in the course of proceedings, the extradited person shall only be proceeded against or sentenced in so far as the offence under its new description is shown by its constituent elements to be an offence which would allow extradition.

Article 15 – Re-extradition to a third state

Except as provided for in Article 14, paragraph 1.b, the requesting Party shall not, without the consent of the requested Party, surrender to another Party or to a third State a person surrendered to the requesting Party and sought by the said other Party or third State in respect of offences committed before his surrender. The requested Party may request the production of the documents mentioned in Article 12, paragraph 2.

Article 16 – Provisional arrest

1   In case of urgency the competent authorities of the requesting Party may request the provisional arrest of the person sought. The competent authorities of the requested Party shall decide the matter in accordance with its law.

2   The request for provisional arrest shall state that one of the documents mentioned in Article 12, paragraph 2.a, exists and that it is intended to send a request for extradition. It shall also state for what offence extradition will be requested and when and where such offence was committed and shall so far as possible give a description of the person sought.

3   A request for provisional arrest shall be sent to the competent authorities of the requested Party either through the diplomatic channel or direct by post or telegraph or through the International Criminal Police Organisation (Interpol) or by any other means affording evidence in writing or accepted by the requested Party. The requesting authority shall be informed without delay of the result of its request.

4   Provisional arrest may be terminated if, within a period of 18 days after arrest, the requested Party has not received the request for extradition and the documents mentioned in Article 12. It shall not, in any event, exceed 40 days from the date of such arrest. The possibility of provisional release at any time is not excluded, but the requested Party shall take any measures which it considers necessary to prevent the escape of the person sought.

5   Release shall not prejudice re-arrest and extradition if a request for extradition is received subsequently.

Article 17 – Conflicting requests

If extradition is requested concurrently by more than one State, either for the same offence or for different offences, the requested Party shall make its decision having regard to all the circumstances and especially the relative seriousness and place of commission of the offences, the respective dates of the requests, the nationality of the person claimed and the possibility of subsequent extradition to another State.

Article 18 – Surrender of the person to be extradited

1   The requested Party shall inform the requesting Party by the means mentioned in Article 12, paragraph 1, of its decision with regard to the extradition.

2   Reasons shall be given for any complete or partial rejection.

3   If the request is agreed to, the requesting Party shall be informed of the place and date of surrender and of the length of time for which the person claimed was detained with a view to surrender.

4   Subject to the provisions of paragraph 5 of this article, if the person claimed has not been taken over on the appointed date, he may be released after the expiry of 15 days and shall in any case be released after the expiry of 30 days. The requested Party may refuse to extradite him for the same offence.

5   If circumstances beyond its control prevent a Party from surrendering or taking over the person to be extradited, it shall notify the other Party. The two Parties shall agree a new date for surrender and the provisions of paragraph 4 of this article shall apply.

Article 19 – Postponed or conditional surrender

1   The requested Party may, after making its decision on the request for extradition, postpone the surrender of the person claimed in order that he may be proceeded against by that Party or, if he has already been convicted, in order that he may serve his sentence in the territory of that Party for an offence other than that for which extradition is requested.

2   The requested Party may, instead of postponing surrender, temporarily surrender the person claimed to the requesting Party in accordance with conditions to be determined by mutual agreement between the Parties.

Article 20 – Handing over of property

1   The requested Party shall, in so far as its law permits and at the request of the requesting Party, seize and hand over property:

a   which may be required as evidence, or

b   which has been acquired as a result of the offence and which, at the time of the arrest, is found in the possession of the person claimed or is discovered subsequently.

2   The property mentioned in paragraph 1 of this article shall be handed over even if extradition, having been agreed to, cannot be carried out owing to the death or escape of the person claimed.

3   When the said property is liable to seizure or confiscation in the territory of the requested Party, the latter may, in connection with pending criminal proceedings, temporarily retain it or hand it over on condition that it is returned.

4   Any rights which the requested Party or third parties may have acquired in the said property shall be preserved. Where these rights exist, the

property shall be returned without charge to the requested Party as soon as possible after the trial.

Article 21 – Transit

1   Transit through the territory of one of the Contracting Parties shall be granted on submission of a request by the means mentioned in Article 12, paragraph 1, provided that the offence concerned is not considered by the Party requested to grant transit as an offence of a political or purely military character having regard to Articles 3 and 4 of this Convention.

2   Transit of a national, within the meaning of Article 6, of a country requested to grant transit may be refused.

3   Subject to the provisions of paragraph 4 of this article, it shall be necessary to produce the documents mentioned in Article 12, paragraph 2.

4   If air transport is used, the following provisions shall apply:

   a   when it is not intended to land, the requesting Party shall notify the Party over whose territory the flight is to be made and shall certify that one of the documents mentioned in Article 12, paragraph 2.a exists. In the case of an unscheduled landing, such notification shall have the effect of a request for provisional arrest as provided for in Article 16, and the requesting Party shall submit a formal request for transit;

   b   when it is intended to land, the requesting Party shall submit a formal request for transit.

5   A Party may, however, at the time of signature or of the deposit of its instrument of ratification of, or accession to, this Convention, declare that it will only grant transit of a person on some or all of the conditions on which it grants extradition. In that event, reciprocity may be applied.

6   The transit of the extradited person shall not be carried out through any territory where there is reason to believe that his life or his freedom may be threatened by reason of his race, religion, nationality or political opinion.

Article 22 – Procedure

Except where this Convention otherwise provides, the procedure with regard to extradition and provisional arrest shall be governed solely by the law of the requested Party.

Article 23 – Language to be used

The documents to be produced shall be in the language of the requesting or requested Party. The requested Party may require a translation into one of the official languages of the Council of Europe to be chosen by it.

Article 24 – Expenses

1   Expenses incurred in the territory of the requested Party by reason of extradition shall be borne by that Party.

2   Expenses incurred by reason of transit through the territory of a Party requested to grant transit shall be borne by the requesting Party.

3   In the event of extradition from a non-metropolitan territory of the requested Party, the expenses occasioned by travel between that territory and the metropolitan territory of the requesting Party shall be borne by the latter. The same rule shall apply to expenses occasioned by travel between the non-metropolitan territory of the requested Party and its metropolitan territory.

Article 25 – Definition of "detention order"

For the purposes of this Convention, the expression "detention order" means any order involving deprivation of liberty which has been made by a criminal court in addition to or instead of a prison sentence.

Article 26 – Reservations

1   Any Contracting Party may, when signing this Convention or when depositing its instrument of ratification or accession, make a reservation in respect of any provision or provisions of the Convention.

2   Any Contracting Party which has made a reservation shall withdraw it as soon as circumstances permit. Such withdrawal shall be made by notification to the Secretary General of the Council of Europe.

3   A Contracting Party which has made a reservation in respect of a provision of the Convention may not claim application of the said provision by another Party save in so far as it has itself accepted the provision.

Article 27 – Territorial application

1   This Convention shall apply to the metropolitan territories of the Contracting Parties.

2   In respect of France, it shall also apply to Algeria and to the overseas Departments and, in respect of the United Kingdom of Great Britain and Northern Ireland, to the Channel Islands and to the Isle of Man.

3   The Federal Republic of Germany may extend the application of this Convention to the *Land* of Berlin by notice addressed to the Secretary General of the Council of Europe, who shall notify the other Parties of such declaration.

4   By direct arrangement between two or more Contracting Parties, the application of this Convention may be extended, subject to the conditions laid down in the arrangement, to any territory of such Parties, other than the territories mentioned in paragraphs 1, 2 and 3 of this article, for whose international relations any such Party is responsible.

Article 28 – Relations between this Convention and bilateral Agreements

1   This Convention shall, in respect of those countries to which it applies, supersede the provisions of any bilateral treaties, conventions or agreements governing extradition between any two Contracting Parties.

2   The Contracting Parties may conclude between themselves bilateral or multilateral agreements only in order to supplement the provisions of this Convention or to facilitate the application of the principles contained therein.

3   Where, as between two or more Contracting Parties, extradition takes place on the basis of a uniform law, the Parties shall be free to regulate their mutual relations in respect of extradition exclusively in accordance with such a system notwithstanding the provisions of this Convention. The same principle shall apply as between two or more Contracting Parties each of which has in force a law providing for the execution in its territory of warrants of arrest issued in the territory of the other Party or Parties. Contracting Parties which exclude or may in the future exclude the application of this Convention as between themselves in accordance with this paragraph shall notify the Secretary General of the Council of Europe accordingly. The Secretary General shall inform the other Contracting Parties of any notification received in accordance with this paragraph.

Article 29 – Signature, ratification and entry into force

1   This Convention shall be open to signature by the members of the Council of Europe. It shall be ratified. The instruments of ratification shall be deposited with the Secretary General of the Council.

2   The Convention shall come into force 90 days after the date of deposit of the third instrument of ratification.

3   As regards any signatory ratifying subsequently the Convention shall come into force 90 days after the date of the deposit of its instrument of ratification.

Article 30 – Accession

1   The Committee of Ministers of the Council of Europe may invite any State not a member of the Council to accede to this Convention, provided that the resolution containing such invitation receives the unanimous agreement of the members of the Council who have ratified the Convention.

2   Accession shall be by deposit with the Secretary General of the Council of an instrument of accession, which shall take effect 90 days after the date of its deposit.

Article 31 – Denunciation

Any Contracting Party may denounce this Convention in so far as it is concerned by giving notice to the Secretary General of the Council of Europe. Denunciation shall take effect six months after the date when the Secretary General of the Council received such notification.

Article 32 – Notifications

The Secretary General of the Council of Europe shall notify the members of the Council and the government of any State which has acceded to this Convention of:

a   the deposit of any instrument of ratification or accession;

b   the date of entry into force of this Convention;

c   any declaration made in accordance with the provisions of Article 6, paragraph 1, and of Article 21, paragraph 5;

d   any reservation made in accordance with Article 26, paragraph 1;

e   the withdrawal of any reservation in accordance with Article 26, paragraph 2;

f   any notification of denunciation received in accordance with the provisions of Article 31 and by the date on which such denunciation will take effect.

In witness whereof the undersigned, being duly authorised thereto, have signed this Convention.

Done at Paris, this 13th day of December 1957, in English and French, both texts being equally authentic, in a single copy which shall remain deposited in the archives of the Council of Europe. The Secretary General of the Council of Europe shall transmit certified copies to the signatory governments.

Additional Protocol to the
European Convention on Extradition (ETS No. 86)

The member States of the Council of Europe, signatory to this Protocol,

Having regard to the provisions of the European Convention on Extradition opened for signature in Paris on 13 December 1957 (hereinafter referred to as "the Convention") and in particular Articles 3 and 9 thereof;

Considering that it is desirable to supplement these Articles with a view to strengthening the protection of humanity and of individuals,

Have agreed as follows:

Chapter I

Article 1

For the application of Article 3 of the Convention, political offences shall not be considered to include the following:

a   the crimes against humanity specified in the Convention on the Prevention and Punishment of the Crime of Genocide adopted on 9 December 1948 by the General Assembly of the United Nations;

b   the violations specified in Article 50 of the 1949 Geneva Convention for the Amelioration of the Condition of the Wounded and Sick in Armed Forces in the Field, Article 51 of the 1949 Geneva Convention for the Amelioration of the Condition of Wounded, Sick and Shipwrecked members of Armed Forces at Sea, Article 130 of the 1949 Geneva Convention relative to the Treatment of Prisoners of War and Article 147 of the 1949 Geneva Convention relative to the Protection of Civilian Persons in Time of War;

c   any comparable violations of the laws of war having effect at the time when this Protocol enters into force and of customs of war existing at that time, which are not already provided for in the above-mentioned provisions of the Geneva Conventions.

Chapter II

Article 2

Article 9 of the Convention shall be supplemented by the following text, the original Article 9 of the Convention becoming paragraph 1 and the under-mentioned provisions becoming paragraphs 2, 3 and 4:

"2. The extradition of a person against whom a final judgment has been rendered in a third State, Contracting Party to the Convention, for the offence or offences in respect of which the claim was made, shall not be granted:

a   if the afore-mentioned judgment resulted in his acquittal;

b   if the term of imprisonment or other measure to which he was sentenced:

    i   has been completely enforced;

    ii   has been wholly, or with respect to the part not enforced, the subject of a pardon or an amnesty;

c   if the court convicted the offender without imposing a sanction.

3   However, in the cases referred to in paragraph 2, extradition may be granted:

a   if the offence in respect of which judgment has been rendered was committed against a person, an institution or any thing having public status in the requesting State;

b   if the person on whom judgment was passed had himself a public status in the requesting State;

c   if the offence in respect of which judgment was passed was committed completely or partly in the territory of the requesting State or in a place treated as its territory.

4   The provisions of paragraphs 2 and 3 shall not prevent the application of wider domestic provisions relating to the effect of *ne bis in idem* attached to foreign criminal judgments."

Chapter III

Article 3

1   This Protocol shall be open to signature by the member States of the Council of Europe which have signed the Convention. It shall be subject to ratification, acceptance or approval. Instruments of ratification, acceptance or approval shall be deposited with the Secretary General of the Council of Europe.

2   The Protocol shall enter into force 90 days after the date of the deposit of the third instrument of ratification, acceptance or approval.

3   In respect of a signatory State ratifying, accepting or approving subsequently, the Protocol shall enter into force 90 days after the date of the deposit of its instrument of ratification, acceptance or approval.

4   A member State of the Council of Europe may not ratify, accept or approve this Protocol without having, simultaneously or previously, ratified the Convention.

Article 4

1   Any State which has acceded to the Convention may accede to this Protocol after the Protocol has entered into force.

2   Such accession shall be effected by depositing with the Secretary General of the Council of Europe an instrument of accession which shall take effect 90 days after the date of its deposit.

Article 5

1   Any State may, at the time of signature or when depositing its instrument of ratification, acceptance, approval or accession, specify the territory or territories to which this Protocol shall apply.

2   Any State may, when depositing its instrument of ratification, acceptance, approval or accession or at any later date, by declaration addressed to the Secretary General of the Council of Europe, extend this Protocol to any other territory or territories specified in the declaration and for whose international relations it is responsible or on whose behalf it is authorised to give undertakings.

3   Any declaration made in pursuance of the preceding paragraph may, in respect of any territory mentioned in such declaration, be withdrawn according to the procedure laid down in Article 8 of this Protocol.

Article 6

1   Any State may, at the time of signature or when depositing its instrument of ratification, acceptance, approval or accession, declare that it does not accept one or the other of Chapters I or II.

2   Any Contracting Party may withdraw a declaration it has made in accordance with the foregoing paragraph by means of a declaration addressed to the Secretary General of the Council of Europe which shall become effective as from the date of its receipt.

3   No reservation may be made to the provisions of this Protocol.

Article 7

The European Committee on Crime Problems of the Council of Europe shall be kept informed regarding the application of this Protocol and shall do whatever is needful to facilitate a friendly settlement of any difficulty which may arise out of its execution.

Article 8

1   Any Contracting Party may, in so far as it is concerned, denounce this Protocol by means of a notification addressed to the Secretary General of the Council of Europe.

2   Such denunciation shall take effect six months after the date of receipt by the Secretary General of such notification.

3   Denunciation of the Convention entails automatically denunciation of this Protocol.

Article 9

The Secretary General of the Council of Europe shall notify the member States of the Council and any State which has acceded to the Convention of:

a   any signature;

b   any deposit of an instrument of ratification, acceptance, approval or accession;

c   any date of entry into force of this Protocol in accordance with Article 3 thereof;

d   any declaration received in pursuance of the provisions of Article 5 and any withdrawal of such a declaration;

e   any declaration made in pursuance of the provisions of Article 6, paragraph 1;

f   the withdrawal of any declaration carried out in pursuance of the provisions of Article 6, paragraph 2;

g   any notification received in pursuance of the provisions of Article 8 and the date on which denunciation takes effect.

In witness whereof, the undersigned, being duly authorised thereto, have signed this Protocol.

Done at Strasbourg, this 15th day of October 1975, in English and French, both texts being equally authoritative, in a single copy which shall remain deposited in the archives of the Council of Europe. The Secretary General of the Council of Europe shall transmit certified copies to each of the signatory and acceding States.

Second Additional Protocol to the
European Convention on Extradition (ETS No. 98)

The member States of the Council of Europe, signatory to this Protocol,

Desirous of facilitating the application of the European Convention on Extradition opened for signature in Paris on 13 December 1977 (hereinafter referred to as "the Convention") in the field of fiscal offences;

Considering it also desirable to supplement the Convention in certain other respects,

Have agreed as follows:

Chapter I

Article 1

Paragraph 2 of Article 2 of the Convention shall be supplemented by the following provision:

"This right shall also apply to offences which are subject only to pecuniary sanctions."

Chapter II

Article 2

Article 5 of the Convention shall be replaced by the following provisions:

"Fiscal offences

1   For offences in connection with taxes, duties, customs and exchange extradition shall take place between the Contracting Parties in accordance with the provisions of the Convention if the offence, under the law of the requested Party, corresponds to an offence of the same nature.

2   Extradition may not be refused on the ground that the law of the requested Party does not impose the same kind of tax or duty or does not contain a tax, duty, custom or exchange regulation of the same kind as the law of the requesting Party."

Chapter III

Article 3

The Convention shall be supplemented by the following provisions:

"Judgments in absentia

1   When a Contracting Party requests from another Contracting Party the extradition of a person for the purpose of carrying out a sentence or detention order imposed by a decision rendered against him *in absentia*, the requested Party may refuse to extradite for this purpose if, in its opinion, the proceedings leading to the judgment did not satisfy the minimum rights of defence recognised as due to everyone charged with criminal offence. However, extradition shall be granted if the requesting Party gives an assurance considered sufficient to guarantee to the person claimed the right to a retrial which safeguards the rights of defence. This decision will authorise the requesting Party either to enforce the judgment in question if the convicted person does not make an opposition or, if he does, to take proceedings against the person extradited.

2   When the requested Party informs the person whose extradition has been requested of the judgment rendered against him *in absentia*, the requesting Party shall not regard this communication as a formal notification for the purposes of the criminal procedure in that State".

Chapter IV

Article 4

The Convention shall be supplemented by the following provisions:

"Amnesty

Extradition shall not be granted for an offence in respect of which an amnesty has been declared in the requested State and which that State had competence to prosecute under its own criminal law."

Chapter V

Article 5

Paragraph 1 of Article 12 of the Convention shall be replaced by the following provisions:

"The request shall be in writing and shall be addressed by the Ministry of Justice of the requesting Party to the Ministry of Justice of the requested Party; however, use of the diplomatic channel is not excluded. Other means of communication may be arranged by direct agreement between two or more Parties."

Chapter VI

Article 6

1   This Protocol shall be open to signature by the member States of the Council of Europe which have signed the Convention. It shall be subject to ratification, acceptance or approval. Instruments of ratification, acceptance or approval shall be deposited with the Secretary General of the Council of Europe.

2   The Protocol shall enter into force 90 days after the date of the deposit of the third instrument of ratification, acceptance or approval.

3   In respect of a signatory State ratifying, accepting or approving subsequently, the Protocol shall enter into force 90 days after the date of the deposit of its instrument of ratification, acceptance or approval.

4   A member State of the Council of Europe may not ratify, accept or approve this Protocol without having, simultaneously or previously, ratified the Convention.

Article 7

1   Any State which has acceded to the Convention may accede to this Protocol after the Protocol has entered into force.

2   Such accession shall be effected by depositing with the Secretary General of the Council of Europe an instrument of accession which shall take effect 90 days after the date of its deposit.

Article 8

1   Any State may, at the time of signature or when depositing its instrument of ratification, acceptance, approval or accession, specify the territory or territories to which this Protocol shall apply.

2   Any State may, when depositing its instrument of ratification, acceptance, approval or accession or at any later date, by declaration addressed to the Secretary General of the Council of Europe, extend this Protocol to any other territory or territories specified in the declaration and for whose international relations it is responsible or on whose behalf it is authorised to give undertakings.

3   Any declaration made in pursuance of the preceding paragraph may, in respect of any territory mentioned in such declaration, be withdrawn by means of a notification addressed to the Secretary General of the Council of Europe. Such withdrawal shall take effect six months after the date of receipt by the Secretary General of the Council of Europe of the notification.

Article 9

1   Reservations made by a State to a provision of the Convention shall be applicable also to this Protocol, unless that State otherwise declares at the time of signature or when depositing its instrument of ratification, acceptance, approval or accession.

2   Any State may, at the time of signature or when depositing its instrument of ratification, acceptance, approval or accession, declare that it reserves the right:

a   not to accept Chapter I;

b   not to accept Chapter II, or to accept it only in respect of certain offences or certain categories of the offences referred to in Article 2;

c   not to accept Chapter III, or to accept only paragraph 1 of Article 3;

d   not to accept Chapter IV;

e   not to accept Chapter V.

3   Any Contracting Party may withdraw a reservation it has made in accordance with the foregoing paragraph by means of declaration addressed to the Secretary General of the Council of Europe which shall become effective as from the date of its receipt.

4   A Contracting Party which has applied to this Protocol a reservation made in respect of a provision of the Convention or which has made a reservation in respect of a provision of this Protocol may not claim the application of that provision by another Contracting Party; it may, however, if its reservation is partial or conditional claim, the application of that provision in so far as it has itself accepted it.

5   No other reservation may be made to the provisions of this Protocol.

Article 10

The European Committee on Crime Problems of the Council of Europe shall be kept informed regarding the application of this Protocol and shall do whatever is needful to facilitate a friendly settlement of any difficulty which may arise out of its execution.

Article 11

1   Any Contracting Party may, in so far as it is concerned, denounce this Protocol by means of a notification addressed to the Secretary General of the Council of Europe.

2   Such denunciation shall take effect six months after the date of receipt by the Secretary General of such notification.

3   Denunciation of the Convention entails automatically denunciation of this Protocol.

Article 12

The Secretary General of the Council of Europe shall notify the member States of the Council and any State which has acceded to the Convention of:

a   any signature of this Protocol;

b   any deposit of an instrument of ratification, acceptance, approval or accession;

c   any date of entry into force of this Protocol in accordance with Articles 6 and 7;

d   any declaration received in pursuance of the provisions of paragraphs 2 and 3 of Article 8;

e   any declaration received in pursuance of the provisions of paragraph 1 of Article 9;

f   any reservation made in pursuance of the provisions of paragraph 2 of Article 9;

g   the withdrawal of any reservation carried out in pursuance of the provisions of paragraph 3 of Article 9;

h   any notification received in pursuance of the provisions of Article 11 and the date on which denunciation takes effect.

In witness whereof the undersigned, being duly authorised thereto, have signed this Protocol.

Done at Strasbourg, this 17th day of March 1978, in English and in French, both texts being equally authoritative, in a single copy which shall remain deposited in the archives of the Council of Europe. The Secretary General of the Council of Europe shall transmit certified copies to each of the signatory and acceding States.

European Convention on
Mutual Assistance in Criminal Matters (ETS No. 30)

Preamble

The governments signatory hereto, being members of the Council of Europe,

Considering that the aim of the Council of Europe is to achieve greater unity among its members;

Believing that the adoption of common rules in the field of mutual assistance in criminal matters will contribute to the attainment of this aim;

Considering that such mutual assistance is related to the question of extradition, which has already formed the subject of a Convention signed on 13th December 1957,

Have agreed as follows:

Chapter I – General provisions

Article 1

1   The Contracting Parties undertake to afford each other, in accordance with the provisions of this Convention, the widest measure of mutual assistance in proceedings in respect of offences the punishment of which, at the time of the request for assistance, falls within the jurisdiction of the judicial authorities of the requesting Party.

2   This Convention does not apply to arrests, the enforcement of verdicts or offences under military law which are not offences under ordinary criminal law.

Article 2

Assistance may be refused:

a   if the request concerns an offence which the requested Party considers a political offence, an offence connected with a political offence, or a fiscal offence;

b   if the requested Party considers that execution of the request is likely to prejudice the sovereignty, security, *ordre public* or other essential interests of its country.

Chapter II – Letters rogatory

Article 3

1   The requested Party shall execute in the manner provided for by its law any letters rogatory relating to a criminal matter and addressed to it by the judicial authorities of the requesting Party for the purpose of procuring evidence or transmitting articles to be produced in evidence, records or documents.

2   If the requesting Party desires witnesses or experts to give evidence on oath, it shall expressly so request, and the requested Party shall comply with the request if the law of its country does not prohibit it.

3   The requested Party may transmit certified copies or certified photostat copies of records or documents requested, unless the requesting Party expressly requests the transmission of originals, in which case the requested Party shall make every effort to comply with the request.

Article 4

On the express request of the requesting Party the requested Party shall state the date and place of execution of the letters rogatory. Officials and interested persons may be present if the requested Party consents.

Article 5

1   Any Contracting Party may, by a declaration addressed to the Secretary General of the Council of Europe, when signing this Convention or depositing its instrument of ratification or accession, reserve the right to make the execution of letters rogatory for search or seizure of property dependent on one or more of the following conditions:

a   that the offence motivating the letters rogatory is punishable under both the law of the requesting Party and the law of the requested Party;

b   that the offence motivating the letters rogatory is an extraditable offence in the requested country;

c   that execution of the letters rogatory is consistent with the law of the requested Party.

2   Where a Contracting Party makes a declaration in accordance with paragraph 1 of this article, any other Party may apply reciprocity.

Article 6

1   The requested Party may delay the handing over of any property, records or documents requested, if it requires the said property, records or documents in connection with pending criminal proceedings.

2   Any property, as well as original records or documents, handed over in execution of letters rogatory shall be returned by the requesting Party to the requested Party as soon as possible unless the latter Party waives the return thereof.

Chapter III – Service of writs and records of judicial verdicts - Appearance of witnesses, experts and prosecuted persons

Article 7

1   The requested Party shall effect service of writs and records of judicial verdicts which are transmitted to it for this purpose by the requesting Party.

Service may be effected by simple transmission of the writ or record to the person to be served. If the requesting Party expressly so requests, service shall be effected by the requested Party in the manner provided for the service of analogous documents under its own law or in a special manner consistent with such law.

2   Proof of service shall be given by means of a receipt dated and signed by the person served or by means of a declaration made by the requested Party that service has been effected and stating the form and date of such service. One or other of these documents shall be sent immediately to the requesting Party. The requested Party shall, if the requesting Party so requests, state whether service has been effected in accordance with the law of the requested Party. If service cannot be effected, the reasons shall be communicated immediately by the requested Party to the requesting Party.

3   Any Contracting Party may, by a declaration addressed to the Secretary General of the Council of Europe, when signing this Convention or depositing its instrument of ratification or accession, request that service of a summons on an accused person who is in its territory be transmitted to its authorities by a certain time before the date set for appearance. This time shall be specified in the aforesaid declaration and shall not exceed 50 days.

This time shall be taken into account when the date of appearance is being fixed and when the summons is being transmitted.

Article 8

A witness or expert who has failed to answer a summons to appear, service of which has been requested, shall not, even if the summons contains a notice of penalty, be subjected to any punishment or measure of restraint, unless subsequently he voluntarily enters the territory of the requesting Party and is there again duly summoned.

Article 9

The allowances, including subsistence, to be paid and the travelling expenses to be refunded to a witness or expert by the requesting Party shall be calculated as from his place of residence and shall be at rates at least equal to those provided for in the scales and rules in force in the country where the hearing is intended to take place.

Article 10

1   If the requesting Party considers the personal appearance of a witness or expert before its judicial authorities especially necessary, it shall so mention in its request for service of the summons and the requested Party shall invite the witness or expert to appear.

The requested Party shall inform the requesting Party of the reply of the witness or expert.

2   In the case provided for under paragraph 1 of this article the request or the summons shall indicate the approximate allowances payable and the travelling and subsistence expenses refundable.

3   If a specific request is made, the requested Party may grant the witness or expert an advance. The amount of the advance shall be endorsed on the summons and shall be refunded by the requesting Party.

Article 11

1   A person in custody whose personal appearance as a witness or for purposes of confrontation is applied for by the requesting Party shall be temporarily transferred to the territory where the hearing is intended to take place, provided that he shall be sent back within the period stipulated by the requested Party and subject to the provisions of Article 12 in so far as these are applicable.

Transfer may be refused:

a   if the person in custody does not consent,

b   if his presence is necessary at criminal proceedings pending in the territory of the requested Party, c   if transfer is liable to prolong his detention, or

d   if there are other overriding grounds for not transferring him to the territory of the requesting Party.

2   Subject to the provisions of Article 2, in a case coming within the immediately preceding paragraph, transit of the person in custody through the territory of a third State, Party to this Convention, shall be granted on application, accompanied by all necessary documents, addressed by the Ministry of Justice of the requesting Party to the Ministry of Justice of the Party through whose territory transit is requested.

A Contracting Party may refuse to grant transit to its own nationals.

3   The transferred person shall remain in custody in the territory of the requesting Party and, where applicable, in the territory of the Party through which transit is requested, unless the Party from whom transfer is requested applies for his release.

Article 12

1   A witness or expert, whatever his nationality, appearing on a summons before the judicial authorities of the requesting Party shall not be prosecuted or detained or subjected to any other restriction of his personal liberty in the territory of that Party in respect of acts or convictions anterior to his departure from the territory of the requested Party.

2   A person, whatever his nationality, summoned before the judicial authorities of the requesting Party to answer for acts forming the subject of proceedings against him, shall not be prosecuted or detained or subjected to any other restriction of his personal liberty for acts or convictions anterior to his departure from the territory of the requested Party and not specified in the summons.

3   The immunity provided for in this article shall cease when the witness or expert or prosecuted person, having had for a period of fifteen consecutive days from the date when his presence is no longer required by the judicial authorities an opportunity of leaving, has nevertheless remained in the territory, or having left it, has returned.

Chapter IV – Judicial records

Article 13

1   A requested Party shall communicate extracts from and information relating to judicial records, requested from it by the judicial authorities of a

Contracting Party and needed in a criminal matter, to the same extent that these may be made available to its own judicial authorities in like case.

2   In any case other than that provided for in paragraph 1 of this article the request shall be complied with in accordance with the conditions provided for by the law, regulations or practice of the requested Party.

Chapter V – Procedure

Article 14

1   Requests for mutual assistance shall indicate as follows:

a   the authority making the request,

b   the object of and the reason for the request,

c   where possible, the identity and the nationality of the person concerned, and

d   where necessary, the name and address of the person to be served.

2   Letters rogatory referred to in Articles 3, 4 and 5 shall, in addition, state the offence and contain a summary of the facts.

Article 15

1   Letters rogatory referred to in Articles 3, 4 and 5 as well as the applications referred to in Article 11 shall be addressed by the Ministry of Justice of the requesting Party to the Ministry of Justice of the requested Party and shall be returned through the same channels.

2   In case of urgency, letters rogatory may be addressed directly by the judicial authorities of the requesting Party to the judicial authorities of the requested Party. They shall be returned together with the relevant documents through the channels stipulated in paragraph 1 of this article.

3   Requests provided for in paragraph 1 of Article 13 may be addressed directly by the judicial authorities concerned to the appropriate authorities of the requested Party, and the replies may be returned directly by those authorities. Requests provided for in paragraph 2 of Article 13 shall be addressed by the Ministry of Justice of the requesting Party to the Ministry of Justice of the requested Party.

4   Requests for mutual assistance, other than those provided for in paragraphs 1 and 3 of this article and, in particular, requests for investigation preliminary to prosecution, may be communicated directly between the judicial authorities.

5   In cases where direct transmission is permitted under this Convention, it may take place through the International Criminal Police Organisation (Interpol).

6   A Contracting Party may, when signing this Convention or depositing its instrument of ratification or accession, by a declaration addressed to the Secretary General of the Council of Europe, give notice that some or all requests for assistance shall be sent to it through channels other than those provided for in this article, or require that, in a case provided for in paragraph 2 of this article, a copy of the letters rogatory shall be transmitted at the same time to its Ministry of Justice.

7   The provisions of this article are without prejudice to those of bilateral agreements or arrangements in force between Contracting Parties which provide for the direct transmission of requests for assistance between their respective authorities.

Article 16

1   Subject to paragraph 2 of this article, translations of requests and annexed documents shall not be required.

2   Each Contracting Party may, when signing or depositing its instrument of ratification or accession, by means of a declaration addressed to the Secretary General of the Council of Europe, reserve the right to stipulate that requests and annexed documents shall be addressed to it accompanied by a translation into its own language or into either of the official languages of the Council of Europe or into one of the latter languages, specified by it. The other Contracting Parties may apply reciprocity.

3   This article is without prejudice to the provisions concerning the translation of requests or annexed documents contained in the agreements or arrangements in force or to be made between two or more Contracting Parties.

Article 17

Evidence or documents transmitted pursuant to this Convention shall not require any form of authentication.

Article 18

Where the authority which receives a request for mutual assistance has no jurisdiction to comply therewith, it shall, *ex officio*, transmit the request to the competent authority of its country and shall so inform the requesting Party through the direct channels, if the request has been addressed through such channels.

Article 19

Reasons shall be given for any refusal of mutual assistance.

Article 20

Subject to the provisions of Article 10, paragraph 3, execution of requests for mutual assistance shall not entail refunding of expenses except those incurred by the attendance of experts in the territory of the requested Party or the transfer of a person in custody carried out under Article 11.

Chapter VI – Laying of information in connection with proceedings

Article 21

1   Information laid by one Contracting Party with a view to proceedings in the courts of another Party shall be transmitted between the Ministries of Justice concerned unless a Contracting Party avails itself of the option provided for in paragraph 6 of Article 15.

2   The requested Party shall notify the requesting Party of any action taken on such information and shall forward a copy of the record of any verdict pronounced.

3   The provisions of Article 16 shall apply to information laid under paragraph 1 of this article.

Chapter VII – Exchange of information from judicial records

Article 22

Each Contracting Party shall inform any other Party of all criminal convictions and subsequent measures in respect of nationals of the latter Party, entered in the judicial records. Ministries of Justice shall communicate such information to one another at least once a year. Where the person concerned is considered a national of two or more other Contracting Parties, the information shall be given to each of these Parties, unless the person is a national of the Party in the territory of which he was convicted.

Chapter VIII – Final provisions

Article 23

1   Any Contracting Party may, when signing this Convention or when depositing its instrument of ratification or accession, make a reservation in respect of any provision or provisions of the Convention.

2   Any Contracting Party which has made a reservation shall withdraw it as soon as circumstances permit. Such withdrawal shall be made by notification to the Secretary General of the Council of Europe.

3   A Contracting Party which has made a reservation in respect of a provision of the Convention may not claim application of the said provision by another Party save in so far as it has itself accepted the provision.

Article 24

A Contracting Party may, when signing the Convention or depositing its instrument of ratification or accession, by a declaration addressed to the Secretary General of the Council of Europe, define what authorities it will, for the purpose of the Convention, deem judicial authorities.

Article 25

1   This Convention shall apply to the metropolitan territories of the Contracting Parties.

2   In respect of France, it shall also apply to Algeria and to the overseas Departments, and, in respect of Italy, it shall also apply to the territory of Somaliland under Italian administration.

3   The Federal Republic of Germany may extend the application of this Convention to the *Land* of Berlin by notice addressed to the Secretary General of the Council of Europe.

4   In respect of the Kingdom of the Netherlands, the Convention shall apply to its European territory. The Netherlands may extend the application of this Convention to the Netherlands Antilles, Surinam and Netherlands New Guinea by notice addressed to the Secretary General of the Council of Europe.

5   By direct arrangement between two or more Contracting Parties and subject to the conditions laid down in the arrangement, the application of this Convention may be extended to any territory, other than the territories mentioned in paragraphs 1, 2, 3 and 4 of this article, of one of these Parties, for the international relations of which any such Party is responsible.

Article 26

1   Subject to the provisions of Article 15, paragraph 7, and Article 16, paragraph 3, this Convention shall, in respect of those countries to which it applies, supersede the provisions of any treaties, conventions or bilateral agreements governing mutual assistance in criminal matters between any two Contracting Parties.

2   This Convention shall not affect obligations incurred under the terms of any other bilateral or multilateral international convention which contains or may contain clauses governing specific aspects of mutual assistance in a given field.

3   The Contracting Parties may conclude between themselves bilateral or multilateral agreements on mutual assistance in criminal matters only in order to supplement the provisions of this Convention or to facilitate the application of the principles contained therein.

4   Where, as between two or more Contracting Parties, mutual assistance in criminal matters is practised on the basis of uniform legislation or of a special system providing for the reciprocal application in their respective territories of measures of mutual assistance, these Parties shall, notwithstanding the provisions of this Convention, be free to regulate their mutual relations in this field exclusively in accordance with such legislation or system. Contracting Parties which, in accordance with this paragraph, exclude as between themselves the application of this Convention shall notify the Secretary General of the Council of Europe accordingly.

Article 27

1   This Convention shall be open to signature by the members of the Council of Europe. It shall be ratified. The instruments of ratification shall be deposited with the Secretary General of the Council.

2   The Convention shall come into force 90 days after the date of deposit of the third instrument of ratification.

3   As regards any signatory ratifying subsequently the Convention shall come into force 90 days after the date of the deposit of its instrument of ratification.

Article 28

1   The Committee of Ministers of the Council of Europe may invite any State not a member of the Council to accede to this Convention, provided that the resolution containing such invitation obtains the unanimous agreement of the members of the Council who have ratified the Convention.

2   Accession shall be by deposit with the Secretary General of the Council of an instrument of accession which shall take effect 90 days after the date of its deposit.

Article 29

Any Contracting Party may denounce this Convention in so far as it is concerned by giving notice to the Secretary General of the Council of Europe. Denunciation shall take effect six months after the date when the Secretary General of the Council received such notification.

Article 30

The Secretary General of the Council of Europe shall notify the members of the Council and the government of any State which has acceded to this Convention of:

a   the names of the signatories and the deposit of any instrument of ratification or accession;

b   the date of entry into force of this Convention;

c   any notification received in accordance with the provisions of Article 5 – paragraph 1, Article 7 – paragraph 3, Article 15 – paragraph 6, Article 16 – paragraph 2, Article 24, Article 25 – paragraphs 3 and 4, Article 26 – paragraph 4;

d   any reservation made in accordance with Article 23, paragraph 1;

e   the withdrawal of any reservation in accordance with Article 23, paragraph 2;

f   any notification of denunciation received in accordance with the provisions of Article 29 and the date on which such denunciation will take effect.

In witness whereof the undersigned, being duly authorised thereto, have signed this Convention.

Done at Strasbourg, this 20th day of April 1959, in English and French, both texts being equally authoritative, in a single copy which shall remain deposited in the archives of the Council of Europe. The Secretary General of the Council of Europe shall transmit certified copies to the signatory and acceding governments.

Additional Protocol to the European Convention on Mutual Assistance in Criminal Matters (ETS No. 99)

The member States of the Council of Europe, signatory to this Protocol,

Desirous of facilitating the application of the European Convention on Mutual Assistance in Criminal Matters opened for signature in Strasbourg on 20th April 1959 (hereinafter referred to as "the Convention") in the field of fiscal offences;

Considering it also desirable to supplement the Convention in certain other respects,

Have agreed as follows:

Chapter I

Article 1

The Contracting Parties shall not exercise the right provided for in Article 2.a of the Convention to refuse assistance solely on the ground that the request concerns an offence which the requested Party considers a fiscal offence.

Article 2

1   In the case where a Contracting Party has made the execution of letters rogatory for search or seizure of property dependent on the condition that the offence motivating the letters rogatory is punishable under both the law of the requesting Party and the law of the requested Party, this condition shall be fulfilled, as regards fiscal offences, if the offence is punishable under the law of the requesting Party and corresponds to an offence of the same nature under the law of the requested Party.

2   The request may not be refused on the ground that the law of the requested Party does not impose the same kind of tax or duty or does not contain a tax, duty, customs and exchange regulation of the same kind as the law of the requesting Party.

Chapter II

Article 3

The Convention shall also apply to:

a   the service of documents concerning the enforcement of a sentence, the recovery of a fine or the payment of costs of proceedings;

b   measures relating to the suspension of pronouncement of a sentence or of its enforcement, to conditional release, to deferment of the commencement of the enforcement of a sentence or to the interruption of such enforcement.

Chapter III

Article 4

Article 22 of the Convention shall be supplemented by the following text, the original Article 22 of the Convention becoming paragraph 1 and the below-mentioned provisions becoming paragraph 2:

"2   Furthermore, any Contracting Party which has supplied the above-mentioned information shall communicate to the Party concerned, on the latter's request in individual cases, a copy of the convictions and measures in question as well as any other information relevant thereto in order to enable it to consider whether they necessitate any measures at national level. This communication shall take place between the Ministries of Justice concerned."

Chapter IV

Article 5

1   This Protocol shall be open to signature by the member States of the Council of Europe which have signed the Convention. It shall be subject to ratification, acceptance or approval. Instruments of ratification, acceptance or approval shall be deposited with the Secretary General of the Council of Europe.

2   The Protocol shall enter into force 90 days after the date of the deposit of the third instrument of ratification, acceptance or approval.

3   In respect of a signatory State ratifying, accepting or approving subsequently, the Protocol shall enter into force 90 days after the date of the deposit of its instrument of ratification, acceptance or approval.

4   A member State of the Council of Europe may not ratify, accept or approve this Protocol without having, simultaneously or previously, ratified the Convention.

Article 6

1   Any State which has acceded to the Convention may accede to this Protocol after the Protocol has entered into force.

2   Such accession shall be effected by depositing with the Secretary General of the Council of Europe an instrument of accession which shall take effect 90 days after the date of its deposit.

Article 7

1   Any State may, at the time of signature or when depositing its instrument of ratification, acceptance, approval or accession, specify the territory or territories to which this Protocol shall apply.

2   Any State may, when depositing its instrument of ratification, acceptance, approval or accession or at any later date, by declaration addressed to the Secretary General of the Council of Europe, extend this Protocol to any other territory or territories specified in the declaration and for whose international relations it is responsible or on whose behalf it is authorised to give undertakings.

3   Any declaration made in pursuance of the preceding paragraph may, in respect of any territory mentioned in such declaration, be withdrawn by means of a notification addressed to the Secretary General of the Council of Europe. Such withdrawal shall take effect six months after the date of receipt by the Secretary General of the Council of Europe of the notification.

Article 8

1   Reservations made by a Contracting Party to a provision of the Convention shall be applicable also to this Protocol, unless that Party otherwise declares at the time of signature or when depositing its instrument of ratification, acceptance, approval or accession. The same shall apply to the declarations made by virtue of Article 24 of the Convention.

2   Any State may, at the time of signature or when depositing its instrument of ratification, acceptance, approval or accession, declare that it reserves the right:

   a   not to accept Chapter I, or to accept it only in respect of certain offences or certain categories of the offences referred to in Article I, or not to comply with letters rogatory for search or seizure of property in respect of fiscal offences;

   b   not to accept Chapter II;

   c   not to accept Chapter III.

3   Any Contracting Party may withdraw a declaration it has made in accordance with the foregoing paragraph by means of a declaration

addressed to the Secretary General of the Council of Europe which shall become effective as from the date of its receipt.

4   A Contracting Party which has applied to this Protocol a reservation made in respect of a provision of the Convention or which has made a reservation in respect of a provision of this Protocol may not claim the application of that provision by another Contracting Party; it may, however, if its reservation is partial or conditional claim the application of that provision in so far as it has itself accepted it.

5   No other reservation may be made to the provisions of this Protocol.

Article 9

The provisions of this Protocol are without prejudice to more extensive regulations in bilateral or multilateral agreements concluded between Contracting Parties in application of Article 26, paragraph 3, of the Convention.

Article 10

The European Committee on Crime Problems of the Council of Europe shall be kept informed regarding the application of this Protocol and shall do whatever is needful to facilitate a friendly settlement of any difficulty which may arise out of its execution.

Article 11

1   Any Contracting Party may, in so far as it is concerned, denounce this Protocol by means of a notification addressed to the Secretary General of the Council of Europe.

2   Such denunciation shall take effect six months after the date of receipt by the Secretary General of such notification.

3   Denunciation of the Convention entails automatically denunciation of this Protocol.

Article 12

The Secretary General of the Council of Europe shall notify the member States of the Council and any State which has acceded to the Convention of:

a   any signature of this Protocol;

b   any deposit of an instrument of ratification, acceptance, approval or accession;

c   any date of entry into force of this Protocol in accordance with Articles 5 and 6;

d   any declaration received in pursuance of the provisions of paragraphs 2 and 3 of Article 7;

e   any declaration received in pursuance of the provisions of paragraph 1 of Article 8;

f   any reservation made in pursuance of the provisions of paragraph 2 of Article 8;

g   the withdrawal of any reservation carried out in pursuance of the provisions of paragraph 3 of Article 8;

h   any notification received in pursuance of the provisions of Article 11 and the date on which denunciation takes effect.

In witness whereof the undersigned, being duly authorised thereto, have signed this Protocol.

Done at Strasbourg, this 17th day of March 1978, in English and in French, both texts being equally authoritative, in a single copy which shall remain deposited in the archives of the Council of Europe. The Secretary General of the Council of Europe shall transmit certified copies to each of the signatory and acceding States.

Second Additional Protocol to the European Convention on Mutual Assistance in Criminal Matters (ETS No. 182)

The member States of the Council of Europe, signatory to this Protocol,

Having regard to their undertakings under the Statute of the Council of Europe;

Desirous of further contributing to safeguard human rights, uphold the rule of law and support the democratic fabric of society;

Considering it desirable to that effect to strengthen their individual and collective ability to respond to crime;

Decided to improve on and supplement in certain aspects the European Convention on Mutual Assistance in Criminal Matters done at Strasbourg on 20 April 1959 (hereinafter referred to as "the Convention"), as well as the Additional Protocol thereto, done at Strasbourg on 17 March 1978;

Taking into consideration the Convention for the Protection of Human Rights and Fundamental Freedoms, done at Rome on 4 November 1950, as well as the Convention for the Protection of Individuals with regard to Automatic Processing of Personal Data, done at Strasbourg on 28 January 1981,

Have agreed as follows:

Chapter I

Article 1 – Scope

Article 1 of the Convention shall be replaced by the following provisions:

"1   The Parties undertake promptly to afford each other, in accordance with the provisions of this Convention, the widest measure of mutual assistance in proceedings in respect of offences the punishment of which, at the time of the request for assistance, falls within the jurisdiction of the judicial authorities of the requesting Party.

2   This Convention does not apply to arrests, the enforcement of verdicts or offences under military law which are not offences under ordinary criminal law.

3   Mutual assistance may also be afforded in proceedings brought by the administrative authorities in respect of acts which are punishable under the national law of the requesting or the requested Party by virtue of being infringements of the rules of law, where the decision may give rise to proceedings before a court having jurisdiction in particular in criminal matters.

4   Mutual assistance shall not be refused solely on the grounds that it relates to acts for which a legal person may be held liable in the requesting Party."

Article 2 – Presence of officials of the requesting Party

Article 4 of the Convention shall be supplemented by the following text, the original Article 4 of the Convention becoming paragraph 1 and the provisions below becoming paragraph 2:

"2   Requests for the presence of such officials or interested persons should not be refused where that presence is likely to render the execution of the request for assistance more responsive to the needs of the requesting Party and, therefore, likely to avoid the need for supplementary requests for assistance."

Article 3 – Temporary transfer of detained persons to the territory of the requesting Party

Article 11 of the Convention shall be replaced by the following provisions:

"1   A person in custody whose personal appearance for evidentiary purposes other than for standing trial is applied for by the requesting Party shall be temporarily transferred to its territory, provided that he or she shall be sent back within the period stipulated by the requested Party and subject to the provisions of Article 12 of this Convention, in so far as these are applicable.

Transfer may be refused if:

a   the person in custody does not consent;

b   his or her presence is necessary at criminal proceedings pending in the territory of the requested Party;

c   transfer is liable to prolong his or her detention, or

d   there are other overriding grounds for not transferring him or her to the territory of the requesting Party.

2   Subject to the provisions of Article 2 of this Convention, in a case coming within paragraph 1, transit of the person in custody through the territory of a third Party, shall be granted on application, accompanied by all necessary documents, addressed by the Ministry of Justice of the requesting Party to the Ministry of Justice of the Party through whose territory transit is requested. A Party may refuse to grant transit to its own nationals.

3   The transferred person shall remain in custody in the territory of the requesting Party and, where applicable, in the territory of the Party through which transit is requested, unless the Party from whom transfer is requested applies for his or her release."

Article 4 – Channels of communication

Article 15 of the Convention shall be replaced by the following provisions:

"1   Requests for mutual assistance, as well as spontaneous information, shall be addressed in writing by the Ministry of Justice of the requesting Party to the Ministry of Justice of the requested Party and shall be returned through the same channels. However, they may be forwarded directly by the judicial authorities of the requesting Party to the judicial authorities of the requested Party and returned through the same channels.

2   Applications as referred to in Article 11 of this Convention and Article 13 of the Second Additional Protocol to this Convention shall in all cases be addressed by the Ministry of Justice of the requesting Party to the Ministry of Justice of the requested Party and shall be returned through the same channels.

3   Requests for mutual assistance concerning proceedings as mentioned in paragraph 3 of Article 1 of this Convention may also be forwarded directly by the administrative or judicial authorities of the requesting Party to the administrative or judicial authorities of the requested Party, as the case may be, and returned through the same channels.

4   Requests for mutual assistance made under Articles 18 and 19 of the Second Additional Protocol to this Convention may also be forwarded directly by the competent authorities of the requesting Party to the competent authorities of the requested Party.

5   Requests provided for in paragraph 1 of Article 13 of this Convention may be addressed directly by the judicial authorities concerned to the appropriate authorities of the requested Party, and the replies may be returned directly by those authorities. Requests provided for in paragraph 2 of Article 13 of this Convention shall be addressed by the Ministry of Justice of the requesting Party to the Ministry of Justice of the requested Party.

6   Requests for copies of convictions and measures as referred to in Article 4 of the Additional Protocol to the Convention may be made directly to the competent authorities. Any Contracting State may, at any time, by a declaration addressed to the Secretary General of the Council of Europe, define what authorities it will, for the purpose of this paragraph, deem competent authorities.

7   In urgent cases, where direct transmission is permitted under this Convention, it may take place through the International Criminal Police Organisation (Interpol).

8   Any Party may, at any time, by a declaration addressed to the Secretary General of the Council of Europe, reserve the right to make the execution of requests, or specified requests, for mutual assistance dependent on one or more of the following conditions:

       a   that a copy of the request be forwarded to the central authority designated in that declaration;

       b   that requests, except urgent requests, be forwarded to the central authority designated in that declaration;

       c   that, in case of direct transmission for reasons of urgency, a copy shall be transmitted at the same time to its Ministry of Justice;

       d   that some or all requests for assistance shall be sent to it through channels other than those provided for in this article.

9   Requests for mutual assistance and any other communications under this Convention or its Protocols may be forwarded through any electronic or other means of telecommunication provided that the requesting Party is prepared, upon request, to produce at any time a written record of it and the original. However, any Contracting State, may by a declaration addressed at any time to the Secretary General of the Council of Europe, establish the conditions under which it shall be willing to accept and execute requests received by electronic or other means of telecommunication.

10   The provisions of this article are without prejudice to those of bilateral agreements or arrangements in force between Parties which provide for the direct transmission of requests for assistance between their respective authorities."

Article 5 – Costs

Article 20 of the Convention shall be replaced by the following provisions:

"1   Parties shall not claim from each other the refund of any costs resulting from the application of this Convention or its Protocols, except:

       a   costs incurred by the attendance of experts in the territory of the requested Party;

    b   costs incurred by the transfer of a person in custody carried out under Articles 13 or 14 of the Second Additional Protocol to this Convention, or Article 11 of this Convention;

    c   costs of a substantial or extraordinary nature.

2   However, the cost of establishing a video or telephone link, costs related to the servicing of a video or telephone link in the requested Party, the remuneration of interpreters provided by it and allowances to witnesses and their travelling expenses in the requested Party shall be refunded by the requesting Party to the requested Party, unless the Parties agree otherwise.

3   Parties shall consult with each other with a view to making arrangements for the payment of costs claimable under paragraph 1.c above.

4   The provisions of this article shall apply without prejudice to the provisions of Article 10, paragraph 3, of this Convention."

Article 6 – Judicial authorities

Article 24 of the Convention shall be replaced by the following provisions:

"Any State shall at the time of signature or when depositing its instrument of ratification, acceptance, approval or accession, by means of a declaration addressed to the Secretary General of the Council of Europe, define what authorities it will, for the purpose of the Convention, deem judicial authorities. It subsequently may, at any time and in the same manner, change the terms of its declaration."

Chapter II

Article 7 – Postponed execution of requests

1   The requested Party may postpone action on a request if such action would prejudice investigations, prosecutions or related proceedings by its authorities.

2   Before refusing or postponing assistance, the requested Party shall, where appropriate after having consulted with the requesting Party, consider whether the request may be granted partially or subject to such conditions as it deems necessary.

3   If the request is postponed, reasons shall be given for the postponement. The requested Party shall also inform the requesting Party of any reasons that render impossible the execution of the request or are likely to delay it significantly.

Article 8 – Procedure

Notwithstanding the provisions of Article 3 of the Convention, where requests specify formalities or procedures which are necessary under the law of the requesting Party, even if unfamiliar to the requested Party, the latter shall comply with such requests to the extent that the action sought is not contrary to fundamental principles of its law, unless otherwise provided for in this Protocol.

Article 9 – Hearing by video conference

1   If a person is in one Party's territory and has to be heard as a witness or expert by the judicial authorities of another Party, the latter may, where it is not desirable or possible for the person to be heard to appear in its territory in person, request that the hearing take place by video conference, as provided for in paragraphs 2 to 7.

2   The requested Party shall agree to the hearing by video conference provided that the use of the video conference is not contrary to fundamental principles of its law and on condition that it has the technical means to carry out the hearing. If the requested Party has no access to the technical means for video conferencing, such means may be made available to it by the requesting Party by mutual agreement.

3   Requests for a hearing by video conference shall contain, in addition to the information referred to in Article 14 of the Convention, the reason why it is not desirable or possible for the witness or expert to attend in person, the name of the judicial authority and of the persons who will be conducting the hearing.

4   The judicial authority of the requested Party shall summon the person concerned to appear in accordance with the forms laid down by its law.

5   With reference to hearing by video conference, the following rules shall apply:

a   a judicial authority of the requested Party shall be present during the hearing, where necessary assisted by an interpreter, and shall also be responsible for ensuring both the identification of the person to be heard and respect for the fundamental principles of the law of the requested Party. If the judicial authority of the requested Party is of the view that during the hearing the fundamental principles of the law of the requested Party are being infringed, it shall immediately take the necessary measures to ensure that the hearing continues in accordance with the said principles;

b   measures for the protection of the person to be heard shall be agreed, where necessary, between the competent authorities of the requesting and the requested Parties;

c   the hearing shall be conducted directly by, or under the direction of, the judicial authority of the requesting Party in accordance with its own laws;

d   at the request of the requesting Party or the person to be heard, the requested Party shall ensure that the person to be heard is assisted by an interpreter, if necessary;

e   the person to be heard may claim the right not to testify which would accrue to him or her under the law of either the requested or the requesting Party.

6   Without prejudice to any measures agreed for the protection of persons, the judicial authority of the requested Party shall on the conclusion of the hearing draw up minutes indicating the date and place of the hearing, the identity of the person heard, the identities and functions of all other persons in the requested Party participating in the hearing, any oaths taken and the technical conditions under which the hearing took place. The document shall be forwarded by the competent authority of the requested Party to the competent authority of the requesting Party.

7   Each Party shall take the necessary measures to ensure that, where witnesses or experts are being heard within its territory, in accordance with this article, and refuse to testify when under an obligation to testify or do not testify according to the truth, its national law applies in the same way as if the hearing took place in a national procedure.

8   Parties may at their discretion also apply the provisions of this article, where appropriate and with the agreement of their competent judicial authorities, to hearings by video conference involving the accused person or the suspect. In this case, the decision to hold the video conference, and the manner in which the video conference shall be carried out, shall be subject to agreement between the Parties concerned, in accordance with their national law and relevant international instruments. Hearings involving the accused person or the suspect shall only be carried out with his or her consent.

9   Any Contracting State may, at any time, by means of a declaration addressed to the Secretary General of the Council of Europe, declare that it will not avail itself of the possibility provided in paragraph 8 above of also applying the provisions of this article to hearings by video conference involving the accused person or the suspect.

Article 10 – Hearing by telephone conference

1   If a person is in one Party's territory and has to be heard as a witness or expert by judicial authorities of another Party, the latter may, where its national law so provides, request the assistance of the former Party to enable the hearing to take place by telephone conference, as provided for in paragraphs 2 to 6.

2   A hearing may be conducted by telephone conference only if the witness or expert agrees that the hearing take place by that method.

3   The requested Party shall agree to the hearing by telephone conference where this is not contrary to fundamental principles of its law.

4   A request for a hearing by telephone conference shall contain, in addition to the information referred to in Article 14 of the Convention, the name of the judicial authority and of the persons who will be conducting the hearing and an indication that the witness or expert is willing to take part in a hearing by telephone conference.

5   The practical arrangements regarding the hearing shall be agreed between the Parties concerned. When agreeing such arrangements, the requested Party shall undertake to:

a   notify the witness or expert concerned of the time and the venue of the hearing;

b   ensure the identification of the witness or expert;

c   verify that the witness or expert agrees to the hearing by telephone conference.

6   The requested Party may make its agreement subject, fully or in part, to the relevant provisions of Article 9, paragraphs 5 and 7.

Article 11 – Spontaneous information

1   Without prejudice to their own investigations or proceedings, the competent authorities of a Party may, without prior request, forward to the competent authorities of another Party information obtained within the framework of their own investigations, when they consider that the disclosure of such information might assist the receiving Party in initiating or carrying out investigations or proceedings, or might lead to a request by that Party under the Convention or its Protocols.

2   The providing Party may, pursuant to its national law, impose conditions on the use of such information by the receiving Party.

3   The receiving Party shall be bound by those conditions.

4   However, any Contracting State may, at any time, by means of a declaration addressed to the Secretary General of the Council of Europe, declare that it reserves the right not to be bound by the conditions imposed by the providing Party under paragraph 2 above, unless it receives prior notice of the nature of the information to be provided and agrees to its transmission.

Article 12 – Restitution

1   At the request of the requesting Party and without prejudice to the rights of bona fide third parties, the requested Party may place articles obtained by criminal means at the disposal of the requesting Party with a view to their return to their rightful owners.

2   In applying Articles 3 and 6 of the Convention, the requested Party may waive the return of articles either before or after handing them over to the requesting Party if the restitution of such articles to the rightful owner may be facilitated thereby. The rights of bona fide third parties shall not be affected.

3   In the event of a waiver before handing over the articles to the requesting Party, the requested Party shall exercise no security right or other right of recourse under tax or customs legislation in respect of these articles.

4   A waiver as referred to in paragraph 2 shall be without prejudice to the right of the requested Party to collect taxes or duties from the rightful owner.

Article 13 – Temporary transfer of detained persons to the requested Party

1   Where there is agreement between the competent authorities of the Parties concerned, a Party which has requested an investigation for which the presence of a person held in custody on its own territory is required may temporarily transfer that person to the territory of the Party in which the investigation is to take place.

2   The agreement shall cover the arrangements for the temporary transfer of the person and the date by which the person must be returned to the territory of the requesting Party.

3   Where consent to the transfer is required from the person concerned, a statement of consent or a copy thereof shall be provided promptly to the requested Party.

4   The transferred person shall remain in custody in the territory of the requested Party and, where applicable, in the territory of the Party

through which transit is requested, unless the Party from which the person was transferred applies for his or her release.

5   The period of custody in the territory of the requested Party shall be deducted from the period of detention which the person concerned is or will be obliged to undergo in the territory of the requesting Party.

6   The provisions of Article 11, paragraph 2, and Article 12 of the Convention shall apply mutatis mutandis.

7   Any Contracting State may at any time, by means of a declaration addressed to the Secretary General of the Council of Europe, declare that before an agreement is reached under paragraph 1 of this article, the consent referred to in paragraph 3 of this article will be required, or will be required under certain conditions indicated in the declaration.

Article 14 – Personal appearance of transferred sentenced persons

The provisions of Articles 11 and 12 of the Convention shall apply mutatis mutandis also to persons who are in custody in the requested Party, pursuant to having been transferred in order to serve a sentence passed in the requesting Party, where their personal appearance for purposes of review of the judgement is applied for by the requesting Party.

Article 15 – Language of procedural documents and judicial decisions to be served

1   The provisions of this article shall apply to any request for service under Article 7 of the Convention or Article 3 of the Additional Protocol thereto.

2   Procedural documents and judicial decisions shall in all cases be transmitted in the language, or the languages, in which they were issued.

3   Notwithstanding the provisions of Article 16 of the Convention, if the authority that issued the papers knows or has reasons to believe that the addressee understands only some other language, the papers, or at least the most important passages thereof, shall be accompanied by a translation into that other language.

4   Notwithstanding the provisions of Article 16 of the Convention, procedural documents and judicial decisions shall, for the benefit of the authorities of the requested Party, be accompanied by a short summary of their contents translated into the language, or one of the languages, of that Party.

Article 16 – Service by post

1   The competent judicial authorities of any Party may directly address, by post, procedural documents and judicial decisions, to persons who are in the territory of any other Party.

2   Procedural documents and judicial decisions shall be accompanied by a report stating that the addressee may obtain information from the authority identified in the report, regarding his or her rights and obligations concerning the service of the papers. The provisions of paragraph 3 of Article 15 above shall apply to that report.

3   The provisions of Articles 8, 9 and 12 of the Convention shall apply mutatis mutandis to service by post.

4   The provisions of paragraphs 1, 2 and 3 of Article 15 above shall also apply to service by post.

Article 17 – Cross-border observations

1   Police officers of one of the Parties who, within the framework of a criminal investigation, are keeping under observation in their country a person who is presumed to have taken part in a criminal offence to which extradition may apply, or a person who it is strongly believed will lead to the identification or location of the above-mentioned person, shall be authorised to continue their observation in the territory of another Party where the latter has authorised cross-border observation in response to a request for assistance which has previously been submitted. Conditions may be attached to the authorisation.

On request, the observation will be entrusted to officers of the Party in whose territory it is carried out.

The request for assistance referred to in the first sub-paragraph must be sent to an authority designated by each Party and having jurisdiction to grant or to forward the requested authorisation.

2   Where, for particularly urgent reasons, prior authorisation of the other Party cannot be requested, the officers conducting the observation within the framework of a criminal investigation shall be authorised to continue beyond the border the observation of a person presumed to have committed offences listed in paragraph 6, provided that the following conditions are met:

   a   the authorities of the Party designated under paragraph 4, in whose territory the observation is to be continued, must be notified immediately, during the observation, that the border has been crossed;

b a request for assistance submitted in accordance with paragraph 1 and outlining the grounds for crossing the border without prior authorisation shall be submitted without delay.

Observation shall cease as soon as the Party in whose territory it is taking place so requests, following the notification referred to in a. or the request referred to in b. or where authorisation has not been obtained within five hours of the border being crossed.

3 The observation referred to in paragraphs 1 and 2 shall be carried out only under the following general conditions:

a The officers conducting the observation must comply with the provisions of this article and with the law of the Party in whose territory they are operating; they must obey the instructions of the local responsible authorities.

b Except in the situations provided for in paragraph 2, the officers shall, during the observation, carry a document certifying that authorisation has been granted.

c The officers conducting the observation must be able at all times to provide proof that they are acting in an official capacity.

d The officers conducting the observation may carry their service weapons during the observation, save where specifically otherwise decided by the requested Party; their use shall be prohibited save in cases of legitimate self-defence.

e Entry into private homes and places not accessible to the public shall be prohibited.

f The officers conducting the observation may neither stop and question, nor arrest, the person under observation.

g All operations shall be the subject of a report to the authorities of the Party in whose territory they took place; the officers conducting the observation may be required to appear in person.

h The authorities of the Party from which the observing officers have come shall, when requested by the authorities of the Party in whose territory the observation took place, assist the enquiry subsequent to the operation in which they took part, including legal proceedings.

4 Parties shall at the time of signature or when depositing their instrument of ratification, acceptance, approval or accession, by means of a declaration addressed to the Secretary General of the Council of Europe, indicate both the officers and authorities that they designate for the

purposes of paragraphs 1 and 2 of this article. They subsequently may, at any time and in the same manner, change the terms of their declaration.

5   The Parties may, at bilateral level, extend the scope of this article and adopt additional measures in implementation thereof.

6   The observation referred to in paragraph 2 may take place only for one of the following criminal offences:

    –   assassination;
    –   murder;
    –   rape;
    –   arson;
    –   counterfeiting;
    –   armed robbery and receiving of stolen goods;
    –   extortion;
    –   kidnapping and hostage taking;
    –   traffic in human beings;
    –   illicit traffic in narcotic drugs and psychotropic substances;
    –   breach of the laws on arms and explosives;
    –   use of explosives;
    –   illicit carriage of toxic and dangerous waste;
    –   smuggling of aliens;
    –   sexual abuse of children.

Article 18 – Controlled delivery

1   Each Party undertakes to ensure that, at the request of another Party, controlled deliveries may be permitted on its territory in the framework of criminal investigations into extraditable offences.

2   The decision to carry out controlled deliveries shall be taken in each individual case by the competent authorities of the requested Party, with due regard to the national law of that Party.

3   Controlled deliveries shall take place in accordance with the procedures of the requested Party. Competence to act, direct and control operations shall lie with the competent authorities of that Party.

4   Parties shall at the time of signature or when depositing their instrument of ratification, acceptance, approval or accession, by means of a declaration addressed to the Secretary General of the Council of Europe, indicate the authorities that are competent for the purposes of this article. They subsequently may, at any time and in the same manner, change the terms of their declaration.

Article 19 – Covert investigations

1   The requesting and the requested Parties may agree to assist one another in the conduct of investigations into crime by officers acting under covert or false identity (covert investigations).

2   The decision on the request is taken in each individual case by the competent authorities of the requested Party with due regard to its national law and procedures. The duration of the covert investigation, the detailed conditions, and the legal status of the officers concerned during covert investigations shall be agreed between the Parties with due regard to their national law and procedures.

3   Covert investigations shall take place in accordance with the national law and procedures of the Party on the territory of which the covert investigation takes place. The Parties involved shall co-operate to ensure that the covert investigation is prepared and supervised and to make arrangements for the security of the officers acting under covert or false identity.

4   Parties shall at the time of signature or when depositing their instrument of ratification, acceptance, approval or accession, by means of a declaration addressed to the Secretary General of the Council of Europe, indicate the authorities that are competent for the purposes of paragraph 2 of this article. They subsequently may, at any time and in the same manner, change the terms of their declaration.

Article 20 – Joint investigation teams

1   By mutual agreement, the competent authorities of two or more Parties may set up a joint investigation team for a specific purpose and a limited period, which may be extended by mutual consent, to carry out criminal investigations in one or more of the Parties setting up the team. The composition of the team shall be set out in the agreement.

A joint investigation team may, in particular, be set up where:

a   a Party's investigations into criminal offences require difficult and demanding investigations having links with other Parties;

b   a number of Parties are conducting investigations into criminal offences in which the circumstances of the case necessitate co-ordinated, concerted action in the Parties involved.

A request for the setting up of a joint investigation team may be made by any of the Parties concerned. The team shall be set up in one of the Parties in which the investigations are expected to be carried out.

2   In addition to the information referred to in the relevant provisions of Article 14 of the Convention, requests for the setting up of a joint investigation team shall include proposals for the composition of the team.

3   A joint investigation team shall operate in the territory of the Parties setting up the team under the following general conditions:

   a   the leader of the team shall be a representative of the competent authority participating in criminal investigations from the Party in which the team operates. The leader of the team shall act within the limits of his or her competence under national law;

   b   the team shall carry out its operations in accordance with the law of the Party in which it operates. The members and seconded members of the team shall carry out their tasks under the leadership of the person referred to in sub-paragraph a, taking into account the conditions set by their own authorities in the agreement on setting up the team;

   c   the Party in which the team operates shall make the necessary organisational arrangements for it to do so.

4   In this article, members of the joint investigation team from the Party in which the team operates are referred to as "members", while members from Parties other than the Party in which the team operates are referred to as "seconded members".

5   Seconded members of the joint investigation team shall be entitled to be present when investigative measures are taken in the Party of operation. However, the leader of the team may, for particular reasons, in accordance with the law of the Party where the team operates, decide otherwise.

6   Seconded members of the joint investigation team may, in accordance with the law of the Party where the team operates, be entrusted by the leader of the team with the task of taking certain investigative measures where this has been approved by the competent authorities of the Party of operation and the seconding Party.

7   Where the joint investigation team needs investigative measures to be taken in one of the Parties setting up the team, members seconded to the team by that Party may request their own competent authorities to take those measures. Those measures shall be considered in that Party under the conditions which would apply if they were requested in a national investigation.

8   Where the joint investigation team needs assistance from a Party other than those which have set up the team, or from a third State, the request

for assistance may be made by the competent authorities of the State of operation to the competent authorities of the other State concerned in accordance with the relevant instruments or arrangements.

9   A seconded member of the joint investigation team may, in accordance with his or her national law and within the limits of his or her competence, provide the team with information available in the Party which has seconded him or her for the purpose of the criminal investigations conducted by the team.

10   Information lawfully obtained by a member or seconded member while part of a joint investigation team which is not otherwise available to the competent authorities of the Parties concerned may be used for the following purposes:

a   for the purposes for which the team has been set up;

b   subject to the prior consent of the Party where the information became available, for detecting, investigating and prosecuting other criminal offences. Such consent may be withheld only in cases where such use would endanger criminal investigations in the Party concerned or in respect of which that Party could refuse mutual assistance;

c   for preventing an immediate and serious threat to public security, and without prejudice to sub-paragraph b. if subsequently a criminal investigation is opened;

d   for other purposes to the extent that this is agreed between Parties setting up the team.

11   This article shall be without prejudice to any other existing provisions or arrangements on the setting up or operation of joint investigation teams.

12   To the extent that the laws of the Parties concerned or the provisions of any legal instrument applicable between them permit, arrangements may be agreed for persons other than representatives of the competent authorities of the Parties setting up the joint investigation team to take part in the activities of the team. The rights conferred upon the members or seconded members of the team by virtue of this article shall not apply to these persons unless the agreement expressly states otherwise.

Article 21 – Criminal liability regarding officials

During the operations referred to in Articles 17, 18, 19 or 20, unless otherwise agreed upon by the Parties concerned, officials from a Party other than the Party of operation shall be regarded as officials of the

Party of operation with respect to offences committed against them or by them.

Article 22 – Civil liability regarding officials

1   Where, in accordance with Articles 17, 18, 19 or 20, officials of a Party are operating in another Party, the first Party shall be liable for any damage caused by them during their operations, in accordance with the law of the Party in whose territory they are operating.

2   The Party in whose territory the damage referred to in paragraph 1 was caused shall make good such damage under the conditions applicable to damage caused by its own officials.

3   The Party whose officials have caused damage to any person in the territory of another Party shall reimburse the latter in full any sums it has paid to the victims or persons entitled on their behalf.

4   Without prejudice to the exercise of its rights vis-à-vis third parties and with the exception of paragraph 3, each Party shall refrain in the case provided for in paragraph 1 from requesting reimbursement of damages it has sustained from another Party.

5   The provisions of this article shall apply subject to the proviso that the Parties did not agree otherwise.

Article 23 – Protection of witnesses

Where a Party requests assistance under the Convention or one of its Protocols in respect of a witness at risk of intimidation or in need of protection, the competent authorities of the requesting and requested Parties shall endeavour to agree on measures for the protection of the person concerned, in accordance with their national law.

Article 24 – Provisional measures

1   At the request of the requesting Party, the requested Party, in accordance with its national law, may take provisional measures for the purpose of preserving evidence, maintaining an existing situation or protecting endangered legal interests.

2   The requested Party may grant the request partially or subject to conditions, in particular time limitation.

Article 25 – Confidentiality

The requesting Party may require that the requested Party keep confidential the fact and substance of the request, except to the extent necessary to execute the request. If the requested Party cannot comply with the requirement of confidentiality, it shall promptly inform the requesting Party.

Article 26 – Data protection

1 Personal data transferred from one Party to another as a result of the execution of a request made under the Convention or any of its Protocols, may be used by the Party to which such data have been transferred, only:

   a for the purpose of proceedings to which the Convention or any of its Protocols apply;

   b for other judicial and administrative proceedings directly related to the proceedings mentioned under (a);

   c for preventing an immediate and serious threat to public security.

2 Such data may however be used for any other purpose if prior consent to that effect is given by either the Party from which the data had been transferred, or the data subject.

3 Any Party may refuse to transfer personal data obtained as a result of the execution of a request made under the Convention or any of its Protocols where

   – such data is protected under its national legislation, and

   – the Party to which the data should be transferred is not bound by the Convention for the Protection of Individuals with regard to Automatic Processing of Personal Data, done at Strasbourg on 28 January 1981, unless the latter Party undertakes to afford such protection to the data as is required by the former Party.

4 Any Party that transfers personal data obtained as a result of the execution of a request made under the Convention or any of its Protocols may require the Party to which the data have been transferred to give information on the use made with such data.

5 Any Party may, by a declaration addressed to the Secretary General of the Council of Europe, require that, within the framework of procedures for which it could have refused or limited the transmission or the use of personal data in accordance with the provisions of the Convention or one of its Protocols, personal data transmitted to another Party not be used by the latter for the purposes of paragraph 1 unless with its previous consent.

Article 27 – Administrative authorities

Parties may at any time, by means of a declaration addressed to the Secretary General of the Council of Europe, define what authorities they will deem administrative authorities for the purposes of Article 1, paragraph 3, of the Convention.

Article 28 – Relations with other treaties

The provisions of this Protocol are without prejudice to more extensive regulations in bilateral or multilateral agreements concluded between Parties in application of Article 26, paragraph 3, of the Convention.

Article 29 – Friendly settlement

The European Committee on Crime Problems shall be kept informed regarding the interpretation and application of the Convention and its Protocols, and shall do whatever is necessary to facilitate a friendly settlement of any difficulty which may arise out of their application.

Chapter III

Article 30 – Signature and entry into force

1   This Protocol shall be open for signature by the member States of the Council of Europe which are a Party to or have signed the Convention. It shall be subject to ratification, acceptance or approval. A signatory may not ratify, accept or approve this Protocol unless it has previously or simultaneously ratified, accepted or approved the Convention. Instruments of ratification, acceptance or approval shall be deposited with the Secretary General of the Council of Europe.

2   This Protocol shall enter into force on the first day of the month following the expiration of a period of three months after the deposit of the third instrument of ratification, acceptance or approval.

3   In respect of any signatory State which subsequently deposits its instrument of ratification, acceptance or approval, the Protocol shall enter into force on the first day of the month following the expiration of a period of three months after the date of deposit.

Article 31 – Accession

1   Any non-member State, which has acceded to the Convention, may accede to this Protocol after it has entered into force.

2   Such accession shall be effected by depositing with the Secretary General of the Council of Europe an instrument of accession.

3   In respect of any acceding State, the Protocol shall enter into force on the first day of the month following the expiration of a period of three months after the date of the deposit of the instrument of accession.

Article 32 – Territorial application

1   Any State may at the time of signature or when depositing its instrument of ratification, acceptance, approval or accession, specify the territory or territories to which this Protocol shall apply.

2   Any State may, at any later date, by declaration addressed to the Secretary General of the Council of Europe, extend the application of this Protocol to any other territory specified in the declaration. In respect of such territory the Protocol shall enter into force on the first day of the month following the expiration of a period of three months after the date of receipt of such declaration by the Secretary General.

3   Any declaration made under the two preceding paragraphs may, in respect of any territory specified in such declaration, be withdrawn by a notification addressed to the Secretary General. The withdrawal shall become effective on the first day of the month following the expiration of a period of three months after the date or receipt of such notification by the Secretary General.

Article 33 – Reservations

1   Reservations made by a Party to any provision of the Convention or its Protocol shall be applicable also to this Protocol, unless that Party otherwise declares at the time of signature or when depositing its instrument of ratification, acceptance, approval or accession. The same shall apply to any declaration made in respect or by virtue of any provision of the Convention or its Protocol.

2   Any State may, at the time of signature or when depositing its instrument of ratification, acceptance, approval or accession, declare that it avails itself of the right not to accept wholly or in part any one or more of Articles 16, 17, 18, 19 and 20. No other reservation may be made.

3   Any State may wholly or partially withdraw a reservation it has made in accordance with the foregoing paragraphs, by means of a declaration addressed to the Secretary General of the Council of Europe, which shall become effective as from the date of its receipt.

4   Any Party which has made a reservation in respect of any of the articles of this Protocol mentioned in paragraph 2 above, may not claim the application of that article by another Party. It may, however, if its reservation is partial or conditional, claim the application of that provision in so far as it has itself accepted it.

Article 34 – Denunciation

1 Any Party may, in so far as it is concerned, denounce this Protocol by means of a notification addressed to the Secretary General of the Council of Europe.

2 Such denunciation shall become effective on the first day of the month following the expiration of a period of three months after the date of receipt of the notification by the Secretary General.

3 Denunciation of the Convention entails automatically denunciation of this Protocol.

Article 35 – Notifications

The Secretary General of the Council of Europe shall notify the member States of the Council of Europe and any State which has acceded to this Protocol of:

a any signature;

b the deposit of any instrument of ratification, acceptance, approval or accession;

c any date of entry into force of this Protocol in accordance with Articles 30 and 31;

d any other act, declaration, notification or communication relating to this Protocol.

In witness whereof the undersigned, being duly authorised thereto, have signed this Protocol.

Done at Strasbourg, this 8th day of November 2001, in English and in French, both texts being equally authentic, in a single copy which shall be deposited in the archives of the Council of Europe. The Secretary General of the Council of Europe shall transmit certified copies to each member State of the Council of Europe and to the non-member States which have acceded to the Convention.

European Convention on the
Transfer of Proceedings in Criminal Matters (ETS No. 73)

The member States of the Council of Europe, signatory hereto,

Considering that the aim of the Council of Europe is the achievement of greater unity between its members;

Desiring to supplement the work which they have already accomplished in the field of criminal law with a view to arriving at more just and efficient sanctions;

Considering it useful to this end to ensure, in a spirit of mutual confidence, the organisation of criminal proceedings on the international level, in particular, by avoiding the disadvantages resulting from conflicts of competence,

Have agreed as follows:

Part I – Definitions

Article 1

For the purposes of this Convention:

a   "offence" comprises acts dealt with under the criminal law and those dealt with under the legal provisions listed in Appendix III to this Convention on condition that where an administrative authority is competent to deal with the offence it must be possible for the person concerned to have the case tried by a court;

b   "sanction" means any punishment or other measure incurred or pronounced in respect of an offence or in respect of a violation of the legal provisions listed in Appendix III.

Part II – Competence

Article 2

1   For the purposes of applying this Convention, any Contracting State shall have competence to prosecute under its own criminal law any offence to which the law of another Contracting State is applicable.

2   The competence conferred on a Contracting State exclusively by virtue of paragraph 1 of this Article may be exercised only pursuant to a request for proceedings presented by another Contracting State.

Article 3

Any Contracting State having competence under its own law to prosecute an offence may, for the purposes of applying this Convention, waive or desist from proceedings against a suspected person who is being or will be prosecuted for the same offence by another Contracting State. Having regard to Article 21, paragraph 2, any such decision to waive or to desist from proceedings shall be provisional pending a final decision in the other Contracting State.

Article 4

The requested State shall discontinue proceedings exclusively grounded on Article 2 when to its knowledge the right of punishment is extinguished under the law of the requesting State for a reason other than time-limitation, to which Articles 10.c, 11.f and g, 22, 23 and 26 in particular apply.

Article 5

The provisions of Part III of this Convention do not limit the competence given to a requested State by its municipal law in regard to prosecutions.

Part III – Transfer of proceedings

Section 1 – Request for proceedings

Article 6

1   When a person is suspected of having committed an offence under the law of a Contracting State, that State may request another Contracting State to take proceedings in the cases and under the conditions provided for in this Convention.

2   If under the provisions of this Convention a Contracting State may request another Contracting State to take proceedings, the competent authorities of the first State shall take that possibility into consideration.

Article 7

1   Proceedings may not be taken in the requested State unless the offence in respect of which the proceedings are requested would be an offence if committed in its territory and when, under these circumstances, the offender would be liable to sanction under its own law also.

2   If the offence was committed by a person of public status or against a person, an institution or any thing of public status in the requesting State, it shall be considered in the requested State as having been committed by a person of public status or against such a person, an institution or any

thing corresponding, in the latter State, to that against which it was actually committed.

Article 8

1   A Contracting State may request another Contracting State to take proceedings in any one or more of the following cases:

a   if the suspected person is ordinarily resident in the requested State;

b   if the suspected person is a national of the requested State or if that State is his State of origin;

c   if the suspected person is undergoing or is to undergo a sentence involving deprivation of liberty in the requested State;

d   if proceedings for the same or other offences are being taken against the suspected person in the requested State;

e   if it considers that transfer of the proceedings is warranted in the interests of arriving at the truth and in particular that the most important items of evidence are located in the requested State;

f   if it considers that the enforcement in the requested State of a sentence if one were passed is likely to improve the prospects for the social rehabilitation of the person sentenced;

g   if it considers that the presence of the suspected person cannot be ensured at the hearing of proceedings in the requesting State and that his presence in person at the hearing of proceedings in the requested State can be ensured;

h   if it considers that it could not itself enforce a sentence if one were passed, even by having recourse to extradition, and that the requested State could do so;

2   Where the suspected person has been finally sentenced in a Contracting State, that State may request the transfer of proceedings in one or more of the cases referred to in paragraph 1 of this article only if it cannot itself enforce the sentence, even by having recourse to extradition, and if the other Contracting State does not accept enforcement of a foreign judgment as a matter of principle or refuses to enforce such sentence.

Article 9

1   The competent authorities in the requested State shall examine the request for proceedings made in pursuance of the preceding articles. They shall decide, in accordance with their own law, what action to take thereon.

2   Where the law of the requested State provides for the punishment of the offence by an administrative authority, that State shall, as soon as possible, so inform the requesting State unless the requested State has made a declaration under paragraph 3 of this article.

3   Any Contracting State may at the time of signature, or when depositing its instrument of ratification, acceptance or accession, or at any later date indicate, by declaration addressed to the Secretary General of the Council of Europe, the conditions under which its domestic law permits the punishment of certain offences by an administrative authority. Such a declaration shall replace the notification envisaged in paragraph 2 of this article.

Article 10

The requested State shall not take action on the request:

a   if the request does not comply with the provisions of Articles 6, paragraph 1, and 7, paragraph 1;

b   if the institution of proceedings is contrary to the provisions of Article 35;

c   if, at the date on the request, the time-limit for criminal proceedings has already expired in the requesting State under the legislation of that State.

Article 11

Save as provided for in Article 10 the requested State may not refuse acceptance of the request in whole or in part, except in any one or more of the following cases:

a   if it considers that the grounds on which the request is based under Article 8 are not justified;

b   if the suspected person is not ordinarily resident in the requested State;

c   if the suspected person is not a national of the requested State and was not ordinarily resident in the territory of that State at the time of the offence;

d   if it considers that the offence for which proceedings are requested is an offence of a political nature or a purely military or fiscal one;

e if it considers that there are substantial grounds for believing that the request for proceedings was motivated by considerations of race, religion, nationality or political opinion;

f if its own law is already applicable to the offence and if at the time of the receipt of the request proceedings were precluded by lapse of time according to that law; Article 26, paragraph 2, shall not apply in such a case;

g if its competence is exclusively grounded on Article 2 and if at the time of the receipt of the request proceedings would be precluded by lapse of time according to its law, the prolongation of the time-limit by six months under the terms of Article 23 being taken into consideration;

h if the offence was committed outside the territory of the requesting State;

i if proceedings would be contrary to the international undertakings of the requested State;

j if proceedings would be contrary to the fundamental principles of the legal system of the requested State;

k if the requesting State has violated a rule of procedure laid down in this Convention.

Article 12

1 The requested State shall withdraw its acceptance of the request if, subsequent to this acceptance, a ground mentioned in Article 10 of this Convention for not taking action on the request becomes apparent.

2 The requested State may withdraw its acceptance of the request:

a if it becomes apparent that the presence in person of the suspected person cannot be ensured at the hearing of the proceedings in that State or that any sentence, which might be passed, could not be enforced in that State;

b if one of the grounds for refusal mentioned in Article 11 becomes apparent before the case is brought before a court; or

c in other cases, if the requesting State agrees.

Section 2 – Transfer procedure

Article 13

1   All requests specified in this Convention shall be made in writing. They, and all communications necessary for the application of this Convention, shall be sent either by the Ministry of Justice of the requesting State to the Ministry of Justice of the requested State or, by virtue of special mutual arrangement, direct by the authorities of the requesting State to those of the requested State; they shall be returned by the same channel.

2   In urgent cases, requests and communications may be sent through the International Criminal Police Organisation (Interpol).

3   Any Contracting State may, by declaration addressed to the Secretary General of the Council of Europe, give notice of its intention to adopt in so far as it itself is concerned rules of transmission other than those laid down in paragraph 1 of this article.

Article 14

If a Contracting State considers that the information supplied by another Contracting State is not adequate to enable it to apply this Convention, it shall ask for the necessary additional information. It may prescribe a date for the receipt of such information.

Article 15

1   A request for proceedings shall be accompanied by the original, or a certified copy, of the criminal file and all other necessary documents. However, if the suspected person is remanded in custody in accordance with the provisions of Section 5 and if the requesting State is unable to transmit these documents at the same time as the request for proceedings, the documents may be sent subsequently.

2   The requesting State shall also inform the requested State in writing of any procedural acts performed or measures taken in the requesting State after the transmission of the request which have a bearing on the proceedings. This communication shall be accompanied by any relevant documents.

Article 16

1   The requested State shall promptly communicate its decision on the request for proceedings to the requesting State.

2   The requested State shall also inform the requesting State of a waiver of proceedings or of the decision taken as a result of proceedings. A

certified copy of any written decision shall be transmitted to the requesting State.

Article 17

If the competence of the requested State is exclusively grounded on Article 2 that State shall inform the suspected person of the request for proceedings with a view to allowing him to present his views on the matter before that State has taken a decision on the request.

Article 18

1   Subject to paragraph 2 of this article, no translation of the documents relating to the application of this Convention shall be required.

2   Any Contracting State may, at the time of signature or when depositing its instrument of ratification, acceptance or accession, by declaration addressed to the Secretary General of the Council of Europe, reserve the right to require that, with the exception of the copy of the written decision referred to in Article 16, paragraph 2, the said documents be accompanied by a translation. The other Contracting States shall send the translations in either the national language of the receiving State or such one of the official languages of the Council of Europe as the receiving State shall indicate. However, such an indication is not obligatory. The other Contracting States may claim reciprocity.

3   This article shall be without prejudice to any provisions concerning translation of requests and supporting documents that may be contained in agreements or arrangements now in force or that may be concluded between two or more Contracting States.

Article 19

Documents transmitted in application of this Convention need not be authenticated.

Article 20

Contracting Parties shall not claim from each other the refund of any expenses resulting from the application of this Convention.

Section 3 – Effects in the requesting State of a request for proceedings

Article 21

1   When the requesting State has requested proceedings, it can no longer prosecute the suspected person for the offence in respect of which the proceedings have been requested or enforce a judgment which has been

pronounced previously in that State against him for that offence. Until the requested State's decision on the request for proceedings has been received, the requesting State shall, however, retain its right to take all steps in respect of prosecution, short of bringing the case to trial, or, as the case may be, allowing the competent administrative authority to decide on the case.

2   The right of prosecution and of enforcement shall revert to the requesting State:

a   if the requested State informs it of a decision in accordance with Article 10 not to take action on the request;

b   if the requested State informs it of a decision in accordance with Article 11 to refuse acceptance of the request;

c   if the requested State informs it of a decision in accordance with Article 12 to withdraw acceptance of the request;

d   if the requested State informs it of a decision not to institute proceedings or discontinue them;

e   if it withdraws its request before the requested State has informed it of a decision to take action on the request.

Article 22

A request for proceedings, made in accordance with the provisions of this Part, shall have the effect in the requesting State of prolonging the time-limit for proceedings by six months.

Section 4 – Effects in the requested State of a request for proceedings

Article 23

If the competence of the requested State is exclusively grounded on Article 2 the time-limit for proceedings in that State shall be prolonged by six months.

Article 24

1   If proceedings are dependent on a complaint in both States the complaint brought in the requesting State shall have equal validity with that brought in the requested State.

2   If a complaint is necessary only in the requested State, that State may take proceedings even in the absence of a complaint if the person who is empowered to bring the complaint has not objected within a period of one

month from the date of receipt by him of notice from the competent authority informing him of his right to object.

Article 25

In the requested State the sanction applicable to the offence shall be that prescribed by its own law unless that law provides otherwise. Where the competence of the requested State is exclusively grounded on Article 2, the sanction pronounced in that State shall not be more severe than that provided for in the law of the requesting State.

Article 26

1   Any act with a view to proceedings, taken in the requesting State in accordance with its law and regulations, shall have the same validity in the requested State as if it had been taken by the authorities of that State, provided that assimilation does not give such act a greater evidential weight than it has in the requesting State.

2   Any act which interrupts time-limitation and which has been validly performed in the requesting State shall have the same effects in the requested State and vice versa.

Section 5 – Provisional measures in the requested State

Article 27

1   When the requesting State announces its intention to transmit a request for proceedings, and if the competence of the requested State would be exclusively grounded on Article 2, the requested State may, on application by the requesting State and by virtue of this Convention, provisionally arrest the suspected person:

a   if the law of the requested States authorises remand in custody for the offence, and

b   if there are reasons to fear that the suspected person will abscond or that he will cause evidence to be suppressed.

2   The application for provisional arrest shall state that there exists a warrant of arrest or other order having the same effect, issued in accordance with the procedure laid down in the law of the requesting State; it shall also state for what offence proceedings will be requested and when and where such offence was committed and it shall contain as accurate a description of the suspected person as possible. It shall also contain a brief statement of the circumstances of the case.

3   An application for provisional arrest shall be sent direct by the authorities in the requesting State mentioned in Article 13 to the corresponding

authorities in the requested State, by post or telegram or by any other means affording evidence in writing or accepted by the requested State. The requesting State shall be informed without delay of the result of its application.

Article 28

Upon receipt of a request for proceedings accompanied by the documents referred to in Article 15, paragraph 1, the requested State shall have jurisdiction to apply all such provisional measures, including remand in custody of the suspected person and seizure of property, as could be applied under its own law if the offence in respect of which proceedings are requested had been committed in its territory.

Article 29

1   The provisional measures provided in Articles 27 and 28 shall be governed by the provisions of this Convention and the law of the requested State. The law of that State, or the Convention shall also determine the conditions on which the measures may lapse.

2   These measures shall lapse in the cases referred to in Article 21, paragraph 2.

3   A person in custody shall in any event be released if he is arrested in pursuance of Article 27 and the requested State does not receive the request for proceedings within 18 days from the date of the arrest.

4   A person in custody shall in any event be released if he is arrested in pursuance of Article 27 and the documents which should accompany the request for proceedings have not been received by the requested State within 15 days from the receipt of the request for proceedings.

5   The period of custody applied exclusively by virtue of Article 27 shall not in any event exceed 40 days.

Part IV – Plurality of criminal proceedings

Article 30

1   Any Contracting State which, before the institution or in the course of proceedings for an offence which it considers to be neither of a political nature nor a purely military one, is aware of proceedings pending in another Contracting State against the same person in respect of the same offence shall consider whether it can either waive or suspend its own proceedings, or transfer them to the other State.

2   If it deems it advisable in the circumstances not to waive or suspend its own proceedings it shall so notify the other State in good time and in any event before judgment is given on the merits.

Article 31

1   In the eventuality referred to in Article 30, paragraph 2, the States concerned shall endeavour as far as possible to determine, after evaluation in each of the circumstances mentioned in Article 8, which of them alone shall continue to conduct proceedings. During this consultative procedure the States concerned shall postpone judgment on the merits without however being obliged to prolong such postponement beyond a period of 30 days as from the despatch of the notification provided for in Article 30, paragraph 2.

2   The provisions of paragraph 1 shall not be binding:

a   on the State despatching the notification provided for in Article 30, paragraph 2, if the main trial has been declared open there in the presence of the accused before despatch of the notification;

b   on the State to which the notification is addressed, if the main trial has been declared open there in the presence of the accused before receipt of the notification.

Article 32

In the interests of arriving at the truth and with a view to the application of an appropriate sanction, the States concerned shall examine whether it is expedient that one of them alone shall conduct proceedings and, if so, endeavour to determine which one, when:

a   several offences which are materially distinct and which fall under the criminal law of each of those States are ascribed either to a single person or to several persons having acted in unison;

b   a single offence which falls under the criminal law of each of those States is ascribed to several persons having acted in unison.

Article 33

All decisions reached in accordance with Articles 31, paragraph 1, and 32 shall entail, as between the States concerned, all the consequences of a transfer of proceedings as provided for in this Convention. The State which waives its own proceedings shall be deemed to have transferred them to the other State.

Article 34

The transfer procedure provided for in Section 2 of Part III shall apply in so far as its provisions are compatible with those contained in the present Part.

Part V – *Ne bis in idem*

Article 35

1   A person in respect of whom a final and enforceable criminal judgment has been rendered may for the same act neither be prosecuted nor sentenced nor subjected to enforcement of a sanction in another Contracting State:

a   if he was acquitted;

b   if the sanction imposed:

  i   has been completely enforced or is being enforced, or

  ii   has been wholly, or with respect to the part not enforced, the subject of a pardon or an amnesty, or

  iii   can no longer be enforced because of lapse of time;

c   if the court convicted the offender without imposing a sanction.

2   Nevertheless, a Contracting State shall not, unless it has itself requested the proceedings, be obliged to recognise the effect of *ne bis in idem* if the act which gave rise to the judgment was directed against either a person or an institution or any thing having public status in that State, or if the subject of the judgment had himself a public status in that State.

3   Furthermore, a Contracting State where the act was committed or considered as such according to the law of that State shall not be obliged to recognise the effect of *ne bis in idem* unless that State has itself requested the proceedings.

Article 36

If new proceedings are instituted against a person who in another Contracting State has been sentenced for the same act, then any period of deprivation of liberty arising from the sentence enforced shall be deducted from the sanction which may be imposed.

Article 37

This Part shall not prevent the application of wider domestic provisions relating to the effect of *ne bis in idem* attached to foreign criminal judgments.

Part VI – Final clauses

Article 38

1   This Convention shall be open to signature by the member States of the Council of Europe. It shall be subject to ratification or acceptance. Instruments of ratification or acceptance shall be deposited with the Secretary General of the Council of Europe.

2   This Convention shall enter into force three months after the date of the deposit of the third instrument of ratification or acceptance.

3   In respect of a signatory State ratifying or accepting subsequently, the Convention shall come into force three months after the date of the deposit of its instrument of ratification or acceptance.

Article 39

1   After the entry into force of this Convention, the Committee of Ministers of the Council of Europe may invite any non-member State to accede thereto provided that the resolution containing such invitation received the unanimous agreement of the Members of the Council who have ratified the Convention.

2   Such accession shall be effected by depositing with the Secretary General of the Council of Europe an instrument of accession which shall take effect three months after the date of its deposit.

Article 40

1   Any Contracting State may, at the time of signature or when depositing its instrument of ratification, acceptance or accession, specify the territory or territories to which this Convention shall apply.

2   Any Contracting State may, when depositing its instrument of ratification, acceptance or accession or at any later date, by declaration addressed to the Secretary General of the Council of Europe, extend this Convention to any other territory or territories specified in the declaration and for whose international relations it is responsible or on whose behalf it is authorised to give undertakings.

3   Any declaration made in pursuance of the preceding paragraph may, in respect of any territory mentioned in such declaration, be withdrawn according to the procedure laid down in Article 45 of this Convention.

Article 41

1   Any Contracting State may, at the time of signature or when depositing its instrument of ratification, acceptance or accession, declare that it avails itself of one or more of the reservations provided for in Appendix I or make a declaration provided for in Appendix II to this Convention.

2   Any Contracting State may wholly or partly withdraw a reservation or declaration it has made in accordance with the foregoing paragraph by means of a declaration addressed to the Secretary General of the Council of Europe which shall become effective as from the date of its receipt.

3   A Contracting State which has made a reservation in respect of any provision of this Convention may not claim the application of that provision by any other Contracting State; it may, however, if its reservation is partial or conditional, claim the application of that provision in so far as it has itself accepted it.

Article 42

1   Any Contracting State may at any time, by declaration addressed to the Secretary General of the Council of Europe, set out the legal provisions to be included in Appendix III to this Convention.

2   Any change of the national provisions listed in Appendix III shall be notified to the Secretary General of the Council of Europe if such a change renders the information in this appendix incorrect.

3   Any changes made in Appendix III in application of the preceding paragraphs shall take effect in each Contracting State one month after the date of their notification by the Secretary General of the Council of Europe.

Article 43

1   This Convention affects neither the rights and the undertakings derived from extradition treaties and international multilateral conventions concerning special matters, nor provisions concerning matters which are dealt with in the present Convention and which are contained in other existing conventions between Contracting States.

2   The Contracting States may not conclude bilateral or multilateral agreements with one another on the matters dealt with in this

Convention, except in order to supplement its provisions or facilitate application of the principles embodied in it.

3   Should two or more Contracting States, however, have already established their relations in this matter on the basis of uniform legislation, or instituted a special system of their own, or should they in future do so, they shall be entitled to regulate those relations accordingly, notwithstanding the terms of this Convention.

4   Contracting States ceasing to apply the terms of this Convention to their mutual relations in this matter in accordance with the provisions of the preceding paragraph shall notify the Secretary General of the Council of Europe to that effect.

Article 44

The European Committee on Crime Problems of the Council of Europe shall be kept informed regarding the application of this Convention and shall do whatever is needful to facilitate a friendly settlement of any difficulty which may arise out of its execution.

Article 45

1   This Convention shall remain in force indefinitely.

2   Any Contracting State may, in so far as it is concerned, denounce this Convention by means of a notification addressed to the Secretary General of the Council of Europe.

3   Such denunciation shall take effect six months after the date of receipt by the Secretary General of such notification.

Article 46

The Secretary General of the Council of Europe shall notify the member States of the Council and any State which has acceded to this Convention of:

a   any signature;

b   any deposit of an instrument of ratification, acceptance or accession;

c   any date of entry into force of this Convention in accordance with Article 38 thereof;

d   any declaration received in pursuance of the provisions of Article 9, paragraph 3;

e   any declaration received in pursuance of the provisions of Article 13, paragraph 3;

f   any declaration received in pursuance of the provisions of Article 18, paragraph 2;

g   any declaration received in pursuance of the provisions of Article 40, paragraphs 2 and 3;

h   any reservation or declaration made in pursuance of the provisions of Article 41, paragraph 1;

i   the withdrawal of any reservation or declaration carried out in pursuance of the provisions of Article 41, paragraph 2;

j   any declaration received in pursuance of Article 42, paragraph 1, and any subsequent notification received in pursuance of paragraph 2 of that article;

k   any notification received in pursuance of the provisions of Article 43, paragraph 4;

l   any notification received in pursuance of the provisions of Article 45 and the date on which denunciation takes effect.

Article 47

This Convention and the notifications and declarations authorised thereunder shall apply only to offences committed after the Convention comes into effect for the Contracting States involved.

In witness whereof, the undersigned, being duly authorised thereto, have signed this Convention.

Done at Strasbourg, this 15th day of May, 1972, in English and in French, both texts being equally authoritative, in a single copy, which shall remain deposited in the archives of the Council of Europe. The Secretary General shall transmit certified copies to each of the signatory and acceding governments.

Appendix I

Each Contracting State may declare that it reserves the right:

a   to refuse a request for proceedings, if it considers that the offence is a purely religious offence;

b   to refuse a request for proceedings for an act the sanctions for which, in accordance with its own law, can be imposed only by an administrative authority;

c   not to accept Article 22;

d   not to accept Article 23;

e   not to accept the provisions contained in the second sentence of Article 25 for constitutional reasons;

f   not to accept the provisions laid down in Article 26, paragraph 2, where it is competent by virtue of its own law;

g   not to apply Articles 30 and 31 in respect of an act for which the sanctions, in accordance with its own law or that of the other State concerned, can be imposed only by an administrative authority.

h   not to accept Part V.

Appendix II

Any Contracting State may declare that for reasons arising out of its constitutional law it can make or receive requests for proceedings only in circumstances specified in its municipal law.

Any Contracting State may, by means of a declaration, define as far as it is concerned the term "national" within the meaning of this Convention.

Appendix III

List of offences other than offences dealt with under criminal law

The following offences shall be assimilated to offences under criminal law

—   in France:

any unlawful behaviour sanctioned by a *contravention de grande voirie*.

—   in the Federal Republic of Germany:

any unlawful behaviour dealt with according to the procedure laid down in the Act of Violations of Regulations (*Gesetz über Ordnungswidrigkeiten* of 24 May 1968 - BGB1 1968, I, 481).

—   in Italy:

any unlawful behaviour to which is applicable Act No. 317 of 3 March 1967.

European Convention on the
Compensation of Victims of Violent Crimes (ETS No. 116)

The member States of the Council of Europe, signatory hereto,

Considering that the aim of the Council of Europe is to achieve a greater unity between its members;

Considering that for reasons of equity and social solidarity it is necessary to deal with the situation of victims of intentional crimes of violence who have suffered bodily injury or impairment of health and of dependants of persons who have died as a result of such crimes;

Considering that it is necessary to introduce or develop schemes for the compensation of these victims by the State in whose territory such crimes were committed, in particular when the offender has not been identified or is without resources;

Considering that it is necessary to establish minimum provisions in this field;

Having regard to Resolution (77) 27 of the Committee of Ministers of the Council of Europe on the compensation of victims of crime,

Have agreed as follows:

Part I – Basic principles

Article 1

The Parties undertake to take the necessary steps to give effect to the principles set out in Part I of this Convention.

Article 2

1   When compensation is not fully available from other sources the State shall contribute to compensate:

    a   those who have sustained serious bodily injury or impairment of health directly attributable to an intentional crime of violence;

    b   the dependants of persons who have died as a result of such crime.

2   Compensation shall be awarded in the above cases even if the offender cannot be prosecuted or punished.

Article 3

Compensation shall be paid by the State on whose territory the crime was committed:

a   to nationals of the States party to this Convention;

b   to nationals of all member States of the Council of Europe who are permanent residents in the State on whose territory the crime was committed.

Article 4

Compensation shall cover, according to the case under consideration, at least the following items: loss of earnings, medical and hospitalisation expenses and funeral expenses, and, as regards dependants, loss of maintenance.

Article 5

The compensation scheme may, if necessary, set for any or all elements of compensation an upper limit above which and a minimum threshold below which such compensation shall not be granted.

Article 6

The compensation scheme may specify a period within which any application for compensation must be made.

Article 7

Compensation may be reduced or refused on account of the applicant's financial situation.

Article 8

1   Compensation may be reduced or refused on account of the victim's or the applicant's conduct before, during or after the crime, or in relation to the injury or death.

2   Compensation may also be reduced or refused on account of the victim's or the applicant's involvement in organised crime or his membership of an organisation which engages in crimes of violence.

3   Compensation may also be reduced or refused if an award or a full award would be contrary to a sense of justice or to public policy (*ordre public*).

Article 9

With a view to avoiding double compensation, the State or the competent authority may deduct from the compensation awarded or reclaim from the person compensated any amount of money received, in consequence of the injury or death, from the offender, social security or insurance, or coming from any other source.

Article 10

The State or the competent authority may be subrogated to the rights of the person compensated for the amount of the compensation paid.

Article 11

Each Party shall take appropriate steps to ensure that information about the scheme is available to potential applicants.

Part II – International co-operation

Article 12

Subject to the application of bilateral or multilateral agreements on mutual assistance concluded between Contracting States, the competent authorities of each Party shall, at the request of the appropriate authorities of any other Party, give the maximum possible assistance in connection with the matters covered by this Convention. To this end, each Contracting State shall designate a central authority to receive, and to take action on, requests for such assistance, and shall inform thereof the Secretary General of the Council of Europe when depositing its instrument of ratification, acceptance, approval or accession.

Article 13

1   The European Committee on Crime Problems (CDPC) of the Council of Europe shall be kept informed regarding the application of the Convention.

2   To this end, each Party shall transmit to the Secretary General of the Council of Europe any relevant information about its legislative or regulatory provisions concerning the matters covered by the Convention.

Part III – Final clauses

Article 14

This Convention shall be open for signature by the member States of the Council of Europe. It is subject to ratification, acceptance or approval.

Instruments of ratification, acceptance or approval shall be deposited with the Secretary General of the Council of Europe.

Article 15

1   This Convention shall enter into force on the first day of the month following the expiration of a period of three months after the date on which three member States of the Council of Europe have expressed their consent to be bound by the Convention in accordance with the provisions of Article 14.

2   In respect of any member State which subsequently expresses its consent to be bound by it, the Convention shall enter into force on the first day of the month following the expiration of a period of three months after the date of the deposit of the instrument of ratification, acceptance or approval.

Article 16

1   After the entry into force of this Convention, the Committee of Ministers of the Council of Europe may invite any State not a member of the Council of Europe to accede to this Convention by a decision taken by the majority provided for in Article 20.d of the Statute of the Council of Europe and by the unanimous vote of the representatives of the Contracting States entitled to sit on the Committee.

2   In respect of any acceding State, the Convention shall enter into force on the first day of the month following the expiration of a period of three months after the date of deposit of the instrument of accession with the Secretary General of the Council of Europe.

Article 17

1   Any State may at the time of signature or when depositing its instrument of ratification, acceptance, approval or accession, specify the territory or territories to which this Convention shall apply.

2   Any State may at any later date, by a declaration addressed to the Secretary General of the Council of Europe, extend the application of this Convention to any other territory specified in the declaration. In respect of such territory the Convention shall enter into force on the first day of the month following the expiration of a period of three months after the date of receipt of such declaration by the Secretary General.

3   Any declaration made under the two preceding paragraphs may, in respect of any territory specified in such declaration, be withdrawn by a notification addressed to the Secretary General. The withdrawal shall become effective on the first day of the month following the expiration of a

period of six months after the date of receipt of such notification by the Secretary General.

Article 18

1 Any State may, at the time of signature or when depositing its instrument of ratification, acceptance, approval or accession, declare that it avails itself of one or more reservations.

2 Any Contracting State which has made a reservation under the preceding paragraph may wholly or partly withdraw it by means of a notification addressed to the Secretary General of the Council of Europe. The withdrawal shall take effect on the date of receipt of such notification by the Secretary General.

3 A Party which has made a reservation in respect of a provision of this Convention may not claim the application of that provision by any other Party; it may, however, if its reservation is partial or conditional, claim the application of that provision in so far as it has itself accepted it.

Article 19

1 Any Party may at any time denounce this Convention by means of a notification addressed to the Secretary General of the Council of Europe.

2 Such a denunciation shall become effective on the first day of the month following the expiration of a period of six months after the date of receipt of the notification by the Secretary General.

Article 20

The Secretary General of the Council of Europe shall notify the member States of the Council and any State which has acceded to this Convention, of:

a any signature;

b the deposit of any instrument of ratification, acceptance, approval or accession;

c any date of entry into force of this Convention in accordance with Articles 15, 16 and 17;

d any other act, notification or communication relating to this Convention.

In witness whereof the undersigned, being duly authorised thereto, have signed this Convention.

Done at Strasbourg, this 24th day of November 1983, in English and French, both texts being equally authentic, in a single copy which shall be deposited in the archives of the Council of Europe. The Secretary General of the Council of Europe shall transmit certified copies to each member State of the Council of Europe and to any State invited to accede to this Convention.

European Convention on Laundering, Search, Seizure and Confiscation of the Proceeds from Crime (ETS No. 141)

Preamble

The member States of the Council of Europe and the other States signatory hereto,

Considering that the aim of the Council of Europe is to achieve a greater unity between its members;

Convinced of the need to pursue a common criminal policy aimed at the protection of society;

Considering that the fight against serious crime, which has become an increasingly international problem, calls for the use of modern and effective methods on an international scale;

Believing that one of these methods consists in depriving criminals of the proceeds from crime;

Considering that for the attainment of this aim a well-functioning system of international co-operation also must be established,

Have agreed as follows:

Chapter I – Use of terms

Article I – Use of terms

For the purposes of this Convention:

a   "proceeds" means any economic advantage from criminal offences. It may consist of any property as defined in sub-paragraph b of this article;

b   "property" includes property of any description, whether corporeal or incorporeal, movable or immovable, and legal documents or instruments evidencing title to, or interest in such property;

c   "instrumentalities" means any property used or intended to be used, in any manner, wholly or in part, to commit a criminal offence or criminal offences;

d   "confiscation" means a penalty or a measure, ordered by a court following proceedings in relation to a criminal offence or criminal offences resulting in the final deprivation of property;

e   "predicate offence" means any criminal offence as a result of which proceeds were generated that may become the subject of an offence as defined in Article 6 of this Convention.

Chapter II – Measures to be taken at national level

Article 2 – Confiscation measures

1   Each Party shall adopt such legislative and other measures as may be necessary to enable it to confiscate instrumentalities and proceeds or property the value of which corresponds to such proceeds.

2   Each Party may, at the time of signature or when depositing its instrument of ratification, acceptance, approval or accession, by a declaration addressed to the Secretary General of the Council of Europe, declare that paragraph 1 of this article applies only to offences or categories of offences specified in such declaration.

Article 3 – Investigative and provisional measures

Each Party shall adopt such legislative and other measures as may be necessary to enable it to identify and trace property which is liable to confiscation pursuant to Article 2, paragraph 1, and to prevent any dealing in, transfer or disposal of such property.

Article 4 – Special investigative powers and techniques

1   Each Party shall adopt such legislative and other measures as may be necessary to empower its courts or other competent authorities to order that bank, financial or commercial records be made available or be seized in order to carry out the actions referred to in Articles 2 and 3. A Party shall not decline to act under the provisions of this article on grounds of bank secrecy.

2   Each Party shall consider adopting such legislative and other measures as may be necessary to enable it to use special investigative techniques facilitating the identification and tracing of proceeds and the gathering of evidence related thereto. Such techniques may include monitoring orders, observation, interception of telecommunications, access to computer systems and orders to produce specific documents.

Article 5 – Legal remedies

Each Party shall adopt such legislative and other measures as may be necessary to ensure that interested parties affected by measures under Articles 2 and 3 shall have effective legal remedies in order to preserve their rights.

Article 6 – Laundering offences

1   Each Party shall adopt such legislative and other measures as may be necessary to establish as offences under its domestic law, when committed intentionally:

   a   the conversion or transfer of property, knowing that such property is proceeds, for the purpose of concealing or disguising the illicit origin of the property or of assisting any person who is involved in the commission of the predicate offence to evade the legal consequences of his actions;

   b   the concealment or disguise of the true nature, source, location, disposition, movement, rights with respect to, or ownership of, property, knowing that such property is proceeds; and, subject to its constitutional principles and the basic concepts of its legal system;

   c   the acquisition, possession or use of property, knowing, at the time of receipt, that such property was proceeds;

   d   participation in, association or conspiracy to commit, attempts to commit and aiding, abetting, facilitating and counselling the commission of any of the offences established in accordance with this article.

2   For the purposes of implementing or applying paragraph 1 of this article:

   a   it shall not matter whether the predicate offence was subject to the criminal jurisdiction of the Party;

   b   it may be provided that the offences set forth in that paragraph do not apply to the persons who committed the predicate offence;

   c   knowledge, intent or purpose required as an element of an offence set forth in that paragraph may be inferred from objective, factual circumstances.

3   Each Party may adopt such measures as it considers necessary to establish also as offences under its domestic law all or some of the acts referred to in paragraph 1 of this article, in any or all of the following cases where the offender:

   a   ought to have assumed that the property was proceeds;

   b   acted for the purpose of making profit;

   c   acted for the purpose of promoting the carrying on of further criminal activity.

4   Each Party may, at the time of signature or when depositing its instrument of ratification, acceptance, approval or accession, by declaration addressed to the Secretary General of the Council of Europe declare that paragraph 1 of this article applies only to predicate offences or categories of such offences specified in such declaration.

Chapter III – International co-operation

Section 1 – Principles of international co-operation

Article 7 – General principles and measures for international co-operation

1   The Parties shall co-operate with each other to the widest extent possible for the purposes of investigations and proceedings aiming at the confiscation of instrumentalities and proceeds.

2   Each Party shall adopt such legislative or other measures as may be necessary to enable it to comply, under the conditions provided for in this chapter, with requests:

a   for confiscation of specific items of property representing proceeds or instrumentalities, as well as for confiscation of proceeds consisting in a requirement to pay a sum of money corresponding to the value of proceeds;

b   for investigative assistance and provisional measures with a view to either form of confiscation referred to under a above.

Section 2 – Investigative assistance

Article 8 – Obligation to assist

The Parties shall afford each other, upon request, the widest possible measure of assistance in the identification and tracing of instrumentalities, proceeds and other property liable to confiscation. Such assistance shall include any measure providing and securing evidence as to the existence, location or movement, nature, legal status or value of the aforementioned property.

Article 9 – Execution of assistance

The assistance pursuant to Article 8 shall be carried out as permitted by and in accordance with the domestic law of the requested Party and, to the extent not incompatible with such law, in accordance with the procedures specified in the request.

Article 10 – Spontaneous information

Without prejudice to its own investigations or proceedings, a Party may without prior request forward to another Party information on instrumentalities and proceeds, when it considers that the disclosure of such information might assist the receiving Party in initiating or carrying out investigations or proceedings or might lead to a request by that Party under this chapter.

Section 3 – Provisional measures

Article 11 – Obligation to take provisional measures

1   At the request of another Party which has instituted criminal proceedings or proceedings for the purpose of confiscation, a Party shall take the necessary provisional measures, such as freezing or seizing, to prevent any dealing in, transfer or disposal of property which, at a later stage, may be the subject of a request for confiscation or which might be such as to satisfy the request.

2   A Party which has received a request for confiscation pursuant to Article 13 shall, if so requested, take the measures mentioned in paragraph 1 of this article in respect of any property which is the subject of the request or which might be such as to satisfy the request.

Article 12 – Execution of provisional measures

1   The provisional measures mentioned in Article 11 shall be carried out as permitted by and in accordance with the domestic law of the requested Party and, to the extent not incompatible with such law, in accordance with the procedures specified in the request.

2   Before lifting any provisional measure taken pursuant to this article, the requested Party shall, wherever possible, give the requesting Party an opportunity to present its reasons in favour of continuing the measure.

Section 4 – Confiscation

Article 13 – Obligation to confiscate

1   A Party, which has received a request made by another Party for confiscation concerning instrumentalities or proceeds, situated in its territory, shall:

a enforce a confiscation order made by a court of a requesting Party in relation to such instrumentalities or proceeds; or b	submit the request to its competent authorities for the purpose of obtaining an order of confiscation and, if such order is granted, enforce it.

2	For the purposes of applying paragraph 1.b of this article, any Party shall whenever necessary have competence to institute confiscation proceedings under its own law.

3	The provisions of paragraph 1 of this article shall also apply to confiscation consisting in a requirement to pay a sum of money corresponding to the value of proceeds, if property on which the confiscation can be enforced is located in the requested Party. In such cases, when enforcing confiscation pursuant to paragraph 1, the requested Party shall, if payment is not obtained, realise the claim on any property available for that purpose.

4	If a request for confiscation concerns a specific item of property, the Parties may agree that the requested Party may enforce the confiscation in the form of a requirement to pay a sum of money corresponding to the value of the property.

Article 14 – Execution of confiscation

1	The procedures for obtaining and enforcing the confiscation under Article 13 shall be governed by the law of the requested Party.

2	The requested Party shall be bound by the findings as to the facts in so far as they are stated in a conviction or judicial decision of the requesting Party or in so far as such conviction or judicial decision is implicitly based on them.

3	Each Party may, at the time of signature or when depositing its instrument of ratification, acceptance, approval or accession, by a declaration addressed to the Secretary General of the Council of Europe, declare that paragraph 2 of this article applies only subject to its constitutional principles and the basic concepts of its legal system.

4	If the confiscation consists in the requirement to pay a sum of money, the competent authority of the requested Party shall convert the amount thereof into the currency of that Party at the rate of exchange ruling at the time when the decision to enforce the confiscation is taken.

5	In the case of Article 13, paragraph 1.a, the requesting Party alone shall have the right to decide on any application for review of the confiscation order.

Article 15 – Confiscated property

Any property confiscated by the requested Party shall be disposed of by that Party in accordance with its domestic law, unless otherwise agreed by the Parties concerned.

Article 16 – Right of enforcement and maximum amount of confiscation

1   A request for confiscation made under Article 13 does not affect the right of the requesting Party to enforce itself the confiscation order.

2   Nothing in this Convention shall be so interpreted as to permit the total value of the confiscation to exceed the amount of the sum of money specified in the confiscation order. If a Party finds that this might occur, the Parties concerned shall enter into consultations to avoid such an effect.

Article 17 – Imprisonment in default

The requested Party shall not impose imprisonment in default or any other measure restricting the liberty of a person as a result of a request under Article 13, if the requesting Party has so specified in the request.

Section 5 – Refusal and postponement of co-operation

Article 18 – Grounds for refusal

1   Co-operation under this chapter may be refused if:

a   the action sought would be contrary to the fundamental principles of the legal system of the requested Party; or

b   the execution of the request is likely to prejudice the sovereignty, security, *ordre public* or other essential interests of the requested Party; or

c   in the opinion of the requested Party, the importance of the case to which the request relates does not justify the taking of the action sought; or

d   the offence to which the request relates is a political or fiscal offence; or

e   the requested Party considers that compliance with the action sought would be contrary to the principle of *ne bis in idem*; or

f   the offence to which the request relates would not be an offence under the law of the requested Party if committed within its jurisdiction. However, this ground for refusal applies to co-operation under Section 2 only in so far as the assistance sought involves coercive action.

2   Co-operation under Section 2, in so far as the assistance sought involves coercive action, and under Section 3 of this chapter, may also be refused if the measures sought could not be taken under the domestic law of the requested Party for the purposes of investigations or proceedings, had it been a similar domestic case.

3   Where the law of the requested Party so requires, co-operation under Section 2, in so far as the assistance sought involves coercive action, and under Section 3 of this chapter may also be refused if the measures sought or any other measures having similar effects would not be permitted under the law of the requesting Party, or, as regards the competent authorities of the requesting Party, if the request is not authorised by either a judge or another judicial authority, including public prosecutors, any of these authorities acting in relation to criminal offences.

4   Co-operation under Section 4 of this chapter may also be refused if:

a   under the law of the requested Party confiscation is not provided for in respect of the type of offence to which the request relates; or

b   without prejudice to the obligation pursuant to Article 13, paragraph 3, it would be contrary to the principles of the domestic laws of the requested Party concerning the limits of confiscation in respect of the relationship between an offence and:

   i   an economic advantage that might be qualified as its proceeds; or

   ii   property that might be qualified as its instrumentalities; or

c   under the law of the requested Party confiscation may no longer be imposed or enforced because of the lapse of time; or

d   the request does not relate to a previous conviction, or a decision of a judicial nature or a statement in such a decision that an offence or several offences have been committed, on the basis of which the confiscation has been ordered or is sought; or

e   confiscation is either not enforceable in the requesting Party, or it is still subject to ordinary means of appeal; or

f   the request relates to a confiscation order resulting from a decision rendered *in absentia* of the person against whom the order was issued and, in the opinion of the requested Party, the proceedings conducted by the requesting Party leading to such decision did not satisfy the minimum rights of defence recognised as due to everyone against whom a criminal charge is made.

5   For the purpose of paragraph 4.f of this article a decision is not considered to have been rendered *in absentia* if:

a   it has been confirmed or pronounced after opposition by the person concerned; or

b   it has been rendered on appeal, provided that the appeal was lodged by the person concerned.

6   When considering, for the purposes of paragraph 4.f of this article if the minimum rights of defence have been satisfied, the requested Party shall take into account the fact that the person concerned has deliberately sought to evade justice or the fact that that person, having had the possibility of lodging a legal remedy against the decision made *in absentia*, elected not to do so. The same will apply when the person concerned, having been duly served with the summons to appear, elected not to do so nor to ask for adjournment.

7   A Party shall not invoke bank secrecy as a ground to refuse any co-operation under this chapter. Where its domestic law so requires, a Party may require that a request for co-operation which would involve the lifting of bank secrecy be authorised by either a judge or another judicial authority, including public prosecutors, any of these authorities acting in relation to criminal offences.

8   Without prejudice to the ground for refusal provided for in paragraph 1.a of this article:

a   the fact that the person under investigation or subjected to a confiscation order by the authorities of the requesting Party is a legal person shall not be invoked by the requested Party as an obstacle to affording any co-operation under this chapter;

b   the fact that the natural person against whom an order of confiscation of proceeds has been issued has subsequently died or the fact that a legal person against whom an order of confiscation of proceeds has been issued has subsequently been dissolved shall not be invoked as an obstacle to render assistance in accordance with Article 13, paragraph 1.a.

Article 19 – Postponement

The requested Party may postpone action on a request if such action would prejudice investigations or proceedings by its authorities.

Article 20 – Partial or conditional granting of a request

Before refusing or postponing co-operation under this chapter, the requested Party shall, where appropriate after having consulted the requesting Party, consider whether the request may be granted partially or subject to such conditions as it deems necessary.

Section 6 – Notification and protection of third parties' rights

Article 21 – Notification of documents

1   The Parties shall afford each other the widest measure of mutual assistance in the serving of judicial documents to persons affected by provisional measures and confiscation.

2   Nothing in this article is intended to interfere with:

a   the possibility of sending judicial documents, by postal channels, directly to persons abroad;

b   the possibility for judicial officers, officials or other competent authorities of the Party of origin to effect service of judicial documents directly through the consular authorities of that Party or through judicial officers, officials or other competent authorities of the Party of destination,

unless the Party of destination makes a declaration to the contrary to the Secretary General of the Council of Europe at the time of signature or when depositing its instrument of ratification, acceptance, approval or accession.

3   When serving judicial documents to persons abroad affected by provisional measures or confiscation orders issued in the sending Party, this Party shall indicate what legal remedies are available under its law to such persons.

Article 22 – Recognition of foreign decisions

1   When dealing with a request for co-operation under Sections 3 and 4, the requested Party shall recognise any judicial decision taken in the requesting Party regarding rights claimed by third parties.

2   Recognition may be refused if:

a   third parties did not have adequate opportunity to assert their rights; or

b   the decision is incompatible with a decision already taken in the requested Party on the same matter; or c   it is incompatible with the *ordre public* of the requested Party; or

d   the decision was taken contrary to provisions on exclusive jurisdiction provided for by the law of the requested Party.

Section 7 – Procedural and other general rules

Article 23 – Central authority

1   The Parties shall designate a central authority or, if necessary, authorities, which shall be responsible for sending and answering requests made under this chapter, the execution of such requests or the transmission of them to the authorities competent for their execution.

2   Each Party shall, at the time of signature or when depositing its instrument of ratification, acceptance, approval or accession, communicate to the Secretary General of the Council of Europe the names and addresses of the authorities designated in pursuance of paragraph 1 of this article.

Article 24 – Direct communication

1   The central authorities shall communicate directly with one another.

2   In the event of urgency, requests or communications under this chapter may be sent directly by the judicial authorities, including public prosecutors, of the requesting Party to such authorities of the requested Party. In such cases a copy shall be sent at the same time to the central authority of the requested Party through the central authority of the requesting Party.

3   Any request or communication under paragraphs 1 and 2 of this article may be made through the International Criminal Police Organisation (Interpol).

4   Where a request is made pursuant to paragraph 2 of this article and the authority is not competent to deal with the request, it shall refer the request to the competent national authority and inform directly the requesting Party that it has done so.

5   Requests or communications under Section 2 of this chapter, which do not involve coercive action, may be directly transmitted by the competent authorities of the requesting Party to the competent authorities of the requested Party.

Article 25 – Form of request and languages

1   All requests under this chapter shall be made in writing. Modern means of telecommunications, such as telefax, may be used.

2   Subject to the provisions of paragraph 3 of this article, translations of the requests or supporting documents shall not be required.

3   At the time of signature or when depositing its instrument of ratification, acceptance, approval or accession, any Party may communicate to the Secretary General of the Council of Europe a declaration that it reserves the right to require that requests made to it and documents supporting such requests be accompanied by a translation into its own language or into one of the official languages of the Council of Europe or into such one of these languages as it shall indicate. It may on that occasion declare its readiness to accept translations in any other language as it may specify. The other Parties may apply the reciprocity rule.

Article 26 – Legalisation

Documents transmitted in application of this chapter shall be exempt from all legalisation formalities.

Article 27 – Content of request

1   Any request for co-operation under this chapter shall specify:

a   the authority making the request and the authority carrying out the investigations or proceedings;

b   the object of and the reason for the request;

c   the matters, including the relevant facts (such as date, place and circumstances of the offence) to which the investigations or proceedings relate, except in the case of a request for notification;

d   in so far as the co-operation involves coercive action:

   i   the text of the statutory provisions or, where this is not possible, a statement of the relevant law applicable; and

   ii   an indication that the measure sought or any other measures having similar effects could be taken in the territory of the requesting Party under its own law;

e   where necessary and in so far as possible:

	i	details of the person or persons concerned, including name, date and place of birth, nationality and location, and, in the case of a legal person, its seat; and

	ii	the property in relation to which co-operation is sought, its location, its connection with the person or persons concerned, any connection with the offence, as well as any available information about other persons, interests in the property; and

    f   any particular procedure the requesting Party wishes to be followed.

2   A request for provisional measures under Section 3 in relation to seizure of property on which a confiscation order consisting in the requirement to pay a sum of money may be realised shall also indicate a maximum amount for which recovery is sought in that property.

3   In addition to the indications mentioned in paragraph 1, any request under Section 4 shall contain:

    a   in the case of Article 13, paragraph 1.a:

	i	a certified true copy of the confiscation order made by the court in the requesting Party and a statement of the grounds on the basis of which the order was made, if they are not indicated in the order itself;

	ii	an attestation by the competent authority of the requesting Party that the confiscation order is enforceable and not subject to ordinary means of appeal;

	iii	information as to the extent to which the enforcement of the order is requested; and

	iv	information as to the necessity of taking any provisional measures;

    b   in the case of Article 13, paragraph 1.b, a statement of the facts relied upon by the requesting Party sufficient to enable the requested Party to seek the order under its domestic law;

    c   when third parties have had the opportunity to claim rights, documents demonstrating that this has been the case.

Article 28 – Defective requests

1   If a request does not comply with the provisions of this chapter or the information supplied is not sufficient to enable the requested Party to deal with the request, that Party may ask the requesting Party to amend the request or to complete it with additional information.

2   The requested Party may set a time-limit for the receipt of such amendments or information.

3   Pending receipt of the requested amendments or information in relation to a request under Section 4 of this chapter, the requested Party may take any of the measures referred to in Sections 2 or 3 of this chapter.

Article 29 – Plurality of requests

1   Where the requested Party receives more than one request under Sections 3 or 4 of this chapter in respect of the same person or property, the plurality of requests shall not prevent that Party from dealing with the requests involving the taking of provisional measures.

2   In the case of plurality of requests under Section 4 of this chapter, the requested Party shall consider consulting the requesting Parties.

Article 30 – Obligation to give reasons

The requested Party shall give reasons for any decision to refuse, postpone or make conditional any co-operation under this chapter.

Article 31 – Information

1   The requested Party shall promptly inform the requesting Party of:

a   the action initiated on a request under this chapter;

b   the final result of the action carried out on the basis of the request;

c   a decision to refuse, postpone or make conditional, in whole or in part, any co-operation under this chapter;

d   any circumstances which render impossible the carrying out of the action sought or are likely to delay it significantly; and

e   in the event of provisional measures taken pursuant to a request under Sections 2 or 3 of this chapter, such provisions of its domestic law as would automatically lead to the lifting of the provisional measure.

2   The requesting Party shall promptly inform the requested Party of:

a   any review, decision or any other fact by reason of which the confiscation order ceases to be wholly or partially enforceable; and

b   any development, factual or legal, by reason of which any action under this chapter is no longer justified.

3   Where a Party, on the basis of the same confiscation order, requests confiscation in more than one Party, it shall inform all Parties which are affected by an enforcement of the order about the request.

Article 32 – Restriction of use

1   The requested Party may make the execution of a request dependent on the condition that the information or evidence obtained will not, without its prior consent, be used or transmitted by the authorities of the requesting Party for investigations or proceedings other than those specified in the request.

2   Each Party may, at the time of signature or when depositing its instrument of ratification, acceptance, approval or accession, by declaration addressed to the Secretary General of the Council of Europe, declare that, without its prior consent, information or evidence provided by it under this chapter may not be used or transmitted by the authorities of the requesting Party in investigations or proceedings other than those specified in the request.

Article 33 – Confidentiality

1   The requesting Party may require that the requested Party keep confidential the facts and substance of the request, except to the extent necessary to execute the request. If the requested Party cannot comply with the requirement of confidentiality, it shall promptly inform the requesting Party.

2   The requesting Party shall, if not contrary to basic principles of its national law and if so requested, keep confidential any evidence and information provided by the requested Party, except to the extent that its disclosure is necessary for the investigations or proceedings described in the request.

3   Subject to the provisions of its domestic law, a Party which has received spontaneous information under Article 10 shall comply with any requirement of confidentiality as required by the Party which supplies the information. If the other Party cannot comply with such requirement, it shall promptly inform the transmitting Party.

Article 34 – Costs

The ordinary costs of complying with a request shall be borne by the requested Party. Where costs of a substantial or extraordinary nature are necessary to comply with a request, the Parties shall consult in order to agree the conditions on which the request is to be executed and how the costs shall be borne.

Article 35 – Damages

1   When legal action on liability for damages resulting from an act or omission in relation to co-operation under this chapter has been initiated by a person, the Parties concerned shall consider consulting each other, where appropriate, to determine how to apportion any sum of damages due.

2   A Party which has become subject of a litigation for damages shall endeavour to inform the other Party of such litigation if that Party might have an interest in the case.

Chapter IV – Final provisions

Article 36 – Signature and entry into force

1   This Convention shall be open for signature by the member States of the Council of Europe and non-member States which have participated in its elaboration. Such States may express their consent to be bound by:

a   signature without reservation as to ratification, acceptance or approval; or

b   signature subject to ratification, acceptance or approval, followed by ratification, acceptance or approval.

2   Instruments of ratification, acceptance or approval shall be deposited with the Secretary General of the Council of Europe.

3   This Convention shall enter into force on the first day of the month following the expiration of a period of three months after the date on which three States, of which at least two are member States of the Council of Europe, have expressed their consent to be bound by the Convention in accordance with the provisions of paragraph 1.

4   In respect of any signatory State which subsequently expresses its consent to be bound by it, the Convention shall enter into force on the first day of the month following the expiration of a period of three months after the date of the expression of its consent to be bound by the Convention in accordance with the provisions of paragraph 1.

Article 37 – Accession to the Convention

1   After the entry into force of this Convention, the Committee of Ministers of the Council of Europe, after consulting the Contracting States to the Convention, may invite any State not a member of the Council and not having participated in its elaboration to accede to this Convention, by a decision taken by the majority provided for in Article 20.d. of the Statute

of the Council of Europe and by the unanimous vote of the representatives of the Contracting States entitled to sit on the Committee.

2   In respect of any acceding State the Convention shall enter into force on the first day of the month following the expiration of a period of three months after the date of deposit of the instrument of accession with the Secretary General of the Council of Europe.

Article 38 – Territorial application

1   Any State may, at the time of signature or when depositing its instrument of ratification, acceptance, approval or accession, specify the territory or territories to which this Convention shall apply.

2   Any State may, at any later date, by a declaration addressed to the Secretary General of the Council of Europe, extend the application of this Convention to any other territory specified in the declaration. In respect of such territory the Convention shall enter into force on the first day of the month following the expiration of a period of three months after the date of receipt of such declaration by the Secretary General.

3   Any declaration made under the two preceding paragraphs may, in respect of any territory specified in such declaration, be withdrawn by a notification addressed to the Secretary General. The withdrawal shall become effective on the first day of the month following the expiration of a period of three months after the date of receipt of such notification by the Secretary General.

Article 39 – Relationship to other conventions and agreements

1   This Convention does not affect the rights and undertakings derived from international multilateral conventions concerning special matters.

2   The Parties to the Convention may conclude bilateral or multilateral agreements with one another on the matters dealt with in this Convention, for purposes of supplementing or strengthening its provisions or facilitating the application of the principles embodied in it.

3   If two or more Parties have already concluded an agreement or treaty in respect of a subject which is dealt with in this Convention or otherwise have established their relations in respect of that subject, they shall be entitled to apply that agreement or treaty or to regulate those relations accordingly, in lieu of the present Convention, if it facilitates international co-operation.

Article 40 – Reservations

1   Any State may, at the time of signature or when depositing its instrument of ratification, acceptance, approval or accession, declare that it avails

itself of one or more of the reservations provided for in Article 2, paragraph 2, Article 6, paragraph 4, Article 14, paragraph 3, Article 21, paragraph 2, Article 25, paragraph 3 and Article 32, paragraph 2. No other reservation may be made.

2   Any State which has made a reservation under the preceding paragraph may wholly or partly withdraw it by means of a notification addressed to the Secretary General of the Council of Europe. The withdrawal shall take effect on the date of receipt of such notification by the Secretary General.

3   A Party which has made a reservation in respect of a provision of this Convention may not claim the application of that provision by any other Party; it may, however, if its reservation is partial or conditional, claim the application of that provision in so far as it has itself accepted it.

Article 41 – Amendments

1   Amendments to this Convention may be proposed by any Party, and shall be communicated by the Secretary General of the Council of Europe to the member States of the Council of Europe and to every non-member State which has acceded to or has been invited to accede to this Convention in accordance with the provisions of Article 37.

2   Any amendment proposed by a Party shall be communicated to the European Committee on Crime Problems which shall submit to the Committee of Ministers its opinion on that proposed amendment.

3   The Committee of Ministers shall consider the proposed amendment and the opinion submitted by the European Committee on Crime Problems and may adopt the amendment.

4   The text of any amendment adopted by the Committee of Ministers in accordance with paragraph 3 of this article shall be forwarded to the Parties for acceptance.

5   Any amendment adopted in accordance with paragraph 3 of this article shall come into force on the thirtieth day after all Parties have informed the Secretary General of their acceptance thereof.

Article 42 – Settlement of disputes

1   The European Committee on Crime Problems of the Council of Europe shall be kept informed regarding the interpretation and application of this Convention.

2   In case of a dispute between Parties as to the interpretation or application of this Convention, they shall seek a settlement of the dispute through negotiation or any other peaceful means of their choice, including submission of the dispute to the European Committee on Crime

Problems, to an arbitral tribunal whose decisions shall be binding upon the Parties, or to the International Court of Justice, as agreed upon by the Parties concerned.

Article 43 – Denunciation

1   Any Party may, at any time, denounce this Convention by means of a notification addressed to the Secretary General of the Council of Europe.

2   Such denunciation shall become effective on the first day of the month following the expiration of a period of three months after the date of receipt of the notification by the Secretary General.

3   The present Convention shall, however, continue to apply to the enforcement under Article 14 of confiscation for which a request has been made in conformity with the provisions of this Convention before the date on which such a denunciation takes effect.

Article 44 – Notifications

The Secretary General of the Council of Europe shall notify the member States of the Council and any State which has acceded to this Convention of:

a   any signature;

b   the deposit of any instrument of ratification, acceptance, approval or accession;

c   any date of entry into force of this Convention in accordance with Articles 36 and 37;

d   any reservation made under Article 40, paragraph 1;

e   any other act, notification or communication relating to this Convention.

In witness whereof the undersigned, being duly authorised thereto, have signed this Convention.

Done at Strasbourg, the 8th day of November 1990, in English and in French, both texts being equally authentic, in a single copy which shall be deposited in the archives of the Council of Europe. The Secretary General of the Council of Europe shall transmit certified copies to each member State of the Council of Europe, to the non-member States which have participated in the elaboration of this Convention, and to any State invited to accede to it.

European Convention on Cybercrime (ETS No. 185)

Preamble

The member States of the Council of Europe and the other States signatory hereto,

Considering that the aim of the Council of Europe is to achieve a greater unity between its members;

Recognising the value of fostering co-operation with the other States parties to this Convention;

Convinced of the need to pursue, as a matter of priority, a common criminal policy aimed at the protection of society against cybercrime, inter alia, by adopting appropriate legislation and fostering international co-operation;

Conscious of the profound changes brought about by the digitalisation, convergence and continuing globalisation of computer networks;

Concerned by the risk that computer networks and electronic information may also be used for committing criminal offences and that evidence relating to such offences may be stored and transferred by these networks;

Recognising the need for co-operation between States and private industry in combating cybercrime and the need to protect legitimate interests in the use and development of information technologies;

Believing that an effective fight against cybercrime requires increased, rapid and well-functioning international co-operation in criminal matters;

Convinced that the present Convention is necessary to deter action directed against the confidentiality, integrity and availability of computer systems, networks and computer data as well as the misuse of such systems, networks and data by providing for the criminalisation of such conduct, as described in this Convention, and the adoption of powers sufficient for effectively combating such criminal offences, by facilitating their detection, investigation and prosecution at both the domestic and international levels and by providing arrangements for fast and reliable international co-operation;

Mindful of the need to ensure a proper balance between the interests of law enforcement and respect for fundamental human rights as enshrined in the 1950 Council of Europe Convention for the Protection of Human Rights and Fundamental Freedoms, the 1966 United Nations International Covenant on Civil and Political Rights and other applicable international human rights treaties, which reaffirm the right of everyone to hold opinions without interference, as well as the right to freedom of expression, including the freedom to seek, receive, and impart information and ideas of all kinds, regardless of frontiers, and the rights concerning the respect for privacy;

Mindful also of the right to the protection of personal data, as conferred, for example, by the 1981 Council of Europe Convention for the Protection of Individuals with regard to Automatic Processing of Personal Data;

Considering the 1989 United Nations Convention on the Rights of the Child and the 1999 International Labour Organization Worst Forms of Child Labour Convention;

Taking into account the existing Council of Europe conventions on co-operation in the penal field, as well as similar treaties which exist between Council of Europe member States and other States, and stressing that the present Convention is intended to supplement those conventions in order to make criminal investigations and proceedings concerning criminal offences related to computer systems and data more effective and to enable the collection of evidence in electronic form of a criminal offence;

Welcoming recent developments which further advance international understanding and co-operation in combating cybercrime, including action taken by the United Nations, the OECD, the European Union and the G8;

Recalling Committee of Ministers Recommendations No. R (85) 10 concerning the practical application of the European Convention on Mutual Assistance in Criminal Matters in respect of letters rogatory for the interception of telecommunications, No. R (88) 2 on piracy in the field of copyright and neighbouring rights, No. R (87) 15 regulating the use of personal data in the police sector, No. R (95) 4 on the protection of personal data in the area of telecommunication services, with particular reference to telephone services, as well as No. R (89) 9 on computer-related crime providing guidelines for national legislatures concerning the definition of certain computer crimes and No. R (95) 13 concerning problems of criminal procedural law connected with information technology;

Having regard to Resolution No. 1 adopted by the European Ministers of Justice at their 21st Conference (Prague, 10 and 11 June 1997), which recommended that the Committee of Ministers support the work on cybercrime carried out by the European Committee on Crime Problems (CDPC) in order to bring domestic criminal law provisions closer to each other and enable the use of effective means of investigation into such offences, as well as to Resolution No. 3 adopted at the 23rd Conference of the European Ministers of Justice (London, 8 and 9 June 2000), which encouraged the negotiating parties to pursue their efforts with a view to finding appropriate solutions to enable the largest possible number of States to become parties to the Convention and acknowledged the need for a swift and efficient system of international co-operation, which duly takes into account the specific requirements of the fight against cybercrime;

Having also regard to the Action Plan adopted by the Heads of State and Government of the Council of Europe on the occasion of their Second Summit (Strasbourg, 10 and 11 October 1997), to seek common responses to the development of the new information technologies based on the standards and values of the Council of Europe;

Have agreed as follows:

Chapter I – Use of terms

Article 1 – Definitions

For the purposes of this Convention:

a   "computer system" means any device or a group of interconnected or related devices, one or more of which, pursuant to a program, performs automatic processing of data;

b   "computer data" means any representation of facts, information or concepts in a form suitable for processing in a computer system, including a program suitable to cause a computer system to perform a function;

c   "service provider" means:

    i   any public or private entity that provides to users of its service the ability to communicate by means of a computer system, and

    ii   any other entity that processes or stores computer data on behalf of such communication service or users of such service;

d   "traffic data" means any computer data relating to a communication by means of a computer system, generated by a computer system that formed a part in the chain of communication, indicating the communication's origin, destination, route, time, date, size, duration, or type of underlying service.

Chapter II – Measures to be taken at the national level

Section 1 – Substantive criminal law

Title 1 – Offences against the confidentiality, integrity and availability of computer data and systems

Article 2 – Illegal access

Each Party shall adopt such legislative and other measures as may be necessary to establish as criminal offences under its domestic law, when committed intentionally, the access to the whole or any part of a computer system without right. A Party may require that the offence be committed by infringing security measures, with the intent of obtaining computer data or other dishonest intent, or in relation to a computer system that is connected to another computer system.

Article 3 – Illegal interception

Each Party shall adopt such legislative and other measures as may be necessary to establish as criminal offences under its domestic law, when committed intentionally, the interception without right, made by technical means, of non-public transmissions of computer data to, from or within a computer system, including electromagnetic emissions from a computer system carrying such computer data. A Party may require that the offence be committed with dishonest intent, or in relation to a computer system that is connected to another computer system.

Article 4 – Data interference

1   Each Party shall adopt such legislative and other measures as may be necessary to establish as criminal offences under its domestic law, when committed intentionally, the damaging, deletion, deterioration, alteration or suppression of computer data without right.

2   A Party may reserve the right to require that the conduct described in paragraph 1 result in serious harm.

Article 5 – System interference

Each Party shall adopt such legislative and other measures as may be necessary to establish as criminal offences under its domestic law, when committed intentionally, the serious hindering without right of the functioning of a computer system by inputting, transmitting, damaging, deleting, deteriorating, altering or suppressing computer data.

Article 6 – Misuse of devices

1   Each Party shall adopt such legislative and other measures as may be necessary to establish as criminal offences under its domestic law, when committed intentionally and without right:

a   the production, sale, procurement for use, import, distribution or otherwise making available of:

   i   a device, including a computer program, designed or adapted primarily for the purpose of committing any of the offences established in accordance with the above Articles 2 through 5;

   ii   a computer password, access code, or similar data by which the whole or any part of a computer system is capable of being accessed,

   with intent that it be used for the purpose of committing any of the offences established in Articles 2 through 5; and

b   the possession of an item referred to in paragraphs a.i or ii above, with intent that it be used for the purpose of committing any of the offences established in Articles 2 through 5. A Party may require by law that a number of such items be possessed before criminal liability attaches.

2   This article shall not be interpreted as imposing criminal liability where the production, sale, procurement for use, import, distribution or otherwise making available or possession referred to in paragraph 1 of this article is not for the purpose of committing an offence established in accordance with Articles 2 through 5 of this Convention, such as for the authorised testing or protection of a computer system.

3   Each Party may reserve the right not to apply paragraph 1 of this article, provided that the reservation does not concern the sale, distribution or otherwise making available of the items referred to in paragraph 1 a.ii of this article.

Title 2 – Computer-related offences

Article 7 – Computer-related forgery

Each Party shall adopt such legislative and other measures as may be necessary to establish as criminal offences under its domestic law, when committed intentionally and without right, the input, alteration, deletion, or suppression of computer data, resulting in inauthentic data with the intent that it be considered or acted upon for legal purposes as if it were authentic, regardless whether or not the data is directly readable and intelligible. A Party may require an intent to defraud, or similar dishonest intent, before criminal liability attaches.

Article 8 – Computer-related fraud

Each Party shall adopt such legislative and other measures as may be necessary to establish as criminal offences under its domestic law, when committed intentionally and without right, the causing of a loss of property to another person by:

a   any input, alteration, deletion or suppression of computer data;

b   any interference with the functioning of a computer system,

with fraudulent or dishonest intent of procuring, without right, an economic benefit for oneself or for another person.

Title 3 – Content-related offences

Article 9 – Offences related to child pornography

1   Each Party shall adopt such legislative and other measures as may be necessary to establish as criminal offences under its domestic law, when committed intentionally and without right, the following conduct:

a   producing child pornography for the purpose of its distribution through a computer system;

b   offering or making available child pornography through a computer system;

c   distributing or transmitting child pornography through a computer system;

d   procuring child pornography through a computer system for oneself or for another person;

e   possessing child pornography in a computer system or on a computer-data storage medium.

2   For the purpose of paragraph 1 above, the term "child pornography" shall include pornographic material that visually depicts:

a   a minor engaged in sexually explicit conduct;

b   a person appearing to be a minor engaged in sexually explicit conduct;

c   realistic images representing a minor engaged in sexually explicit conduct.

3   For the purpose of paragraph 2 above, the term "minor" shall include all persons under 18 years of age. A Party may, however, require a lower age-limit, which shall be not less than 16 years.

4   Each Party may reserve the right not to apply, in whole or in part, paragraphs 1, sub-paragraphs d. and e, and 2, sub-paragraphs b. and c.

Title 4 – Offences related to infringements of copyright and related rights

Article 10 – Offences related to infringements of copyright and related rights

1   Each Party shall adopt such legislative and other measures as may be necessary to establish as criminal offences under its domestic law the infringement of copyright, as defined under the law of that Party, pursuant to the obligations it has undertaken under the Paris Act of 24 July 1971 revising the Bern Convention for the Protection of Literary and Artistic Works, the Agreement on Trade-Related Aspects of Intellectual Property Rights and the WIPO Copyright Treaty, with the exception of any moral rights conferred by such conventions, where such acts are committed wilfully, on a commercial scale and by means of a computer system.

2   Each Party shall adopt such legislative and other measures as may be necessary to establish as criminal offences under its domestic law the infringement of related rights, as defined under the law of that Party, pursuant to the obligations it has undertaken under the International Convention for the Protection of Performers, Producers of Phonograms and Broadcasting Organisations (Rome Convention), the Agreement on Trade-Related Aspects of Intellectual Property Rights and the WIPO Performances and Phonograms Treaty, with the exception of any moral rights conferred by such conventions, where such acts are committed wilfully, on a commercial scale and by means of a computer system.

3   A Party may reserve the right not to impose criminal liability under paragraphs 1 and 2 of this article in limited circumstances, provided that other effective remedies are available and that such reservation does not derogate from the Party's international obligations set forth in the international instruments referred to in paragraphs 1 and 2 of this article.

Title 5 – Ancillary liability and sanctions

Article 11 – Attempt and aiding or abetting

1   Each Party shall adopt such legislative and other measures as may be necessary to establish as criminal offences under its domestic law, when

committed intentionally, aiding or abetting the commission of any of the offences established in accordance with Articles 2 through 10 of the present Convention with intent that such offence be committed.

2   Each Party shall adopt such legislative and other measures as may be necessary to establish as criminal offences under its domestic law, when committed intentionally, an attempt to commit any of the offences established in accordance with Articles 3 through 5, 7, 8, and 9.1.a and c. of this Convention.

3   Each Party may reserve the right not to apply, in whole or in part, paragraph 2 of this article.

Article 12 – Corporate liability

1   Each Party shall adopt such legislative and other measures as may be necessary to ensure that legal persons can be held liable for a criminal offence established in accordance with this Convention, committed for their benefit by any natural person, acting either individually or as part of an organ of the legal person, who has a leading position within it, based on:

a   a power of representation of the legal person;

b   an authority to take decisions on behalf of the legal person;

c   an authority to exercise control within the legal person.

2   In addition to the cases already provided for in paragraph 1 of this article, each Party shall take the measures necessary to ensure that a legal person can be held liable where the lack of supervision or control by a natural person referred to in paragraph 1 has made possible the commission of a criminal offence established in accordance with this Convention for the benefit of that legal person by a natural person acting under its authority.

3   Subject to the legal principles of the Party, the liability of a legal person may be criminal, civil or administrative.

4   Such liability shall be without prejudice to the criminal liability of the natural persons who have committed the offence.

Article 13 – Sanctions and measures

1   Each Party shall adopt such legislative and other measures as may be necessary to ensure that the criminal offences established in accordance with Articles 2 through 11 are punishable by effective, proportionate and dissuasive sanctions, which include deprivation of liberty.

2   Each Party shall ensure that legal persons held liable in accordance with Article 12 shall be subject to effective, proportionate and dissuasive criminal or non-criminal sanctions or measures, including monetary sanctions.

Section 2 – Procedural law

Title 1 – Common provisions

Article 14 – Scope of procedural provisions

1   Each Party shall adopt such legislative and other measures as may be necessary to establish the powers and procedures provided for in this section for the purpose of specific criminal investigations or proceedings.

2   Except as specifically provided otherwise in Article 21, each Party shall apply the powers and procedures referred to in paragraph 1 of this article to:

a   the criminal offences established in accordance with Articles 2 through 11 of this Convention;

b   other criminal offences committed by means of a computer system; and

c   the collection of evidence in electronic form of a criminal offence.

3   a   Each Party may reserve the right to apply the measures referred to in Article 20 only to offences or categories of offences specified in the reservation, provided that the range of such offences or categories of offences is not more restricted than the range of offences to which it applies the measures referred to in Article 21. Each Party shall consider restricting such a reservation to enable the broadest application of the measure referred to in Article 20.

b   Where a Party, due to limitations in its legislation in force at the time of the adoption of the present Convention, is not able to apply the measures referred to in Articles 20 and 21 to communications being transmitted within a computer system of a service provider, which system:

i   is being operated for the benefit of a closed group of users, and

ii   does not employ public communications networks and is not connected with another computer system, whether public or private,

that Party may reserve the right not to apply these measures to such communications. Each Party shall consider restricting such a reservation to enable the broadest application of the measures referred to in Articles 20 and 21.

Article 15 – Conditions and safeguards

1 Each Party shall ensure that the establishment, implementation and application of the powers and procedures provided for in this Section are subject to conditions and safeguards provided for under its domestic law, which shall provide for the adequate protection of human rights and liberties, including rights arising pursuant to obligations it has undertaken under the 1950 Council of Europe Convention for the Protection of Human Rights and Fundamental Freedoms, the 1966 United Nations International Covenant on Civil and Political Rights, and other applicable international human rights instruments, and which shall incorporate the principle of proportionality.

2 Such conditions and safeguards shall, as appropriate in view of the nature of the procedure or power concerned, inter alia, include judicial or other independent supervision, grounds justifying application, and limitation of the scope and the duration of such power or procedure.

3 To the extent that it is consistent with the public interest, in particular the sound administration of justice, each Party shall consider the impact of the powers and procedures in this section upon the rights, responsibilities and legitimate interests of third parties.

Title 2 – Expedited preservation of stored computer data

Article 16 – Expedited preservation of stored computer data

1 Each Party shall adopt such legislative and other measures as may be necessary to enable its competent authorities to order or similarly obtain the expeditious preservation of specified computer data, including traffic data, that has been stored by means of a computer system, in particular where there are grounds to believe that the computer data is particularly vulnerable to loss or modification.

2 Where a Party gives effect to paragraph 1 above by means of an order to a person to preserve specified stored computer data in the person's possession or control, the Party shall adopt such legislative and other measures as may be necessary to oblige that person to preserve and maintain the integrity of that computer data for a period of time as long as necessary, up to a maximum of ninety days, to enable the competent authorities to seek its disclosure. A Party may provide for such an order to be subsequently renewed.

3 Each Party shall adopt such legislative and other measures as may be necessary to oblige the custodian or other person who is to preserve the

computer data to keep confidential the undertaking of such procedures for the period of time provided for by its domestic law.

4   The powers and procedures referred to in this article shall be subject to Articles 14 and 15.

Article 17 – Expedited preservation and partial disclosure of traffic data

1   Each Party shall adopt, in respect of traffic data that is to be preserved under Article 16, such legislative and other measures as may be necessary to:

a   ensure that such expeditious preservation of traffic data is available regardless of whether one or more service providers were involved in the transmission of that communication; and

b   ensure the expeditious disclosure to the Party's competent authority, or a person designated by that authority, of a sufficient amount of traffic data to enable the Party to identify the service providers and the path through which the communication was transmitted.

2   The powers and procedures referred to in this article shall be subject to Articles 14 and 15.

Title 3 – Production order

Article 18 – Production order

1   Each Party shall adopt such legislative and other measures as may be necessary to empower its competent authorities to order:

a   a person in its territory to submit specified computer data in that person's possession or control, which is stored in a computer system or a computer-data storage medium; and

b   a service provider offering its services in the territory of the Party to submit subscriber information relating to such services in that service provider's possession or control.

2   The powers and procedures referred to in this article shall be subject to Articles 14 and 15.

3   For the purpose of this article, the term "subscriber information" means any information contained in the form of computer data or any other form that is held by a service provider, relating to subscribers of its services other than traffic or content data and by which can be established:

a   the type of communication service used, the technical provisions taken thereto and the period of service;

b   the subscriber's identity, postal or geographic address, telephone and other access number, billing and payment information, available on the basis of the service agreement or arrangement;

c   any other information on the site of the installation of communication equipment, available on the basis of the service agreement or arrangement.

Title 4 – Search and seizure of stored computer data

Article 19 – Search and seizure of stored computer data

1   Each Party shall adopt such legislative and other measures as may be necessary to empower its competent authorities to search or similarly access:

a   a computer system or part of it and computer data stored therein; and

b   a computer-data storage medium in which computer data may be stored

in its territory.

2   Each Party shall adopt such legislative and other measures as may be necessary to ensure that where its authorities search or similarly access a specific computer system or part of it, pursuant to paragraph 1.a, and have grounds to believe that the data sought is stored in another computer system or part of it in its territory, and such data is lawfully accessible from or available to the initial system, the authorities shall be able to expeditiously extend the search or similar accessing to the other system.

3   Each Party shall adopt such legislative and other measures as may be necessary to empower its competent authorities to seize or similarly secure computer data accessed according to paragraphs 1 or 2. These measures shall include the power to:

a   seize or similarly secure a computer system or part of it or a computer-data storage medium;

b   make and retain a copy of those computer data;

c   maintain the integrity of the relevant stored computer data;

d   render inaccessible or remove those computer data in the accessed computer system.

4   Each Party shall adopt such legislative and other measures as may be necessary to empower its competent authorities to order any person who has knowledge about the functioning of the computer system or measures applied to protect the computer data therein to provide, as is reasonable, the necessary information, to enable the undertaking of the measures referred to in paragraphs 1 and 2.

5   The powers and procedures referred to in this article shall be subject to Articles 14 and 15.

Title 5 – Real-time collection of computer data

Article 20 – Real-time collection of traffic data

1   Each Party shall adopt such legislative and other measures as may be necessary to empower its competent authorities to:

a   collect or record through the application of technical means on the territory of that Party, and

b   compel a service provider, within its existing technical capability:

   i   to collect or record through the application of technical means on the territory of that Party; or

   ii   to co-operate and assist the competent authorities in the collection or recording of,

   traffic data, in real-time, associated with specified communications in its territory transmitted by means of a computer system.

2   Where a Party, due to the established principles of its domestic legal system, cannot adopt the measures referred to in paragraph 1.a, it may instead adopt legislative and other measures as may be necessary to ensure the real-time collection or recording of traffic data associated with specified communications transmitted in its territory, through the application of technical means on that territory.

3   Each Party shall adopt such legislative and other measures as may be necessary to oblige a service provider to keep confidential the fact of the execution of any power provided for in this article and any information relating to it.

4   The powers and procedures referred to in this article shall be subject to Articles 14 and 15.

Article 21 – Interception of content data

1   Each Party shall adopt such legislative and other measures as may be necessary, in relation to a range of serious offences to be determined by domestic law, to empower its competent authorities to:

    a   collect or record through the application of technical means on the territory of that Party, and

    b   compel a service provider, within its existing technical capability:

        i   to collect or record through the application of technical means on the territory of that Party, or

        ii   to co-operate and assist the competent authorities in the collection or recording of,

    content data, in real-time, of specified communications in its territory transmitted by means of a computer system.

2   Where a Party, due to the established principles of its domestic legal system, cannot adopt the measures referred to in paragraph 1.a, it may instead adopt legislative and other measures as may be necessary to ensure the real-time collection or recording of content data on specified communications in its territory through the application of technical means on that territory.

3   Each Party shall adopt such legislative and other measures as may be necessary to oblige a service provider to keep confidential the fact of the execution of any power provided for in this article and any information relating to it.

4   The powers and procedures referred to in this article shall be subject to Articles 14 and 15.

Section 3 – Jurisdiction

Article 22 – Jurisdiction

1   Each Party shall adopt such legislative and other measures as may be necessary to establish jurisdiction over any offence established in accordance with Articles 2 through 11 of this Convention, when the offence is committed:

    a   in its territory; or

    b   on board a ship flying the flag of that Party; or

    c   on board an aircraft registered under the laws of that Party; or d   by one of its nationals, if the offence is punishable under criminal law where it was committed or if the offence is committed outside the territorial jurisdiction of any State.

2   Each Party may reserve the right not to apply or to apply only in specific cases or conditions the jurisdiction rules laid down in paragraphs 1.b through 1.d of this article or any part thereof.

3   Each Party shall adopt such measures as may be necessary to establish jurisdiction over the offences referred to in Article 24, paragraph 1, of this Convention, in cases where an alleged offender is present in its territory and it does not extradite him or her to another Party, solely on the basis of his or her nationality, after a request for extradition.

4   This Convention does not exclude any criminal jurisdiction exercised by a Party in accordance with its domestic law.

5   When more than one Party claims jurisdiction over an alleged offence established in accordance with this Convention, the Parties involved shall, where appropriate, consult with a view to determining the most appropriate jurisdiction for prosecution.

Chapter III – International co-operation

Section 1 – General principles

Title 1 – General principles relating to international co-operation

Article 23 – General principles relating to international co-operation

The Parties shall co-operate with each other, in accordance with the provisions of this chapter, and through the application of relevant international instruments on international co-operation in criminal matters, arrangements agreed on the basis of uniform or reciprocal legislation, and domestic laws, to the widest extent possible for the purposes of investigations or proceedings concerning criminal offences related to computer systems and data, or for the collection of evidence in electronic form of a criminal offence.

Title 2 – Principles relating to extradition

Article 24 – Extradition

1   a   This article applies to extradition between Parties for the criminal offences established in accordance with Articles 2 through 11 of this Convention, provided that they are punishable under the laws of both Parties concerned by deprivation of liberty for a maximum period of at least one year, or by a more severe penalty.

b   Where a different minimum penalty is to be applied under an arrangement agreed on the basis of uniform or reciprocal legislation or an extradition treaty, including the European Convention on Extradition (ETS No. 24), applicable between two or more parties, the minimum penalty provided for under such arrangement or treaty shall apply.

2   The criminal offences described in paragraph 1 of this article shall be deemed to be included as extraditable offences in any extradition treaty existing between or among the Parties. The Parties undertake to include such offences as extraditable offences in any extradition treaty to be concluded between or among them.

3   If a Party that makes extradition conditional on the existence of a treaty receives a request for extradition from another Party with which it does not have an extradition treaty, it may consider this Convention as the legal basis for extradition with respect to any criminal offence referred to in paragraph 1 of this article.

4   Parties that do not make extradition conditional on the existence of a treaty shall recognise the criminal offences referred to in paragraph 1 of this article as extraditable offences between themselves.

5   Extradition shall be subject to the conditions provided for by the law of the requested Party or by applicable extradition treaties, including the grounds on which the requested Party may refuse extradition.

6   If extradition for a criminal offence referred to in paragraph 1 of this article is refused solely on the basis of the nationality of the person sought, or because the requested Party deems that it has jurisdiction over the offence, the requested Party shall submit the case at the request of the requesting Party to its competent authorities for the purpose of prosecution and shall report the final outcome to the requesting Party in due course. Those authorities shall take their decision and conduct their investigations and proceedings in the same manner as for any other offence of a comparable nature under the law of that Party.

7   a   Each Party shall, at the time of signature or when depositing its instrument of ratification, acceptance, approval or accession, communicate to the Secretary General of the Council of Europe the name and address of each authority responsible for making or receiving requests for extradition or provisional arrest in the absence of a treaty.

    b   The Secretary General of the Council of Europe shall set up and keep updated a register of authorities so designated by the Parties. Each Party shall ensure that the details held on the register are correct at all times.

Title 3 – General principles relating to mutual assistance

Article 25 – General principles relating to mutual assistance

1   The Parties shall afford one another mutual assistance to the widest extent possible for the purpose of investigations or proceedings concerning criminal offences related to computer systems and data, or for the collection of evidence in electronic form of a criminal offence.

2   Each Party shall also adopt such legislative and other measures as may be necessary to carry out the obligations set forth in Articles 27 through 35.

3   Each Party may, in urgent circumstances, make requests for mutual assistance or communications related thereto by expedited means of communication, including fax or e-mail, to the extent that such means provide appropriate levels of security and authentication (including the use of encryption, where necessary), with formal confirmation to follow, where required by the requested Party. The requested Party shall accept and respond to the request by any such expedited means of communication.

4   Except as otherwise specifically provided in articles in this chapter, mutual assistance shall be subject to the conditions provided for by the law of the requested Party or by applicable mutual assistance treaties, including the grounds on which the requested Party may refuse co-operation. The requested Party shall not exercise the right to refuse mutual assistance in relation to the offences referred to in Articles 2 through 11 solely on the ground that the request concerns an offence which it considers a fiscal offence.

5   Where, in accordance with the provisions of this chapter, the requested Party is permitted to make mutual assistance conditional upon the existence of dual criminality, that condition shall be deemed fulfilled, irrespective of whether its laws place the offence within the same category of offence or denominate the offence by the same terminology as the requesting Party, if the conduct underlying the offence for which assistance is sought is a criminal offence under its laws.

Article 26 – Spontaneous information

1   A Party may, within the limits of its domestic law and without prior request, forward to another Party information obtained within the framework of its own investigations when it considers that the disclosure of such information might assist the receiving Party in initiating or carrying out investigations or proceedings concerning criminal offences established in accordance with this Convention or might lead to a request for co-operation by that Party under this chapter.

2   Prior to providing such information, the providing Party may request that it be kept confidential or only used subject to conditions. If the receiving Party cannot comply with such request, it shall notify the providing Party, which shall then determine whether the information should nevertheless be provided. If the receiving Party accepts the information subject to the conditions, it shall be bound by them.

Title 4 – Procedures pertaining to mutual assistance requests in the absence of applicable international agreements

Article 27 – Procedures pertaining to mutual assistance requests in the absence of applicable international agreements

1   Where there is no mutual assistance treaty or arrangement on the basis of uniform or reciprocal legislation in force between the requesting and requested Parties, the provisions of paragraphs 2 through 9 of this article shall apply. The provisions of this article shall not apply where such treaty, arrangement or legislation exists, unless the Parties concerned agree to apply any or all of the remainder of this article in lieu thereof.

2   a   Each Party shall designate a central authority or authorities responsible for sending and answering requests for mutual assistance, the execution of such requests or their transmission to the authorities competent for their execution.

      b   The central authorities shall communicate directly with each other;

      c   Each Party shall, at the time of signature or when depositing its instrument of ratification, acceptance, approval or accession, communicate to the Secretary General of the Council of Europe the names and addresses of the authorities designated in pursuance of this paragraph;

      d   The Secretary General of the Council of Europe shall set up and keep updated a register of central authorities designated by the Parties. Each Party shall ensure that the details held on the register are correct at all times.

3   Mutual assistance requests under this article shall be executed in accordance with the procedures specified by the requesting Party, except where incompatible with the law of the requested Party.

4   The requested Party may, in addition to the grounds for refusal established in Article 25, paragraph 4, refuse assistance if:

      a   the request concerns an offence which the requested Party considers a political offence or an offence connected with a political offence, or b   it considers that execution of the request is likely to prejudice its sovereignty, security, ordre public or other essential interests.

5   The requested Party may postpone action on a request if such action would prejudice criminal investigations or proceedings conducted by its authorities.

6   Before refusing or postponing assistance, the requested Party shall, where appropriate after having consulted with the requesting Party, consider whether the request may be granted partially or subject to such conditions as it deems necessary.

7   The requested Party shall promptly inform the requesting Party of the outcome of the execution of a request for assistance. Reasons shall be given for any refusal or postponement of the request. The requested Party shall also inform the requesting Party of any reasons that render impossible the execution of the request or are likely to delay it significantly.

8   The requesting Party may request that the requested Party keep confidential the fact of any request made under this chapter as well as its subject, except to the extent necessary for its execution. If the requested Party cannot comply with the request for confidentiality, it shall promptly inform the requesting Party, which shall then determine whether the request should nevertheless be executed.

9   a   In the event of urgency, requests for mutual assistance or communications related thereto may be sent directly by judicial authorities of the requesting Party to such authorities of the requested Party. In any such cases, a copy shall be sent at the same time to the central authority of the requested Party through the central authority of the requesting Party.

    b   Any request or communication under this paragraph may be made through the International Criminal Police Organisation (Interpol).

    c   Where a request is made pursuant to sub-paragraph a. of this article and the authority is not competent to deal with the request, it shall refer the request to the competent national authority and inform directly the requesting Party that it has done so.

    d   Requests or communications made under this paragraph that do not involve coercive action may be directly transmitted by the competent authorities of the requesting Party to the competent authorities of the requested Party.

    e   Each Party may, at the time of signature or when depositing its instrument of ratification, acceptance, approval or accession, inform the Secretary General of the Council of Europe that, for reasons of efficiency, requests made under this paragraph are to be addressed to its central authority.

Article 28 – Confidentiality and limitation on use

1   When there is no mutual assistance treaty or arrangement on the basis of uniform or reciprocal legislation in force between the requesting and the requested Parties, the provisions of this article shall apply. The provisions of this article shall not apply where such treaty, arrangement or legislation exists, unless the Parties concerned agree to apply any or all of the remainder of this article in lieu thereof.

2   The requested Party may make the supply of information or material in response to a request dependent on the condition that it is:

a   kept confidential where the request for mutual legal assistance could not be complied with in the absence of such condition, or

b   not used for investigations or proceedings other than those stated in the request.

3   If the requesting Party cannot comply with a condition referred to in paragraph 2, it shall promptly inform the other Party, which shall then determine whether the information should nevertheless be provided. When the requesting Party accepts the condition, it shall be bound by it.

4   Any Party that supplies information or material subject to a condition referred to in paragraph 2 may require the other Party to explain, in relation to that condition, the use made of such information or material.

Section 2 – Specific provisions

Title 1 – Mutual assistance regarding provisional measures

Article 29 – Expedited preservation of stored computer data

1   A Party may request another Party to order or otherwise obtain the expeditious preservation of data stored by means of a computer system, located within the territory of that other Party and in respect of which the requesting Party intends to submit a request for mutual assistance for the search or similar access, seizure or similar securing, or disclosure of the data.

2   A request for preservation made under paragraph 1 shall specify:

a   the authority seeking the preservation;

b   the offence that is the subject of a criminal investigation or proceedings and a brief summary of the related facts;

c   the stored computer data to be preserved and its relationship to the offence;

d   any available information identifying the custodian of the stored computer data or the location of the computer system;

e   the necessity of the preservation; and

f   that the Party intends to submit a request for mutual assistance for the search or similar access, seizure or similar securing, or disclosure of the stored computer data.

3   Upon receiving the request from another Party, the requested Party shall take all appropriate measures to preserve expeditiously the specified data in accordance with its domestic law. For the purposes of responding to a request, dual criminality shall not be required as a condition to providing such preservation.

4   A Party that requires dual criminality as a condition for responding to a request for mutual assistance for the search or similar access, seizure or similar securing, or disclosure of stored data may, in respect of offences other than those established in accordance with Articles 2 through 11 of this Convention, reserve the right to refuse the request for preservation under this article in cases where it has reasons to believe that at the time of disclosure the condition of dual criminality cannot be fulfilled.

5   In addition, a request for preservation may only be refused if:

a   the request concerns an offence which the requested Party considers a political offence or an offence connected with a political offence, or

b   the requested Party considers that execution of the request is likely to prejudice its sovereignty, security, ordre public or other essential interests.

6   Where the requested Party believes that preservation will not ensure the future availability of the data or will threaten the confidentiality of or otherwise prejudice the requesting Party's investigation, it shall promptly so inform the requesting Party, which shall then determine whether the request should nevertheless be executed.

7   Any preservation effected in response to the request referred to in paragraph 1 shall be for a period not less than sixty days, in order to enable the requesting Party to submit a request for the search or similar access, seizure or similar securing, or disclosure of the data. Following

the receipt of such a request, the data shall continue to be preserved pending a decision on that request.

Article 30 – Expedited disclosure of preserved traffic data

1   Where, in the course of the execution of a request made pursuant to Article 29 to preserve traffic data concerning a specific communication, the requested Party discovers that a service provider in another State was involved in the transmission of the communication, the requested Party shall expeditiously disclose to the requesting Party a sufficient amount of traffic data to identify that service provider and the path through which the communication was transmitted.

2   Disclosure of traffic data under paragraph 1 may only be withheld if:

a   the request concerns an offence which the requested Party considers a political offence or an offence connected with a political offence; or

b   the requested Party considers that execution of the request is likely to prejudice its sovereignty, security, ordre public or other essential interests.

Title 2 – Mutual assistance regarding investigative powers

Article 31 – Mutual assistance regarding accessing of stored computer data

1   A Party may request another Party to search or similarly access, seize or similarly secure, and disclose data stored by means of a computer system located within the territory of the requested Party, including data that has been preserved pursuant to Article 29.

2   The requested Party shall respond to the request through the application of international instruments, arrangements and laws referred to in Article 23, and in accordance with other relevant provisions of this chapter.

3   The request shall be responded to on an expedited basis where:

a   there are grounds to believe that relevant data is particularly vulnerable to loss or modification; or

b   the instruments, arrangements and laws referred to in paragraph 2 otherwise provide for expedited co-operation.

Article 32 – Trans-border access to stored computer data with consent or where publicly available

A Party may, without the authorisation of another Party:

a   access publicly available (open source) stored computer data, regardless of where the data is located geographically; or

b   access or receive, through a computer system in its territory, stored computer data located in another Party, if the Party obtains the lawful and voluntary consent of the person who has the lawful authority to disclose the data to the Party through that computer system.

Article 33 – Mutual assistance in the real-time collection of traffic data

1   The Parties shall provide mutual assistance to each other in the real-time collection of traffic data associated with specified communications in their territory transmitted by means of a computer system. Subject to the provisions of paragraph 2, this assistance shall be governed by the conditions and procedures provided for under domestic law.

2   Each Party shall provide such assistance at least with respect to criminal offences for which real-time collection of traffic data would be available in a similar domestic case.

Article 34 – Mutual assistance regarding the interception of content data

The Parties shall provide mutual assistance to each other in the real-time collection or recording of content data of specified communications transmitted by means of a computer system to the extent permitted under their applicable treaties and domestic laws.

Title 3 – 24/7 Network

Article 35 – 24/7 Network

1   Each Party shall designate a point of contact available on a twenty-four hour, seven-day-a-week basis, in order to ensure the provision of immediate assistance for the purpose of investigations or proceedings concerning criminal offences related to computer systems and data, or for the collection of evidence in electronic form of a criminal offence. Such assistance shall include facilitating, or, if permitted by its domestic law and practice, directly carrying out the following measures:

a   the provision of technical advice;

b   the preservation of data pursuant to Articles 29 and 30;

c   the collection of evidence, the provision of legal information, and locating of suspects.

2   a   A Party's point of contact shall have the capacity to carry out communications with the point of contact of another Party on an expedited basis.

      b   If the point of contact designated by a Party is not part of that Party's authority or authorities responsible for international mutual assistance or extradition, the point of contact shall ensure that it is able to co-ordinate with such authority or authorities on an expedited basis.

      3   Each Party shall ensure that trained and equipped personnel are available, in order to facilitate the operation of the network.

Chapter IV – Final provisions

Article 36 – Signature and entry into force

1   This Convention shall be open for signature by the member States of the Council of Europe and by non-member States which have participated in its elaboration.

2   This Convention is subject to ratification, acceptance or approval. Instruments of ratification, acceptance or approval shall be deposited with the Secretary General of the Council of Europe.

3   This Convention shall enter into force on the first day of the month following the expiration of a period of three months after the date on which five States, including at least three member States of the Council of Europe, have expressed their consent to be bound by the Convention in accordance with the provisions of paragraphs 1 and 2.

4   In respect of any signatory State which subsequently expresses its consent to be bound by it, the Convention shall enter into force on the first day of the month following the expiration of a period of three months after the date of the expression of its consent to be bound by the Convention in accordance with the provisions of paragraphs 1 and 2.

Article 37 – Accession to the Convention

1   After the entry into force of this Convention, the Committee of Ministers of the Council of Europe, after consulting with and obtaining the unanimous consent of the Contracting States to the Convention, may invite any State which is not a member of the Council and which has not participated in its elaboration to accede to this Convention. The decision shall be taken by the majority provided for in Article 20.d. of the Statute of the Council of Europe and by the unanimous vote of the representatives of the Contracting States entitled to sit on the Committee of Ministers.

2   In respect of any State acceding to the Convention under paragraph 1 above, the Convention shall enter into force on the first day of the month following the expiration of a period of three months after the date of deposit of the instrument of accession with the Secretary General of the Council of Europe.

Article 38 – Territorial application

1   Any State may, at the time of signature or when depositing its instrument of ratification, acceptance, approval or accession, specify the territory or territories to which this Convention shall apply.

2   Any State may, at any later date, by a declaration addressed to the Secretary General of the Council of Europe, extend the application of this Convention to any other territory specified in the declaration. In respect of such territory the Convention shall enter into force on the first day of the month following the expiration of a period of three months after the date of receipt of the declaration by the Secretary General.

3   Any declaration made under the two preceding paragraphs may, in respect of any territory specified in such declaration, be withdrawn by a notification addressed to the Secretary General of the Council of Europe. The withdrawal shall become effective on the first day of the month following the expiration of a period of three months after the date of receipt of such notification by the Secretary General.

Article 39 – Effects of the Convention

1   The purpose of the present Convention is to supplement applicable multilateral or bilateral treaties or arrangements as between the Parties, including the provisions of:

–   the European Convention on Extradition, opened for signature in Paris, on 13 December 1957 (ETS No. 24);

–   the European Convention on Mutual Assistance in Criminal Matters, opened for signature in Strasbourg, on 20 April 1959 (ETS No. 30);

–   the Additional Protocol to the European Convention on Mutual Assistance in Criminal Matters, opened for signature in Strasbourg, on 17 March 1978 (ETS No. 99).

2   If two or more Parties have already concluded an agreement or treaty on the matters dealt with in this Convention or have otherwise established their relations on such matters, or should they in future do so, they shall also be entitled to apply that agreement or treaty or to regulate those relations accordingly. However, where Parties establish their relations in respect of the matters dealt with in the present Convention other than as

regulated therein, they shall do so in a manner that is not inconsistent with the Convention's objectives and principles.

3   Nothing in this Convention shall affect other rights, restrictions, obligations and responsibilities of a Party.

Article 40 – Declarations

By a written notification addressed to the Secretary General of the Council of Europe, any State may, at the time of signature or when depositing its instrument of ratification, acceptance, approval or accession, declare that it avails itself of the possibility of requiring additional elements as provided for under Articles 2, 3, 6 paragraph 1.b, 7, 9 paragraph 3, and 27, paragraph 9.e.

Article 41 – Federal clause

1   A federal State may reserve the right to assume obligations under Chapter II of this Convention consistent with its fundamental principles governing the relationship between its central government and constituent States or other similar territorial entities provided that it is still able to co-operate under Chapter III.

2   When making a reservation under paragraph 1, a federal State may not apply the terms of such reservation to exclude or substantially diminish its obligations to provide for measures set forth in Chapter II. Overall, it shall provide for a broad and effective law enforcement capability with respect to those measures.

3   With regard to the provisions of this Convention, the application of which comes under the jurisdiction of constituent States or other similar territorial entities, that are not obliged by the constitutional system of the federation to take legislative measures, the federal government shall inform the competent authorities of such States of the said provisions with its favourable opinion, encouraging them to take appropriate action to give them effect.

Article 42 – Reservations

By a written notification addressed to the Secretary General of the Council of Europe, any State may, at the time of signature or when depositing its instrument of ratification, acceptance, approval or accession, declare that it avails itself of the reservation(s) provided for in Article 4, paragraph 2, Article 6, paragraph 3, Article 9, paragraph 4, Article 10, paragraph 3, Article 11, paragraph 3, Article 14, paragraph 3, Article 22, paragraph 2, Article 29, paragraph 4, and Article 41, paragraph 1. No other reservation may be made.

Article 43 – Status and withdrawal of reservations

1   A Party that has made a reservation in accordance with Article 42 may wholly or partially withdraw it by means of a notification addressed to the Secretary General of the Council of Europe. Such withdrawal shall take effect on the date of receipt of such notification by the Secretary General. If the notification states that the withdrawal of a reservation is to take effect on a date specified therein, and such date is later than the date on which the notification is received by the Secretary General, the withdrawal shall take effect on such a later date.

2   A Party that has made a reservation as referred to in Article 42 shall withdraw such reservation, in whole or in part, as soon as circumstances so permit.

3   The Secretary General of the Council of Europe may periodically enquire with Parties that have made one or more reservations as referred to in Article 42 as to the prospects for withdrawing such reservation(s).

Article 44 – Amendments

1   Amendments to this Convention may be proposed by any Party, and shall be communicated by the Secretary General of the Council of Europe to the member States of the Council of Europe, to the non-member States which have participated in the elaboration of this Convention as well as to any State which has acceded to, or has been invited to accede to, this Convention in accordance with the provisions of Article 37.

2   Any amendment proposed by a Party shall be communicated to the European Committee on Crime Problems (CDPC), which shall submit to the Committee of Ministers its opinion on that proposed amendment.

3   The Committee of Ministers shall consider the proposed amendment and the opinion submitted by the CDPC and, following consultation with the non-member States Parties to this Convention, may adopt the amendment.

4   The text of any amendment adopted by the Committee of Ministers in accordance with paragraph 3 of this article shall be forwarded to the Parties for acceptance.

5   Any amendment adopted in accordance with paragraph 3 of this article shall come into force on the thirtieth day after all Parties have informed the Secretary General of their acceptance thereof.

Article 45 – Settlement of disputes

1   The European Committee on Crime Problems (CDPC) shall be kept informed regarding the interpretation and application of this Convention.

2   In case of a dispute between Parties as to the interpretation or application of this Convention, they shall seek a settlement of the dispute through negotiation or any other peaceful means of their choice, including submission of the dispute to the CDPC, to an arbitral tribunal whose decisions shall be binding upon the Parties, or to the International Court of Justice, as agreed upon by the Parties concerned.

Article 46 – Consultations of the Parties

1   The Parties shall, as appropriate, consult periodically with a view to facilitating:

a   the effective use and implementation of this Convention, including the identification of any problems thereof, as well as the effects of any declaration or reservation made under this Convention;

b   the exchange of information on significant legal, policy or technological developments pertaining to cybercrime and the collection of evidence in electronic form;

c   consideration of possible supplementation or amendment of the Convention.

2   The European Committee on Crime Problems (CDPC) shall be kept periodically informed regarding the result of consultations referred to in paragraph 1.

3   The CDPC shall, as appropriate, facilitate the consultations referred to in paragraph 1 and take the measures necessary to assist the Parties in their efforts to supplement or amend the Convention. At the latest three years after the present Convention enters into force, the European Committee on Crime Problems (CDPC) shall, in co-operation with the Parties, conduct a review of all of the Convention's provisions and, if necessary, recommend any appropriate amendments.

4   Except where assumed by the Council of Europe, expenses incurred in carrying out the provisions of paragraph 1 shall be borne by the Parties in the manner to be determined by them.

5   The Parties shall be assisted by the Secretariat of the Council of Europe in carrying out their functions pursuant to this article.

Article 47 – Denunciation

1 Any Party may, at any time, denounce this Convention by means of a notification addressed to the Secretary General of the Council of Europe.

2 Such denunciation shall become effective on the first day of the month following the expiration of a period of three months after the date of receipt of the notification by the Secretary General.

Article 48 – Notification

The Secretary General of the Council of Europe shall notify the member States of the Council of Europe, the non-member States which have participated in the elaboration of this Convention as well as any State which has acceded to, or has been invited to accede to, this Convention of:

a any signature;

b the deposit of any instrument of ratification, acceptance, approval or accession;

c any date of entry into force of this Convention in accordance with Articles 36 and 37;

d any declaration made under Article 40 or reservation made in accordance with Article 42;

e any other act, notification or communication relating to this Convention.

In witness whereof the undersigned, being duly authorised thereto, have signed this Convention.

Done at Budapest, this 23rd day of November 2001, in English and in French, both texts being equally authentic, in a single copy which shall be deposited in the archives of the Council of Europe. The Secretary General of the Council of Europe shall transmit certified copies to each member State of the Council of Europe, to the non-member States which have participated in the elaboration of this Convention, and to any State invited to accede to it.

Additional Protocol to the European Convention on Cybercrime, concerning the criminalisation of acts of a racist and xenophobic nature committed through computer systems (ETS No. 189)

The member States of the Council of Europe and the other States Parties to the Convention on Cybercrime, opened for signature in Budapest on 23 November 2001, signatory hereto;

Considering that the aim of the Council of Europe is to achieve a greater unity between its members;

Recalling that all human beings are born free and equal in dignity and rights;

Stressing the need to secure a full and effective implementation of all human rights without any discrimination or distinction, as enshrined in European and other international instruments;

Convinced that acts of a racist and xenophobic nature constitute a violation of human rights and a threat to the rule of law and democratic stability;

Considering that national and international law need to provide adequate legal responses to propaganda of a racist and xenophobic nature committed through computer systems;

Aware of the fact that propaganda to such acts is often subject to criminalisation in national legislation;

Having regard to the Convention on Cybercrime, which provides for modern and flexible means of international co-operation and convinced of the need to harmonise substantive law provisions concerning the fight against racist and xenophobic propaganda;

Aware that computer systems offer an unprecedented means of facilitating freedom of expression and communication around the globe;

Recognising that freedom of expression constitutes one of the essential foundations of a democratic society, and is one of the basic conditions for its progress and for the development of every human being;

Concerned, however, by the risk of misuse or abuse of such computer systems to disseminate racist and xenophobic propaganda;

Mindful of the need to ensure a proper balance between freedom of expression and an effective fight against acts of a racist and xenophobic nature;

Recognising that this Protocol is not intended to affect established principles relating to freedom of expression in national legal systems;

Taking into account the relevant international legal instruments in this field, and in particular the Convention for the Protection of Human Rights and Fundamental Freedoms and its Protocol No. 12 concerning the general prohibition of discrimination, the existing Council of Europe conventions on co-operation in the penal field, in particular the Convention on Cybercrime, the United Nations International Convention on the Elimination of All Forms of Racial Discrimination of 21 December 1965, the European Union Joint Action of 15 July 1996 adopted by the Council on the basis of Article K.3 of the Treaty on European Union, concerning action to combat racism and xenophobia;

Welcoming the recent developments which further advance international understanding and co-operation in combating cybercrime and racism and xenophobia;

Having regard to the Action Plan adopted by the Heads of State and Government of the Council of Europe on the occasion of their Second Summit (Strasbourg, 10-11 October 1997) to seek common responses to the developments of the new technologies based on the standards and values of the Council of Europe;

Have agreed as follows:

Chapter I – Common provisions

Article 1 – Purpose

The purpose of this Protocol is to supplement, as between the Parties to the Protocol, the provisions of the Convention on Cybercrime, opened for signature in Budapest on 23 November 2001 (hereinafter referred to as "the Convention"), as regards the criminalisation of acts of a racist and xenophobic nature committed through computer systems.

Article 2 – Definition

1 For the purposes of this Protocol:

"racist and xenophobic material" means any written material, any image or any other representation of ideas or theories, which advocates, promotes or incites hatred, discrimination or violence, against any individual or group of individuals, based on race, colour, descent or national or ethnic origin, as well as religion if used as a pretext for any of these factors.

2 The terms and expressions used in this Protocol shall be interpreted in the same manner as they are interpreted under the Convention.

Chapter II – Measures to be taken at national level

Article 3 – Dissemination of racist and xenophobic material through computer systems

1   Each Party shall adopt such legislative and other measures as may be necessary to establish as criminal offences under its domestic law, when committed intentionally and without right, the following conduct:

distributing, or otherwise making available, racist and xenophobic material to the public through a computer system.

2   A Party may reserve the right not to attach criminal liability to conduct as defined by paragraph 1 of this article, where the material, as defined in Article 2, paragraph 1, advocates, promotes or incites discrimination that is not associated with hatred or violence, provided that other effective remedies are available.

3   Notwithstanding paragraph 2 of this article, a Party may reserve the right not to apply paragraph 1 to those cases of discrimination for which, due to established principles in its national legal system concerning freedom of expression, it cannot provide for effective remedies as referred to in the said paragraph 2.

Article 4 – Racist and xenophobic motivated threat

Each Party shall adopt such legislative and other measures as may be necessary to establish as criminal offences under its domestic law, when committed intentionally and without right, the following conduct:

threatening, through a computer system, with the commission of a serious criminal offence as defined under its domestic law, (i) persons for the reason that they belong to a group, distinguished by race, colour, descent or national or ethnic origin, as well as religion, if used as a pretext for any of these factors, or (ii) a group of persons which is distinguished by any of these characteristics.

Article 5 – Racist and xenophobic motivated insult

1   Each Party shall adopt such legislative and other measures as may be necessary to establish as criminal offences under its domestic law, when committed intentionally and without right, the following conduct:

insulting publicly, through a computer system, (i) persons for the reason that they belong to a group distinguished by race, colour, descent or national or ethnic origin, as well as religion, if used as a pretext for any of these factors; or (ii) a group of persons which is distinguished by any of these characteristics.

2   A Party may either:

a   require that the offence referred to in paragraph 1 of this article has the effect that the person or group of persons referred to in paragraph 1 is exposed to hatred, contempt or ridicule; or

b   reserve the right not to apply, in whole or in part, paragraph 1 of this article.

Article 6 – Denial, gross minimisation, approval or justification of genocide or crimes against humanity

1   Each Party shall adopt such legislative measures as may be necessary to establish the following conduct as criminal offences under its domestic law, when committed intentionally and without right:

distributing or otherwise making available, through a computer system to the public, material which denies, grossly minimises, approves or justifies acts constituting genocide or crimes against humanity, as defined by international law and recognised as such by final and binding decisions of the International Military Tribunal, established by the London Agreement of 8 August 1945, or of any other international court established by relevant international instruments and whose jurisdiction is recognised by that Party.

2   A Party may either

a   require that the denial or the gross minimisation referred to in paragraph 1 of this article is committed with the intent to incite hatred, discrimination or violence against any individual or group of individuals, based on race, colour, descent or national or ethnic origin, as well as religion if used as a pretext for any of these factors, or otherwise

b   reserve the right not to apply, in whole or in part, paragraph 1 of this article.

Article 7 – Aiding and abetting

Each Party shall adopt such legislative and other measures as may be necessary to establish as criminal offences under its domestic law, when committed intentionally and without right, aiding or abetting the commission of any of the offences established in accordance with this Protocol, with intent that such offence be committed.

Chapter III — Relations between the Convention and this Protocol

Article 8 – Relations between the Convention and this Protocol

1   Articles 1, 12, 13, 22, 41, 44, 45 and 46 of the Convention shall apply, mutatis mutandis, to this Protocol.

2   The Parties shall extend the scope of application of the measures defined in Articles 14 to 21 and Articles 23 to 35 of the Convention, to Articles 2 to 7 of this Protocol.

Chapter IV – Final provisions

Article 9 – Expression of consent to be bound

1   This Protocol shall be open for signature by the States which have signed the Convention, which may express their consent to be bound by either:

a   signature without reservation as to ratification, acceptance or approval; or

b   signature subject to ratification, acceptance or approval, followed by ratification, acceptance or approval.

2   A State may not sign this Protocol without reservation as to ratification, acceptance or approval, or deposit an instrument of ratification, acceptance or approval, unless it has already deposited or simultaneously deposits an instrument of ratification, acceptance or approval of the Convention.

3   The instruments of ratification, acceptance or approval shall be deposited with the Secretary General of the Council of Europe.

Article 10 – Entry into force

1   This Protocol shall enter into force on the first day of the month following the expiration of a period of three months after the date on which five States have expressed their consent to be bound by the Protocol, in accordance with the provisions of Article 9.

2   In respect of any State which subsequently expresses its consent to be bound by it, the Protocol shall enter into force on the first day of the month following the expiration of a period of three months after the date of its signature without reservation as to ratification, acceptance or approval or deposit of its instrument of ratification, acceptance or approval.

Article 11 – Accession

1   After the entry into force of this Protocol, any State which has acceded to the Convention may also accede to the Protocol.

2   Accession shall be effected by the deposit with the Secretary General of the Council of Europe of an instrument of accession which shall take effect on the first day of the month following the expiration of a period of three months after the date of its deposit.

Article 12 – Reservations and declarations

1   Reservations and declarations made by a Party to a provision of the Convention shall be applicable also to this Protocol, unless that Party declares otherwise at the time of signature or when depositing its instrument of ratification, acceptance, approval or accession.

2   By a written notification addressed to the Secretary General of the Council of Europe, any Party may, at the time of signature or when depositing its instrument of ratification, acceptance, approval or accession, declare that it avails itself of the reservation(s) provided for in Articles 3, 5 and 6 of this Protocol. At the same time, a Party may avail itself, with respect to the provisions of this Protocol, of the reservation(s) provided for in Article 22, paragraph 2, and Article 41, paragraph 1, of the Convention, irrespective of the implementation made by that Party under the Convention. No other reservations may be made.

3   By a written notification addressed to the Secretary General of the Council of Europe, any State may, at the time of signature or when depositing its instrument of ratification, acceptance, approval or accession, declare that it avails itself of the possibility of requiring additional elements as provided for in Article 5, paragraph 2.a, and Article 6, paragraph 2.a, of this Protocol.

Article 13 – Status and withdrawal of reservations

1   A Party that has made a reservation in accordance with Article 12 above shall withdraw such reservation, in whole or in part, as soon as circumstances so permit. Such withdrawal shall take effect on the date of receipt of a notification addressed to the Secretary General of the Council of Europe. If the notification states that the withdrawal of a reservation is to take effect on a date specified therein, and such date is later than the date on which the notification is received by the Secretary General, the withdrawal shall take effect on such a later date.

2   The Secretary General of the Council of Europe may periodically enquire with Parties that have made one or more reservations in accordance with Article 12 as to the prospects for withdrawing such reservation(s).

Article 14 – Territorial application

1   Any Party may at the time of signature or when depositing its instrument of ratification, acceptance, approval or accession, specify the territory or territories to which this Protocol shall apply.

2   Any Party may, at any later date, by a declaration addressed to the Secretary General of the Council of Europe, extend the application of this Protocol to any other territory specified in the declaration. In respect of such territory, the Protocol shall enter into force on the first day of the month following the expiration of a period of three months after the date of receipt of the declaration by the Secretary General.

3   Any declaration made under the two preceding paragraphs may, in respect of any territory specified in such declaration, be withdrawn by a notification addressed to the Secretary General of the Council of Europe. The withdrawal shall become effective on the first day of the month following the expiration of a period of three months after the date of receipt of such notification by the Secretary General.

Article 15 – Denunciation

1   Any Party may, at any time, denounce this Protocol by means of a notification addressed to the Secretary General of the Council of Europe.

2   Such denunciation shall become effective on the first day of the month following the expiration of a period of three months after the date of receipt of the notification by the Secretary General.

Article 16 – Notification

The Secretary General of the Council of Europe shall notify the member States of the Council of Europe, the non-member States which have participated in the elaboration of this Protocol as well as any State which has acceded to, or has been invited to accede to, this Protocol of:

a   any signature;

b   the deposit of any instrument of ratification, acceptance, approval or accession;

c   any date of entry into force of this Protocol in accordance with its Articles 9, 10 and 11;

d   any other act, notification or communication relating to this Protocol.

In witness whereof the undersigned, being duly authorised thereto, have signed this Protocol.

Done at Strasbourg, this 28 January 2003, in English and in French, both texts being equally authentic, in a single copy which shall be deposited in the archives of the Council of Europe. The Secretary General of the Council of Europe shall transmit certified copies to each member State of the Council of Europe, to the non-member States which have participated in the elaboration of this Protocol, and to any State invited to accede to it.

Council of Europe Convention on the Prevention of Terrorism (CETS No. 196)

The member States of the Council of Europe and the other Signatories hereto,

Considering that the aim of the Council of Europe is to achieve greater unity between its members;

Recognising the value of reinforcing co-operation with the other Parties to this Convention;

Wishing to take effective measures to prevent terrorism and to counter, in particular, public provocation to commit terrorist offences and recruitment and training for terrorism;

Aware of the grave concern caused by the increase in terrorist offences and the growing terrorist threat;

Aware of the precarious situation faced by those who suffer from terrorism, and in this connection reaffirming their profound solidarity with the victims of terrorism and their families;

Recognising that terrorist offences and the offences set forth in this Convention, by whoever perpetrated, are under no circumstances justifiable by considerations of a political, philosophical, ideological, racial, ethnic, religious or other similar nature, and recalling the obligation of all Parties to prevent such offences and, if not prevented, to prosecute and ensure that they are punishable by penalties which take into account their grave nature;

Recalling the need to strengthen the fight against terrorism and reaffirming that all measures taken to prevent or suppress terrorist offences have to respect the rule of law and democratic values, human rights and fundamental freedoms as well as other provisions of international law, including, where applicable, international humanitarian law;

Recognising that this Convention is not intended to affect established principles relating to freedom of expression and freedom of association;

Recalling that acts of terrorism have the purpose by their nature or context to seriously intimidate a population or unduly compel a government or an international organisation to perform or abstain from performing any act or seriously destabilise or destroy the fundamental political, constitutional, economic or social structures of a country or an international organisation;

Have agreed as follows:

Article 1 – Terminology

1   For the purposes of this Convention, "terrorist offence" means any of the offences within the scope of and as defined in one of the treaties listed in the Appendix.

2   On depositing its instrument of ratification, acceptance, approval or accession, a State or the European Community which is not a party to a treaty listed in the Appendix may declare that, in the application of this Convention to the Party concerned, that treaty shall be deemed not to be included in the Appendix. This declaration shall cease to have effect as soon as the treaty enters into force for the Party having made such a declaration, which shall notify the Secretary General of the Council of Europe of this entry into force.

Article 2 – Purpose

The purpose of the present Convention is to enhance the efforts of Parties in preventing terrorism and its negative effects on the full enjoyment of human rights, in particular the right to life, both by measures to be taken at national level and through international co-operation, with due regard to the existing applicable multilateral or bilateral treaties or agreements between the Parties.

Article 3 – National prevention policies

1   Each Party shall take appropriate measures, particularly in the field of training of law enforcement authorities and other bodies, and in the fields of education, culture, information, media and public awareness raising, with a view to preventing terrorist offences and their negative effects while respecting human rights obligations as set forth in, where applicable to that Party, the Convention for the Protection of Human Rights and Fundamental Freedoms, the International Covenant on Civil and Political Rights, and other obligations under international law.

2   Each Party shall take such measures as may be necessary to improve and develop the co-operation among national authorities with a view to preventing terrorist offences and their negative effects by, *inter alia*:

a   exchanging information;

b   improving the physical protection of persons and facilities;

c   enhancing training and coordination plans for civil emergencies.

3   Each Party shall promote tolerance by encouraging inter-religious and cross-cultural dialogue involving, where appropriate, non-governmental organisations and other elements of civil society with a view to

preventing tensions that might contribute to the commission of terrorist offences.

4   Each Party shall endeavour to promote public awareness regarding the existence, causes and gravity of and the threat posed by terrorist offences and the offences set forth in this Convention and consider encouraging the public to provide factual, specific help to its competent authorities that may contribute to preventing terrorist offences and offences set forth in this Convention.

Article 4 – International co-operation on prevention

Parties shall, as appropriate and with due regard to their capabilities, assist and support each other with a view to enhancing their capacity to prevent the commission of terrorist offences, including through exchange of information and best practices, as well as through training and other joint efforts of a preventive character.

Article 5 – Public provocation to commit a terrorist offence

1   For the purposes of this Convention, "public provocation to commit a terrorist offence" means the distribution, or otherwise making available, of a message to the public, with the intent to incite the commission of a terrorist offence, where such conduct, whether or not directly advocating terrorist offences, causes a danger that one or more such offences may be committed.

2   Each Party shall adopt such measures as may be necessary to establish public provocation to commit a terrorist offence, as defined in paragraph 1, when committed unlawfully and intentionally, as a criminal offence under its domestic law.

Article 6 – Recruitment for terrorism

1   For the purposes of this Convention, "recruitment for terrorism" means to solicit another person to commit or participate in the commission of a terrorist offence, or to join an association or group, for the purpose of contributing to the commission of one or more terrorist offences by the association or the group.

2   Each Party shall adopt such measures as may be necessary to establish recruitment for terrorism, as defined in paragraph 1, when committed unlawfully and intentionally, as a criminal offence under its domestic law.

Article 7 – Training for terrorism

1   For the purposes of this Convention, "training for terrorism" means to provide instruction in the making or use of explosives, firearms or other

weapons or noxious or hazardous substances, or in other specific methods or techniques, for the purpose of carrying out or contributing to the commission of a terrorist offence, knowing that the skills provided are intended to be used for this purpose.

2   Each Party shall adopt such measures as may be necessary to establish training for terrorism, as defined in paragraph 1, when committed unlawfully and intentionally, as a criminal offence under its domestic law.

Article 8 – Irrelevance of the commission of a terrorist offence

For an act to constitute an offence as set forth in Articles 5 to 7 of this Convention, it shall not be necessary that a terrorist offence be actually committed.

Article 9 – Ancillary offences

1   Each Party shall adopt such measures as may be necessary to establish as a criminal offence under its domestic law:

a   Participating as an accomplice in an offence as set forth in Articles 5 to 7 of this Convention;

b   Organising or directing others to commit an offence as set forth in Articles 5 to 7 of this Convention;

c   Contributing to the commission of one or more offences as set forth in Articles 5 to 7 of this Convention by a group of persons acting with a common purpose. Such contribution shall be intentional and shall either:

i   be made with the aim of furthering the criminal activity or criminal purpose of the group, where such activity or purpose involves the commission of an offence as set forth in Articles 5 to 7 of this Convention; or

ii   be made in the knowledge of the intention of the group to commit an offence as set forth in Articles 5 to 7 of this Convention.

2   Each Party shall also adopt such measures as may be necessary to establish as a criminal offence under, and in accordance with, its domestic law the attempt to commit an offence as set forth in Articles 6 and 7 of this Convention.

Article 10 – Liability of legal entities

1   Each Party shall adopt such measures as may be necessary, in accordance with its legal principles, to establish the liability of legal entities for participation in the offences set forth in Articles 5 to 7 and 9 of this Convention.

2   Subject to the legal principles of the Party, the liability of legal entities may be criminal, civil or administrative.

3   Such liability shall be without prejudice to the criminal liability of the natural persons who have committed the offences.

Article 11 – Sanctions and measures

1   Each Party shall adopt such measures as may be necessary to make the offences set forth in Articles 5 to 7 and 9 of this Convention punishable by effective, proportionate and dissuasive penalties.

2   Previous final convictions pronounced in foreign States for offences set forth in the present Convention may, to the extent permitted by domestic law, be taken into account for the purpose of determining the sentence in accordance with domestic law.

3   Each Party shall ensure that legal entities held liable in accordance with Article 10 are subject to effective, proportionate and dissuasive criminal or non-criminal sanctions, including monetary sanctions.

Article 12 – Conditions and safeguards

1   Each Party shall ensure that the establishment, implementation and application of the criminalisation under Articles 5 to 7 and 9 of this Convention are carried out while respecting human rights obligations, in particular the right to freedom of expression, freedom of association and freedom of religion, as set forth in, where applicable to that Party, the Convention for the Protection of Human Rights and Fundamental Freedoms, the International Covenant on Civil and Political Rights, and other obligations under international law.

2   The establishment, implementation and application of the criminalisation under Articles 5 to 7 and 9 of this Convention should furthermore be subject to the principle of proportionality, with respect to the legitimate aims pursued and to their necessity in a democratic society, and should exclude any form of arbitrariness or discriminatory or racist treatment.

Article 13 – Protection, compensation and support for victims of terrorism

Each Party shall adopt such measures as may be necessary to protect and support the victims of terrorism that has been committed within its own territory. These measures may include, through the appropriate national schemes and subject to domestic legislation, *inter alia*, financial assistance and compensation for victims of terrorism and their close family members.

Article 14 – Jurisdiction

1   Each Party shall take such measures as may be necessary to establish its jurisdiction over the offences set forth in this Convention:

    a   when the offence is committed in the territory of that Party;

    b   when the offence is committed on board a ship flying the flag of that Party, or on board an aircraft registered under the laws of that Party;

    c   when the offence is committed by a national of that Party.

2   Each Party may also establish its jurisdiction over the offences set forth in this Convention:

    a   when the offence was directed towards or resulted in the carrying out of an offence referred to in Article 1 of this Convention, in the territory of or against a national of that Party;

    b   when the offence was directed towards or resulted in the carrying out of an offence referred to in Article 1 of this Convention, against a State or government facility of that Party abroad, including diplomatic or consular premises of that Party;

    c   when the offence was directed towards or resulted in an offence referred to in Article 1 of this Convention, committed in an attempt to compel that Party to do or abstain from doing any act;

    d   when the offence is committed by a stateless person who has his or her habitual residence in the territory of that Party;

    e   when the offence is committed on board an aircraft which is operated by the Government of that Party.

3   Each Party shall take such measures as may be necessary to establish its jurisdiction over the offences set forth in this Convention in the case where the alleged offender is present in its territory and it does not

extradite him or her to a Party whose jurisdiction is based on a rule of jurisdiction existing equally in the law of the requested Party.

4   This Convention does not exclude any criminal jurisdiction exercised in accordance with national law.

5   When more than one Party claims jurisdiction over an alleged offence set forth in this Convention, the Parties involved shall, where appropriate, consult with a view to determining the most appropriate jurisdiction for prosecution.

Article 15 – Duty to investigate

1   Upon receiving information that a person who has committed or who is alleged to have committed an offence set forth in this Convention may be present in its territory, the Party concerned shall take such measures as may be necessary under its domestic law to investigate the facts contained in the information.

2   Upon being satisfied that the circumstances so warrant, the Party in whose territory the offender or alleged offender is present shall take the appropriate measures under its domestic law so as to ensure that person's presence for the purpose of prosecution or extradition.

3   Any person in respect of whom the measures referred to in paragraph 2 are being taken shall be entitled to:

a   communicate without delay with the nearest appropriate representative of the State of which that person is a national or which is otherwise entitled to protect that person's rights or, if that person is a stateless person, the State in the territory of which that person habitually resides;

b   be visited by a representative of that State;

c   be informed of that person's rights under subparagraphs a. and b.

4   The rights referred to in paragraph 3 shall be exercised in conformity with the laws and regulations of the Party in the territory of which the offender or alleged offender is present, subject to the provision that the said laws and regulations must enable full effect to be given to the purposes for which the rights accorded under paragraph 3 are intended.

5   The provisions of paragraphs 3 and 4 shall be without prejudice to the right of any Party having a claim of jurisdiction in accordance with Article 14, paragraphs 1.c and 2.d to invite the International Committee of the Red Cross to communicate with and visit the alleged offender.

Article 16 – Non application of the Convention

This Convention shall not apply where any of the offences established in accordance with Articles 5 to 7 and 9 is committed within a single State, the alleged offender is a national of that State and is present in the territory of that State, and no other State has a basis under Article 14, paragraph 1 or 2 of this Convention, to exercise jurisdiction, it being understood that the provisions of Articles 17 and 20 to 22 of this Convention shall, as appropriate, apply in those cases.

Article 17 – International co-operation in criminal matters

1   Parties shall afford one another the greatest measure of assistance in connection with criminal investigations or criminal or extradition proceedings in respect of the offences set forth in Articles 5 to 7 and 9 of this Convention, including assistance in obtaining evidence in their possession necessary for the proceedings.

2   Parties shall carry out their obligations under paragraph 1 in conformity with any treaties or other agreements on mutual legal assistance that may exist between them. In the absence of such treaties or agreements, Parties shall afford one another assistance in accordance with their domestic law.

3   Parties shall co-operate with each other to the fullest extent possible under relevant law, treaties, agreements and arrangements of the requested Party with respect to criminal investigations or proceedings in relation to the offences for which a legal entity may be held liable in accordance with Article 10 of this Convention in the requesting Party.

4   Each Party may give consideration to establishing additional mechanisms to share with other Parties information or evidence needed to establish criminal, civil or administrative liability pursuant to Article 10.

Article 18 – Extradite or prosecute

1   The Party in the territory of which the alleged offender is present shall, when it has jurisdiction in accordance with Article 14, if it does not extradite that person, be obliged, without exception whatsoever and whether or not the offence was committed in its territory, to submit the case without undue delay to its competent authorities for the purpose of prosecution, through proceedings in accordance with the laws of that Party. Those authorities shall take their decision in the same manner as in the case of any other offence of a serious nature under the law of that Party.

2   Whenever a Party is permitted under its domestic law to extradite or otherwise surrender one of its nationals only upon the condition that the

person will be returned to that Party to serve the sentence imposed as a result of the trial or proceeding for which the extradition or surrender of the person was sought, and this Party and the Party seeking the extradition of the person agree with this option and other terms they may deem appropriate, such a conditional extradition or surrender shall be sufficient to discharge the obligation set forth in paragraph 1.

Article 19 – Extradition

1   The offences set forth in Articles 5 to 7 and 9 of this Convention shall be deemed to be included as extraditable offences in any extradition treaty existing between any of the Parties before the entry into force of this Convention. Parties undertake to include such offences as extraditable offences in every extradition treaty to be subsequently concluded between them.

2   When a Party which makes extradition conditional on the existence of a treaty receives a request for extradition from another Party with which it has no extradition treaty, the requested Party may, if it so decides, consider this Convention as a legal basis for extradition in respect of the offences set forth in Articles 5 to 7 and 9 of this Convention. Extradition shall be subject to the other conditions provided by the law of the requested Party.

3   Parties which do not make extradition conditional on the existence of a treaty shall recognise the offences set forth in Articles 5 to 7 and 9 of this Convention as extraditable offences between themselves, subject to the conditions provided by the law of the requested Party.

4   Where necessary, the offences set forth in Articles 5 to 7 and 9 of this Convention shall be treated, for the purposes of extradition between Parties, as if they had been committed not only in the place in which they occurred but also in the territory of the Parties that have established jurisdiction in accordance with Article 14.

5   The provisions of all extradition treaties and agreements concluded between Parties in respect of offences set forth in Articles 5 to 7 and 9 of this Convention shall be deemed to be modified as between Parties to the extent that they are incompatible with this Convention.

Article 20 – Exclusion of the political exception clause

1   None of the offences referred to in Articles 5 to 7 and 9 of this Convention, shall be regarded, for the purposes of extradition or mutual legal assistance, as a political offence, an offence connected with a political offence, or as an offence inspired by political motives. Accordingly, a request for extradition or for mutual legal assistance based on such an offence may not be refused on the sole ground that it

concerns a political offence or an offence connected with a political offence or an offence inspired by political motives.

2   Without prejudice to the application of Articles 19 to 23 of the Vienna Convention on the Law of Treaties of 23 May 1969 to the other Articles of this Convention, any State or the European Community may, at the time of signature or when depositing its instrument of ratification, acceptance, approval or accession of the Convention, declare that it reserves the right to not apply paragraph 1 of this Article as far as extradition in respect of an offence set forth in this Convention is concerned. The Party undertakes to apply this reservation on a case-by-case basis, through a duly reasoned decision.

3   Any Party may wholly or partly withdraw a reservation it has made in accordance with paragraph 2 by means of a declaration addressed to the Secretary General of the Council of Europe which shall become effective as from the date of its receipt.

4   A Party which has made a reservation in accordance with paragraph 2 of this Article may not claim the application of paragraph 1 of this Article by any other Party; it may, however, if its reservation is partial or conditional, claim the application of this Article in so far as it has itself accepted it.

5   The reservation shall be valid for a period of three years from the day of the entry into force of this Convention in respect of the Party concerned. However, such reservation may be renewed for periods of the same duration.

6   Twelve months before the date of expiry of the reservation, the Secretary General of the Council of Europe shall give notice of that expiry to the Party concerned. No later than three months before expiry, the Party shall notify the Secretary General of the Council of Europe that it is upholding, amending or withdrawing its reservation. Where a Party notifies the Secretary General of the Council of Europe that it is upholding its reservation, it shall provide an explanation of the grounds justifying its continuance. In the absence of notification by the Party concerned, the Secretary General of the Council of Europe shall inform that Party that its reservation is considered to have been extended automatically for a period of six months. Failure by the Party concerned to notify its intention to uphold or modify its reservation before the expiry of that period shall cause the reservation to lapse.

7   Where a Party does not extradite a person in application of this reservation, after receiving an extradition request from another Party, it shall submit the case, without exception whatsoever and without undue delay, to its competent authorities for the purpose of prosecution, unless the requesting Party and the requested Party agree otherwise. The competent authorities, for the purpose of prosecution in the

requested Party, shall take their decision in the same manner as in the case of any offence of a grave nature under the law of that Party. The requested Party shall communicate, without undue delay, the final outcome of the proceedings to the requesting Party and to the Secretary General of the Council of Europe, who shall forward it to the Consultation of the Parties provided for in Article 30.

8   The decision to refuse the extradition request on the basis of this reservation shall be forwarded promptly to the requesting Party. If within a reasonable time no judicial decision on the merits has been taken in the requested Party according to paragraph 7, the requesting Party may communicate this fact to the Secretary General of the Council of Europe, who shall submit the matter to the Consultation of the Parties provided for in Article 30. This Consultation shall consider the matter and issue an opinion on the conformity of the refusal with the Convention and shall submit it to the Committee of Ministers for the purpose of issuing a declaration thereon. When performing its functions under this paragraph, the Committee of Ministers shall meet in its composition restricted to the States Parties.

Article 21 – Discrimination clause

1   Nothing in this Convention shall be interpreted as imposing an obligation to extradite or to afford mutual legal assistance, if the requested Party has substantial grounds for believing that the request for extradition for offences set forth in Articles 5 to 7 and 9 or for mutual legal assistance with respect to such offences has been made for the purpose of prosecuting or punishing a person on account of that person's race, religion, nationality, ethnic origin or political opinion or that compliance with the request would cause prejudice to that person's position for any of these reasons.

2   Nothing in this Convention shall be interpreted as imposing an obligation to extradite if the person who is the subject of the extradition request risks being exposed to torture or to inhuman or degrading treatment or punishment.

3   Nothing in this Convention shall be interpreted either as imposing an obligation to extradite if the person who is the subject of the extradition request risks being exposed to the death penalty or, where the law of the requested Party does not allow for life imprisonment, to life imprisonment without the possibility of parole, unless under applicable extradition treaties the requested Party is under the obligation to extradite if the requesting Party gives such assurance as the requested Party considers sufficient that the death penalty will not be imposed or, where imposed, will not be carried out, or that the person concerned will not be subject to life imprisonment without the possibility of parole.

Article 22 – Spontaneous information

1   Without prejudice to their own investigations or proceedings, the competent authorities of a Party may, without prior request, forward to the competent authorities of another Party information obtained within the framework of their own investigations, when they consider that the disclosure of such information might assist the Party receiving the information in initiating or carrying out investigations or proceedings, or might lead to a request by that Party under this Convention.

2   The Party providing the information may, pursuant to its national law, impose conditions on the use of such information by the Party receiving the information.

3   The Party receiving the information shall be bound by those conditions.

4   However, any Party may, at any time, by means of a declaration addressed to the Secretary General of the Council of Europe, declare that it reserves the right not to be bound by the conditions imposed by the Party providing the information under paragraph 2 above, unless it receives prior notice of the nature of the information to be provided and agrees to its transmission.

Article 23 – Signature and entry into force

1   This Convention shall be open for signature by the member States of the Council of Europe, the European Community and by non-member States which have participated in its elaboration.

2   This Convention is subject to ratification, acceptance or approval. Instruments of ratification, acceptance or approval shall be deposited with the Secretary General of the Council of Europe.

3   This Convention shall enter into force on the first day of the month following the expiration of a period of three months after the date on which six Signatories, including at least four member States of the Council of Europe, have expressed their consent to be bound by the Convention in accordance with the provisions of paragraph 2.

4   In respect of any Signatory which subsequently expresses its consent to be bound by it, the Convention shall enter into force on the first day of the month following the expiration of a period of three months after the date of the expression of its consent to be bound by the Convention in accordance with the provisions of paragraph 2.

Article 24 – Accession to the Convention

1   After the entry into force of this Convention, the Committee of Ministers of the Council of Europe, after consulting with and obtaining the

unanimous consent of the Parties to the Convention, may invite any State which is not a member of the Council of Europe and which has not participated in its elaboration to accede to this convention. The decision shall be taken by the majority provided for in Article 20.d of the Statute of the Council of Europe and by the unanimous vote of the representatives of the Parties entitled to sit on the Committee of Ministers.

2 In respect of any State acceding to the convention under paragraph 1 above, the Convention shall enter into force on the first day of the month following the expiration of a period of three months after the date of deposit of the instrument of accession with the Secretary General of the Council of Europe.

Article 25 – Territorial application

1 Any State or the European Community may, at the time of signature or when depositing its instrument of ratification, acceptance, approval or accession, specify the territory or territories to which this Convention shall apply.

2 Any Party may, at any later date, by a declaration addressed to the Secretary General of the Council of Europe, extend the application of this Convention to any other territory specified in the declaration. In respect of such territory the Convention shall enter into force on the first day of the month following the expiration of a period of three months after the date of receipt of the declaration by the Secretary General.

3 Any declaration made under the two preceding paragraphs may, in respect of any territory specified in such declaration, be withdrawn by a notification addressed to the Secretary General of the Council of Europe. The withdrawal shall become effective on the first day of the month following the expiration of a period of three months after the date of receipt of such notification by the Secretary General.

Article 26 – Effects of the Convention

1 The present Convention supplements applicable multilateral or bilateral treaties or agreements between the Parties, including the provisions of the following Council of Europe treaties:

－ European Convention on Extradition, opened for signature, in Paris, on 13 December 1957 (ETS No. 24);

－ European Convention on Mutual Assistance in Criminal Matters, opened for signature, in Strasbourg, on 20 April 1959 (ETS No. 30);

- European Convention on the Suppression of Terrorism, opened for signature, in Strasbourg, on 27 January 1977 (ETS No. 90);

- Additional Protocol to the European Convention on Mutual Assistance in Criminal Matters, opened for signature in Strasbourg on 17 March 1978 (ETS No. 99);

- Second Additional Protocol to the European Convention on Mutual Assistance in Criminal Matters, opened for signature in Strasbourg on 8 November 2001 (ETS No. 182);

- Protocol amending the European Convention on the Suppression of Terrorism, opened for signature in Strasbourg on 15 May 2003 (ETS No. 190).

2   If two or more Parties have already concluded an agreement or treaty on the matters dealt with in this Convention or have otherwise established their relations on such matters, or should they in future do so, they shall also be entitled to apply that agreement or treaty or to regulate those relations accordingly. However, where Parties establish their relations in respect of the matters dealt with in the present Convention other than as regulated therein, they shall do so in a manner that is not inconsistent with the Convention's objectives and principles.

3   Parties which are members of the European Union shall, in their mutual relations, apply Community and European Union rules in so far as there are Community or European Union rules governing the particular subject concerned and applicable to the specific case, without prejudice to the object and purpose of the present Convention and without prejudice to its full application with other Parties.

4   Nothing in this Convention shall affect other rights, obligations and responsibilities of a Party and individuals under international law, including international humanitarian law.

5   The activities of armed forces during an armed conflict, as those terms are understood under international humanitarian law, which are governed by that law, are not governed by this Convention, and the activities undertaken by military forces of a Party in the exercise of their official duties, inasmuch as they are governed by other rules of international law, are not governed by this Convention.

Article 27 – Amendments to the Convention

1   Amendments to this Convention may be proposed by any Party, the Committee of Ministers of the Council of Europe or the Consultation of the Parties.

2   Any proposal for amendment shall be communicated by the Secretary General of the Council of Europe to the Parties.

3   Moreover, any amendment proposed by a Party or the Committee of Ministers shall be communicated to the Consultation of the Parties, which shall submit to the Committee of Ministers its opinion on the proposed amendment.

4   The Committee of Ministers shall consider the proposed amendment and any opinion submitted by the Consultation of the Parties and may approve the amendment.

5   The text of any amendment approved by the Committee of Ministers in accordance with paragraph 4 shall be forwarded to the Parties for acceptance.

6   Any amendment approved in accordance with paragraph 4 shall come into force on the thirtieth day after all Parties have informed the Secretary General of their acceptance thereof.

Article 28 – Revision of the Appendix

1   In order to update the list of treaties in the Appendix, amendments may be proposed by any Party or by the Committee of Ministers. These proposals for amendment shall only concern universal treaties concluded within the United Nations system dealing specifically with international terrorism and having entered into force. They shall be communicated by the Secretary General of the Council of Europe to the Parties.

2   After having consulted the non-member Parties, the Committee of Ministers may adopt a proposed amendment by the majority provided for in Article 20.d of the Statute of the Council of Europe. The amendment shall enter into force following the expiry of a period of one year after the date on which it has been forwarded to the Parties. During this period, any Party may notify the Secretary General of the Council of Europe of any objection to the entry into force of the amendment in respect of that Party.

3   If one third of the Parties notifies the Secretary General of the Council of Europe of an objection to the entry into force of the amendment, the amendment shall not enter into force.

4   If less than one third of the Parties notifies an objection, the amendment shall enter into force for those Parties which have not notified an objection.

5   Once an amendment has entered into force in accordance with paragraph 2 and a Party has notified an objection to it, this amendment

shall come into force in respect of the Party concerned on the first day of the month following the date on which it notifies the Secretary General of the Council of Europe of its acceptance.

Article 29 – Settlement of disputes

In the event of a dispute between Parties as to the interpretation or application of this Convention, they shall seek a settlement of the dispute through negotiation or any other peaceful means of their choice, including submission of the dispute to an arbitral tribunal whose decisions shall be binding upon the Parties to the dispute, or to the International Court of Justice, as agreed upon by the Parties concerned.

Article 30 – Consultation of the Parties

1   The Parties shall consult periodically with a view to:

   a   making proposals to facilitate or improve the effective use and implementation of this Convention, including the identification of any problems and the effects of any declaration made under this Convention;

   b   formulating its opinion on the conformity of a refusal to extradite which is referred to them in accordance with Article 20, paragraph 8;

   c   making proposals for the amendment of this Convention in accordance with Article 27;

   d   formulating their opinion on any proposal for the amendment of this Convention which is referred to them in accordance with Article 27, paragraph 3;

   e   expressing an opinion on any question concerning the application of this Convention and facilitating the exchange of information on significant legal, policy or technological developments.

2   The Consultation of the Parties shall be convened by the Secretary General of the Council of Europe whenever he finds it necessary and in any case when a majority of the Parties or the Committee of Ministers request its convocation.

3   The Parties shall be assisted by the Secretariat of the Council of Europe in carrying out their functions pursuant to this Article.

Article 31 – Denunciation

1 Any Party may, at any time, denounce this Convention by means of a notification addressed to the Secretary General of the Council of Europe.

2 Such denunciation shall become effective on the first day of the month following the expiration of a period of three months after the date of receipt of the notification by the Secretary General.

Article 32 – Notification

The Secretary General of the Council of Europe shall notify the member States of the Council of Europe, the European Community, the non-member States which have participated in the elaboration of this Convention as well as any State which has acceded to, or has been invited to accede to, this Convention of:

a   any signature;

b   the deposit of any instrument of ratification, acceptance, approval or accession;

c   any date of entry into force of this Convention in accordance with Article 23;

d   any declaration made under Article 1, paragraph 2, 22, paragraph 4, and 25 ;

e   any other act, notification or communication relating to this Convention.

In witness whereof the undersigned, being duly authorised thereto, have signed this Convention.

Done at Warsaw, this 16th day of May 2005, in English and in French, both texts being equally authentic, in a single copy which shall be deposited in the archives of the Council of Europe. The Secretary General of the Council of Europe shall transmit certified copies to each member State of the Council of Europe, to the European Community, to the non-member States which have participated in the elaboration of this Convention, and to any State invited to accede to it.

Appendix

1   Convention for the Suppression of Unlawful Seizure of Aircraft, signed at The Hague on 16 December 1970;

2   Convention for the Suppression of Unlawful Acts Against the Safety of Civil Aviation, concluded at Montreal on 23 September 1971;

3   Convention on the Prevention and Punishment of Crimes Against Internationally Protected Persons, Including Diplomatic Agents, adopted in New York on 14 December 1973;

4   International Convention Against the Taking of Hostages, adopted in New York on 17 December 1979;

5   Convention on the Physical Protection of Nuclear Material, adopted in Vienna on 3 March 1980;

6   Protocol for the Suppression of Unlawful Acts of Violence at Airports Serving International Civil Aviation, done at Montreal on 24 February 1988;

7   Convention for the Suppression of Unlawful Acts Against the Safety of Maritime Navigation, done at Rome on 10 March 1988;

8   Protocol for the Suppression of Unlawful Acts Against the Safety of Fixed Platforms Located on the Continental Shelf, done at Rome on 10 March 1988;

9   International Convention for the Suppression of Terrorist Bombings, adopted in New York on 15 December 1997;

10 International Convention for the Suppression of the Financing of Terrorism, adopted in New York on 9 December 1999.

Council of Europe Convention on Laundering, Search, Seizure and Confiscation of the Proceeds from Crime and on the Financing of Terrorism (CETS No. 198)

Preamble

The member States of the Council of Europe and the other Signatories hereto,

Considering that the aim of the Council of Europe is to achieve a greater unity between its members;

Convinced of the need to pursue a common criminal policy aimed at the protection of society;

Considering that the fight against serious crime, which has become an increasingly international problem, calls for the use of modern and effective methods on an international scale;

Believing that one of these methods consists in depriving criminals of the proceeds from crime and instrumentalities;

Considering that for the attainment of this aim a well-functioning system of international co-operation also must be established;

Bearing in mind the Council of Europe Convention on Laundering, Search, Seizure and Confiscation of the Proceeds from Crime (ETS No. 141 – hereinafter referred to as "the 1990 Convention");

Recalling also Resolution 1373 g(2001) on threats to international peace and security caused by terrorist acts adopted by the Security Council of the United Nations on 28 September 2001, and particularly its paragraph 3.d;

Recalling the International Convention for the Suppression of the Financing of Terrorism, adopted by the General Assembly of the United Nations on 9 December 1999 and particularly its Articles 2 and 4, which oblige States Parties to establish the financing of terrorism as a criminal offence;

Convinced of the necessity to take immediate steps to ratify and to implement fully the International Convention for the Suppression of the Financing of Terrorism, cited above,

Have agreed as follows:

Chapter I – Use of terms

Article 1 – Use of terms

For the purposes of this Convention:

a   "proceeds" means any economic advantage, derived from or obtained, directly or indirectly, from criminal offences. It may consist of any property as defined in sub-paragraph b of this article;

b   "property" includes property of any description, whether corporeal or incorporeal, movable or immovable, and legal documents or instruments evidencing title to or interest in such property;

c   "instrumentalities" means any property used or intended to be used, in any manner, wholly or in part, to commit a criminal offence or criminal offences;

d   "confiscation" means a penalty or a measure, ordered by a court following proceedings in relation to a criminal offence or criminal offences resulting in the final deprivation of property;

e   "predicate offence" means any criminal offence as a result of which proceeds were generated that may become the subject of an offence as defined in Article 9 of this Convention.

f   "financial intelligence unit" (hereinafter referred to as "FIU") means a central, national agency responsible for receiving (and, as permitted, requesting), analysing and disseminating to the competent authorities, disclosures of financial information

    i   concerning suspected proceeds and potential financing of terrorism, or

    ii   required by national legislation or regulation,

in order to combat money laundering and financing of terrorism;

g   "freezing" or "seizure" means temporarily prohibiting the transfer, destruction, conversion, disposition or movement of property or temporarily assuming custody or control of property on the basis of an order issued by a court or other competent authority;

h   "financing of terrorism" means the acts set out in Article 2 of the International Convention for the Suppression of the Financing of Terrorism, cited above.

Chapter II – Financing of terrorism

Article 2 – Application of the Convention to the financing of terrorism

1 Each Party shall adopt such legislative and other measures as may be necessary to enable it to apply the provisions contained in Chapters III, IV and V of this Convention to the financing of terrorism.

2 In particular, each Party shall ensure that it is able to search, trace, identify, freeze, seize and confiscate property, of a licit or illicit origin, used or allocated to be used by any means, in whole or in part, for the financing of terrorism, or the proceeds of this offence, and to provide co-operation to this end to the widest possible extent.

Chapter III – Measures to be taken at national level

Section 1 – General provisions

Article 3 – Confiscation measures

1 Each Party shall adopt such legislative and other measures as may be necessary to enable it to confiscate instrumentalities and proceeds or property the value of which corresponds to such proceeds and laundered property.

2 Provided that paragraph 1 of this article applies to money laundering and to the categories of offences in the appendix to the Convention, each Party may, at the time of signature or when depositing its instrument of ratification, acceptance, approval or accession, by a declaration addressed to the Secretary General of the Council of Europe, declare that paragraph 1 of this article applies

   a only in so far as the offence is punishable by deprivation of liberty or a detention order for a maximum of more than one year. However, each Party may make a declaration on this provision in respect of the confiscation of the proceeds from tax offences for the sole purpose of being able to confiscate such proceeds, both nationally and through international cooperation, under national and international tax-debt recovery legislation; and/or

   b only to a list of specified offences.

3 Parties may provide for mandatory confiscation in respect of offences which are subject to the confiscation regime. Parties may in particular include in this provision the offences of money laundering, drug trafficking, trafficking in human beings and any other serious offence.

4   Each Party shall adopt such legislative or other measures as may be necessary to require that, in respect of a serious offence or offences as defined by national law, an offender demonstrates the origin of alleged proceeds or other property liable to confiscation to the extent that such a requirement is consistent with the principles of its domestic law.

Article 4 – Investigative and provisional measures

Each Party shall adopt such legislative and other measures as may be necessary to enable it to identify, trace, freeze or seize rapidly property which is liable to confiscation pursuant to Article 3, in order in particular to facilitate the enforcement of a later confiscation.

Article 5 – Freezing, seizure and confiscation

Each Party shall adopt such legislative and other measures as may be necessary to ensure that the measures to freeze, seize and confiscate also encompass:

a   the property into which the proceeds have been transformed or converted;

b   property acquired from legitimate sources, if proceeds have been intermingled, in whole or in part, with such property, up to the assessed value of the intermingled proceeds;

c   income or other benefits derived from proceeds, from property into which proceeds of crime have been transformed or converted or from property with which proceeds of crime have been intermingled, up to the assessed value of the intermingled proceeds, in the same manner and to the same extent as proceeds.

Article 6 – Management of frozen or seized property

Each Party shall adopt such legislative or other measures as may be necessary to ensure proper management of frozen or seized property in accordance with Articles 4 and 5 of this Convention.

Article 7 – Investigative powers and techniques

1   Each Party shall adopt such legislative and other measures as may be necessary to empower its courts or other competent authorities to order that bank, financial or commercial records be made available or be seized in order to carry out the actions referred to in Articles 3, 4 and 5. A Party shall not decline to act under the provisions of this article on grounds of bank secrecy.

2   Without prejudice to paragraph 1, each Party shall adopt such legislative and other measures as may be necessary to enable it to:

a   determine whether a natural or legal person is a holder or beneficial owner of one or more accounts, of whatever nature, in any bank located in its territory and, if so obtain all of the details of the identified accounts;

b   obtain the particulars of specified bank accounts and of banking operations which have been carried out during a specified period through one or more specified accounts, including the particulars of any sending or recipient account;

c   monitor, during a specified period, the banking operations that are being carried out through one or more identified accounts; and,

d   ensure that banks do not disclose to the bank customer concerned or to other third persons that information has been sought or obtained in accordance with sub-paragraphs a, b, or c, or that an investigation is being carried out.

Parties shall consider extending this provision to accounts held in non-bank financial institutions.

3   Each Party shall consider adopting such legislative and other measures as may be necessary to enable it to use special investigative techniques facilitating the identification and tracing of proceeds and the gathering of evidence related thereto, such as observation, interception of telecommunications, access to computer systems and order to produce specific documents.

Article 8 – Legal remedies

Each Party shall adopt such legislative and other measures as may be necessary to ensure that interested parties affected by measures under Articles 3, 4 and 5 and such other provisions in this Section as are relevant, shall have effective legal remedies in order to preserve their rights.

Article 9 – Laundering offences

1   Each Party shall adopt such legislative and other measures as may be necessary to establish as offences under its domestic law, when committed intentionally:

a   the conversion or transfer of property, knowing that such property is proceeds, for the purpose of concealing or disguising the illicit origin of the property or of assisting any person who is involved in the commission of the predicate offence to evade the legal consequences of his actions;

b   the concealment or disguise of the true nature, source, location, disposition, movement, rights with respect to, or ownership of, property, knowing that such property is proceeds;

and, subject to its constitutional principles and the basic concepts of its legal system;

c   the acquisition, possession or use of property, knowing, at the time of receipt, that such property was proceeds;

d   participation in, association or conspiracy to commit, attempts to commit and aiding, abetting, facilitating and counselling the commission of any of the offences established in accordance with this article.

2   For the purposes of implementing or applying paragraph 1 of this article:

a   it shall not matter whether the predicate offence was subject to the criminal jurisdiction of the Party;

b   it may be provided that the offences set forth in that paragraph do not apply to the persons who committed the predicate offence;

c   knowledge, intent or purpose required as an element of an offence set forth in that paragraph may be inferred from objective, factual circumstances.

3   Each Party may adopt such legislative and other measures as may be necessary to establish as an offence under its domestic law all or some of the acts referred to in paragraph 1 of this Article, in either or both of the following cases where the offender

a   suspected that the property was proceeds,

b   ought to have assumed that the property was proceeds.

4   Provided that paragraph 1 of this article applies to the categories of predicate offences in the appendix to the Convention, each State or the European Community may, at the time of signature or when depositing its instrument of ratification, acceptance, approval or accession, by a declaration addressed to the Secretary General of the Council of Europe, declare that paragraph 1 of this article applies:

a   only in so far as the predicate offence is punishable by deprivation of liberty or a detention order for a maximum of more than one year, or for those Parties that have a minimum threshold for offences in their legal system, in so far as the offence is punishable by deprivation of liberty or a detention order for a minimum of more than six months; and/or b   only to a list of specified predicate offences; and/or

c   to a category of serious offences in the national law of the Party.

5   Each Party shall ensure that a prior or simultaneous conviction for the predicate offence is not a prerequisite for a conviction for money laundering.

6   Each Party shall ensure that a conviction for money laundering under this Article is possible where it is proved that the property, the object of paragraph 1.a or b of this article, originated from a predicate offence, without it being necessary to establish precisely which offence.

7   Each Party shall ensure that predicate offences for money laundering extend to conduct that occurred in another State, which constitutes an offence in that State, and which would have constituted a predicate offence had it occurred domestically. Each Party may provide that the only prerequisite is that the conduct would have constituted a predicate offence had it occurred domestically.

Article 10 – Corporate liability

1   Each Party shall adopt such legislative and other measures as may be necessary to ensure that legal persons can be held liable for the criminal offences of money laundering established in accordance with this Convention, committed for their benefit by any natural person, acting either individually or as part of an organ of the legal person, who has a leading position within the legal person, based on:

a   a power of representation of the legal person; or

b   an authority to take decisions on behalf of the legal person; or

c   an authority to exercise control within the legal person,

as well as for involvement of such a natural person as accessory or instigator in the above-mentioned offences.

2   Apart from the cases already provided for in paragraph 1, each Party shall take the necessary measures to ensure that a legal person can be held liable where the lack of supervision or control by a natural person referred to in paragraph 1 has made possible the commission of the criminal offences mentioned in paragraph 1 for the benefit of that legal person by a natural person under its authority.

3   Liability of a legal person under this Article shall not exclude criminal proceedings against natural persons who are perpetrators, instigators of, or accessories to, the criminal offences mentioned in paragraph 1.

4   Each Party shall ensure that legal persons held liable in accordance with this Article, shall be subject to effective, proportionate and dissuasive criminal or non-criminal sanctions, including monetary sanctions.

Article 11 – Previous decisions

Each Party shall adopt such legislative and other measures as may be necessary to provide for the possibility of taking into account, when determining the penalty, final decisions against a natural or legal person taken in another Party in relation to offences established in accordance with this Convention.

Section 2 - Financial intelligence unit (FIU) and prevention

Article 12 – Financial intelligence unit (FIU)

1   Each Party shall adopt such legislative and other measures as may be necessary to establish an FIU as defined in this Convention.

2   Each Party shall adopt such legislative and other measures as may be necessary to ensure that its FIU has access, directly or indirectly, on a timely basis to the financial, administrative and law enforcement information that it requires to properly undertake its functions, including the analysis of suspicious transaction reports.

Article 13 – Measures to prevent money laundering

1   Each Party shall adopt such legislative and other measures as may be necessary to institute a comprehensive domestic regulatory and supervisory or monitoring regime to prevent money laundering and shall take due account of applicable international standards, including in particular the recommendations adopted by the Financial Action Task Force on Money Laundering (FATF).

2   In that respect, each Party shall adopt, in particular, such legislative and other measures as may be necessary to:

a   require legal and natural persons which engage in activities which are particularly likely to be used for money laundering purposes, and as far as these activities are concerned, to:

i   identify and verify the identity of their customers and, where applicable, their ultimate beneficial owners, and to conduct ongoing due diligence on the business relationship, while taking into account a risk based approach;

ii   report suspicions on money laundering subject to safeguard;

iii take supporting measures, such as record keeping on customer identification and transactions, training of personnel and the establishment of internal policies and procedures, and if appropriate, adapted to their size and nature of business;

b prohibit, as appropriate, the persons referred to in sub-paragraph a from disclosing the fact that a suspicious transaction report or related information has been transmitted or that a money laundering investigation is being or may be carried out;

c ensure that the persons referred to in sub-paragraph a are subject to effective systems for monitoring, and where applicable supervision, with a view to ensure their compliance with the requirements to combat money laundering, where appropriate on a risk sensitive basis.

3 In that respect, each Party shall adopt such legislative or other measures as may be necessary to detect the significant physical cross border transportation of cash and appropriate bearer negotiable instruments.

Article 14 – Postponement of domestic suspicious transactions

Each Party shall adopt such legislative and other measures as may be necessary to permit urgent action to be taken by the FIU or, as appropriate, by any other competent authorities or body, when there is a suspicion that a transaction is related to money laundering, to suspend or withhold consent to a transaction going ahead in order to analyse the transaction and confirm the suspicion. Each party may restrict such a measure to cases where a suspicious transaction report has been submitted. The maximum duration of any suspension or withholding of consent to a transaction shall be subject to any relevant provisions in national law.

Chapter IV – International co-operation

Section 1 – Principles of international co-operation

Article 15 – General principles and measures for international co-operation

1 The Parties shall mutually co-operate with each other to the widest extent possible for the purposes of investigations and proceedings aiming at the confiscation of instrumentalities and proceeds.

2 Each Party shall adopt such legislative or other measures as may be necessary to enable it to comply, under the conditions provided for in this chapter, with requests:

a   for confiscation of specific items of property representing proceeds or instrumentalities, as well as for confiscation of proceeds consisting in a requirement to pay a sum of money corresponding to the value of proceeds;

b   for investigative assistance and provisional measures with a view to either form of confiscation referred to under a above.

3   Investigative assistance and provisional measures sought in paragraph 2.b shall be carried out as permitted by and in accordance with the internal law of the requested Party. Where the request concerning one of these measures specifies formalities or procedures which are necessary under the law of the requesting Party, even if unfamiliar to the requested Party, the latter shall comply with such requests to the extent that the action sought is not contrary to the fundamental principles of its law.

4   Each Party shall adopt such legislative or other measures as may be necessary to ensure that the requests coming from other Parties in order to identify, trace, freeze or seize the proceeds and instrumentalities, receive the same priority as those made in the framework of internal procedures.

Section 2 – Investigative assistance

Article 16 – Obligation to assist

The Parties shall afford each other, upon request, the widest possible measure of assistance in the identification and tracing of instrumentalities, proceeds and other property liable to confiscation. Such assistance shall include any measure providing and securing evidence as to the existence, location or movement, nature, legal status or value of the aforementioned property.

Article 17 – Requests for information on bank accounts

1   Each Party shall, under the conditions set out in this article, take the measures necessary to determine, in answer to a request sent by another Party, whether a natural or legal person that is the subject of a criminal investigation holds or controls one or more accounts, of whatever nature, in any bank located in its territory and, if so, provide the particulars of the identified accounts.

2   The obligation set out in this article shall apply only to the extent that the information is in the possession of the bank keeping the account.

3   In addition to the requirements of Article 37, the requesting party shall, in the request:

a   state why it considers that the requested information is likely to be of substantial value for the purpose of the criminal investigation into the offence;

b   state on what grounds it presumes that banks in the requested Party hold the account and specify, to the widest extent possible, which banks and/or accounts may be involved; and

c   include any additional information available which may facilitate the execution of the request.

4   The requested Party may make the execution of such a request dependant on the same conditions as it applies in respect of requests for search and seizure.

5   Each State or the European Community may, at the time of signature or when depositing its instrument of ratification, acceptance, approval or accession, by a declaration addressed to the Secretary General of the Council of Europe, declare that this article applies only to the categories of offences specified in the list contained in the appendix to this Convention.

6   Parties may extend this provision to accounts held in non-bank financial institutions. Such extension may be made subject to the principle of reciprocity.

Article 18 – Requests for information on banking transactions

1   On request by another Party, the requested Party shall provide the particulars of specified bank accounts and of banking operations which have been carried out during a specified period through one or more accounts specified in the request, including the particulars of any sending or recipient account.

2   The obligation set out in this Article shall apply only to the extent that the information is in the possession of the bank holding the account.

3   In addition to the requirements of Article 37, the requesting Party shall in its request indicate why it considers the requested information relevant for the purpose of the criminal investigation into the offence.

4   The requested Party may make the execution of such a request dependant on the same conditions as it applies in respect of requests for search and seizure.

5   Parties may extend this provision to accounts held in non-bank financial institutions. Such extension may be made subject to the principle of reciprocity.

Article 19 – Requests for the monitoring of banking transactions

1   Each Party shall ensure that, at the request of another Party, it is able to monitor, during a specified period, the banking operations that are being carried out through one or more accounts specified in the request and communicate the results thereof to the requesting Party.

2   In addition to the requirements of Article 37, the requesting Party shall in its request indicate why it considers the requested information relevant for the purpose of the criminal investigation into the offence.

3   The decision to monitor shall be taken in each individual case by the competent authorities of the requested Party, with due regard for the national law of that Party.

4   The practical details regarding the monitoring shall be agreed between the competent authorities of the requesting and requested Parties.

5   Parties may extend this provision to accounts held in non-bank financial institutions.

Article 20 – Spontaneous information

Without prejudice to its own investigations or proceedings, a Party may without prior request forward to another Party information on instrumentalities and proceeds, when it considers that the disclosure of such information might assist the receiving Party in initiating or carrying out investigations or proceedings or might lead to a request by that Party under this chapter.

Section 3 – Provisional measures

Article 21 – Obligation to take provisional measures

1   At the request of another Party which has instituted criminal proceedings or proceedings for the purpose of confiscation, a Party shall take the necessary provisional measures, such as freezing or seizing, to prevent any dealing in, transfer or disposal of property which, at a later stage, may be the subject of a request for confiscation or which might be such as to satisfy the request.

2   A Party which has received a request for confiscation pursuant to Article 23 shall, if so requested, take the measures mentioned in paragraph 1 of this article in respect of any property which is the subject of the request or which might be such as to satisfy the request.

Article 22 – Execution of provisional measures

1   After the execution of the provisional measures requested in conformity with paragraph 1 of Article 21, the requesting Party shall provide spontaneously and as soon as possible to the requested Party all information which may question or modify the extent of these measures. The requesting Party shall also provide without delays all complementary information requested by the requested Party and which is necessary for the implementation of and the follow up to the provisional measures.

2   Before lifting any provisional measure taken pursuant to this article, the requested Party shall, wherever possible, give the requesting Party an opportunity to present its reasons in favour of continuing the measure.

Section 4 – Confiscation

Article 23 – Obligation to confiscate

1   A Party, which has received a request made by another Party for confiscation concerning instrumentalities or proceeds, situated in its territory, shall:

a   enforce a confiscation order made by a court of a requesting Party in relation to such instrumentalities or proceeds; or

b   submit the request to its competent authorities for the purpose of obtaining an order of confiscation and, if such order is granted, enforce it.

2   For the purposes of applying paragraph 1.b of this article, any Party shall whenever necessary have competence to institute confiscation proceedings under its own law.

3   The provisions of paragraph 1 of this article shall also apply to confiscation consisting in a requirement to pay a sum of money corresponding to the value of proceeds, if property on which the confiscation can be enforced is located in the requested Party. In such cases, when enforcing confiscation pursuant to paragraph 1, the requested Party shall, if payment is not obtained, realise the claim on any property available for that purpose.

4   If a request for confiscation concerns a specific item of property, the Parties may agree that the requested Party may enforce the confiscation in the form of a requirement to pay a sum of money corresponding to the value of the property.

5   The Parties shall co-operate to the widest extent possible under their domestic law with those Parties which request the execution of measures equivalent to confiscation leading to the deprivation of property, which are

not criminal sanctions, in so far as such measures are ordered by a judicial authority of the requesting Party in relation to a criminal offence, provided that it has been established that the property constitutes proceeds or other property in the meaning of Article 5 of this Convention.

Article 24 – Execution of confiscation

1   The procedures for obtaining and enforcing the confiscation under Article 23 shall be governed by the law of the requested Party.

2   The requested Party shall be bound by the findings as to the facts in so far as they are stated in a conviction or judicial decision of the requesting Party or in so far as such conviction or judicial decision is implicitly based on them.

3   Each State or the European Community may, at the time of signature or when depositing its instrument of ratification, acceptance, approval or accession, by a declaration addressed to the Secretary General of the Council of Europe, declare that paragraph 2 of this article applies only subject to its constitutional principles and the basic concepts of its legal system.

4   If the confiscation consists in the requirement to pay a sum of money, the competent authority of the requested Party shall convert the amount thereof into the currency of that Party at the rate of exchange ruling at the time when the decision to enforce the confiscation is taken.

5   In the case of Article 23, paragraph 1.a, the requesting Party alone shall have the right to decide on any application for review of the confiscation order.

Article 25 – Confiscated property

1   Property confiscated by a Party pursuant to Articles 23 and 24 of this Convention, shall be disposed of by that Party in accordance with its domestic law and administrative procedures.

2   When acting on the request made by another Party in accordance with Articles 23 and 24 of this Convention, Parties shall, to the extent permitted by domestic law and if so requested, give priority consideration to returning the confiscated property to the requesting Party so that it can give compensation to the victims of the crime or return such property to their legitimate owners.

3   When acting on the request made by another Party in accordance with Articles 23 and 24 of this Convention, a Party may give special consideration to concluding agreements or arrangements on sharing with other Parties, on a regular or case-by-case basis, such property, in accordance with its domestic law or administrative procedures.

Article 26 – Right of enforcement and maximum amount of confiscation

1   A request for confiscation made under Articles 23 and 24 does not affect the right of the requesting Party to enforce itself the confiscation order.

2   Nothing in this Convention shall be so interpreted as to permit the total value of the confiscation to exceed the amount of the sum of money specified in the confiscation order. If a Party finds that this might occur, the Parties concerned shall enter into consultations to avoid such an effect.

Article 27 – Imprisonment in default

The requested Party shall not impose imprisonment in default or any other measure restricting the liberty of a person as a result of a request under Article 23, if the requesting Party has so specified in the request.

Section 5 – Refusal and postponement of co-operation

Article 28 – Grounds for refusal

1   Co-operation under this chapter may be refused if:

a   the action sought would be contrary to the fundamental principles of the legal system of the requested Party; or

b   the execution of the request is likely to prejudice the sovereignty, security, ordre public or other essential interests of the requested Party; or

c   in the opinion of the requested Party, the importance of the case to which the request relates does not justify the taking of the action sought; or

d   the offence to which the request relates is a fiscal offence, with the exception of the financing of terrorism;

e   the offence to which the request relates is a political offence, with the exception of the financing of terrorism; or

f   the requested Party considers that compliance with the action sought would be contrary to the principle of *ne bis in idem*; or

g   the offence to which the request relates would not be an offence under the law of the requested Party if committed within its jurisdiction. However, this ground for refusal applies to co-operation under Section 2 only in so far as the assistance sought involves coercive action. Where dual criminality is required for co-operation under this chapter, that requirement shall be deemed to be satisfied regardless of whether both Parties place the offence within the same category of offences or denominate the offence by the same terminology, provided that both Parties criminalise the conduct underlying the offence.

2   Co-operation under Section 2, in so far as the assistance sought involves coercive action, and under Section 3 of this chapter, may also be refused if the measures sought could not be taken under the domestic law of the requested Party for the purposes of investigations or proceedings, had it been a similar domestic case.

3   Where the law of the requested Party so requires, co-operation under Section 2, in so far as the assistance sought involves coercive action, and under Section 3 of this chapter may also be refused if the measures sought or any other measures having similar effects would not be permitted under the law of the requesting Party, or, as regards the competent authorities of the requesting Party, if the request is not authorised by either a judge or another judicial authority, including public prosecutors, any of these authorities acting in relation to criminal offences.

4   Co-operation under Section 4 of this chapter may also be refused if:

a   under the law of the requested Party confiscation is not provided for in respect of the type of offence to which the request relates; or

b   without prejudice to the obligation pursuant to Article 23, paragraph 3, it would be contrary to the principles of the domestic law of the requested Party concerning the limits of confiscation in respect of the relationship between an offence and:

i   an economic advantage that might be qualified as its proceeds; or

ii   property that might be qualified as its instrumentalities; or

c   under the law of the requested Party confiscation may no longer be imposed or enforced because of the lapse of time; or

d   without prejudice to Article 23, paragraph 5, the request does not relate to a previous conviction, or a decision of a judicial nature or a statement in such a decision that an offence or several offences have been committed, on the basis of which the confiscation has been ordered or is sought; or

e   confiscation is either not enforceable in the requesting Party, or it is still subject to ordinary means of appeal; or f   the request relates to a confiscation order resulting from a decision rendered in absentia of the person against whom the order was issued and, in the opinion of the requested Party, the proceedings conducted by the requesting Party leading to such decision did not satisfy the minimum rights of defence recognised as due to everyone against whom a criminal charge is made.

5   For the purpose of paragraph 4.f of this article a decision is not considered to have been rendered *in absentia* if:

a   it has been confirmed or pronounced after opposition by the person concerned; or

b   it has been rendered on appeal, provided that the appeal was lodged by the person concerned.

6   When considering, for the purposes of paragraph 4.f of this article if the minimum rights of defence have been satisfied, the requested Party shall take into account the fact that the person concerned has deliberately sought to evade justice or the fact that that person, having had the possibility of lodging a legal remedy against the decision made *in absentia*, elected not to do so. The same will apply when the person concerned, having been duly served with the summons to appear, elected not to do so nor to ask for adjournment.

7   A Party shall not invoke bank secrecy as a ground to refuse any co-operation under this chapter. Where its domestic law so requires, a Party may require that a request for co-operation which would involve the lifting of bank secrecy be authorised by either a judge or another judicial authority, including public prosecutors, any of these authorities acting in relation to criminal offences.

8   Without prejudice to the ground for refusal provided for in paragraph 1.a of this article:

a   the fact that the person under investigation or subjected to a confiscation order by the authorities of the requesting Party is a legal person shall not be invoked by the requested Party as an obstacle to affording any co-operation under this chapter;

b   the fact that the natural person against whom an order of confiscation of proceeds has been issued has died or the fact that a legal person against whom an order of confiscation of proceeds has been issued has subsequently been dissolved shall not be invoked as an obstacle to render assistance in accordance with Article 23, paragraph 1.a.

c   the fact that the person under investigation or subjected to a confiscation order by the authorities of the requesting Party is mentioned in the request both as the author of the underlying criminal offence and of the offence of money laundering, in accordance with Article 9.2.b of this Convention, shall not be invoked by the requested Party as an obstacle to affording any co-operation under this chapter.

Article 29 – Postponement

The requested Party may postpone action on a request if such action would prejudice investigations or proceedings by its authorities.

Article 30 – Partial or conditional granting of a request

Before refusing or postponing co-operation under this chapter, the requested Party shall, where appropriate after having consulted the requesting Party, consider whether the request may be granted partially or subject to such conditions as it deems necessary.

Section 6 – Notification and protection of third parties' rights

Article 31 – Notification of documents

1   The Parties shall afford each other the widest measure of mutual assistance in the serving of judicial documents to persons affected by provisional measures and confiscation.

2   Nothing in this article is intended to interfere with:

a   the possibility of sending judicial documents, by postal channels, directly to persons abroad;

b   the possibility for judicial officers, officials or other competent authorities of the Party of origin to effect service of judicial documents directly through the consular authorities of that Party or through judicial officers, officials or other competent authorities of the Party of destination,

unless the Party of destination makes a declaration to the contrary to the Secretary General of the Council of Europe at the time of signature or when depositing its instrument of ratification, acceptance, approval or accession.

3   When serving judicial documents to persons abroad affected by provisional measures or confiscation orders issued in the sending Party, this Party shall indicate what legal remedies are available under its law to such persons.

Article 32 – Recognition of foreign decisions

1   When dealing with a request for co-operation under Sections 3 and 4, the requested Party shall recognise any judicial decision taken in the requesting Party regarding rights claimed by third parties.

2   Recognition may be refused if:

   a   third parties did not have adequate opportunity to assert their rights; or

   b   the decision is incompatible with a decision already taken in the requested Party on the same matter; or

   c   it is incompatible with the ordre public of the requested Party; or

   d   the decision was taken contrary to provisions on exclusive jurisdiction provided for by the law of the requested Party.

Section 7 – Procedural and other general rules

Article 33 – Central authority

1   The Parties shall designate a central authority or, if necessary, authorities, which shall be responsible for sending and answering requests made under this chapter, the execution of such requests or the transmission of them to the authorities competent for their execution.

2   Each Party shall, at the time of signature or when depositing its instrument of ratification, acceptance, approval or accession, communicate to the Secretary General of the Council of Europe the names and addresses of the authorities designated in pursuance of paragraph 1 of this article.

Article 34 – Direct communication

1   The central authorities shall communicate directly with one another.

2   In the event of urgency, requests or communications under this chapter may be sent directly by the judicial authorities, including public prosecutors, of the requesting Party to such authorities of the requested Party. In such cases a copy shall be sent at the same time to the central authority of the requested Party through the central authority of the requesting Party.

3   Any request or communication under paragraphs 1 and 2 of this article may be made through the International Criminal Police Organisation (Interpol).

4   Where a request is made pursuant to paragraph 2 of this article and the authority is not competent to deal with the request, it shall refer the request to the competent national authority and inform directly the requesting Party that it has done so.

5   Requests or communications under Section 2 of this chapter, which do not involve coercive action, may be directly transmitted by the competent authorities of the requesting Party to the competent authorities of the requested Party.

6   Draft requests or communications under this chapter may be sent directly by the judicial authorities of the requesting Party to such authorities of the requested Party prior to a formal request to ensure that it can be dealt with efficiently upon receipt and contains sufficient information and supporting documentation for it to meet the requirements of the legislation of the requested Party.

Article 35 – Form of request and languages

1   All requests under this chapter shall be made in writing. They may be transmitted electronically, or by any other means of telecommunication, provided that the requesting Party is prepared, upon request, to produce at any time a written record of such communication and the original. However each Party may, at any time, by a declaration addressed to the Secretary General of the Council of Europe, indicate the conditions in which it is ready to accept and execute requests received electronically or by any other means of communication.

2   Subject to the provisions of paragraph 3 of this article, translations of the requests or supporting documents shall not be required.

3   At the time of signature or when depositing its instrument of ratification, acceptance, approval or accession, any State or the European Community may communicate to the Secretary General of the Council of Europe a declaration that it reserves the right to require that requests made to it and documents supporting such requests be accompanied by a translation into its own language or into one of the official languages of the Council of Europe or into such one of these languages as it shall indicate. It may on that occasion declare its readiness to accept translations in any other language as it may specify. The other Parties may apply the reciprocity rule.

Article 36 – Legalisation

Documents transmitted in application of this chapter shall be exempt from all legalisation formalities.

Article 37 – Content of request

1   Any request for co-operation under this chapter shall specify:

a   the authority making the request and the authority carrying out the investigations or proceedings;

b   the object of and the reason for the request;

c   the matters, including the relevant facts (such as date, place and circumstances of the offence) to which the investigations or proceedings relate, except in the case of a request for notification;

d   in so far as the co-operation involves coercive action:

i   the text of the statutory provisions or, where this is not possible, a statement of the relevant law applicable; and

ii   an indication that the measure sought or any other measures having similar effects could be taken in the territory of the requesting Party under its own law;

e   where necessary and in so far as possible:

i   details of the person or persons concerned, including name, date and place of birth, nationality and location, and, in the case of a legal person, its seat; and

ii   the property in relation to which co-operation is sought, its location, its connection with the person or persons concerned, any connection with the offence, as well as any available information about other persons, interests in the property; and

f   any particular procedure the requesting Party wishes to be followed.

2   A request for provisional measures under Section 3 in relation to seizure of property on which a confiscation order consisting in the requirement to pay a sum of money may be realised shall also indicate a maximum amount for which recovery is sought in that property.

3   In addition to the indications mentioned in paragraph 1, any request under Section 4 shall contain:

a   in the case of Article 23, paragraph 1.a:

i   a certified true copy of the confiscation order made by the court in the requesting Party and a statement of the grounds on the basis of which the order was made, if they are not indicated in the order itself;

    ii   an attestation by the competent authority of the requesting Party that the confiscation order is enforceable and not subject to ordinary means of appeal;

    iii   information as to the extent to which the enforcement of the order is requested; and

    iv   information as to the necessity of taking any provisional measures;

b   in the case of Article 23, paragraph 1.b, a statement of the facts relied upon by the requesting Party sufficient to enable the requested Party to seek the order under its domestic law;

c   when third parties have had the opportunity to claim rights, documents demonstrating that this has been the case.

Article 38 – Defective requests

1   If a request does not comply with the provisions of this chapter or the information supplied is not sufficient to enable the requested Party to deal with the request, that Party may ask the requesting Party to amend the request or to complete it with additional information.

2   The requested Party may set a time-limit for the receipt of such amendments or information.

3   Pending receipt of the requested amendments or information in relation to a request under Section 4 of this chapter, the requested Party may take any of the measures referred to in Sections 2 or 3 of this chapter.

Article 39 – Plurality of requests

1   Where the requested Party receives more than one request under Sections 3 or 4 of this chapter in respect of the same person or property, the plurality of requests shall not prevent that Party from dealing with the requests involving the taking of provisional measures.

2   In the case of plurality of requests under Section 4 of this chapter, the requested Party shall consider consulting the requesting Parties.

Article 40 – Obligation to give reasons

The requested Party shall give reasons for any decision to refuse, postpone or make conditional any co-operation under this chapter.

Article 41 – Information

1   The requested Party shall promptly inform the requesting Party of:

a   the action initiated on a request under this chapter;

b   the final result of the action carried out on the basis of the request;

c   a decision to refuse, postpone or make conditional, in whole or in part, any co-operation under this chapter;

d   any circumstances which render impossible the carrying out of the action sought or are likely to delay it significantly; and

e   in the event of provisional measures taken pursuant to a request under Sections 2 or 3 of this chapter, such provisions of its domestic law as would automatically lead to the lifting of the provisional measure.

2   The requesting Party shall promptly inform the requested Party of:

a   any review, decision or any other fact by reason of which the confiscation order ceases to be wholly or partially enforceable; and

b   any development, factual or legal, by reason of which any action under this chapter is no longer justified.

3   Where a Party, on the basis of the same confiscation order, requests confiscation in more than one Party, it shall inform all Parties which are affected by an enforcement of the order about the request.

Article 42 – Restriction of use

1   The requested Party may make the execution of a request dependent on the condition that the information or evidence obtained will not, without its prior consent, be used or transmitted by the authorities of the requesting Party for investigations or proceedings other than those specified in the request.

2   Each State or the European Community may, at the time of signature or when depositing its instrument of ratification, acceptance, approval or accession, by declaration addressed to the Secretary General of the Council of Europe, declare that, without its prior consent, information or evidence provided by it under this chapter may not be used or transmitted by the authorities of the requesting Party in investigations or proceedings other than those specified in the request.

Article 43 – Confidentiality

1   The requesting Party may require that the requested Party keep confidential the facts and substance of the request, except to the extent necessary to execute the request. If the requested Party cannot comply with the requirement of confidentiality, it shall promptly inform the requesting Party.

2   The requesting Party shall, if not contrary to basic principles of its national law and if so requested, keep confidential any evidence and information provided by the requested Party, except to the extent that its disclosure is necessary for the investigations or proceedings described in the request.

3   Subject to the provisions of its domestic law, a Party which has received spontaneous information under Article 20 shall comply with any requirement of confidentiality as required by the Party which supplies the information. If the other Party cannot comply with such requirement, it shall promptly inform the transmitting Party.

Article 44 – Costs

The ordinary costs of complying with a request shall be borne by the requested Party. Where costs of a substantial or extraordinary nature are necessary to comply with a request, the Parties shall consult in order to agree the conditions on which the request is to be executed and how the costs shall be borne.

Article 45 – Damages

1   When legal action on liability for damages resulting from an act or omission in relation to co-operation under this chapter has been initiated by a person, the Parties concerned shall consider consulting each other, where appropriate, to determine how to apportion any sum of damages due.

2   A Party which has become subject of a litigation for damages shall endeavour to inform the other Party of such litigation if that Party might have an interest in the case.

Chapter V – Co-operation between FIUs

Article 46 – Co-operation between FIUs

1   Parties shall ensure that FIUs, as defined in this Convention, shall cooperate for the purpose of combating money laundering, to assemble and analyse, or, if appropriate, investigate within the FIU relevant information on any fact which might be an indication of money laundering in accordance with their national powers.

2   For the purposes of paragraph 1, each Party shall ensure that FIUs exchange, spontaneously or on request and either in accordance with this Convention or in accordance with existing or future memoranda of understanding compatible with this Convention, any accessible information that may be relevant to the processing or analysis of information or, if appropriate, to investigation by the FIU regarding financial transactions related to money laundering and the natural or legal persons involved.

3   Each Party shall ensure that the performance of the functions of the FIUs under this article shall not be affected by their internal status, regardless of whether they are administrative, law enforcement or judicial authorities.

4   Each request made under this article shall be accompanied by a brief statement of the relevant facts known to the requesting FIU. The FIU shall specify in the request how the information sought will be used.

5   When a request is made in accordance with this article, the requested FIU shall provide all relevant information, including accessible financial information and requested law enforcement data, sought in the request, without the need for a formal letter of request under applicable conventions or agreements between the Parties.

6   An FIU may refuse to divulge information which could lead to impairment of a criminal investigation being conducted in the requested Party or, in exceptional circumstances, where divulging the information would be clearly disproportionate to the legitimate interests of a natural or legal person or the Party concerned or would otherwise not be in accordance with fundamental principles of national law of the requested Party. Any such refusal shall be appropriately explained to the FIU requesting the information.

7   Information or documents obtained under this article shall only be used for the purposes laid down in paragraph 1. Information supplied by a counterpart FIU shall not be disseminated to a third party, nor be used by the receiving FIU for purposes other than analysis, without prior consent of the supplying FIU.

8   When transmitting information or documents pursuant to this article, the transmitting FIU may impose restrictions and conditions on the use of information for purposes other than those stipulated in paragraph 7. The receiving FIU shall comply with any such restrictions and conditions.

9   Where a Party wishes to use transmitted information or documents for criminal investigations or prosecutions for the purposes laid down in paragraph 7, the transmitting FIU may not refuse its consent to such use unless it does so on the basis of restrictions under its national law

or conditions referred to in paragraph 6. Any refusal to grant consent shall be appropriately explained.

10   FIUs shall undertake all necessary measures, including security measures, to ensure that information submitted under this article is not accessible by any other authorities, agencies or departments.

11   The information submitted shall be protected, in conformity with the Council of Europe Convention of 28 January 1981 for the Protection of Individuals with regard to Automatic Processing of Personal Data (ETS No. 108) and taking account of Recommendation No R(87)15 of 15 September 1987 of the Committee of Ministers of the Council of Europe Regulating the Use of Personal Data in the Police Sector, by at least the same rules of confidentiality and protection of personal data as those that apply under the national legislation applicable to the requesting FIU.

12   The transmitting FIU may make reasonable enquiries as to the use made of information provided and the receiving FIU shall, whenever practicable, provide such feedback.

13   Parties shall indicate the unit which is an FIU within the meaning of this article.

Article 47 – International co-operation for postponement of suspicious transactions

1   Each Party shall adopt such legislative or other measures as may be necessary to permit urgent action to be initiated by a FIU, at the request of a foreign FIU, to suspend or withhold consent to a transaction going ahead for such periods and depending on the same conditions as apply in its domestic law in respect of the postponement of transactions.

2   The action referred to in paragraph 1 shall be taken where the requested FIU is satisfied, upon justification by the requesting FIU, that:

a   the transaction is related to money laundering; and

b   the transaction would have been suspended, or consent to the transaction going ahead would have been withheld, if the transaction had been the subject of a domestic suspicious transaction report.

Chapter VI – Monitoring mechanism and settlement of disputes

Article 48 – Monitoring mechanism and settlement of disputes

1   The Conference of the Parties (COP) shall be responsible for following the implementation of the Convention. The COP:

a   shall monitor the proper implementation of the Convention by the Parties;

b   shall, at the request of a Party, express an opinion on any question concerning the interpretation and application of the Convention.

2   The COP shall carry out the functions under paragraph 1.a above by using any available Select Committee of Experts on the Evaluation of Anti-Money Laundering Measures (Moneyval) public summaries (for Moneyval countries) and any available FATF public summaries (for FATF countries), supplemented by periodic self assessment questionnaires, as appropriate. The monitoring procedure will deal with areas covered by this Convention only in respect of those areas which are not covered by other relevant international standards on which mutual evaluations are carried out by the FATF and Moneyval.

3   If the COP concludes that it requires further information in the discharge of its functions, it shall liaise with the Party concerned, taking advantage, if so required by the COP, of the procedure and mechanism of Moneyval. The Party concerned shall then report back to the COP. The COP shall on this basis decide whether or not to carry out a more in-depth assessment of the position of the Party concerned. This may, but need not necessarily, involve, a country visit by an evaluation team.

4   In case of a dispute between Parties as to the interpretation or application of the Convention, they shall seek a settlement of the dispute through negotiation or any other peaceful means of their choice, including submission of the dispute to the COP, to an arbitral tribunal whose decisions shall be binding upon the Parties, or to the International Court of Justice, as agreed upon by the Parties concerned.

5   The COP shall adopt its own rules of procedure.

6   The Secretary General of the Council of Europe shall convene the COP not later than one year following the entry into force of this Convention. Thereafter, regular meetings of the COP shall be held in accordance with the rules of procedure adopted by the COP.

Chapter VII – Final Provisions

Article 49 – Signature and entry into force

1   The Convention shall be open for signature by the member States of the Council of Europe, the European Community and non-member States which have participated in its elaboration. Such States or the European Community may express their consent to be bound by:

a   signature without reservation as to ratification, acceptance or approval; or b   signature subject to ratification, acceptance or approval, followed by ratification, acceptance or approval.

2   Instruments of ratification, acceptance or approval shall be deposited with the Secretary General of the Council of Europe.

3   This Convention shall enter into force on the first day of the month following the expiration of a period of three months after the date on which 6 signatories, of which at least four are member States of the Council of Europe, have expressed their consent to be bound by the Convention in accordance with the provisions of paragraph 1.

4   In respect of any Signatory which subsequently expresses its consent to be bound by it, the Convention shall enter into force on the first day of the month following the expiration of a period of three months after the date of the expression of its consent to be bound by the Convention in accordance with the provisions of paragraph 1.

5   No Party to the 1990 Convention may ratify, accept or approve this Convention without considering itself bound by at least the provisions corresponding to the provisions of the 1990 Convention to which it is bound.

6   As from its entry into force, Parties to this Convention, which are at the same time Parties to the 1990 Convention:

a   shall apply the provisions of this Convention in their mutual relationships;

b   shall continue to apply the provisions of the 1990 Convention in their relations with other Parties to the said Convention, but not to the present Convention.

Article 50 – Accession to the Convention

1   After the entry into force of this Convention, the Committee of Ministers of the Council of Europe, after consulting the Parties to the Convention, may invite any State not a member of the Council and not having participated in its elaboration to accede to this Convention, by a decision taken by the majority provided for in Article 20.d. of the Statute of the Council of Europe and by the unanimous vote of the representatives of the Parties entitled to sit on the Committee.

2   In respect of any acceding State, the Convention shall enter into force on the first day of the month following the expiration of a period of three months after the date of deposit of the instrument of accession with the Secretary General of the Council of Europe.

Article 51 – Territorial application

1   Any State or the European Community may, at the time of signature or when depositing its instrument of ratification, acceptance, approval or accession, specify the territory or territories to which the Convention shall apply.

2   Any Party may, at any later date, by a declaration addressed to the Secretary General of the Council of Europe, extend the application of the Convention to any other territory specified in the declaration. In respect of such territory the Convention shall enter into force on the first day of the month following the expiration of a period of three months after the date of receipt of such declaration by the Secretary General.

3   Any declaration made under the two preceding paragraphs may, in respect of any territory specified in such declaration, be withdrawn by a notification addressed to the Secretary General. The withdrawal shall become effective on the first day of the month following the expiration of a period of three months after the date of receipt of such notification by the Secretary General.

Article 52 – Relationship to other conventions and agreements

1   This Convention does not affect the rights and undertakings of Parties derived from international multilateral instruments concerning special matters.

2   The Parties to this Convention may conclude bilateral or multilateral agreements with one another on the matters dealt with in this Convention, for the purposes of supplementing or strengthening its provisions or facilitating the application of the principles embodied in it.

3   If two or more Parties have already concluded an agreement or treaty in respect of a subject which is dealt with in this Convention or otherwise have established their relations in respect of that subject, they shall be entitled to apply that agreement or treaty or to regulate these relations accordingly, in lieu of the Convention, if it facilitates international co-operation.

4   Parties which are members of the European Union shall, in their mutual relations, apply Community and European Union rules in so far as there are Community or European Union rules governing the particular subject concerned and applicable to the specific case, without prejudice to the object and purpose of the present Convention and without prejudice to its full application with other Parties.

Article 53 – Declarations and reservations

1   Any State or the European Community may, at the time of signature or when depositing its instrument of ratification, acceptance, approval or accession, make one or more of the declaration provided for in Article 3, paragraph 2, Article 9, paragraph 4, Article 17, paragraph 5, Article 24, paragraph 3, Article 31, paragraph 2, Article 35, paragraphs 1 and 3 and Article 42, paragraph 2.

2   Any State or the European Community may also, at the time of signature or when depositing its instrument of ratification, acceptance, approval or accession, by a declaration addressed to the Secretary General, reserve its right not to apply, in part or in whole, the provisions of Article 7, paragraph 2, sub-paragraph c; Article 9, paragraph 6; Article 46, paragraph 5; and Article 47.

3   Any State or the European Community may, at the time of signature or when depositing its instrument of ratification, acceptance, approval or accession, declare the manner in which it intends to apply Articles 17 and 19 of this Convention, particularly taking into account applicable international agreements in the field of international co-operation in criminal matters. It shall notify any changes in this information to the Secretary General of the Council of Europe.

4   Any State or the European Community may, at the time of signature or when depositing its instrument of ratification, acceptance, approval or accession, declare:

a   that it will not apply Article 3, paragraph 4 of this Convention; or

b   that it will apply Article 3, paragraph 4 of this Convention only partly; or

c   the manner in which it intends to apply Article 3, paragraph 4 of this Convention.

It shall notify any changes in this information to the Secretary General of the Council of Europe.

5   No other reservation may be made.

6   Any Party which has made a reservation under this article may wholly or partly withdraw it by means of a notification addressed to the Secretary General of the Council of Europe. The withdrawal shall take effect on the date of receipt of such notification by the Secretary General.

7   A Party which has made a reservation in respect of a provision of the Convention may not claim the application of that provision by any other

Party; it may, however, if its reservation is partial or conditional, claim the application of that provision in so far as it has itself accepted it.

Article 54 – Amendments

1   Amendments to the Convention may be proposed by any Party, and shall be communicated by the Secretary General of the Council of Europe to the member States of the Council of Europe, to the European Community and to every non-member State which has acceded to or has been invited to accede to this Convention in accordance with the provisions of Article 50.

2   Any amendment proposed by a Party shall be communicated to the European Committee on Crime Problems (CDPC) which shall submit to the Committee of Ministers its opinion on that proposed amendment.

3   The Committee of Ministers shall consider the proposed amendment and the opinion submitted by the CDPC and may adopt the amendment by the majority provided for in Article 20.d of the Statute of the Council of Europe.

4   The text of any amendment adopted by the Committee of Ministers in accordance with paragraph 3 of this article shall be forwarded to the Parties for acceptance.

5   Any amendment adopted in accordance with paragraph 3 of this article shall come into force on the thirtieth day after all Parties have informed the Secretary General of their acceptance thereof.

6   In order to update the categories of offences contained in the appendix, as well as amend Article 13, amendments may be proposed by any Party or by the Committee of Ministers. They shall be communicated by the Secretary General of the Council of Europe to the Parties.

7   After having consulted the Parties which are not members of the Council of Europe and, if necessary the CDPC, the Committee of Ministers may adopt an amendment proposed in accordance with paragraph 6 by the majority provided for in Article 20.d of the Statute of the Council of Europe. The amendment shall enter into force following the expiry of a period of one year after the date on which it has been forwarded to the Parties. During this period, any Party may notify the Secretary General of any objection to the entry into force of the amendment in its respect.

8   If one-third of the Parties notifies the Secretary General of an objection to the entry into force of the amendment, the amendment shall not enter into force.

9   If less than one-third of the Parties notifies an objection, the amendment shall enter into force for those Parties which have not notified an objection.

10   Once an amendment has entered into force in accordance with paragraphs 6 to 9 of this article and a Party has notified an objection to it, this amendment shall come into force in respect of the Party concerned on the first day of the month following the date on which it has notified the Secretary General of the Council of Europe of its acceptance. A Party which has made an objection may withdraw it at any time by notifying it to the Secretary General of the Council of Europe.

11   If an amendment has been adopted by the Committee of Ministers, a State or the European Community may not express their consent to be bound by the Convention, without accepting at the same time the amendment.

Article 55 – Denunciation

1   Any Party may, at any time, denounce the Convention by means of a notification addressed to the Secretary General of the Council of Europe.

2   Such denunciation shall become effective on the first day of the month following the expiration of a period of three months after the date of receipt of the notification by the Secretary General.

3   The present Convention shall, however, continue to apply to the enforcement under Article 23 of confiscation for which a request has been made in conformity with the provisions of the Convention before the date on which such a denunciation takes effect.

Article 56 – Notifications

The Secretary General of the Council of Europe shall notify the member States of the Council of Europe, the European Community, the non-member States which have participated in the elaboration of the Convention, any State invited to accede to it and any other Party to the Convention of:

a   any signature;

b   the deposit of any instrument of ratification, acceptance, approval or accession;

c   any date of entry into force of the Convention in accordance with Articles 49 and 50;

d   any declaration or reservation made under Article 53;

e   any other act, notification or communication relating to the Convention.

In witness whereof the undersigned, being duly authorised thereto, have signed this Convention.

Done at Warsaw, this 16th day of May 2005, in English and in French, both texts being equally authentic, in a single copy which shall be deposited in the archives of the Council of Europe. The Secretary General of the Council of Europe shall transmit certified copies to each member State of the Council of Europe, to the European Community, to the non-member States which have participated in the elaboration of the Convention and to any State invited to accede to it.

Appendix

a   participation in an organised criminal group and racketeering;

b   terrorism, including financing of terrorism;

c   trafficking in human beings and migrant smuggling;

d   sexual exploitation, including sexual exploitation of children;

e   illicit trafficking in narcotic drugs and psychotropic substances;

f   illicit arms trafficking;

g   illicit trafficking in stolen and other goods;

h   corruption and bribery;

i   fraud;

j   counterfeiting currency;

k   counterfeiting and piracy of products;

l   environmental crime;

m   murder, grievous bodily injury;

n   kidnapping, illegal restraint and hostage-taking;

o   robbery or theft;

p   smuggling;

q   extortion;

r   forgery;

s   piracy; and

t   insider trading and market manipulation.

Committee of Ministers

Resolution (74) 3 on international terrorism

(Adopted by the Committee of Ministers on 24 January 1974 at its 53rd Session)

The Committee of Ministers,

Considering the recommendations of the Consultative Assembly on international terrorism and in particular Recommendation 703 (1973) ;

Aware of the growing concern caused by the multiplication of acts of international terrorism which jeopardise the safety of persons ;

Desirous that effective measures be taken in order that the authors of such acts do not escape punishment ;

Convinced that extradition is a particularly effective measure for achieving this result and that the political motive alleged by the authors of certain acts of terrorism should not have as a result that they are neither extradited nor punished,

Recommends that governments of member states be guided by the following principles :

1.   When they receive a request for extradition concerning offences covered by the Conventions of The Hague for the suppression of unlawful seizure of aircraft and of Montreal for the suppression of unlawful acts against the safety of civil aviation, offences against diplomatic agents and other internationally protected persons, the taking of hostages or any terrorist act, they should, when applying international agreements or conventions on the subject, and especially the European Convention on Extradition, or when applying their domestic law, take into consideration the particularly serious nature of these acts, inter alia:

-   when they create a collective danger to human life, liberty or safety ;

-   when they affect innocent persons foreign to the motives behind them;

-   when cruel or vicious means are used in the commission of those acts.

2.   If it refuses extradition in a case of the kind mentioned above and if its jurisdiction rules permit, the government of the requested state should submit the case to its competent authorities for the purpose of prosecution. Those authorities should take their decision in the same manner as in the case of any ordinary offence of a serious nature under the law of that state.

3.   The governments of member states in which such jurisdiction is lacking should envisage the possibility of establishing it.

Declaration on terrorism (1978)

(Adopted by the Committee of Ministers at its 63rd Session, on 23 November 1978)

The Committee of Ministers of the Council of Europe,

1. Mindful of the recent increase in acts of terrorism in certain member states;

2. Considering that the prevention and suppression of such acts are indispensable to the maintenance of the democratic structure of member states;

3. Noting that the European Convention on the Suppression of Terrorism entered into force on 4 August 1978;

4. Considering that this convention represents an important contribution tot the fight against terrorism;

5. Convinced that it is necessary further to develop and to strengthen international co-operation in this field,

I. Reaffirms the important role of the Council of Europe in the fight against terrorism as an Organisation of democratic states founded on the rule of law and committed to the protection of human rights and fundamental freedoms;

II. Emphasises the importance of the work being undertaken in the Council of Europe with a view to intensifying European co-operation in the fight against terrorism;

III. Decides that in this work priority should be given to the examination of the following questions:

  a. means of rendering existing practices of international co-operation between the competent authorities simpler and more expeditious;

  b. means of improving and speeding up the communication of information to any state concerned relating to the circumstances in which an act of terrorism was committed, the measures taken against its author, the outcome of any judicial proceedings against him and the enforcement of any sentence passed;

  c. problems arising where acts of terrorism have been committed within the jurisdiction of several states.

Recommendation No. R (82) 1
concerning international co-operation in the prosecution and punishment of acts of terrorism

(Adopted by the Committee of Ministers on 15 January 1982 at the 342nd meeting of the Ministers' Deputies)

The Committee of Ministers, under the terms of Article 15.*b* of the Statute of the Council of Europe,

Considering that the aim of the Council of Europe is to achieve greater unity among its members;

Concerned at the increased number of acts of terrorism committed in certain member states;

Considering the prevention and suppression of such acts to be indispensable to the maintenance of the democratic institutions of member states;

Having regard to Council of Europe initiatives[1] in the past aimed at the suppression of terrorism, which represent important contributions to the fight against this threat to society;

Convinced that it is necessary further to develop and to strengthen international co-operation in this field;

Desirous of rendering existing procedures of international judicial co-operation simpler and more expeditious, of improving the exchange of information between the competent authorities of member states, particularly between those with a common border, and of facilitating the prosecution and punishment of acts of terrorism;

---

[1] In particular:
- European Convention on Extradition (1957) with two Additional Protocols (1975 and 1978);
- European Convention on Mutual Assistance in Criminal Matters (1959) and Additional Protocol (1978);
- European Convention on the Suppression of Terrorism (1977);
- Resolution (74) 3 on international terrorism adopted by the Committee of Ministers at its 53rd Session (January 1974);
- Declaration on Terrorism adopted by the Committee of Ministers at its 63rd Session (November 1978);
- Communiqués of the Committee of Ministers at its 67th (October 1980), 68th (May 1981) and 69th (November 1981) Sessions;
- Assembly Recommendations 684 (1972), 703 (1973), 852 (1979) and 916 (1981);
- Conference on the "Defence of democracy against terrorism in Europe - Tasks and problems" (November 1980).

Having regard to existing co-operation and channels of communication between the police forces of member states;

Recalling the Declaration on Terrorism adopted by the Committee of Ministers on 23 November 1978;

Emphasising that any measure of international co-operation must be fully compatible with the protection of human rights and particularly with the principles contained in the Convention for the Protection of Human Rights and Fundamental Freedoms signed in Rome on 4 November 1950,

Recommends the governments of member states to give effect, by the most appropriate means, to the following measures aimed at improving international co-operation in the prosecution and punishment of acts of terrorism directed against the life, physical integrity or liberty of persons, or against property where they create a collective danger for persons, including, in accordance with domestic law, attempts at, or threats of, or participation as an accomplice in, these acts (referred to as "acts of terrorism" in the present recommendation).

I. *Channels of communication for mutual judicial assistance in criminal matters*

1.   Direct communication, between the authorities concerned in the requesting and the requested state, of requests for judicial assistance and the replies thereto, should be encouraged in all cases where it is permitted by the law of these states or by any treaty to which these states are party, if it is likely to render mutual judicial assistance more expeditious.

2.   Where direct transmission is permitted, cases involving acts of terrorism should be treated with urgency according to the procedure provided by Article 15.2 of the European Convention on Mutual Assistance in Criminal Matters or by other treaties in force between member states or by the law of these states, so that letters rogatory may be addressed by the authority concerned in the requesting state directly to the authority concerned in the requested state, it being understood that the requested state may require a copy to be sent to its Ministry of Justice or other competent ministry.

3.   Where requests for assistance and the replies thereto may be communicated directly between the authorities concerned in the requesting and the requested state, their transmission should be effected as rapidly as possible, either through Interpol National Central Bureaux, in so far as this is not contrary to Interpol's Constitution, or by other existing ways of transmission.

4.   Where communication is effected between Ministries of Justice or other competent ministries, the authority concerned in the requesting state should be allowed directly to provide the authority concerned in the requested state with an advance copy of the request. The authority concerned in the

requested state should be advised that the sole purpose of transmitting the copy is to enable it to prepare for the execution of the request.

II. *Exchange of information*

5. Exchanges of information between member states should be improved and reinforced. To that end, the competent authorities should, in so far as this is not contrary to domestic law, be enabled to furnish, of their own accord, information in their possession on such matters as:

    i.   measures concerning the prosecution of the alleged offender (e.g. arrest, indictment);

    ii.   the outcome of any judicial or administrative proceedings (e.g. conviction, decision on extradition);

    iii.   the enforcement of any sentence (including pardon, conditional release);

    iv.   other relevant information relating to the whereabouts of the person concerned (e.g. expulsion, escape, execution of an extradition decision)

to the authorities of any member state concerned as, for instance, the state where the act of terrorism was committed, the state which has jurisdiction over the offence, the state of which the offender is a national, the state where the offender has his habitual residence, or any other state likely to have an interest in the particular element of information.

6. The exchange of this information should be effected with all necessary expediency either through Interpol National Central Bureaux, in so far as this is not contrary to Interpol's Constitution, of by other existing ways of transmission.

III. *Prosecution and trial of offences of an international character*

7. Where one or several acts of terrorism have been committed in the territory of two or several member states and there is a link between those acts or their authors, the member states concerned should examine the possibility of having the prosecution and the trial conducted in only one state. To that end, the states concerned should agree on the competent state, in accordance with existing international treaties and their internal law. The same should apply, if possible, where one or several acts of terrorism of an international character have been committed in the territory of a single state by several persons acting in unison who have been apprehended in various states. In negotiating such agreements on the competent state, the states concerned should, with a view to ensuring that prosecution and trial take place in the state best suited for conducting the proceedings, take into account the number of offences committed in each state, the seriousness of the offences,

the availability of evidence, the personal circumstances of the alleged offender, in particular his nationality and habitual residence, and the prospects of rehabilitation.

Explanatory Memorandum

Introduction

1.   In the context of the initiatives undertaken by the Council of Europe in the fight against terrorism, the "Committee of Experts to examine the problems raised by certain new forms of concerted acts of violence", which had prepared the European Convention on the Suppression of Terrorism, continued examining further measures of facilitating international co-operation with regard to the prosecution and punishment of terrorists, in pursuance of new terms of reference which had been assigned to it in November 1977 by the Committee of Ministers on the proposal of the European Committee on Crime Problems (CDPC).

2.   Recommendation No. R (82) 1 concerning international co-operation in the prosecution and punishment of acts of terrorism is the result of this work. It was prepared by the Committee of Experts at its 5th to 9th meetings, held from 5 to 8 June 1978,11 to 13 December 1978, 19 to 22 June 1979, 23 to 26 June 1980 and 10 to 13 February 1981 respectively, under the chairmanship of Mr R. Linke (Austria). The draft recommendation was approved by the European Committee on Crime Problems (CDPC) at its 30th plenary Session in March 1981, revised, at the request of the Committee of Ministers, at the tenth meeting of the Committee of Experts from 20 to 23 October 1981 and adopted by the Committee of Ministers at the 342nd meeting of their Deputies on 15 January 1982.

General considerations

3.   One of the characteristics of terrorist crimes is their increasing internationalisation, that is to say that their perpetrators frequently plan their crimes on the territory of a state other than that where the crimes are to be committed, or take refuge, and are apprehended, beyond the frontiers of the state where the crimes have been committed. For that reason international co-operation in the prosecution and punishment of the authors of terrorist crimes is essential for effectively combating terrorism. The European Convention on the Suppression of Terrorism, as a means of international co-operation in the prosecution and punishment of such crimes, is a contribution of outstanding importance to the fight against terrorism.

4.   The Recommendation aims at furthering this objective by setting out a number of measures which, if endorsed by the governments of member states, will contribute to developing and strengthening international co-operation in this field, pending ratification of the European Convention on the Suppression of Terrorism by all member states. The Recommendation extends to three areas of co-operation which, in a Declaration on Terrorism adopted on 23 November 1978, were singled out by the Committee of Ministers as requiring priority attention:

i.   means of rendering existing practices of mutual judicial assistance simpler and more expeditious (Chapter I);

ii.   means of improving and speeding up the exchange of relevant information between the competent authorities of member states (Chapter II);

iii.   means of co-ordinating prosecution and trial in cases where terrorist crimes have an international character (Chapter III).

5.   In several respects, the Recommendation is complementary to the European Convention on Mutual Assistance in Criminal Matters; it is, in fact, to a large degree inspired by the rules contained in that convention.

6.   The measures of international co-operation which the Recommendation proposes are aimed at reinforcing the protection of human rights to which the member states of the Council of Europe are committed. By suggesting means of improving international co-operation in the prosecution and punishment of terrorists, the Recommendation seeks to contribute to combating terrorism, a form of criminality which is often accompanied by a particularly ruthless disregard for the human rights of its victims or potential victims. At the same time, the Committee of Experts has, when drafting the different recommendations, carefully examined their possible repercussions on the human rights of the accused, particularly his procedural rights - in the belief that terrorism can be most effectively fought when the measures taken against terrorists are in full conformity with the requirements of human rights protection as they are reflected in the European Convention on Human Rights. In this context, the committee took note of the Parliamentary Assembly's Recommendation 852 on terrorism in Europe which, in its paragraph 8, stresses "that anti-terrorist strategies, if they are vital for the preservation of democratic institutions, must also be compatible with them, and must always be subject to national constitutions and the European Convention on Human Rights". The committee fully endorsed this statement and, to ensure that its own recommendations complied with them, examined the relevant case-law of the European Commission of Human Rights. To underline the paramount importance of this consideration, a reference to it has been included in the preamble.

7.   As regards the Recommendation's scope of application, it does not define the category of offences in respect of which the different measures of improved international co-operation are intended to apply, nor does it set out a list of offences which are considered to be acts of terrorism. It simply refers to "acts of terrorism directed against the life, physical integrity or liberty of persons, or against property where they create a collective danger for persons, including, in accordance with domestic law, attempts at, or threats of, or participation as an accomplice in, these acts".

8.   With a view to ascertaining whether international police co-operation required improvement, the Committee of Experts, assisted by an observer

from the International Criminal Police Organisation (Interpol), examined existing practices of co-operation between police forces of member states, and it concluded that international police co-operation - particularly through Interpol - worked satisfactorily.

The purpose of the Recommendation is not therefore to improve international police co-operation as such. In some member states, however, the police act as an authority responsible for the prosecution of authors of acts of terrorism. So far as those countries are concerned, the recommendations contained in Chapter II would apply to the police.

Moreover, in recommendations 1.3 and 11.6 reference is made to Interpol's communication channels.

9.   The Recommendation is confined to setting out a number of measures which are likely to strengthen, improve and facilitate international co-operation between member states. The Recommendation does not indicate how these measures may be implemented at national level. It is for each government to decide on the means which, having regard to its internal administration of justice, it considers to be the most appropriate for implementing the different recommendations.

Commentary on the recommendations

I.   *Channels of communication for mutual judicial assistance in criminal matters*

10.   Chapter I concerns the Recommendation's first objective which is to render existing practices of international judicial co-operation simpler and more expeditious. Improving communication channels is one of the means most likely to achieve that aim.

11.   The recommendations contained in Chapter I have been drafted against the background of the European Convention on Mutual Assistance in Criminal Matters. They are, however, intended, generally, to apply to all communications effected between authorities of member states for the purpose of mutual assistance in cases involving terrorist offences, irrespective of whether the state concerned is a Contracting Party to this convention. The general aim of the measures proposed in Chapter I is not to modify any of the provisions of the Mutual Assistance Convention with regard to channels of communication (an aim which in any case could not be achieved by means of a recommendation), but to encourage the use of more expedient ways of communication - namely the direct transmission of requests and replies between the authorities concerned - in all instances where treaties or domestic law allow it.

12. The rapid transmission of requests for assistance and replies is of paramount importance for two reasons: firstly, by ensuring that perpetrators of terrorist crimes are swiftly brought to justice it contributes to effectively fighting terrorism; secondly, it helps to speed up the assistance procedure and to enable judicial authorities to try the offender "within a reasonable time", in conformity with Article 6.1 of the European Convention on Human Rights.

13. For these reasons, recommendation I.1 encourages the use of direct communication, between the authorities concerned, of requests for assistance and replies thereto. However, this recommendation is subject to a double proviso: the direct communication must be permitted (by domestic law or by an international treaty to which the state concerned is a party), and it must be likely to render mutual judicial assistance more expeditious. The latter proviso reflects a divergency of opinion within the Committee of Experts. Whereas the majority considered the direct communication between the authorities concerned to be generally conducive to the speedy transmission of requests and replies, other experts doubted whether the principle of direct communication could be applied in a general way, without regard to the special circumstances of the case in question and without due consideration of the internal organisation and rules of procedure of the state concerned: apart from truly urgent cases, there might be good reason for not excluding the competent ministry - Ministry of Justice or Ministry of Foreign Affairs - from the channels of communication. It was pointed out that irrespective of whether they fall to be regarded as political or non-political for the purpose of mutual assistance, cases involving terrorist offences often raised delicate questions of a political nature. Furthermore, ministries had wide practical experience in channelling assistance requests, particularly with regard to verifying formal requirements and providing translations. In this context, it was pointed out that for precisely these reasons several States Parties to the Mutual Assistance Convention had deemed it necessary to exclude the use of direct transmission channels even where they are allowed under the convention.

14. Recommendation 1.1 takes these considerations into account. It reflects the opinion that, as a general rule, states should encourage the use of direct communications between the authorities concerned as being conducive to rendering existing practices simpler and more expeditious. It acknowledges, however, that there might be good reasons for not applying this rule in all cases: the recommendation is therefore subject to the proviso that direct communication between the authorities concerned must, in fact, contribute to rendering assistance more expeditious.

I.2

15. Recommendation I.2 concerns the transmission of letters rogatory. In accordance with the Recommendation's general aim - to render practices of mutual assistance more expeditious - it seeks to accelerate the transmission of letters rogatory in cases involving acts of terrorism by inviting member

states to treat these cases with urgency and allow the requesting authority directly to address letters rogatory to the requested authority.

16. The recommendation is inspired by the provisions of Article 15.2 of the European Convention on Mutual Assistance in Criminal Matters. By inviting states to treat cases involving acts of terrorism as urgent cases, the recommendation encourages those states which are parties to that convention to apply its Article 15.2, and those states which are not parties to the convention to adopt a similar procedure, with the result that letters rogatory may be communicated directly between the authorities concerned.

I.3

17. If mutual assistance is effectively to contribute to the prosecution of terrorist crimes, it is not sufficient that the authorities concerned communicate directly with each other; it is equally important that these communications be effected speedily. Recommendation 1.3 therefore emphasises the importance of rapid transmission of assistance requests and replies.

18. The use of Interpol channels is mentioned as one of the means for achieving that aim, in particular where a request for assistance concerning the acts referred to in the Recommendation emanates from another member state of the Council of Europe. This reflects the opinion of the Committee of Experts that, from the point of view of rapid communication, transmission through Interpol National Central Bureaux would, as a rule, be preferable to other channels of communication such as, for instance, diplomatic channels.

Interpol is already involved in the functioning of international co-operation agreements, for example by virtue of Article 16 of the European Convention on Extradition and Article 15 of the European Convention on Mutual Assistance in Criminal Matters. However, as far as acts of terrorism are concerned, Interpol's intervention might be conditioned by Article 3 of its Constitution. Although that provision does not expressly refer to "terrorism", it might have an incidence on Interpol's possibilities of contributing to the kind of measures to which the recommendation applies; for it precludes Interpol from acting in cases of political offences. For this reason, the recommended use of Interpol channels has been made subject to the proviso that it "is not contrary to Interpol's Constitution". However, Article 3 of Interpol's Constitution should be considered in the light of a resolution adopted in 1951 by Interpol's General Assembly which limits the scope of Article 3, with regard to political offences, to crimes of a predominantly political nature, as well as in the light of the practice followed by Interpol, including its National Central Bureaux, in accordance with the aforementioned resolution.

I.4

19. Recommendation 1.4 applies in cases where requests for assistance or replies, or both, cannot be communicated directly between the authorities concerned, but have to be conveyed through the Ministries of Justice or other

competent ministries. To render mutual assistance in these cases more expeditious, particularly to enable the requested authority to make the necessary preparatory arrangements for the execution of the request, it is recommended that the requesting authority be allowed to send directly an advance copy of the request to the requested authority. The purpose of this procedure is to make the requested authority aware of an impending request. To avoid misunderstandings as to the nature of this copy, the requested authority must be advised that the sole purpose of transmitting the copy is to enable it to prepare for the execution of the request. The requested authority is not to treat the advance copy as the request proper; if the ministry concerned of the requesting state does not transmit the request, the requested authority may not act on it.

II. Exchange of information

20. Chapter II is concerned with improving the international exchange of information concerning perpetrators or alleged perpetrators of terrorist crimes, in so far as this is not contrary to domestic law. It applies to information on such matters as prosecutions, judicial or administrative proceedings, enforcement of sentences and the whereabouts of the person concerned. The aim of the measures set out in this part of the Recommendation is to remedy a shortcoming of international co-operation in the fight against terrorism: the authorities responsible for the prosecution and punishment of terrorist crimes are often unaware of proceedings and measures taken against the offender in other countries although this information is of direct interest to them; it might be relevant to proceedings they conduct themselves or be of importance in connection with measures they have taken or might wish to take with regard to the offender or alleged offender. The main purpose of conveying such information to a foreign authority is to enable it to address a request for assistance to the authority which has supplied the information in question. An exchange of information such as that recommended in Chapter II will therefore facilitate mutual assistance and render the fight against terrorism more effective.

21. The text is inspired by the provisions of Article 11 of the Hague Convention for the Suppression of Unlawful Seizure of Aircraft (of 16 December 1970) and Article 13 of the Montreal Convention for the Suppression of Unlawful Acts against the Safety of Civil Aviation (of 23 September 1971). However, as opposed to these two conventions drawn up by the International Civil Aviation Organisation, Chapter II of the Recommendation does not envisage the setting up of a clearing house, but provides for the relevant information to be exchanged directly between the competent authorities of member states.

22. The term "competent authority" is not defined in the Recommendation. It is, therefore, for each member state to determine which authorities are "competent authorities" for the purposes of the recommended exchange of information.

23. As conceived by recommendation II.5, the exchange of information is based on the following three elements:

- The competent authority supplies the information of its own accord, that is without having received a request from the foreign authority to which the information is to be furnished.

- Information may be furnished only in so far as this is not contrary to domestic law (for example data protection legislation).

- The competent authority holding the information has discretion in deciding whether it is necessary to convey a given element of information to an authority in another state, as well as in deciding to which foreign authority the information is to be supplied.

24. The authority's discretion with regard to the choice of the recipient authority follows from the wording of recommendation II.5 ("authorities of any member state concerned"). The notion is but indirectly defined in the last part of the sentence: a "member state concerned" is any state likely to have an interest in the particular element of information. To give some guidance to the informing authority, a number of states likely to be "concerned", that is to have an interest in the information, are enumerated by way of example; they include the state which has jurisdiction over the offence, the state of which the offender is a national, and the state where the offender has his habitual residence.

25. The exchange of information extends to all matters relating to the prosecution or punishment of persons who have committed, or are alleged to have committed, acts of terrorism within the meaning of the Recommendation. The most relevant of these matters - grouped in four categories, relating to prosecution, judicial or administrative decisions, enforcement of sentences and the whereabouts of the person concerned - are enumerated by way of example. Here again an authority which disposes of information has discretion in deciding whether it is information likely to interest the authority in another member state. The list of matters contained in recommendation II.5 is not exhaustive; it is intended to give some indication of the nature of the information to be furnished to foreign authorities.

26. It follows from one of the considerations expressed in the preamble - that any measure of international co-operation must be fully compatible with the protection of human rights - that any information received in application of the Recommendation is to be used in such a way as to be in full conformity with the requirements of the European Convention on Human Rights, in particular with its Article 6.2.

27. This recommendation being essentially the same as that made for the transmission of requests for judicial assistance, the commentary on recommendation 1.3 applies *mutatis mutandis.*

III.   *Prosecution and trial of offences of an international character*

28.   Chapter III concerns the concentration of prosecution and trial in cases where terrorist offences have an international character, either because they have been committed in different states and there is a link between them or because, although committed within the same state, they involve several authors who have acted in concert, but who have been apprehended in different states. The recommendation that member states co-operate, by common agreement, in the prosecution and the trial of international acts of terrorism is applicable to three different situations: 1. where one offence has been committed, by one or several persons, in several states; 2. where one person has committed several offences in different states; and 3. where several persons have committed one or several offences in only one state, but are apprehended in different states.

29.   The recommendations contained in Chapter III pursue two main objectives:

One concerns the conduct of the prosecution and the trial which the recommendations seek to render more efficient. As regards the establishment of truth, the prosecution of the same person in several states might involve difficulties of evidence, as it will not always be possible for the offender to appear in person in all states concerned. Where several persons have been involved in the offences, it is important that all the statements made by these persons are available to the authority concerned. Moreover, the recommendation to concentrate, whenever possible, prosecution and trial in only one state aims at facilitating the application of an appropriate sanction. In order to determine the most appropriate sanction to be applied against the offender, the court must be able to take account of all the offences committed by that offender. If some of the offences are tried in one state, and the others in another state, the total sanction imposed on the offender might be more severe than if judgment had been given in only one state. Where several persons are involved in the same complex of offences, adjudication in different states might, because of differing ranges of sanctions, lead to unsatisfactory results.

The other objective of the provisions contained in Chapter III is to safeguard the principle of *non bis in idem,* that is to prevent anyone from being accused and brought to trial more than once for the same offences. For that reason, it is recommended to member states to agree on the conduct, in one state alone, of proceedings in respect of different punishable acts which are subject to the criminal law of several states and which have been committed by the same person or by several persons acting in concert, or of one punishable act committed by several persons acting in concert.

III.7

30. To achieve concentration of prosecution and trial in the cases described in paragraph 28 above, it is recommended that the states concerned decide, by common agreement, in which state the proceedings are to be conducted.

31. The reason why the recommendation invites states only "to examine the possibility" of having the prosecution and the trial conducted in only one state is that it will not always be practicable to do so. If, for instance, among several different cases one is of a less serious character so that only a minor sanction is likely to be imposed, it will normally not be reasonable to engage in negotiations on a single competence. Furthermore, where a single offence has been committed by several persons, agreement on a single prosecution and trial is usually not possible if the offenders have been apprehended in their respective home countries.

32. It follows from the reference to "internal law" as well as from the Recommendation's legal nature that the measures mentioned under III.7 in no way affect the right of states to prosecute and try any offence in accordance with their own rules of competence.
Moreover, any agreement on the competent state must be in accordance with existing international - bilateral or multilateral – treaties such as, for instance, the European Convention on the Transfer of Proceedings in Criminal Matters.

33. Finally, prosecution and trial should take place in the state best suited for conducting the proceedings. By listing a number of elements to be taken into account, the recommendation provides guidance to governments in respect of the choice they are called upon to make. None of the elements listed calls for any specific comment.

Declaration on terrorist acts (1986)

(Adopted by the Committee of Ministers on 8 September 1986, at the 399th meeting of the Ministers' Deputies)

Terrorism: strong reaction from Council of Europe

Committee of Ministers' Chairman, Italian Foreign Minister Giulio ANREOTTI, Parliamentary Assembly President Louis JUNG and Secretary General Marcelino OREJA have condemned in the strongest terms the terrorist acts of the last few days which, in the case of Turkey, affect yet again one of the Council's member States. They denounce the escalation of these barbaric acts which strike down innocent victims, and reassert that terrorism must be condemned unreservedly. Since terrorism aims at destabilising democracies by attacking the life and liberty of citizens it must be met with firmness and increased co-operation among democratic countries. The forthcoming should mark a decisive step for the co-ordination of efforts and policies among the democratic community of the 21 member countries of the Council of Europe.

Declaration on the Fight against International Terrorism (2001)

(Adopted by the Committee of Ministers on 12 September 2001 at the 763rd meeting of the Ministers' Deputies)

1.   The Committee of Ministers of the Council of Europe condemns with the utmost force the terrorist attacks of unprecedented violence committed against the American people, to whom it expresses sympathy and solidarity.

These crimes do not strike only the United States but affect us all.   These barbaric acts violate human rights, in particular the right to life, democracy and the search for peace.

Such monstrous acts demand resolute reaction from all states committed to uphold civilised values.

The Council of Europe, which unites the continent around these values, has a particular interest and responsibility to contribute to such a reaction.

2.   The Committee of Ministers decides to hold a special meeting on 21 September with the following agenda:

  i.   strengthening of the fight against terrorism, using the specific expertise and instruments of the Council of Europe, and improving the mechanisms and means for co-operation with other international organisations and the Observer states;

  ii.   inviting the member states to give increased effectiveness to the existing pan-European co-operation, for example, to accede, where they have not done so, to conventions on mutual assistance in criminal matters;

  iii.   examining the scope for updating the European Convention on the Suppression of Terrorism;

  iv.   the inclusion of the fight against terrorism in the Council of Europe's integrated project on the struggle against violence in everyday life in a democratic society.

Recommendation (2001) 11
concerning Guiding Principles on the Fight against Organised Crime

(Adopted by the Committee of Ministers
on 19 September 2001
at the 765th meeting of the Ministers' Deputies)

The Committee of Ministers, under the terms of Article 15.*b* of the Statute of the Council of Europe,

Recalling that the aim of the Council of Europe is to achieve a greater unity among its members;

Aware of the need for member states to develop a common crime policy in relation to organised crime by determining ways that ensure greater effectiveness in their legislation and enhance international co-operation in this area;

Emphasising that organised crime represents, by its economic power, transnational connections and sophisticated techniques and methods, a major threat to society, the rule of law and democracy to which states need to react with a common strategy;

Considering that a common strategy requires a firm commitment by states to join efforts, share experience and take common action both at national and international levels;

Bearing in mind the multifaceted nature of organised crime and its interaction with economic crime, including in particular corruption, money laundering and fraud;

Convinced therefore that a common strategy against organised crime also requires common action against corruption and money laundering, and noting with satisfaction the results so far achieved in these fields, notably the adoption of Resolution (97) 24 on the twenty guiding principles for the fight against corruption, the agreement establishing the group of states against corruption (GRECO) and the Criminal Law Convention on Corruption (ETS No.173), as well as the increasing ratification of the Convention on Laundering, Search, Seizure and Confiscation of the Proceeds of Crime (ETS No. 141), and the setting up of a mutual evaluation mechanism for anti-money laundering regimes;

Taking into account Recommendation No. R (97) 13 on the intimidation of witnesses and the rights of the defence and Recommendation No. R (96) 8 on crime policy in Europe in a time of change;

Taking also into account the "best practice surveys" elaborated by the Council of Europe on various measures applied successfully by some member states in the fight against organised crime, which have proved instrumental not only in stimulating other countries' legislation and practice, but equally in the drawing up of the present recommendation;

Mindful of member states' obligations to maintain a fair balance between the interests of society in law enforcement and the rights of individuals, as enshrined in the provisions of the European Convention on Human Rights and the case-law of its organs;

Bearing in mind Resolution No. 1 of the European Ministers of Justice adopted at their 21st Conference (Prague, June 1997) on the links between corruption and organised crime as well as the Final Declaration and Action Plan adopted by the 2nd Summit of Heads of State and Government (Strasbourg, October 1997) calling on the Council of Europe to step up action against corruption, money laundering and organised crime;

Taking into account global and regional initiatives in this field, such as actions by the United Nations, the Financial Action Task Force on Money Laundering (FATF), the G7 and the European Union;

Welcoming the adoption of the United Nations Convention against Transnational Organized Crime open for signature from 12 to 15 December 2000 in Palermo,

Recommends that governments of member states:

–   review their criminal policy, legislation and practice in the light of the principles appended to this recommendation;

–   ensure that these principles are disseminated to all interested bodies, such as law enforcement agencies, bar associations, judicial organs and other private or public sector institutions involved in the prevention or repression of organised crime.

Appendix to Recommendation (2001) 11

I. *Definitions*

For the purposes of this recommendation:

—   "organised crime group" shall mean a structured group of three or more persons, existing for a period of time and acting in concert with the aim of committing one or more serious crimes, in order to obtain, directly or indirectly, a financial or material benefit;

—   "serious crime", shall mean conduct constituting an offence punishable by a maximum deprivation of liberty of at least four years or a more serious penalty;

—   "law enforcement agency" shall mean any public body entrusted with the investigation and/or prosecution of criminal offences in accordance with its legal mandate.

II. *Principles relating to general prevention*

1.   Member states should take measures to prevent natural and legal persons from covering up the conversion of the proceeds of crime into other property through use of substantial cash payments and cash currency exchanges.

2.   Member states should take measures to prevent the use of financial centres and offshore facilities for laundering money and conducting illegal financial transactions. For that purpose, member states should allow, *inter alia*, the inspection of financial transactions which have no apparent commercial purpose and require the identification of the direct or ultimate parties involved.

3.   Member states should establish requirements for vulnerable professions, to "know their customers" and to report suspicious transactions when such professionals are acting as financial intermediaries on behalf of their clients.

4.   Member states should identify in their legislation those provisions, which are or can be abused by organised crime groups for their own purpose, in areas such as export/import, licensing, fiscal and customs regulations, and take steps to strengthen legislation and to prevent abuse. In particular, member states should ensure mutual consistency of provisions and should have these provisions regularly tested by independent auditors to assess their "resistance" to abuse, such as fraud.

5.   Member states should ensure that the increasing use of information technology in the financial sector, such as cyber-payment methods or transactions through virtual banks, is accompanied by appropriate security features that prevent or reduce opportunities for illegal use.

6.   Member states should establish common standards of good governance and financial discipline that enhance transparency and accountability in public administration, and should encourage the adoption of codes of conduct to prevent illegal practices, such as corruption, in the commercial and financial sectors, including public procurement.

7.   Member states should encourage the emergence of a corporate culture based on responsibility and zero tolerance *vis-à-vis* illegal practices. In particular, Member states should establish standards for the protection of "whistle-blowers" who report corruption or other suspected criminal activities committed on behalf of or within legal persons.

III.   *Principles relating to the criminal justice system*

8.   Member states should strive to criminalise the participation of any person in an organised crime group, as defined above, irrespective of the place in the Council of Europe member states in which the group is concentrated or carries out its criminal activities.

9.   Member states should criminalise the laundering of any kind of criminal proceeds, in particular those originating from organised crime.

10.   Member states should penalise the intentional failure to report suspicious financial transactions when committed by those bank and non-bank institutions and professions, which are under a reporting obligation.

11.   Member states should, subject to compliance with fundamental constitutional principles, provide for legal measures to deprive persons of assets which are reasonably suspected to originate from organised criminal activity.

12.   Member states should ensure that legal persons can be held liable for offences committed on their behalf and linked to organised crime.

13.   Member states should pay special attention to tax or fiscal offences linked with organised crime and ensure that they are investigated and prosecuted in an effective manner.

14.   Member states should establish investigative strategies that target the assets of organised crime groups through inter-connected financial investigations; as part of such strategies, Member states should set up quick legal mechanisms to lift bank secrecy and adopt provisions under which bankers, fiduciaries, accountants, notaries and lawyers may be compelled by judicial order to produce financial records or statements and, if necessary, give testimony, under appropriate safeguards.

15.   Member states should adopt legislative measures for the tracing, freezing, seizure and confiscation or forfeiture of assets originating from organised crime activities.

16. Member states should introduce the possibility of confiscation or asset forfeiture in relation to the proceeds of organised crime by means of judicial procedures that may be independent from other proceedings and, exceptionally, may involve mitigating the onus of proof regarding the illicit origin of the assets.

17. Member states should provide effective, physical and other, protection for witnesses and collaborators of justice who require such protection because they have given or agreed to provide information and/or give testimony or other evidence in relation to organised crime. Similarly, such protection measures should be available for those who participate in or have agreed to participate in the investigation or the prosecution of organised crime as well as for the relatives and associates of the individuals who require protection.

18. Member states should adopt appropriate measures to ensure, both within and outside the country of trial, the protection of witnesses prior to, during or after criminal proceedings.

19. Member states should introduce legislation allowing or extending the use of investigative measures that enable law enforcement agencies to gain insight, in the course of criminal investigations, into the activities of organised crime groups, including surveillance, interception of communications, undercover operations, controlled deliveries and the use of informants. To enable the implementation of such techniques, member states should provide law enforcement agencies with the required technology and appropriate training.

20. Member states should develop new methods of police work by shifting focus from reactive policing to pro-active policing, including the use of strategic intelligence and crime analysis.

21. Member states should consider the creation of specialised multidisciplinary teams to investigate and prosecute economic and organised crime. Such multidisciplinary work requires the improvement of the co-ordination, communication and exchange of information within the criminal justice system and with other relevant public authorities.

IV. *Principles relating to international co-operation*

22. Member states should, for the purpose of facilitating the investigation of the economic background of organised crime groups, enable legally and operationally the exchange of information between their relevant authorities with respect to legal persons and other legal entities registered in their jurisdiction and the natural persons involved in their creation, ownership, direction and funding.

23. Member states should introduce provisions in domestic law or in bilateral or multilateral agreements to enable asset sharing among those countries

involved in the tracing, freezing, seizure and confiscation or forfeiture of assets originating from organised crime activities.

24. Member states should make their domestic witness protection schemes/programmes available to foreign witnesses, for example, by entering into bilateral or multilateral agreements providing for such assistance and specifying the applicable conditions.

25. Member states should quickly ratify and implement international legal instruments aiming at fostering police and judicial co-operation among member states, including through bilateral agreements and eliminating obstacles to effective co-operation, for example by :

- lifting their reservations entered into the conventions to which they are parties;

- reducing grounds of refusal, especially those related to fiscal or political offences ;

- ensuring that the procedural requirements of the requesting state are taken into account when executing its request for mutual legal assistance, to enable it to make easier use of the evidence collected on its behalf in criminal proceedings;

- identifying, within nationally existing structures, central contact points to facilitate contacts with foreign operational agencies;

- appointing, subject to their legal systems, judicial contact points, other than the central authority, for a quicker identification of the requested judicial authorities and for enabling direct transmission of requests for mutual legal assistance in cases of urgency or for the exchange of information;

- ensuring that joint police and law enforcement operations may be carried out with foreign liaison officers and magistrates, and considering posting liaison officers and magistrates in other member states;

- ensuring that a response is promptly given to all requests for mutual legal assistance related to offences committed by organised crime groups;

- ensuring co-ordination of police and judicial co-operation by establishing channels and methods of direct and swift international co-operation and information and intelligence exchange.

V.   Principles relating to data collection, research and training

26.   Member states should ensure that data is systematically collected and analysed concerning the criminal activities, the organisation, financial background and geographical scope of organised crime groups operating on their territories as well as their connections to other domestic or foreign groups. National systems of data collection and of criminal statistics should take into account the specific features of organised crime and have adequate resources and staff.

27.   Member states should support research and the institutions which carry out research on organised crime.

28.   Member states should provide the necessary means for training law enforcement agencies and, where appropriate, other components of the criminal justice system, in the area of financial investigations and new methods of investigation.

Appendix - List of legal instruments concerning international co-operation in criminal matters which member states should ratify

ETS No. 24   European Convention on Extradition (1957);

ETS No. 86   Additional Protocol to the European Convention on Extradition (1975);

ETS No. 98   Second Additional Protocol to the European Convention on Extradition(1978);

ETS No. 30   European Convention on Mutual Assistance in Criminal Matters (1959);

ETS No. 99   Additional Protocol to the European Convention on Mutual Assistance in Criminal Matters (1978);

ETS No. 73   European Convention on the Transfer of Proceedings in Criminal Matters (1972);

ETS No. 90   European Convention on the Suppression of Terrorism (1977);

ETS No. 97   Additional Protocol to the European Convention on Information on Foreign Law (1978);

ETS No. 141   Convention on Laundering, Search, Seizure and Confiscation of the Proceeds from Crime (1990);

ETS No. 156   Agreement on Illicit Traffic by Sea, implementing Article 17 of the United Nations Convention against Illicit Traffic in Narcotic Drugs and Psychotropic Substances (1995);

ETS No. 172   Convention on the Protection of the Environment through Criminal Law (1998);

ETS No. 173   Criminal Law Convention on Corruption (1998).

Explanatory memorandum

I. Introduction

1. Why adopt another Recommendation on organised crime ? Because organised crime is increasingly, as noted by another European institution[1], a threat to society as we know it and wish to preserve it. Criminal behaviour is no longer the domain of individuals only, but also of organisations that pervade the various structures of civil society, and indeed society as a whole. Crime is increasingly organising itself across national borders, also taking advantage of the free movement of goods, capital, services and persons. Technological innovations, such as Internet and electronic banking have become extremely convenient vehicles either for committing crimes or for transferring the resulting profits into seemingly licit activities. Fraud and corruption take on massive proportions, defrauding citizens and public institutions alike. In comparison, effective means of preventing and repressing these criminal activities are developing at a slow pace, almost always one step behind. It was therefore time for the Council of Europe to react, firmly and with determination. The present Guiding Principles – prepared by an expert committee on organised crime – reflect the ideas of both practitioners and policy-makers who would like to take reasonably effective measures against organised crime and thus contribute to making society safer.

2. Following a decision of the Committee of Ministers (587th meeting, 1 April 1997) the Committee of experts on criminological and criminal law aspects of organised crime (PC-CO) was set up. The purpose of this Committee was to analyse, under the authority of the European Committee on Crime Problems (CDPC), the characteristics of organised crime in the member States of the Council of Europe, to assess the counter-measures adopted and to identify means of improving the effectiveness of both national responses and international co-operation in this respect.

3. The PC-CO held three plenary meetings and six working group meetings, between April 1997 and December 1999. It first drew up a questionnaire which was circulated each year, with some amendments, to member States. On the basis of the replies provided, Committee PC-CO produced and submitted to the CDPC three annual reports on the organised crime situation in the member States (1996-1998). In addition, it carried out three best practice surveys, on witness protection, the reversal of the burden of proof in confiscation proceedings and intrusive surveillance measures, respectively. Finally, the PC-CO drew up the present recommendation containing guiding principles on the fight against organised crime and the explanatory memorandum attached to it.

---

[1] European Union - Action Plan to combat organised crime, adopted by the Council on 28 April 1997, 97/C 251/01.

4.   The draft recommendation was first submitted to the CDPC at its 49th plenary session in June 2000. However, the CDPC decided to postpone, for lack of time, the examination of the draft and referred the matter to its Bureau. At its meeting of 7-8 March 2001, the Bureau examined and revised the draft Recommendation, taking into account comments made by CDPC Heads of delegation in writing. The revised text was approved by the CDPC at its 50th Plenary meeting, held from 18 to 22 June 2001. The draft explanatory memorandum was adopted on the same occasion. The Committee of Ministers adopted the text as Recommendation Rec(2001).. at the ..th meeting of the Ministers' Deputies and authorised the publication of this explanatory memorandum thereto.

5.   The Committee's terms of reference were as follows:

"Examine, in the light of Recommendation N° R (96) 8 on crime policy in a time of change, with a view to preparing a report and, if appropriate, recommendations, the following questions :

a.   Characteristics of organised crime

analysis, with a view to providing explanation, of the current situation of organised crime, from a qualitative as well as a quantitative viewpoint, with particular emphasis on:

-   the political, social (environmental) economic, legal and regulatory factors that facilitate the emergence and/or unrelenting level of organised crime;

-   the description of offences committed, including the modus operandi of the organisations committing these offences (taking into account their national or transnational character);

-   the description of the degree of organisation (e.g. ad hoc criminal groups, structured criminal networks, mafia-type organisations);

-   the description of offenders (young people or adults, nationals or aliens, legal persons, national or transnational).

b.   Measures with a view to preventing and combating organised crime

Assessment of the domestic responses to organised crime, implemented or envisaged, the resources necessary for them (material as well as know-how), and the means of information and evaluation available. In this context, in particular the following should be taken into account, in relation to the phenomena referred to under (a) above :

-   legislative measures;

-       social (prevention) measures (e.g. social and economic policy, education, information, welfare);

-       situational (prevention) measures (e.g. measures to reduce the opportunities and means of committing offences);

-       improvement in the working of the criminal justice system (e.g. training and specialisation, simplification of procedures, elaboration of new investigative techniques or intervention of new actors such as financial institutions).

c.   Study of national legislation in relation to organised crime

To the extent that it appears necessary for preventing or combating organised crime, national legislations in this area should be studied in order to :

-       identify existing solutions that could serve as examples;

-       ascertain the criteria used in national legislations to qualify offences as "committed in an organised manner", "conspiracy" or "association de malfaiteurs" with a view to overcoming the difficulties arising, e.g. in international co-operation resulting from differences in these concepts, for example by establishing common criteria;

-       identify lacunae in international co-operation instruments and possible solutions which could be included in such instruments, taking into account the work carried out by the Committee of Experts on the Operation of European Conventions in the Penal Field (PC-OC);

-       prepare common procedural principles, especially in relation to banking secrecy, the admissibility of certain types of evidence or the length and effect of statutory limitation periods;

-       define common objectives of criminal policy in relation to organised crime."

II.   General comments

6.   The text of the Recommendation is divided in four parts:

-       Principles relating to General Prevention (principles 1 - 7);
-       Principles relating to the Criminal Justice System (principles 8 - 21);
-       Principles relating to International Co-operation (principles 22 - 25);
-       Principles relating to Data Collection, Research and Training (principles 26 - 28).

7.   The first part, principles relating to general prevention (1 – 7), has been designed by the experts to draw Governments' attention to the importance of involving various segments of society, which are not related to law enforcement or criminal justice, in the prevention of organised crime activities. These segments seem to be often the "points of connection" which organised crime exploits for furthering or legitimising its activities. They are primarily legitimate corporate structures, e.g. banks and companies, which interact with organised crime for example by handling criminal proceeds or serving as a legal front for criminal activities.   Government structures, whether local or central, can also be involved, e. g. by delivering the necessary permits. Certain professionals, particularly in the financial and legal sector, may also act on behalf of organised crime as facilitators or financial conduits of illegal activities. These different types of institutions or professionals which are addressed in the first set of principles should become players or partners of government strategies against organised crime, e.g. by detecting illegal practices and reporting them to the competent authorities. The first set of principles also deals with certain types of regulations, for example in the area of currency exchange and other administrative matters, which can easily be misused for criminal purposes, often because of their complexity and/or weak controls. Finally, some principles relating to general prevention address those measures which corporations and government institutions can take internally in order to ensure transparency and accountability.

8.   The second set of principles (principles 8–21) is related to the criminal justice system in the broad sense, i.e. it covers issues such as criminalisation of certain behaviour, investigation - including asset-investigations -, confiscation and witness-protection. The rationale behind these principles is that prevention measures can arguably not stop all organised criminal activities and need to be supplemented by repressive measures. The most radical measure which governments are called upon to take is to criminalise certain behaviour, i.e. participation in an organised crime group, the laundering of criminal proceeds and the failure to report suspicious transactions. Some or all of these acts may at present not constitute a criminal offence *per se* in the legislation of member States, but experts of the Committee considered their criminalisation as necessary building blocks in a comprehensive anti-organised crime strategy.

9.   Deprivation of assets generated by organised crime is closely related to the issue of criminalisation, though governments have been suggested various options, including the use of criminal law measures, for dealing with such assets. Measures taken by administrative, e.g. tax authorities would meet the objectives of the principle. Another measure which Governments are invited to take is to pay special attention to fiscal or tax offences, when those are connected with organised crime, however difficult it might be in some cases to prove the link. It is therefore assumed that certain fiscal offences, for example tax evasion or fraud, may well be used against organised criminals, particularly leaders who handle large amounts of criminal proceeds but do not participate directly in illegal activities.

10. In addition to the principles related to criminalisation, the second set also addresses the question of financial investigations, co-operation of certain professionals with the authorities, provisional measures to locate and secure assets originating from organised crime and confiscation of such assets. These principles highlight again the need to focus on the financial dimension of organised crime by making asset-investigations an ordinary feature of anti-organised crime government strategies. Other principles further specify the possible elements of such strategies and recommend the use of protected witnesses, intrusive surveillance measures and covert operations, intelligence-based policing and inter-agency co-ordination to make organised crime-related investigations more effective.

11. A third set of principles (principles 22–25) deals with international co-operation and aims primarily at making formal and informal cross-border co-operation easier, e.g. by eliminating obstacles to existing arrangements and enabling new forms of co-operation. In this regard, the Recommendation contains in its Appendix a list of Council of Europe treaties, which Governments are invited to ratify and implement. Those treaties include instruments related purely to international co-operation, e.g. on extradition and mutual assistance, and sectoral treaties on criminalisation, such as money laundering or corruption.

12. Finally, a fourth set of principles (26-28) concerns ways and means of improving data collection, research and training with respect to organised crime.

III. Previous work

13. The Guiding Principles on the fight against organised crime may well be the first specific Council of Europe instrument which deals exclusively with organised crime, but by no means is it the first which mentions the issue. There are two previous recommendations which are worth recalling in this respect: Recommendations No R (86) 8 on crime policy in Europe in a time of change and No. R (97) 13 on intimidation of witnesses and the rights of the defence.

14. Recommendation No. R (86) 8 contained a number of important principles from which the guiding principles took over ideas. It invited Governments to:

- consider the possibility of making it an offence to belong to or support an organised crime association;

- endeavour to develop a good knowledge of the features of criminal organisations and to share that knowledge with the governments of other member states;

- act on the basis of a strategy, in particular by using intelligence and crime analysis to achieve identified aims;

- create specialised police, investigation and prosecutorial structures vested with means to carry out financial investigation and computerised analysis systems;

- provide adequate protection for witnesses and other participants in proceedings relating to the fight against organised crime;

- envisage the interception of communications – both telecommunications and direct communications - in order to cope better with the requirements of fighting against criminal organisations;

- make money laundering an offence and make provisions for the search, seizure and confiscation of the proceeds of crime;

- envisage the possibility of providing for an investigation/prosecution magistrate with jurisdiction over the entire national territory, or providing for the establishment of a central co-ordination body.

15. Recommendation No. (97) 13 recommended, inter alia, that:

- when designing a framework of measures to combat organised crime, specific rules of procedure should be adopted to cope with intimidation. These measures may also be applicable to other serious offences. Such rules shall ensure the necessary balance in a democratic society between the prevention of disorder or crime and the safeguarding of the right of the accused to a fair trial;

- while ensuring that the defence has adequate opportunity to challenge the evidence given by a witness, the following measures should be, inter alia, considered:

  - recording by audio-visual means of statements made by witnesses during pre-trial examination;

  - using pre-trial statements given before a judicial authority as evidence in court when it is not possible for witnesses to appear before the court or when appearing in court might result in great and actual danger to the life and security of witnesses, their relatives or other persons close to them;

  - revealing the identity of witnesses at the latest possible stage of the proceedings and/or releasing only selected details;

-   excluding the media and/or the public from all or part of the trial.

-   where available and in accordance with domestic law, anonymity of persons who might give evidence should be an exceptional measure. Where the guarantee of anonymity has been requested by such persons and/or temporarily granted by the competent authorities, criminal procedural law should provide for a verification procedure to maintain a fair balance between the needs of criminal proceedings and the rights of the defence. The defence should, through this procedure, have the opportunity to challenge the alleged need for anonymity of the witness, his credibility and the origin of his knowledge;

-   anonymity should only be granted when the competent judicial authority, after hearing the parties, finds that:

    i.   the life or freedom of the person involved is seriously threatened or, in the case of an undercover agent, his potential to work in the future is seriously threatened; and

    ii. the evidence is likely to be significant and the person appears to be credible.

-   where appropriate, further measures should be available to protect witnesses giving evidence, including preventing identification of the witness by the defence e.g. by using screens, disguising his face or distorting his voice;

-   when anonymity has been granted, the conviction shall not be based solely or to a decisive extent on the evidence of such persons;

-   where appropriate, special programmes, such as witness protection programmes, should be set up and made available to witnesses who need protection. The main objective of these programmes should be to safeguard the life and personal security of witnesses, their relatives and other persons close to them;

-   witness protection programmes should offer various methods of protection; this may include giving witnesses and their relatives and other persons close to them an identity change, relocation, assistance in obtaining new jobs, providing them with body-guards and other physical protection;

-   given the prominent role that collaborators of justice play in the fight against organised crime, they should be given adequate consideration, including the possibility of benefiting from measures provided by witness protection programmes. Where necessary, such programmes may also include specific arrangements such as special penitentiary regimes for collaborators of justice serving a prison sentence.

IV. Commentary on the preamble

16. It was noted by the experts of Committee PC-CO when studying responses to the questionnaire 1998, that many - but certainly not all - member States had developed some legislation and taken measures in order to fight organised crime. Individual offences, such as smuggling of human beings or trafficking in illegal drugs, were often criminalised, taking into account the specific features of criminality in a given member State. However, the experts also noted that in many cases neither the interaction between various criminal offences committed in an organised manner, nor the transnational character of such offences was duly considered. This resulted in an apparent lack of organised crime-related offences in criminal statistics and prompted the impression that isolated individuals were behind serious crime. Ultimately, the adequacy of domestic legislation to deal with organised crime seemed, in several cases, questionable.

17. Organised crime appears nowadays as one of the most significant challenges to law enforcement and, in some cases, to the authority of the State. Naturally, the establishment and strength of organised crime may greatly vary from one country to another. As the Annual reports on the situation of organised crime show, some countries are particularly vulnerable to such criminality, whereas others remain relatively protected (e.g. islands). It is generally accepted that one country, however powerful and determined it may be, can hardly eliminate organised crime, given the connections that exist between local and foreign groups and, increasingly, the federation of various domestic groups into "supranational" groups. The Guiding principles are therefore seen by the experts as a necessary "soft-law" instrument to develop a common crime policy with regard to organised crime, both in terms of legislation and co-ordinated action at international level. A common crime policy would be an essential step towards enabling member States to give an international response to organised crime. International co-operation in this respect is not only necessary, but the only key to success. Such co-operation also requires that States share experiences and knowledge about organised crime.

18. When establishing the annual reports on organised crime, the experts of Committee PC-CO noted that there was a strong correlation between organised crime and economic crime, in particular corruption, money laundering and fraud. This relationship was also acknowledged by various national and international definitions of organised crime, or criteria used to identify "organised criminal groups": these invariably recognise corruption and money laundering as closely connected, frequent but not always necessary side-activities of organised crime. Fraud offences, e.g. organised VAT–carousels, are – again - often committed by organised crime and give rise to substantial illicit proceeds. This means that the instruments developed

to combat corruption and money laundering are useful tools against organised crime as well, such as the 1990 Convention on Laundering, Search, Seizure and Confiscation of the Proceeds from Crime (ETS No. 141) or the 1999 Criminal Law Convention on Corruption (ETS No. 173). As the Council of Europe has, so far, devoted relatively little attention to fraud, the experts strongly support the idea, put forward by the General Rapporteur of the 3rd Conference of Specialised Services in the Fight against Corruption (Limassol, October 1999)[2], that it would be useful to examine the possibility of drafting a European Convention on tax fraud, a type of fraud which frequently involves organised crime, with a view to harmonising domestic law provisions and eliminating or reducing obstacles to mutual legal assistance in this area.

19. The experts also highlighted the need for innovative solutions when addressing the issue of organised crime. The idea of "best practice surveys", included in the Committee's terms of reference, emerged out of the simple realisation that certain countries may have designed or implemented measures against organised crime which could prove useful for others as well. Three surveys were carried out between 1997 and 1999: on witness protection measures, on "intrusive surveillance" and on the reversal of the burden of proof in confiscation proceedings. All three provided ideas for the drafting of the Guiding Principles and contained specific recommendations concerning the measures they had dealt with. Reference will be made to those conclusions below, when discussing related issues.

V.   Commentary on the principles contained in the Recommendation

Definitions

20.   The Recommendation contains three definitions, which are designed for the purpose of the text and do not necessarily correspond to any legal or doctrinal definition.

Organised crime group

21.   The Committee PC-CO did not seek to define organised crime. Instead, the Committee felt that it was more appropriate for the purpose of its work to use a list of criteria concerning organised criminal groups. The main objective of this list was to allow member States identify, along the same criteria, certain criminal groups that could qualify as "organised" and thus make it possible to compare national experiences concerning such groups. A list of 11 criteria was used, based on a similar list established by the European Union[3], which, in turn, was largely inspired by the definition[4] of

---

[2] See documents Conf/4 (99)8, Conclusions, item IV/7.

[3] See document Enfopol 161/1994, Appendix C.

[4] "Organised crime is the planned violation of the law for profit or to acquire power, which offences are each, or together, of a major significance, and are carried out by

"organised crime" by the German Bundeskriminalamt (BKA). In the Committee's interpretation, a certain number of minimum characteristics, numbered 1 to 4 ("mandatory criteria"), as well as at least two of the other characteristics ("optional criteria") needed to be present for any criminal group to be classified as organised. The focus was therefore on groups that meet six or more of these eleven criteria. This can refer to traditional criminal groups but also to legal entities or professionals engaged in various forms of crime, e.g. white-collar crime. The following are mandatory criteria:

-   Collaboration of three or more people;

-   For a prolonged or indefinite period of time;

-   Suspected or convicted of committing serious criminal offences;

-   With the objective of pursuing profit and/or power.

22. The following are optional criteria:

-   Having a specific task or role for each participant;

-   Using some form of internal discipline and control;

-   Using violence or other means suitable for intimidation;

-   Exerting influence on politics, the media, public administration, law enforcement, the administration of justice or the economy by corruption or other means;

-   Using commercial or business-like structures;

-   Engaged in money-laundering;

-   Operating on an international level.

23. The definition of "organised criminal group", as formulated in the Recommendation takes into account these criteria, and it formally corresponds to the definition used in the United Nations Convention against Transnational Organized Crime[5]; it is also compatible with that in the Joint

---

more than two participants who co-operate within a division of labour for a long or undetermined timespan, using :
   a.   commercial or commercial-like structures;
   b.   violence or other means of intimidation;
   c.   influence on politics, media, public administration, justice and legitimate economy."
[5]   Article 2 (a) of the United Nations Convention.

Action adopted by the Council of the European Union[6]. As the definition in the United Nations Convention, the one in the Guiding Principles also refers to "serious crime"[7].

Law enforcement agencies

24. The purpose of this functional definition is to include, irrespective of any national definition, those public institutions and agencies that carry out under their legal terms of reference, investigations and/or prosecutions of criminal offences. Police forces, gendarmerie, customs, tax or fiscal police, etc. would normally fall under this definition as investigating authorities. Public prosecutors would also qualify as prosecution agencies. Investigating magistrates would also qualify, either as investigation or prosecution agencies. State security or intelligence agencies which do not investigate criminal offences would fall outside this definition, with the exception of financial intelligence units (FIUs), which - at least in some countries – can also initiate or carry out investigations. Private security or intelligence agencies would not qualify as law enforcement agencies for the purposes of the Recommendation.

Principles relating to general prevention

Use of cash payments (Guiding Principle No. 1)

25. In some countries the economy is still largely based on substantial cash payments and cash currency exchanges are commonplace. This facilitates money-laundering, particularly if administrative controls are weak or non-existent. As proceeds of crime are primarily cash and need to be converted into other financial assets or property in order to disguise their criminal origin – a process which is now commonly called money laundering – large cash payments may be indicators of money laundering by organised crime. Purchase of expensive luxury cars, real estate property, gold or jewellery, works of art, securities or bonds, etc. in cash would normally give rise to suspicion – at least in cash-less economies – and, under certain circumstances, would be reported to the disclosure receiving agency. In addition, customers would be identified for transactions above a certain threshold. This kind of reaction to large cash payments should, over time, become common practice in all Council of Europe member States. It is recalled that Recommendations 22 and 23 of the Financial Action task Force (FATF) suggested already in 1990 that banks and other financial institutions "report all domestic and international currency transactions above a fixed amount" and that measures be taken to "detect or monitor the physical cross-border transportation of cash". Article 3, paragraph 2 of Council

---

[6] See 98/733/JHA Joint Action of 21 December 1998 adopted by the Council on the basis of Article K.3 of the Treaty on European Union, on making it a criminal offence to participate in a criminal organisation in the member States of the European Union – Official Journal L 351, 29 December 1998, p. 1 – 3.

[7] Article 2 (b) of the United Nations Convention.

Directive 91/308/EEC on Prevention of the use of the financial system for the purpose of money laundering (10 June 1991) requires credit and financial institutions within the EU to identify customers in respect of any transaction involving a sum amounting to ECU 15.000 or more.

26. It is therefore important that the above-mentioned measures be implemented in all member States in line with the FATF recommendations and the EC Directive. A specific Council of Europe expert committee[8] was created in 1997 with precisely this purpose and has now carried out the first round of its evaluations[9].

27. What is required by principle 1 is that Governments take measures to prevent natural and legal persons from covering up, through cash payments or cash currency exchanges, the conversion of criminal proceeds into other property. Such policies should include measures to reduce the amount of cash payments, cash currency exchanges and physical cross border transportation of cash through the development of modern techniques of payment. This includes the use of checks, payment cards, direct deposit of salary checks etc. In addition, this principle implies an increased diligence on behalf of bank and financial institutions, as well as those professions, which handle large amounts of cash, to detect suspicious cash transactions.

Use of financial centres (Guiding Principle No. 2)

28. Offshore financial centres are an element of the world economic system. Their number and variety have increased with the globalisation of trade and investment and the development of modern information technologies. The use made of their services by the different actors in economic life has risen dramatically and numerous financial institutions in Council of Europe member States – including States in transition - have in fact established their own subsidiaries in off-shore centres.

29. Offshore centres are jurisdictions where non-residents have the possibility of establishing companies and using financial services for activities outside the centre, offering in most cases advantages such as low taxation rates and/or under-regulation in areas like company, financial, administrative or currency law. The services they offer vary and competition is developing between different offshore centres. Some onshore countries have even found it useful to open offshore zones inside their own jurisdiction. Therefore, the very notion of an offshore centre could be misleading as it covers many different realities and legal orders. Whereas some offshore jurisdictions offer bank secrecy, confidentiality, anonymity, tax avoidance facilities and fail to provide international co-operation in criminal matters, others have introduced measures of supervision and control that

---

[8] Select Committee of Experts on the evaluation of anti-money laundering measures (PC-R-EV).

[9] See the Annual Reports of Committee PC-R-EV for the years 1997 – 1998 and 1998-1999.

easily match, or on occasion may even exceed, those that can be found in some onshore jurisdictions.

30. The services provided by offshore centres are particularly attractive for individuals and companies involved in corruption, money laundering and other criminal transactions. Experience shows that they are often used for the setting-up of slush funds and for the creation of shell companies and there is evidence that large scale laundering operations often involve the use of shell companies or bank accounts domiciled in offshore centres. These operations are facilitated by or intermingled with apparently legal transactions, such as investment through offshore facilities and tax-planning. Often, these operations have no visible commercial purpose, such as deposits of cash into offshore bank accounts with low or no interest rate and subsequent wire transfers to other bank accounts overseas, and lack minimum identification data on the parties involved in the transaction. Customer identification in offshore countries is often limited to local intermediaries, such as lawyers, accountants or trustees, and financial institutions do not seek, as a matter of course, to establish through banks in the prospective customer's country of residence whether his/her background is suitable for entering into a business relationship. Likewise, there is often no identification of the ultimate beneficiary of the transaction, particularly in the case of corporate customers, which is contrary to the due diligence requirements set out by the FATF Recommendations (recommendation N° 11) and the EC Directive (Article 3, paragraph 5). Finally, SWIFT-messages from and to offshore countries often do not contain details of the remitter and/or the recipient of the message, contrary to current international banking practice.

31. Experience and government reports show that organised crime groups take advantage of the global financial markets and flaws in their regulations as much as tax evaders and money launderers do. In addition, offshore financial centres are likely to co-operate with foreign authorities to an undesirable extent. In this regard, the conclusions of the 4th Conference of specialised services in the fight against corruption[10] identified a number of obstacles that create an impediment for international co-operation:

- differences in company laws and other related regulatory norms, in particular the possibility of setting up shell or letter-box companies lacking any commercial or industrial activity which often do not require minimum capital, audited accounts, annual general meetings or even a locally appointed administrator ;

- the fact that such shell or letter-box companies are used for operating outside the territory of offshore centres where they have been created, rendering their control difficult or even impossible ;

---

[10] See footnote No. 4.

- the lack of means to identify the ultimate physical beneficial owner of shell or letter box companies ;

- reluctance to sign, ratify or implement treaties on international co-operation in criminal and administrative matters ;

- insufficient staffing and training of law enforcement personnel ;

- the misuse of rules providing for bank secrecy, confidentiality, professional privilege and immunities.

32. To prevent the use of offshore financial centres for laundering money and conducting illegal financial transactions as well as to overcome some of these obstacles, Principle 2 urges Governments to take appropriate measures and thus also ensure compliance with the international standards. Of course, offshore and onshore countries both need to comply with those standards. The Principle explicitly recommends governments to allow the inspection of financial transactions which have no apparent commercial purpose and require the identification of the direct or ultimate parties involved. Here are some other measures which Governments should take to implement Principle 2:

- Company laws should be brought into line with international "due diligence" standards established by e.g. the Basle Committee, the Financial Action Task Force (FATF), the European Communities requiring, inter alia, the identification of customers, record-keeping, reporting of suspicious transactions, etc;

- Obligations should be established for intermediaries, such as lawyers, accountants, auditors, company formation agents and trustees to require them to comply with minimum professional standards as well as to report suspicious transactions. Effective, proportionate and dissuasive criminal or administrative sanctions should be attached to the non-respect of such obligations;

- Bank secrecy should never be an impediment in criminal investigations and procedures should be established for lifting, without delay, bank secrecy at the request of competent foreign or domestic law enforcement authorities;

- No company should be registered in offshore jurisdictions before obtaining and verifying detailed information about the identity of the ultimate physical beneficial owner(s) and the effective responsible manager, the activities of the company, reliable bank or company references, criminal records, etc.;

- Professionals dealing with the formation and management of companies and trusts should be effectively regulated – including, where appropriate, through compulsory membership of professional associations – and subject to codes of conduct and disciplinary rules;

- Financial institutions should consider as 'suspicious' for the purpose of their reporting obligation, the involvement in a transaction of a shell or letterbox company established in an offshore jurisdiction, which does not take the measures described above;

- Law enforcement personnel should be trained by specialists in the banking and auditing sector concerning the establishment, operation and possibilities of misuse of offshore shell and letterbox companies.

Requirements for vulnerable professions (Guiding Principle No. 3)

33. In some Council of Europe member States, certain professions, such as notaries, accountants, lawyers or tax advisors may and do routinely conduct financial transactions on behalf of their clients. However, as these professions are not subject to "due diligence" requirements – now customary in the traditional financial sector - and are often protected by client confidentiality rules as well as corresponding legal privileges, they do attract dishonest clients (as well) and thus become vulnerable to misuse for illegal transactions. For some of these professions, it is necessary to make a clear distinction between the activities performed on behalf of clients as financial intermediaries (opening bank accounts, accepting cash deposits, authorising bank transfers via clients account etc.) and other professional relationship towards the client (legal representative, defense lawyer, personal asset-manager, etc). Principle 3 should therefore be interpreted as limited to the activities performed by these professions as financial intermediaries. Other professions, such as real estate agents, art dealers, auctioneers, casinos, automobile dealers, transporters of funds or auditors do not have this feature of dual activity but are exposed to misuse for illegal transactions on account of their handling of cash or other financial transactions and the lack of due diligence will be identified as vulnerable ones for the purposes of this Principle.

34. It is recalled that at present no international standards exist to oblige these vulnerable professions to identify their clients, keep business records or report suspicious transactions to a disclosure receiving agency. The 1991 Directive (91/308/EEC) on prevention of the use of the financial system for the purpose of money laundering provided the basis for action at EU level to prevent criminal money entering the financial system, by requiring financial firms (including 'bureaux de change' and money transmitters) to know the identity of their customers when opening an account or safe-deposit facilities or when a single or linked transactions exceed euro15,000, to keep appropriate records and establish anti-money laundering programmes. Most importantly it requires banking secrecy to be suspended whenever necessary and any suspicions of money laundering (even when the

transaction is below the threshold) to be reported to the appropriate authorities, i.e. disclosure receiving agencies. Since the Directive was adopted in 1991, both the money laundering threat and response to that threat have evolved. The EU Member States (in the recommendations of the Amsterdam European Council's Action Plan to combat organised crime) and the European Parliament (in two reports and resolutions) have called for a strengthening and widening of the EU efforts in this crucial area. Most EU and some non-EU countries did already go beyond the requirements of the 1991 Directive, in terms of coverage of non-financial professions. The recently adopted second money laundering directive seeks to enlarge the circle of professions and institutions subject to due diligence requirements. It is based on the realisation that as the money laundering defences of the banking sector have become stronger, money launderers have sought alternative ways of disguising the criminal origin of their funds. This trend has been clearly noted by the Financial Action Task Force and by other international fora, which confirm that the services of lawyers and accountants are being misused to help hide criminal funds. There have also been numerous cases where the real estate sector is used to launder money from criminal activity.

35.   Principle 3 echoes the objectives of the Second European Directive[*] to strengthen the anti-laundering framework and supports the idea that a number of professions and activities should now play a more active role in combating organised crime and the criminal money it generates. The Principle itself does not enumerate the full list of "vulnerable professions". Instead, it leaves it to governments of member States to determine which are the professions they consider "vulnerable" under their anti-laundering regime. Of course, in so doing, governments may wish to take into account the list set up by the second Directive so as to ensure that the same categories of professions observe due diligence regulations in all Council of Europe member States.

36.   The Second Directive contemplates to require the real estate sector, accountants and auditors and casinos to be fully involved in the fight against organised crime. These activities and professions would be obliged to properly identify their clients and report their suspicions of money laundering to the appropriate anti-money laundering authorities established by the Member States. These professions would be given protection against any liability under civil or criminal law arising from the reporting of money from a suspicious source. In the case of notaries and other independent legal professionals the obligations of the Directive would apply in respect of specific financial or company law activities where the money laundering risk is the greatest (e.g. buying and selling of real estate or business entities,

---

[*]   At the moment of the approval of this draft Recommendation by the European Committee on Crime Problems (CDPC) at its 50th plenary session (June 2001), the Second European Directive was not yet finally adopted. Pending its final adoption, the text in these paragraphs is subject to changes which may occur in the Directive's scope and provisions.

handling clients' money, securities or other assets, opening or managing bank, savings or securities accounts, creation, operation or management of companies, trusts or similar structures). Given the particular status of lawyers and their duty of confidentiality, they would be exempted from any reporting requirement in any situation connected with the representation or defence of clients in legal proceedings. To make full allowance for lawyers' professional duty of discretion, it is envisaged that lawyers would have the option to communicate their suspicions of money laundering by organised crime not to the normal anti-money laundering authorities but through their bar association or equivalent professional body.

37. With this special treatment for lawyers, the second European Directive is striving to include this profession in the anti-money laundering effort while safeguarding the special role of the lawyer in our society. This policy is fully endorsed by Principle 3 as well. Under the proposal, potential money launderers who attempted to misuse the services of the lawyer, possibly by providing inaccurate or incomplete information, would be liable to be reported to a higher authority. At the same time, lawyers would have the advantage of not being left to manage alone when faced with a suspicion of serious criminal activity.

Complex administrative rules (Guiding Principle No. 4)

38. The more complex administrative rules are the more likely it is that they will be misused. This is especially the case for areas such as export and import, licensing, fiscal and customs regulations. In most cases the rules in these areas are so complicated that even legal professionals hesitate over what is meant by them. Such complexity creates many possibilities for misuse, particularly for fraud. Various studies[11] and reports[12] on EU-fraud show that losses directly generated by large-scale organised fraud can amount to huge sums (an estimated 1.3 billion ECU in 1996) and point out that one of the usual facilitating factors is the complexity of rules combined with bureaucracy at both national and EU level. Principle 4 invites Governments to identify in their legislation those provisions which are or can be abused by organised crime and to take steps to strengthen legislation to prevent any such abuses. In addition, governments need to ensure consistency among such regulations. Governments' attention is drawn to the fact that regulations in these areas are not only complex but also often inconsistent with each other. Inconsistency creates loopholes that are likely to be exploited by criminals, including those engaged in organised crime.

39. Principle 4 suggests one possible way of dealing with complex administrative regulations, that is by subjecting them to thorough scrutiny by independent auditors who would assess their resistance to criminal misuse,

---

[11] See e.g. Hans de Doelder, Legal Fraud Trends, address given at the University of Trento on 22 October 1998.

[12] See European Commission, Protection of the financial interests of the communities, Fight against fraud, Annual Reports 1996 – 1999.

such as fraud. This pre-enactment scrutiny, frequently done by large audit firms in respect of corporate regulations, could result in the early detection of inconsistencies as well as of opportunities for fraud or corruption under the proposed regulation.

Use of information technology (Guiding Principle No. 5)

40. The use of information technology had and continues to have tremendous impact on all segments of society, including banking. There is an increasing number of large banks in Europe, a tendency which started a few years ago in the Nordic countries, that offer their services through "virtual banks", open 24 hours a day, 7 days a week. These "virtual banks" are set up by way of creating Internet access to a computer system and users may connect to that system to obtain services. No face-to-face relationship is established between the bank and the customer, though some transactions are generally not automated, such as the opening of a bank account.

41. There is, however, a serious risk of misuse with virtual banks, given that customer identification procedures are either rudimentary (the system requires a photocopy of ID) or totally non-existent (as it allegedly happens with some non-European based virtual banks). Anyone can – of course – be a customer of a virtual bank. There are no geographical constraints and personal knowledge of the customer's financial or indeed social background by the bank no longer makes sense (as in the good old times, when the bank established business relationship with trustworthy clients). In the case of corporate clients, which can be registered anywhere in the world, e.g. in under-regulated offshore financial centres, virtual banks have particularly no possibility of checking the corporation's financial background or its very existence, by asking bank references, proof of incorporation, etc. There is, therefore, a serious potential for misuse created by the possible circumvention or non-application of customer identification rules.

42. Once an account has been opened with a "virtual bank", a variety of bank services can be obtained, including electronic wire-transfers to other bank accounts. Financial intelligence reports claim that in some regions of the world, "virtual banks" are mushrooming and significant amounts of money, some of suspicious origin, are wire-transferred by using SWIFT messages. Those reports also confirm the keen interest that organised crime groups have developed over the last couple of years in such virtual bank-based accounts in under-regulated offshore jurisdictions. It therefore seems essential that banks operating "virtual outlets" or "virtual banks" adopt, as a matter of policy, stringent measures, which guarantee that they know who their clients are. The application of the "know your customer" rule would mean that virtual banks do not accept clients without checking, as a traditional bank would do, the identity, existence and financial background of customers and the reliability of the information provided in evidence of those. Other due diligence requirements, such as record-keeping, etc. should naturally apply as well. Furthermore, "virtual banks" should identify the

remitter and the recipient of any SWIFT message and detect, e.g. by controlling the beneficiary's country of location and bank references, any possible misuse of the system for money laundering purposes. Appropriate security features, such as encryption of transaction data, should also be applied to prevent intrusion and misuse of bank-data.

Good Governance (Guiding Principle No. 6)

43. Government and businesses are important players in modern societies. They are the largest employers in most countries and their financial resources are equally significant. Public administration in democratic societies is accountable to Government and, ultimately, to people who voted for the political party (ies) in power. Large businesses can hardly survive in today's global and integrated economy if they do not observe minimum rules of accountability, imposed by regulations, competitive environment, stock-markets and share-holders. It is expected from both Government and businesses that they perform their functions with due respect for rules of good governance, as a "*bonus paterfamilias*" would do. One of the possible and nowadays often used methods to ascertain that common standards apply to employees in both the public and private sector, is to adopt and enforce codes of conduct.

44. Codes of conduct should be clear and concise statements of the guiding principles of conduct by which an organisation expects its members to behave and the values for which it stands. It is both a public document and a message addressed to every individual employee. It is particularly important in the public sector, as it cannot be assumed that a public servant knows what standards of conduct are expected of him if he has never been told what they are. Reliance on some unwritten process of absorption of standards in the working environment is haphazard and insufficient. If the public servant is to be called to account for his conduct, it is essential that he should have been informed of what was expected of him and that he should know in what respects his conduct has fallen short of those expectations. A clear, concise and accessible written statement of the standards by which his working life is to be conducted is a basic requirement. In the private sector, the code may be seen as part of the employment contract and may in such cases be signed by the employee. A subsequent breach of the code can be a breach of the contract of employment and result in disciplinary proceedings or dismissal. Some codes may not provide for any sanctions but may simply make reference to the relevant offences, such as embezzlement or corruption, in existing criminal codes. To a great extent the effectiveness of a code may depend on the sanctions which are provided. The scope for taking disciplinary measures is of course wider than the scope for criminal law measures.

45. Codes of conduct should not be limited to addressing corruption. They should go further and promote high standards of ethical behaviour. They should state general principles covering lawfulness, diligence, efficiency and thrift, transparency, confidentiality and the handling of classified information,

personal responsibility and independent judgement, fair dealing and integrity, and professional training. Their guidance can also be broadly divided into provisions dealing with personal integrity and those dealing with managerial responsibilities for upholding the integrity of the public service or the company, such as devising and putting in place appropriate systems of operation, ensuring that subordinates are informed and aware of their duties, applying systems of supervision and accountability, applying proper selection procedures, enforcing the code of conduct and maintaining discipline. A minimum is that codes of conduct should reflect the standards of the criminal law relating to dishonesty and corruption. Moreover, there should always be a relationship between codes of conduct and the laws and regulations concerned with disciplinary action.

46. The adoption of codes of conduct is particularly important in the area of public procurement, where substantial public funds are spent on expensive public works, and there is a greater risk of corruption or other malpractice. Practice indeed shows that as regards the volume of money, public procurement is by far the most important domain of corruption. The Council of Europe's Programme of Action against Corruption[13] noted that "the main remedies are attribution procedures which render corruption as difficult as possible (by, for example, the splitting of decision competencies between several persons or administrations, submission procedures which put all competitors on an equal footing, the requirement of very detailed estimations by competitors, good technical knowledge of the personnel of the public auditors who scrutinise the offers, etc.) and a *very high degree of transparency at all stages of the process*, including after the procedure has been terminated. Additional remedies include the reliability checks on administrators involved in the decision making in public procurement, etc".

47. The adoption and application of codes of conduct by Government and businesses would, naturally, not only strengthen transparency and ethical values but help render illegal behaviour, including fraud, corruption, misuse of position, money laundering, more visible and, eventually, help eliminate it. Ultimately, organisations which do observe such codes of conduct and uphold the principles of transparency and accountability better resist penetration or control by organised crime.

Whistle-blowing (Guiding Principle No. 7)

48. This Principle is closely related to the previous one. It aims at encouraging ethical behaviour in corporations, by adopting the principles of responsibility and zero tolerance towards illegal practices. The Principle also calls upon Governments to adopt common rules for the protection of whistle-blowers, i.e. persons who report cases of corruption or other suspected criminal activities committed by or within corporations.

---

[13] See document GMC (96) 95.

49. Several documents recently adopted by the Council of Europe drew attention to the need to protect whistle-blowers and thus help emerge a collective attitude towards illegal behaviour within corporations. First, the aforementioned Programme of Action against Corruption pointed out that given the consensual nature of most corruption offences, the co-operation of corporate information-sources with the law enforcement authorities was of vital importance to uncover and prosecute these offences. It admitted, though, that in a large majority of cases persons who have information on corruption offences do not report it to the police, mainly because they would thus incriminate themselves or because of fear of the possible consequences. This is true both in the administration and in private business. Second, Article 22 of the Criminal Convention on Corruption [ETS N° 173] required States to take the necessary measures to provide for an effective and appropriate protection of collaborators of justice and witnesses. The drafters of this Convention, were inspired, *inter alia*, by Recommendation N° R (97) 13[14], which had suggested a comprehensive set of principles to guide national legislations when addressing the problems of witness-intimidation, either in the framework of criminal procedure law or when designing out-of-court protection measures. Both Article 22 of the Convention and Recommendation N° R (97) 13 referred to "witness" in a large sense so that it comprises persons who possess information relevant to criminal proceedings concerning criminal offences, e.g. corruption, and includes whistleblowers.

50. Principle 7 calls for the protection of whistle-blowers. Of course, the level of protection needs to be adapted to the risks, which whistleblowers face. In some cases it could be sufficient, for instance, to maintain their name undisclosed during the proceedings, in other cases they may need more far-reaching protection measures.

51. The third and most recent document which deals with the "reporting" duties of public officials is Recommendation No. R (2000) 10 of the Committee of Ministers to Member states on codes of conduct for public officials. It advised Governments, in Article 12 (Reporting) to ensure, in particular, that:

-   The public official who believes he or she is being required to act in a way which is unlawful, improper or unethical, which involves maladministration, or which is otherwise inconsistent with this Code, should report the matter in accordance with the law.

-   The public official should report to the competent authorities any evidence, allegation or suspicion of unlawful or criminal activity relating to the public service coming to his or her knowledge in the course of, or arising from, his or her employment. The investigation

---

[14] See Recommendation N° R (97) 13 on the intimidation of witnesses and the rights of the defence, adopted by the Committee of Ministers of the Council of Europe on 10 September 1997.

of the reported facts shall be carried out by the competent authorities.

- The public administration should ensure that no prejudice is caused to a public official who reports any of the above on reasonable grounds and in good faith.

Principles relating to the Criminal Justice System

Making the participation in an organised criminal group a criminal offence (Guiding Principle N° 8)

52. There has been much debate lately on the widening gap between the complex criminological reality of organised crime and the individualistic approach of traditional criminal law. This gap – also visible in other areas of the law - has grown large because of the emergence and rapidly changing features of an ever more sophisticated, often entrepreneurial-type, organised crime, which can no longer be captured by the traditional "one man - one crime" offences. It is no longer a matter of a murder, a burglary, a robbery or a sale of contraband goods. One can, in the best of the cases, detect, investigate and prove such offences and obtain the offender's conviction. The problem is that even by adding those individual offences and offenders to each other, the result does not correspond to the reality of organised crime, which, as the name indicates, supposes some "organisation" of crime. As the annual organised crime reports of the Council of Europe clearly show, organised crime can be "organised" along various structures, e.g. pyramidal mafia-type, network-type etc., but what makes it ultimately specific compared to individual crime is the interaction between group members, who set objectives, divide and execute a criminal plan together. In certain cases, this criminal programme becomes permanent and the expression coined by the US legislators "continuing criminal enterprise" describes well the idea of organised crime.

53. As traditional criminal law focuses on individual offences, even if committed by several persons, it usually does not capture the social – organisational dimension of organised crime, for conceptual reasons. Common law countries are in principle better equipped to address such features with the concept of "conspiracy", though it remains unclear to what extent this could apply to offences committed by organised crime. There is, however, an essential element in "conspiracy", which civil law countries do usually have difficulty with: the "agreement" of the conspirators is sufficient to constitute the offence. Something similar is the essence of organised crime: some people agree to commit offences together as part of a long-term criminal programme. However, the agreement itself may not be sufficient for criminalisation under certain laws, and some form of external manifestation may be required. That said, a group of people with such an agreement may divide up for committing offences, some members may only contribute a car, a garage or participate only in preparations (in itself perhaps legal) but what matters is to act towards a common objective. It is therefore not necessary

that all group members commit offences according to an agreed plan – some may only support the group with material help or - as leaders usually do - only give instructions. To make those persons responsible, Principle 8 invites Governments to strive to criminalise membership of criminal organisations as defined under the corresponding definitions in the Guiding Principles (first indent of Part I) irrespective of the place in Council of Europe member States in which the group is concentrated or carries out its criminal activities. The formulation of the Principle is such that it highlights the need to address organised crime groups on a cross-border level.

54. The 1997 Report on the organised crime situation in Council of Europe member States[15] contained a specific chapter on the criminalisation of membership in organised crime groups and indicated that a number of member States had already taken the steps suggested by Principle 8. In Belgium, for example, the law on criminal organisations aims at making any person who is part of a criminal organisation explicitly punishable, even if the person does not intend to commit an offence within that organisation or to get involved in an offence as a co-offender or an accomplice. The Italian Criminal Code has two provisions covering the participation in a criminal association. The first, contained in Article 416, is very similar to the French concept of *"association de malfaiteurs"* and it does not require that specific offences be committed[16]. The second Italian provision is contained in Article *416bis* of the Criminal Code (introduced in 1982, amended in 1992) and it covers the participation in a "mafia-type" criminal association[17]. This provision provides for aggravating circumstances if the association is armed and if the economic activities which the members intend to perform or control are financed in whole or in part by the proceeds of crime.

---

[15] See document PC-CO (1999) 7.

[16] Article 416: "When three or more persons associate for the purpose of committing more than one crime, those who promote, constitute or organise the association shall be punished, for that fact alone, with imprisonment from three to seven years. The punishment for the sole fact of participating in the association shall be imprisonment from one to five years. The leaders shall be subject to the same punishment as is prescribed for the promoters. If the persons associated overrun the countryside or public roads in arms, a term of imprisonment from five to fifteen years shall be imposed. The punishment shall be increased if the number of persons associating is ten or more".

[17] Article 416 bis: "Persons belonging to a Mafia-type association of three or more persons shall be liable to imprisonment for a term from three to six years. A Mafia-type association is an association whose members use the power of intimidation deriving from the bonds of membership and the atmosphere of coercion and conspiracy of silence (omertà) that it engenders to commit offences, to acquire direct or indirect control of economic activities, licences, authorisations, public procurement contracts and services or to obtain unjustified profits or advantages for themselves or others, or to prevent or obstruct the free exercise of the right to vote, or to procure votes for themselves or others at elections...The provisions of this section are also applicable to the Camorra and any other organisations, whatever their names, that make use of the power of intimidation deriving from the bonds of membership to pursue goals which are typical of Mafia-type organisations."

55. The differences between membership of a mafia-type organisation and simple criminal association are worth mentioning. While a simple association only requires the creation of a stable organisation, however rudimentary, for the purposes of committing an indeterminate number of offences, membership of a mafia-type organisation requires in addition the organisation to have acquired a genuine capacity for intimidation in their area. The members of the organisation must also exploit this power to coerce third parties with whom the organisation establishes relations and thus oblige them to enter into a conspiracy of silence. Intimidation may take various forms, from simply exploiting an atmosphere of intimidation already created by the criminal organisation to committing new acts of violence or making threats that reinforce the previously acquired capacity for intimidation. The "mafia-method" (or rather, the whole host of instruments on which it is based) is therefore identified under Italian criminal law by means of three characteristics ("powers of intimidation deriving from the bonds of the organisation", "coercion" and "conspiracy of silence") and all three are essential and necessary aspects of this association offence.

56. In terms of aims, whereas a simple association aims at committing acts defined as criminal offences by the law, a mafia association can also be organised with the aim of obtaining direct or indirect control of economic activities, authorisations, public procurement contracts and services or profits or other unjustified advantages for the organisation or others, or to prevent or obstruct the free exercise of the right to vote or to procure votes for itself or others at elections. In its answer to the 1997 Council of Europe questionnaire on the situation on organised crime, Italy pointed to an important problem that had arisen over the past years, i.e. the need to legally qualify external support to the Mafia. It is the case of politicians, directors, or entrepreneurs co-operating with mafia organisations, i.e. doing each others "favours" (e.g. hiring members of the association in their company in return for protection and development of economic activities, or paying money or "adjusting trials", or granting public contracts in exchange for votes). The question is whether such licit behaviours (very important for the survival and development of mafia associations) can be punished when perpetrated by non-members of mafia associations. The case-law[18] of the Court of Cassation has provided an important answer on this issue, when establishing that if an "external" contribution to the association has a special significance, either because it is a continued contribution or because it occurs at times of crisis of the organisation, such contribution can be equalled to "internal" participation, as far as punishment is concerned. In fact, the Court of Cassation clarified that even when a non-member of a criminal association carries out a single occasional act, and does so for the purpose of accomplishing any one of the aims of the organisation, such conduct must be considered as complicity in the offence.

---

[18] See the judgment rendered by the Joint sections of the Court of Cassation on 5 October 1994 in the Demitri case.

57. At an international level, the European Union addressed the issue of criminalisation of participation in a criminal organisation by a Joint Action of 21 December 1998[19]. The text first defined the term "criminal organisation" as "a structured association, established over a period of time, of more than two persons, acting in concert with a view to committing offences which are punishable by deprivation of liberty or a detention order of a maximum of at least four years or a more serious penalty, whether such offences are an end in themselves or a means of obtaining material benefits and, where appropriate, of improperly influencing the operation of public authorities". It then went on to establish an obligation for EU member States to "undertake, in accordance with the procedure laid down in Article 6, to ensure that one or both of the types of conduct described below are punishable by effective, proportionate and dissuasive criminal penalties:

a.   conduct by any person who, with intent and with knowledge of either the aim and general criminal activity of the organisation or the intention of the organisation to commit the offences in question, actively takes part in:

-   the organisation's criminal activities falling within Article 1, even where that person does not take part in the actual execution of the offences concerned and, subject to the general principles of the criminal law of the Member State concerned, even where the offences concerned are not actually committed,

-   the organisation's other activities in the further knowledge that his participation will contribute to the achievement of the organisation's criminal activities falling within Article 1;

b.   conduct by any person consisting in an agreement with one or more persons that an activity should be pursued which, if carried out, would amount to the commission of offences falling within Article 1, even if that person does not take part in the actual execution of the activity."

58. The text of the Joint Action makes it clear, as does Principle 8, that where in the territory of EU Member States the organisation is based or pursues its criminal activities, has no relevance. (Article 4).

59. At the level of the United Nations, the Convention against Transnational Organized Crime contemplates establishing a similar offence to that in the EU Joint Action or in Principle 8: Article 5 of the Convention ("Criminalization of participation in an organized criminal group") obliges Parties to criminalise

---

[19] See 98/733/JHA Joint Action of 21 December 1998 adopted by the Council on the basis of Article K.3 of the Treaty on European Union, on making it a criminal offence to participate in a criminal organisation in the member States of the European Union – Official Journal L 351, 29 December 1998, p. 1–3.

as a separate offence, inter alia, the agreement between at least two persons to commit a serious crime for obtaining financial or other material benefit and involving an organised criminal group, even if no act was committed in furtherance of it. In addition, the text provides that the agreement can be inferred from objective factual circumstances. An organised criminal group is defined (Article 2/a) as a structured group of three or more persons, existing for a period of time and acting in concert with the aim of committing one or more serious crimes or offences established in accordance with the Convention, in order to obtain, directly or indirectly, a financial or other material benefit.

Criminalisation of the laundering of organised crime proceeds (Guiding Principle No. 9)

60. The purpose of organised crime is primarily to make money. Money helps criminals gain respect, buy legitimacy, bribe officials, etc.: in short, it enables criminals to continue doing business and make it appear legitimate. This process, which is hardly distinct from the normal course of business in many cases, makes it necessary that the direct profits from crime – often large amounts of cash - are turned into legitimate money, goods or other items of financial value. By disguising the illegitimate origin of such proceeds, derived most frequently from a range of illegal activities, such as drugs or other illegal commodities, trafficking, fraud, racketeering, etc., through a process which many call today "money laundering", organised crime obtains clean money that can be used for doing "normal" business, e.g. investing it. This process is a *sine qua non* condition for organised crime to access – and possibly influence – legitimate financial and economic circuits and has been referred to by all existing definitions of organised crime as one of its constituting elements.

61. What is recommended by Principle 9 is that member States criminalise the laundering of any kind of proceeds, as it is required by the 1990 Convention on Laundering, Search, Seizure and Confiscation of Proceeds from Crime [ETS N° 141], including proceeds from organised crime. This would require member States to revisit their money laundering laws and, where necessary, enlarge their lists of predicate offences to any criminal offence[20], but at least include offences, which are usually committed by organised crime and generate significant proceeds. The proceeds of several

---

[20] Article 6 of the Convention contains, in principle, an «all-crime» based money laundering offence, but reservations can be entered by Parties to the Convention to limit the scope of the offence to proceeds of certain specific offences. The 40 FATF Recommendations, revised in 1996, require countries to « extend the offence of drug money laundering to one based on serious offences » (Recommendation 4), whereas the Joint Action of 3 December 1998 of the European Union (98/699/JHA) on money laundering, the identification, tracing, freezing, seizing , and confiscation of instrumentalities and the proceeds from crime requires EU Member States to lift reservations made to Article of the 1990 Laundering Convention so that their laundering offences at minimum cover proceeds from all serious offences, e.g. those punishable by imprisonment for at least 1 year.

activities may be, and often are, laundered together. If anti-money laundering measures are to be effective against organise crime groups which operate across the spectrum of criminal activity, the offence of money laundering must be based on a large number of offences particularly because in practice it is sometimes virtually impossible to know what specific offence the proceeds came from. At any rate, predicate offences should include tax offences as well.

62. Principle 9 echoes therefore an increasing international tendency to make money laundering offences applicable to all possible kinds of predicate offences, which in itself would make prosecutors' work easier when establishing the link between the laundering offence and the offence which generated the proceeds, but stresses particularly the need to criminalise organised crime-based laundering and thus the need to focus on the financial aspects of organised crime.

Criminalisation of the non-reporting of suspicious financial transactions (Guiding Principle No. 10)

63. This Principle is closely related to the reporting obligation of suspected money laundering imposed on financial and non-financial institutions or professions[21] (hereafter reporting entities) by various international standards, e.g. the 40 FATF Recommendations (Recommendation N° 15) and Directive 308/91/EEC (Articles 6 and 12). It also takes into account the forthcoming Second EU Directive. These standards provide a general regulatory framework for dealing with money laundering in the financial and, increasingly, non-financial sectors. The central piece in this framework is the obligation on reporting entities to disclose their suspicions on possible money laundering operations to a designated authority, often called "disclosure receiving agency" or "financial intelligence unit" (FIU), which will process those for further investigations. The reporting entities or their employees have to be protected from any liability, whether criminal or civil, for breach of confidentiality.

64. If, despite their legal duties, the reporting entities intentionally refrain from forwarding information on money laundering suspicions, this may constitute under certain criminal laws aiding and abetting of money laundering. It is, however, rather difficult to prove that the reporting entity knew that the money was proceeds, even if most jurisdictions accept that intent or knowledge can be inferred from factual circumstances. In practice, banks or other financial institutions are seldom convicted for money laundering, whereas supervisory authorities or auditors frequently discover information, which should have been reported. In some cases it might be negligence or lack of training which explains non-reporting, in others, information is deliberately concealed from superiors and in others still, the whole reporting entity may be involved in furthering illegal activity.

---

[21] See observations made under Principle 3.

65. Principle 10 invites member States to penalise the intentional non-reporting of suspicious transactions, i.e. when any reporting entity - including professionals such as lawyers and accountants – wilfully turns a blind eye on a suspicious transaction. Penalising such behaviour in this context implies imposing either criminal or admiminstraive law sanctions. Even if such behaviour amounts, perhaps, to aiding and abetting money laundering, a separate criminal or administrative offence would certainly play a preventative role by making the professions concerned act in a more responsible and careful manner.

Depriving persons from illegal assets (Guiding Principle No. 11)

66. Many criminal organisations generate substantial profits and revenues, in reality proceeds derived from crime, which remain in their possession and are available to support further criminal activities or can be spent on personal consumption. The organisations involved in drugs, prostitution, selling stolen goods and illegal gambling in the UK are estimated to have generated between £ 6.5 billion and £ 11.1 billion in 1996[22]. Other countries estimated much lower profits during the same year: Spain had an estimate of USD 326 million, while Germany one of USD 549 million, generated by identified organised crime groups[23]. Though with a lot of caution, the FATF, IMF and other international organisations put forward enormous figures when estimating drug-generated proceeds, i.e. between USD 500 - 800 billion. Whatever the exact figures may be – if ever they will be known – it seems undisputed that the wealth accumulated by organised crime takes unprecedented proportions.

67. There are various legal avenues for depriving criminals of their wealth, if criminally acquired: these can be criminal, civil or administrative. Criminal law measures may, for example, include making the person responsible criminally for offences involving "illicit enrichment" and, as a consequence, confiscating the illicit assets. Administrative measures could consist of e.g. fiscal sanctions for non-declaration of revenues or wealth. The criminal law avenue remains, at present, very controversial. Even if limited to public officials, whose financial situation is relatively easy to control as they are on the State's payroll and have, in several countries, to declare their assets, an illicit enrichment offence raises various political, constitutional and legal problems. Following the example of the United Kingdom (Corruption Act (1906)), several countries introduced the offence of "illicit enrichment" to curb widespread corruption in the public sector (e.g. Hong Kong), by making public officials criminally liable for a significant increase in their assets which they cannot reasonably explain and account for in relation to their lawful earnings during the performance of their functions. However, assets of persons in the private sector cannot be controlled with the same ease. Any

---

[22] See Recovering the Proceeds of Crime, a PIU Report, Cabinet Office, UK, June 2000, page 10.

[23] See document PC-CO (98) 26 REV : Report on the Organised Crime Situation in Council of Europe Member States – 1996, page 20.

investigation by a public authority into someone's assets, the person not being a public official, needs solid legal grounds, e.g. some level of suspicion of illegal activity, whether criminal or fiscal violation (for example tax avoidance).

68. Guiding Principale 11 is intended to apply, under certain circumstances, to suspected organised criminals who manage to escape prosecution because they do not participate, or cannot be caught for having participated, in the commission of crime. First, there must be some evidence that the person's assets originate from organised crime (e.g. circumstantial or life-style evidence). The Principle requires that such evidence lead to a reasonable suspicion that the person's assets originate from organised criminal activity. Second, if reasonable suspicion is sufficient for criminal law action, for example a non-conviction based confiscation, member States should apply, in conformity with their constitutional principles, such a measure. This may require that the onus of proving the legitimate origin of the assets is reversed and placed on the defendant. If no reasonable explanation is given that the assets have a legitimate origin and the person, under the circumstances (no revenues, etc), appears to have no plausible source of such assets other than crime, this person could be subject to the said criminal sanction.

69. Where the above situation does not justify under the country's constitutional principles criminal law measures, civil or administrative ones may offer an effective alternative; for example, the use of tax sanctions for unaccounted assets/revenues. Tax and revenue authorities in many countries, for example in the Netherlands, do impose enormous fines on suspected organised criminals for non-declaration of revenues and non-payment of taxes. In this scenario, the same conditions apply as above, but the sanction is imposed by administrative authorities. Both solutions require careful consideration of the legal position of the assets and the proprietor's legitimate income and occupation. If, however, serious indicia are at the authorities disposal and their presumption of the assets' illicit origin cannot be rebutted, at least one of these measures, as described above should be made available.

Liability for legal persons (Guiding Principle No. 12)

70. Organised crime often needs corporate structures for committing its primary profit-generating activities (e.g. fraud), for laundering money and for integrating legitimate business. As the 1997 Council of Europe Report on the situation of organised crime noted "one important aspect of organised crime – both in relation to fraud and money laundering - is the use of businesses as a medium of organised crime. Fraudsters will almost by definition have used some commercial vehicle as a 'front' for fraud, and smugglers (of legal and illegal goods and of people) may find it convenient to use corporate mechanisms as a cover for their activities (or because they want to make some extra money from crime to help with living expenses and working capital). Furthermore, extortion not uncommonly leads to the take-over of

the firm itself, as the criminals become shadow directors or even real owners: this enables the racketeers to enter into pseudo-legitimate contracts with their commercial victims"[24].

71. According to the findings of the Report, many Council of Europe member States experience all of the three types of business involvement that the questionnaire asked about, i.e. (1) belonging to already existing lawful companies where one or more employees co-operate with organised crime; (2) exploitation of a company by criminal groups mixing lawful and unlawful business; and (3) utilisation of a front company, including off-shore companies, carrying out no real business. The involvement of such business structures in organised crime was reported by, among others, the "the Former Yugoslav Republic of Macedonia", Hungary, Ireland, Italy, Norway, Poland, Romania and Turkey, while Italy observed « criminal companies » that carry out apparently lawful activities and are perfectly symbiotic with the economic world, concealed by huge structures, and always closely linked to political leadership. Nordic and Baltic countries also acknowledged that organised criminals use real or fictitious front companies for business purposes. Germany reported that actual business structures were used in 257 domestic and 159 overseas proceedings, and that front companies were detected in 108 domestic and 66 overseas proceedings. Portugal mentions the legal businesses used to falsify documents and to recycle stolen securities. One now dismantled organisation mixed its illegal business with legal hotel industry profits of millions of Escudos. Non-trading companies from offshore finance centres, Canada and the US are often used as a front for fraud (as well as for money-laundering purposes, especially at the layering stage). Belgium noted that organised crime's economic benefit totalled nearly BEF 30 billion (about USD 825 million), and that three quarters of detected organised crime groups used an average of 2.3 commercial structures each, with nearly half commingling legal and illegal activities and only 11.3 per cent being mere artificial front companies not doing any real trading. The Netherlands (like Poland) reported substantial real business run by criminals in the transportation, hotel, restaurant and import/export sectors. Dutch private companies, one-man businesses, and Foundations are used to screen off illegal activities, and it is implied that all three types mentioned in the questionnaire occur in the Netherlands.

72. The liability of legal persons for crime has long been on the agenda of international organisations, such as the European Union, OECD and the Council of Europe, particularly in areas of fraud, environmental crime and corruption. The first step was taken in the area of environmental crime (a major source of profit for organised crime in certain countries) by the Council of Europe in 1977, when it called through Resolution (77) 28[25] for "the re-

---

[24] See document PC-CO (1999) 7, pages 28 – 29.

[25] See Resolution (77) 28 on the contribution of criminal law to the protection of the environment and the Report of the European Committee on Crime Problems, Council of Europe 1978.

examination of the principles of criminal liability, with a view, in particular, to the possible introduction in certain cases of the liability of corporate bodies, public or private" (item 2). The attached report noted that a "large part of European criminal legislation still adheres to the principle, established by Roman law, that legal persons cannot be held liable" (*societas delinquere non potest*), only their representatives as natural persons. Later on, at the level of the Council of Europe, more specific and legally binding instruments in the area of environmental crime[26] and corruption[27] gave full recognition to the principle of corporate liability, though they admitted both criminal and non-criminal (e.g. administrative) forms of liability. A similar tendency could be detected at the level of the European Union[28] and the OECD[29].

73. All existing international instruments recognise the conceptual and legal difficulties which some countries may have in introducing corporate *criminal* liability, given, in particular, that criminal guilt supposes some kind of *mens rea* which only physical persons may have. It is therefore left, for the moment, to States' discretion whether under these instruments they introduce *either* criminal *or* administrative liability for legal persons, as long as such liability entails effective, proportionate and dissuasive sanctions or measures for the criminal offences committed within or by the corporation.

74. Principle 12 follows the path of the aforementioned legal instruments and invites member States to introduce corporate liability. This was considered crucial by the experts given organised crime's influence and dependence on corporate structures. What is required is to "ensure that legal persons can be held liable for offences linked to organised crime committed by them", and, as a consequence, appropriate sanctions are applied against them.

Tax or fiscal offences (Guiding Principle No. 13)

75. Governments have different policies regarding tax and fiscal offences, depending on a number of factors, such as the applicable tax-rates, law-abiding and tax-paying culture, legal provisions and enforcement policies, the need and ability of the government to collect taxes, etc. Governments usually regard tax offences as low-priority if tax-payers do pay voluntarily and as high-priority if they do not. Likewise, violations of tax and fiscal regulations are dealt with either under administrative law as minor offences if tax-payers don't need strong incentives, or under criminal law as more serious offences, if they do.

---

[26] See Convention on the protection of the environment through criminal law [ETS N° 172], Article 9

[27] See Criminal Law Convention on Corruption [ETS N° 173], Article 18.

[28] See Second protocol to the Convention on the Protection of the European Communities' financial interests, Council Act of 19 June 1997, 97/C 221/02, Article 4.

[29] See OECD Convention on Combating Bribery of Foreign Public Officials in International Business Transactions signed in Paris on 17 December 1997, Article 2.

76. Tax avoidance or tax evasion are typically individual offences as long as income taxes are concerned, but may turn into serious tax fraud if corporations engage in massive tax violations. In some cases, tax fraud may be directly linked to organised crime, which naturally evades taxes as far as its illegal revenues are concerned, but get increasingly involved in highly sophisticated VAT-carousels (organised VAT-fraud) as well. Professor Savona suggested[30] that EU-fraud, including VAT caroussels, had become attractive for organised crime and losses indicated that these were large-scale organised financial crimes. UCLAF Reports[31] confirm that assumption.

77. Principle 13 therefore invites Governments to pay special attention to those tax and fiscal offences, which though they seem low-priority violations, can be linked to organised criminal activity. Indicators of such a link could be the persons involved, irregularities with the legal entities involved (e.g. registered in under-regulated offshore centres), other illegal activities detected by law enforcement or intelligence agencies, for example money laundering, the scale of the evasion or fraud-offence, etc. These cases, which certainly require from tax authorities an "increased diligence" similar to that in the banking sector to detect laundering operations, should be taken seriously by governments and investigation should take place routinely. To enable an effective prosecution of such cases, obstacles to mutual legal assistance in this area should be eliminated. Furthermore, training programs should be provided to staff of the involved agencies on tax crime related mechanisms and modus operandi.

Financial investigations (Guiding Principle No. 14)

78. Police investigations usually focus on the material elements of crime, e.g. instruments and objects of crime, which can later be produced in evidence at court. Until relatively recently, there has been little attention given to the financial circumstances of the offender during criminal investigations and only if the crime directly involved assets or other financial means was there a seizure order issued for eventually confiscating those. Organised crime, given its fundamental objectives of making profit and gaining power, has an embedded feature of dealing with (dirty) money derived from its criminal activities, e.g. for laundering and re-investing it for further business or for personal consumption of criminals. Virtually every crime committed by organised criminal groups has some financial dimension, which – if properly investigated – may lead to other evidence of crime. Professor Levi and Lisa Osofsky described[32] a number of scenarios

---

[30] Trends of cross-border organised crime in the European Union, Paper presented at EUCOS Seminar (8-9 November 1999), page 11.

[31] European Commission, Protection of the financial interests of the Communities, Fight against fraud, Annual Reports 1996 –1999.

[32] Michal Levi & Lisa Osofsky : Investigating, seizing and confiscating the proceeds of crime, Home Office Police Research Group, Crime Detection and Prevention Series, Paper 61, London 1995, pages 14-15.

where financial investigations were useful in UK-based criminal investigations, including:

- Showing that between the date of the offence and the arrest, the offender spent the equivalent of one third of the proceeds of an armed robbery over and above his legitimate income;

- Ascertaining that large amounts of money had been deposited in a bank account, which had originated from drug trafficking. The offender was arrested and charged with supplying. He asserted that the funds had been accrued as a result of car dealing. Financial investigations rebutted this;

- Establishing income in excess of means, which was appropriate to the goods stolen in an enquiry into professional car theft;

- Linking drug traffickers to substantial amounts of drug proceeds on the basis of deal books and other evidence.

79. Professors van Duyne and Levi further stressed[33] that "the tackling of profit-directed (organised) crime-enterprises by means of the analysis and examination of their financial management (the flow of goods, payments and spendings) can be indicated by the broad concept of 'financial investigation'. This orientation to the 'crime-money connection' can serve several goals:

- Financial investigation can contribute to the generation of evidence against individuals under suspicion, like the payment for the acquisition of smuggling transports (boat, trucks), the payment of bribes or the money-flow versus the invoicing in cross-border VAT-frauds;

- In connection with this search for evidence, financial investigation can add value by establishing a data-base which can help to construct the suspected facilitating networks, including particular lawyers, accountants or seemingly legitimate investment companies which have so far escaped attention;

- It can strip the criminal of his ill-gotten assets and finance (directly or, more commonly such as in the UK, indirectly) the costs of the police investigation;

- Financial investigations can have an added value to the actual prosecuted crime enterprises by contributing to weaken or even disrupt the market network in which they are commercially situated.

---

[33] See Petrus C. van Duyne, Michael Levi – Criminal Financial Investigation, A strategic and tactical approach in the European dimension, doc. PC-CO (97) 15, pages 2 and 3.

80. The purpose of financial investigations, applied to the context of organised crime is, therefore, multiple: scrutinising the assets of suspected criminals to find out whether there is a relation to possible charges, unravelling the paper-trails in a labyrinth of money transactions in order to get a clear picture of the money flows and prove charges; and, ultimately, getting behind the money-flows and assets by uncovering the working and power relations of organised crime groups with a view to proving their existence and eliminating them. In addition, according to Professors van Duyne and Levi[34], the combination of those elements can and should go beyond the tactical objectives of a given investigation and used more for the strategic purpose of "mapping the criminal landscape or market-section in order to find the weak spots which can be used for subsequent investigation". These strategic financial investigations should embrace the basic criminal "acquisition market" (all illegal goods, commodities and services), the "financial processing market" - where crime proceeds are laundered - and the "precipitation of the crime-money", i.e. the markets where criminal investments are made (catering and hotel industry, real estate, etc.) and aim, ultimately, to "hamper the consolidation of the market position of crime-entrepreneurs and/or the acquisition of a sphere of influence or power in the upperworld".

81. The means of financial investigations are, primarily, gathering and analysis of financial intelligence on suspected criminals or corporations, usually before a formal investigation is started. This is increasingly handled by Financial Intelligence Units (FIUs) where money laundering offences are concerned, following disclosures from the financial sector. However, organised crime investigations often do not or cannot benefit from the analysis produced by FIUs, and often asset-investigations and laundering-investigations are carried out by different agencies. Frequently, these agencies ignore each other's investigations because at the stage of their investigations the connections between assets, criminals and laundering activities are not fully understood.

82. What is required by Principle 14 is to enable inter-connected financial investigations into the assets of organised crime, e.g. by using financial intelligence available at other agencies, and making these investigations a primary feature of *any* criminal investigation concerning organised crime. That means, in practical terms, that financial investigations should be undertaken into the assets and properties of any suspect as soon as there is indication of his/her involvement in organised crime or connected offences, e.g. corruption, fraud or laundering of proceeds. This would entail, in accordance with the powers held by the investigating agency, to lift bank secrecy for gaining access to bank information, gathering information from professionals, such financial intermediaries, lawyers, accountants, on the person's assets, investments, income, etc., with due respect to professional privileges.

---

[34] See footnote 35, op. cit., page 3.

83. It is recalled that Article 3 (Investigative and provisional measures) of the 1990 Laundering Convention requires from contracting parties to be able identify and trace property which is liable to confiscation and to prevent any dealing in, transfer or disposal of such property. Article 4 (Special investigative powers and techniques) further requires parties to the Convention to empower its courts or other competent authorities to order that bank, financial or commercial records be made available, e.g. for financial investigations. The explanatory report noted in this respect that in general bank secrecy does not constitute an obstacle to domestic criminal investigations or the taking of provisional measures in the member States of the Council of Europe, in particular when the lifting of bank secrecy is ordered by a judge, a Grand Jury, an investigating judge or a prosecutor. Principle 14 stresses that there should be quick legal mechanisms to lift bank secrecy for the purpose of financial investigations, but also mentions production orders, by which financial institutions or intermediaries could be compelled to produce financial records or statements. Such production orders were also mentioned, inter alia, by the 1990 Laundering Convention (Article 4, paragraph 2).

Confiscation and asset forfeiture (Guiding Principle No. 15)

84. Depriving organised crime of its financial potential, i.e. its means to corrupt, to buy legitimacy and to continue its criminal programme, is one of the few tested successful methods against organised crime. It has been used extensively in a few countries, such as Italy, the United States and Ireland, in the fight against criminal organisations and it is said[35] to have impacted on the target groups by disrupting their financial background. Principle 15 is based on this experience and aims at making the removal of organised crime assets an integral part of any anti-organised crime strategy. The simple philosophy of "hit the criminal where it hurts, in his pockets" is, unfortunately, not yet fully understood and used by all member states at present. It emerged during mutual evaluations carried out by the FATF or by the Council of Europe, both involving monitoring of compliance of domestic anti-laundering regimes with international standards, that many countries have old-fashioned confiscation provisions which can apply only in a limited number of cases, often at the trial court's discretion. Furthermore, some countries still regard confiscation as an accessory penalty, usually applicable if the offender is convicted and he/she has assets as a direct fruit of his/her criminal activity. This approach results sometimes in odd situations, for example when the offender gets convicted for money laundering but his/her assets remain intact or have to be returned after the trial because there is no sufficient evidence of its direct relationship to criminal activity. Principle 15 reminds member States of the fundamental objective of the 1990 Laundering convention, i.e. to enable nationally and internationally the confiscation of proceeds and instrumentalities of crime, in particular drug trafficking and other forms of organised or serious crime. It should be recalled that confiscation may not only concern the sources of wealth constituting illicit

---

[35] See footnote 24, op. cit. pages 18 – 20.

profits, but also those used or planned to be used in committing crimes. Therefore, any sources of wealth possessed by organised crime should be subject to confiscation, including businesses which provide material elements in the organisational-operational structure of an organised crime group, even if it is not possible to reconstruct its criminal origin. Criminal assets, even if intermingled with legitimate ones, should be subject to confiscation, along with instrumentalities and direct criminal proceeds. Only by being systematic, therefore automatic if the conditions are met, will confiscation become what it ought to be: a strategic weapon against the economic and financial background of organised crime and, ultimately, against its very existence.

85. Principle 15 does not only address confiscation but also those provisional measures which enable its undertaking: tracing, freezing and seizing assets. Again, reference is made to the various powers which countries need to introduce in conformity with this Principle, which follows the logic of Article 3 (and 11) of the 1990 Laundering Convention, e.g. restraint and attachment orders, monitoring and tracing orders, seizure or sequestration orders, etc.

Independent confiscation or forfeiture proceedings (Guiding Principle No. 16)

86. As it was pointed out above, confiscation is often considered an accessory penalty which supposes, notably, that the offender be convicted by a criminal court for a criminal offence. It has to be noted that such a traditional concept of confiscation, as implemented by certain member States, cannot be used effectively against organised criminal group members and their leaders. Investigations into organised criminal groups often lead to suspicions about the criminal origin of their wealth, based sometimes on tax data or lifestyle intelligence, but produce little evidence of their involvement in criminal activity.

87. What is proposed by Principle 16 is to cut off confiscation or forfeiture proceedings from the traditional trial proceedings focusing on the supposed offender's guilt and extend civil forfeiture powers. This means that member States should envisage establishing proceedings focusing on the assets to be confiscated/forfeited without necessarily requiring the suspected offender's conviction for a necessary condition of the final confiscation/forfeiture decision. Those countries which are familiar with "in rem" proceedings, could content themselves with some lower level of evidence (e.g. balance of probabilities) of the criminal origins of the assets in the absence of, or insufficient evidence for, criminal conviction of the owner. Other countries - which need a criminal conviction and do not recognise "in rem" proceedings - could introduce separate post-conviction proceedings for confiscation, in which all assets would be assumed to have originated from crime, and the convicted offender could also be required to prove that some or all have not. There is some experience with both systems in Europe, described by the IInd Best Practice Survey on the reversal of the burden of

proof in confiscation proceedings[36], being in all cases limited to serious organised crime cases, such as drug trafficking. The Principle does not require that member States' legislation place the burden of proof regarding the origin of the assets exclusively on the defendant, but it implies that the burden on the prosecution is mitigated, i.e. some information is required from the defendant as well concerning its assets.

88. Civil forfeiture, used as a strategic tool against organised crime is seldom used at present in Europe. As noted by the UK Government policy paper[37] on asset-forfeiture ("recovery of crime proceeds") "civil forfeiture is a significant extension in the powers available to the State to deal with the proceeds of crime. It can be expected to be viewed as controversial by some". There is, therefore, a careful balance to be struck between the civil rights of the individual and the need to ensure that the State has the tools to protect society from crime. Some countries, such as the US, Australia, Italy and Ireland have successfully implemented civil forfeiture legislations and those in the latter countries resisted, so far, challenges under domestic constitutional and European human rights norms[38]. The Irish system seems to be a good model for other countries, in terms of effectiveness and balance with human rights concerns.

Witness protection (Guiding Principles Nos. 17 - 18)

89. Over the past 10-15 years the question of witness-protection has become a major concern for the justice systems of many countries in Europe. This special attention towards witnesses can be related to several different factors. First of all, a noticeable rise in the criminal activities of terrorist and organised crime groups could be registered during this period at both European level and worldwide. These groups increasingly attempt to corrupt and even destroy the normal functioning of the criminal justice system by all possible means, including threats of violence or bribery of justice officials and the systematic intimidation or elimination of witnesses. The protection of witnesses and of their relatives thus became a necessity going beyond the personal interests of the individuals and becoming a duty of public authorities in order to ensure the integrity and effectiveness of criminal justice.

90. Principles 17 and 18 address the question of protecting witnesses or collaborators of justice who accept to provide information or to give testimony in court against organised crime. The measures proposed by these two Principles are identical to those developed in detail by Recommendation No. R (97) 13 on the intimidation of witnesses and the rights of the defence. As this Recommendation observed, "the need to protect witnesses against intimidation has arisen in connection with terrorism,

---

[36] See "Best Practice Survey" No. 2 – Reversal of the burden of proof in confiscation of proceeds of crime – doc. PC-S-CO (2000) 8.

[37] See footnote 22, op.cit. pages 35-36.

[38] See footnote 37, op.cit. pages 8 – 11.

organised crime, drug related crime, crime amongst closed minority groups and violence within the family. Detection of these kinds of crime is often based on the testimony of persons who are closely connected with the organisation, the gang, the group or the family. Such persons are therefore more vulnerable than others to easy intimidation in order to deter them from giving evidence for the prosecution or from answering questions leading to the conviction of the accused. Intimidation and/or threats may be directly exercised either upon the witness or upon his family. Where there are reasonable grounds to believe that a witness may become the victim of an offence against his life, his health or his freedom, the public authorities e.g. the police, should be obliged to inform him of his position and to take appropriate protective measures as required by the situation. This might mean that criminal proceedings will have to be adapted in order to adequately protect witnesses. Here a balance must be found between the rights of the defence and protecting the safety of witnesses and their families. Special protective measures such as disguising the witness, changing his identity, giving him a new job or moving him should be considered."[39]

91. Taking into account both the seriousness of the crimes committed by and the power of intimidation of organised crime groups, it is recommended that States should adopt specific rules of procedure to cope with problems of witness intimidation when devising measures against organised crime. States are recommended, for example, to consider the opportunity or necessity of keeping the personal data and whereabouts of witnesses secret from the defendant or enlarging the admissibility of pre-trial statements. Some States do already have provisions on anonymous witnesses and/or provisions which allow technical measures to make the identification of witnesses more difficult (e.g. Italy, Germany). In the case where anonymity cannot be granted, or is not sufficient to protect the witness, a range of other measures could be envisaged under Principle 18, such giving testimony via telecommunication links, limiting the disclosure of their addresses and other identifying particulars, enlarging the use of pre-trial statements and temporarily relocating witnesses who are in custody. These measures could also require other protective measures that make the identification of the witness by the defence difficult or impossible e.g. by disguising his face or distorting his voice, either while present in the courtroom or by means of audio-visual link. Such hearing via a video-link can offer a number of advantages, in terms of lowering the risk and also costs of protection. These measures should not be seen as disproportionate and should be granted by the court, taking into account the rights of the defence. These measures may also be admissible for countries experiencing constitutional or other difficulties in introducing measures permitting anonymous testimonies in a strict sense.

92. Finally, Principle 17 envisages full witness protection programmes for long-term protection. Witness protection programmes, or crown-witness schemes, apply to witnesses and collaborators of justice who need protection beyond the criminal trial and may last for a limited period or for life. Such

---

[39] See Recommendation No R (97) 13 concerning intimidation of witnesses and the rights of the defence, page 13.

programmes exist in a number of countries, such as Italy, the United States, Canada, Turkey (related to terrorism acts only) and the United Kingdom. It is recalled that a detailed analysis of the organisation and practical functioning of witness protection programmes was contained in the Ist Best Practice Survey on Witness Protection Programmes[40], produced by Committee PC-CO, on the basis of the practical experiences of three Council of Europe member States.

Special investigating techniques (Guiding Principle No. 19)

93. Organised crime evolves over time, as do the societies in which it operates. Yesterday's legendary "men of honour", led by a respectable Godfather, today run multiple billion dollar businesses in a series of criminal markets and their vulnerability to traditional law enforcement methods seems to have shrunk over the years. As a result, traditional street-level policing strategies have proved too limited in their reach. Controlling organised crime requires methods which are necessarily more intrusive than the traditional ones and law enforcement experience in many countries suggests that in order to strengthen investigative capabilities, reduce time needed for building a strong case and gather reliable evidence, it is necessary to rely on information obtained by means of electronic surveillance and interception of telecommunications[41], undercover (sting) operations and covert agents, informants, pentiti ("reformed" or "co-operating" criminals), controlled delivery of drugs or money. Although there is a general agreement among countries concerning the need to empower law enforcement agencies to use such investigative methods in the fight against organised crime, a number of differences appear in their practical implementation[42], in particular as regards undercover operations, controlled delivery and electronic surveillance. It is important to note that all Council of Europe member States which ⬜ uthorize by law or in practice the use of these methods had, at some stage, to resolve the difficult question of striking a balance between the potential benefits of intrusive powers for law enforcement versus the protection of civil rights, including privacy. One will remember that the European Convention on Human Rights authorizes intrusions into privacy (Article 8) under the conditions that the use of powers such as telephone interception is necessary in a democratic society in the interests of e.g. national security or prevention of crime, that is carried out in accordance with the law and is proportionate to the circumstances invoked by the authorities to justify its use.

94. There is a growing list of international instruments calling for the use of special investigative techniques against organised crime or its component

---

[40] Best Practice Survey No. 1 – Witness protection programmes, Council of Europe 1999.

[41] See Best Practice Survey No. 3 – Report on Interception of Communications and Intrusive Surveillance – Council of Europe 2000.

[42] See for a detailed analysis on the various powers used in Council of Europe member States – Report on the organised crime situation in Council of Europe member States – 1997, pages 41 – 45.

crimes, e.g. money laundering or corruption. Recommendation 36 of the FATF's forty recommendations identified controlled delivery of funds as "one valid and effective investigative technique" in relation to assets known or suspected to the proceeds of crime and strongly recommended its use in domestic and cross-border money laundering investigations. Article 11 of the 1988 United Nations Convention against illicit traffic in narcotic drugs and psychotropic substances also suggested using controlled delivery in investigations into drug trafficking and related money laundering offences, whereas Article 4, paragraph 2 of the 1990 Council of Europe Laundering Convention [ETS No. 141] invited countries to consider introducing "special investigating techniques facilitating the identification and tracing of proceeds and the gathering of evidence related thereto." Special techniques explicitly mentioned by the Convention were monitoring orders, observation, interception of telecommunications, access to computer systems and orders to produce specific documents. Article 23 of the Criminal Law Convention on Corruption [ETS No. 173] imposed an obligation on parties to adopt measures permitting the use special investigative techniques in order to facilitate the gathering of evidence related to corruption offences defined by the Convention.

95. Principle 19 is based on the widely accepted idea that organised criminal groups are secretive and closed, therefore difficult to penetrate. It recommends Governments to introduce investigative measures that would enable law enforcement agencies to gain insight into the activities of such groups, by using surveillance, interception of communications, undercover operations, controlled deliveries and informants. Some of these techniques have long been restricted to the investigation of most serious offences, such as terrorism or mafia-type murders, but nowadays their use is usually authorised, under specific conditions, in organised crime-linked investigations, e.g. in drug trafficking cases. Principle 19 invites Governments to make full use of them for penetrating organised crime groups and gathering evidence of their activities, for the purpose of criminal investigations. They need to be used, naturally, with due respect for civil rights and under judicial or other effective control. The use of technology-dependent techniques, e.g. interception of communications or electronic surveillance, requires appropriate equipment, for example interception and decryption devices.

Pro-active policing methods (Guiding Principle No. 20)

96. As it was pointed out above, organised crime should be dealt with by the police in a different way then traditional forms of serious crimes. With crimes such as fraud and drugs trafficking, usually no complaint is made by an actual victim. Forensic evidence (such as bloodstains and fingerprints) is seldom to be found, partly because the crime is not committed in one specific location and at a specific time. This makes it particularly difficult to find substantial evidence or even to find clues which provide a sufficient basis for suspicion within the meaning of the national criminal procedures In combating serious and organised crime a (more) pro-active strategy is

needed. This strategy differs from the traditional way of investigative work, which can be characterised as reactive. Traditionally, detectives concentrate on reported offences and apply routine techniques such as the examination of the scene of the crime in search for forensic evidence, the questioning of witnesses and the interviewing of suspects.

97. In pro-active investigations, detectives focus their attention upon the current behaviour of people thought to be involved in crime and less upon past offences. The investigators listen to rumours in the criminal circuit, and base their actions (using informers, tapping telephones, keeping individuals under surveillance) on these. The focus is less on the gathering of evidence and more on finding clues. This strategy is therefore sometimes called "intelligence-led investigation", as some techniques used in pro-active policing directly come from the arsenal of intelligence (security) agencies. The aim of pro-active investigation is to find out how a criminal organisation is structured, what criminal activities are planned, where they (will) take place, etc. Because of the circumstance that organised criminal groups usually maintain secrecy about their plans and activities and there is a pattern of criminal activities carried out by more then one individual on several locations at different points in time, an extra effort is needed on behalf of law enforcement bodies in order to be able to track, trace and prosecute the individuals involved. The use of strategic intelligence, provided by criminal or financial intelligence units, and crime analysis are primary tools in such pro-active investigations. Apart from criminologists and crime-analysts, they suppose the involvement of analysts from the economic sector (e.g. in macro-economics, market-analysis), intelligence agencies and social sciences (sociologists).

98. Since information is not only gathered on suspects but also on individuals whose involvement in the criminal activities is not (yet) clear, extra attention should be given to the protection of human rights, especially to the right of privacy. Procedural or other guarantees are required to ensure that pro-active investigative methods are applied only when there are clear indications of serious or organised crime being planned or committed.

Inter-agency teams (Guiding Principle No. 21)

99. In most jurisdictions, organised crime may be investigated by a range of different law enforcement agencies, principally because they don't know that their investigations are linked to organised crime. One agency or its criminal investigation department may be dealing with a murder-case, another with corruption of public officials and yet another agency with tax evasion. In such (not so hypothetical) multiple crime cases, it may turn out, eventually, that the murder was committed by contract for someone who wished to take control over some legal or illegal business and had to bribe an official to get licences and evaded paying taxes to avoid detection. The person, in some countries, would be likely to be convicted – if ever caught – for 3 separate offences and it would hardly come to light that these were linked one with the other. In addition, there would be no trace of "organised crime" in

criminal statistics. No co-ordination and no centralisation of offender-related data: these are the primary causes of failures in investigations into organised crime.

100. Another closely related issue is that some countries have many law enforcement agencies - such as the Carabinieri, Guardia di Finanza, Polizia di Stato etc. in Italy – which may all be involved in the investigation of organised or economic crime. They often have special knowledge in a specific area, but their competences may never-the-less overlap. It is not pure fiction that sometimes these agencies fight each other rather than crime and their internal feuds lead to total inefficiency in a given area. Division of tasks and specialisation are therefore as important as co-ordination. Although some Council of Europe member States do not seem to have specialised units to investigate organised crime cases, where resources so permit, there may be value in the creation of one or more (central and regional) multidisciplinary units exclusively or specifically dedicated to the investigation of organised criminal groups, e.g. in the areas of drug trafficking, money laundering and grand corruption.

101. The seeting up of specialised multidisciplinary teams is therefore recommended by Principle 21. Such multidisciplinary work implies close co-ordination, regular communication and sharing of knowledge between the various agencies in the investigation of economic and organised crime to enhance the effectiveness of such investigations. The creation of a centralised data-base containing crime-, offender-, victim- and assets-related data, with nation-wide access by local or regional units, could also improve the management of organised crime investigations by the criminal justice system as a whole.

Principles related to International Co-operation

(Guiding principles Nos. 22 - 25)

102. The liberalisation of trade and capital investment, the scientific and technological revolution, the emergence of world-wide communication networks, increased mobility, the dismantlement of national borders within certain regions and the creation of supranational spaces where persons, goods and services move freely, all positive elements of modern life as they certainly appear to be, are also factors that criminal organisations do not hesitate to exploit to their own benefit. Not so long ago criminal justice was, almost exclusively a national problem. Nowadays, any criminal policy which were not to take full account of the organised, trans-national elements of criminality would be bound to fail. States which intend to successfully combat organised crime have to co-operate, have to share experiences and have to put together their findings and means. International co-operation is, therefore, a key condition to any national policy's success against organised crime. There is growing awareness about this in the international community. The number of bilateral and multilateral agreements on crime, e.g. money laundering, corruption, terrorism etc. or on various forms of international

assistance are evidence of this tendency. Yet, States seem to have been much too slow, certainly slower than criminals, to adapt their law enforcement strategies to the international framework in which modern organised crime is evolving.

103. Principles 22 – 25 mention but a few ideas that States ought to consider if they want to make international co-operation more effective. The following issues are addressed:

- Exchange of information on legal entities: national investigations related to fraud, corruption, money laundering – whether committed by organised crime or not - are often hampered by a lack of information on foreign corporations and other legal entities that seem to have been involved in the facilitating or concealing of a transaction. Principle 22 invites governments to take measures to enable legally and practically such exchange of information across borders, including information about their creation, ownership, direction and funding;

- Asset-sharing agreements: assets confiscated by certain countries often remain there even if they originated from overseas; usually these criminal assets have no other reason of being there other than that of the protection offered by the country's bank secrecy of client-confidentiality regime and confiscation is undertaken on behalf of foreign authorities, on the basis of foreign evidence. Notwithstanding the cases in which such confiscated assets are eventually returned to the country from which they originated, a sadly rare scenario today, it appears that in the majority of large international confiscations, there is no reward for a country which investigates the underlying crime and locates the assets because the confiscating country takes it all upon successful confiscation. Though certain bilateral treaties of memoranda of understanding do exist between some European and North-American jurisdictions, the lack of a multilateral asset-sharing agreements is still a serious impediment for international asset-investigations (which are usually rather costly). Principle 23 therefore invites countries to share the confiscated assets among those jurisdictions which contributed to the confiscation by taking some measures, such as tracing or freezing the assets subject to confiscation;

- Implementing witness protection programmes across borders: in small countries it is virtually impossible to hide persons from organised crime groups. If small countries want persons placed in witness protection programmes to be effectively protected they often need to transfer them to another country. This requires close co-operation, considerable trust and burden-sharing between the requested (receiving) and requesting (sending) countries. So far, this kind of co-operation is not explicitly covered by any international treaty on mutual assistance but the need to create at the level of the Council of Europe such an instrument has been recognised, first by Recommendation N° R (97)13 (item 30) and the Ist Best Practice Survey;

-   Ratifying and implementing international legal instruments of judicial co-operation: Principle 25 gives a number of ideas on how to improve international co-operation in the investigation and prosecution of organised crime, in particular by pointing to possible legal or structural obstacles to co-operation, calling for innovative and constructive co-operation channels and inviting governments to further speed up and rationalise communication between authorities or persons called upon to co-operate. A list of the relevant Council of Europe treaties, which member States should ratify, is appended to the Recommendation.

Principles relating to Data Collection, Research and Training

Data collection (Guiding Principle No. 26)

104. Guiding Principle 26 is based on the realisation that in the absence of a systematic collection and analysis of data related to organised crime, the planning and implementation of national anti-organised crime strategies respond less to the crime situation than to policy objectives. These two elements are, ideally, linked one with the other.

105. It has become clear in the elaboration of PC-CO's annual organised crime reports, that most member States do not have a specific system of data collection in this area and that their general criminal statistics are unable to provide certain types of information required for such annual reports. Principle 26 therefore recognises the need for organised crime-specific data collection, provides some specific criteria for such data-collection (e.g. geographical scope of groups, their organisation, financial background, connections with foreign groups, etc.) and recommends that these be used for analysing organised crime. In addition, it recommends that national systems of data collection and criminal statitistics take into account the specific features of organised crime (see paragraphs 52 and 53) and be properly resourced and staffed.

Research (Guiding Principle No. 27)

106. Guiding Principle 27 supplements the previous one and aims at enhancing research capacities, whether private or public, on organised crime. It invites governments to support institutions, for example universities, foundations or public bodies (police academies), carrying out research in this area. Such support may be funding, but also granting access to files and data relevant for the research activity.

Training (Guiding Principle No. 28)

107. This Principle is a recognition of the fact that new methods usually don't work if people who are supposed to implement them are not familiar with or committed to them. This is particularly true if the new methods, such as financial investigations or pro-active policing, require additional skills, i.e. in accounting, auditing, which are not necessarily accessible to all agents across the law enforcement sector through initial training. Principle 29 therefore invites governments to provide all law enforcement agencies and, where appropriate, personnel of judicial or prosecution bodies, with training on these new investigative methods, both in theory and practice. Training should be both initial and permanent, depending on the nature of the investigating method (interception techniques for example do change over time).

Guidelines of the Committee of Ministers of the Council of Europe on Human Rights and the Fight against Terrorism (2002)

adopted by the Committee of Ministers on 11 July 2002 at the 804th meeting of the Ministers' Deputies

Preamble

The Committee of Ministers,

[a] Considering that terrorism seriously jeopardises human rights, threatens democracy, and aims notably to destabilise legitimately constituted governments and to undermine pluralistic civil society;

[b] Unequivocally condemning all acts, methods and practices of terrorism as criminal and unjustifiable, wherever and by whomever committed;

[c] Recalling that a terrorist act can never be excused or justified by citing motives such as human rights and that the abuse of rights is never protected;

[d] Recalling that it is not only possible, but also absolutely necessary, to fight terrorism while respecting human rights, the rule of law and, where applicable, international humanitarian law;

[e] Recalling the need for States to do everything possible, and notably to co-operate, so that the suspected perpetrators, organisers and sponsors of terrorist acts are brought to justice to answer for all the consequences, in particular criminal and civil, of their acts;

[f] Reaffirming the imperative duty of States to protect their populations against possible terrorist acts;

[g] Recalling the necessity for states, notably for reasons of equity and social solidarity, to ensure that victims of terrorist acts can obtain compensation;

[h] Keeping in mind that the fight against terrorism implies long-term measures with a view to preventing the causes of terrorism, by promoting, in particular, cohesion in our societies and a multicultural and inter-religious dialogue;

[i] Reaffirming States' obligation to respect, in their fight against terrorism, the international instruments for the protection of human rights and, for the member states in particular, the Convention for the Protection of Human Rights and Fundamental Freedoms and the case-law of the European Court of Human Rights;

adopts the following guidelines and invites member States to ensure that they are widely disseminated among all authorities responsible for the fight against terrorism.

I. States' obligation to protect everyone against terrorism

States are under the obligation to take the measures needed to protect the fundamental rights of everyone within their jurisdiction against terrorist acts, especially the right to life. This positive obligation fully justifies States' fight against terrorism in accordance with the present guidelines.

II. Prohibition of arbitrariness

All measures taken by States to fight terrorism must respect human rights and the principle of the rule of law, while excluding any form of arbitrariness, as well as any discriminatory or racist treatment, and must be subject to appropriate supervision.

III. Lawfulness of anti-terrorist measures

1. All measures taken by States to combat terrorism must be lawful.

2. When a measure restricts human rights, restrictions must be defined as precisely as possible and be necessary and proportionate to the aim pursued.

IV. Absolute prohibition of torture

The use of torture or of inhuman or degrading treatment or punishment is absolutely prohibited, in all circumstances, and in particular during the arrest, questioning and detention of a person suspected of or convicted of terrorist activities, irrespective of the nature of the acts that the person is suspected of or for which he/she was convicted.

V. Collection and processing of personal data by any competent authority in the field of State security

Within the context of the fight against terrorism, the collection and the processing of personal data by any competent authority in the field of State security may interfere with the respect for private life only if such collection and processing, in particular:

(i) are governed by appropriate provisions of domestic law;

(ii) are proportionate to the aim for which the collection and the processing were foreseen;

(iii) may be subject to supervision by an external independent authority.

VI. Measures which interfere with privacy

1. Measures used in the fight against terrorism that interfere with privacy (in particular body searches, house searches, bugging, telephone tapping,

surveillance of correspondence and use of undercover agents) must be provided for by law. It must be possible to challenge the lawfulness of these measures before a court.

2.   Measures taken to fight terrorism must be planned and controlled by the authorities so as to minimise, to the greatest extent possible, recourse to lethal force and, within this framework, the use of arms by the security forces must be strictly proportionate to the aim of protecting persons against unlawful violence or to the necessity of carrying out a lawful arrest.

VII. Arrest and police custody

1.   A person suspected of terrorist activities may only be arrested if there are reasonable suspicions. He/she must be informed of the reasons for the arrest.

2.   A person arrested or detained for terrorist activities shall be brought promptly before a judge. Police custody shall be of a reasonable period of time, the length of which must be provided for by law.

3.   A person arrested or detained for terrorist activities must be able to challenge the lawfulness of his/her arrest and of his/her police custody before a court.

VIII. Regular supervision of pre-trial detention

A person suspected of terrorist activities and detained pending trial is entitled to regular supervision of the lawfulness of his or her detention by a court.

IX. Legal proceedings

1.   A person accused of terrorist activities has the right to a fair hearing, within a reasonable time, by an independent, impartial tribunal established by law.

2.   A person accused of terrorist activities benefits from the presumption of innocence.

3.   The imperatives of the fight against terrorism may nevertheless justify certain restrictions to the right of defence, in particular with regard to:

(i)   the arrangements for access to and contacts with counsel;

(ii)   the arrangements for access to the case-file;

(iii)   the use of anonymous testimony.

4.   Such restrictions to the right of defence must be strictly proportionate to their purpose, and compensatory measures to protect the interests of the

accused must be taken so as to maintain the fairness of the proceedings and to ensure that procedural rights are not drained of their substance.

X.   Penalties incurred

1.   The penalties incurred by a person accused of terrorist activities must be provided for by law for any action or omission which constituted a criminal offence at the time when it was committed; no heavier penalty may be imposed than the one that was applicable at the time when the criminal offence was committed.

2.   Under no circumstances may a person convicted of terrorist activities be sentenced to the death penalty; in the event of such a sentence being imposed, it may not be carried out.

XI.   Detention

1.   A person deprived of his/her liberty for terrorist activities must in all circumstances be treated with due respect for human dignity.

2.   The imperatives of the fight against terrorism may nevertheless require that a person deprived of his/her liberty for terrorist activities be submitted to more severe restrictions than those applied to other prisoners, in particular with regard to:

(i)   the regulations concerning communications and surveillance of correspondence, including that between counsel and his/her client;

(ii)   placing persons deprived of their liberty for terrorist activities in specially secured quarters;

(iii) the separation of such persons within a prison or among different prisons,

on condition that the measure taken is proportionate to the aim to be achieved.

XII. Asylum, return ("refoulement") and expulsion

1.   All requests for asylum must be dealt with on an individual basis. An effective remedy must lie against the decision taken. However, when the State has serious grounds to believe that the person who seeks to be granted asylum has participated in terrorist activities, refugee status must be refused to that person.

2.   It is the duty of a State that has received a request for asylum to ensure that the possible return ("*refoulement*") of the applicant to his/her country of origin or to another country will not expose him/her to the death penalty, to torture or to inhuman or degrading treatment or punishment. The same applies to expulsion.

3.   Collective expulsion of aliens is prohibited.

4.   In all cases, the enforcement of the expulsion or return ("*refoulement*") order must be carried out with respect for the physical integrity and for the dignity of the person concerned, avoiding any inhuman or degrading treatment.

XIII. Extradition

1.   Extradition is an essential procedure for effective international co-operation in the fight against terrorism.

2.   The extradition of a person to a country where he/she risks being sentenced to the death penalty may not be granted. A requested State may however grant an extradition if it has obtained adequate guarantees that:

(i)   the person whose extradition has been requested will not be sentenced to death; or

(ii)   in the event of such a sentence being imposed, it will not be carried out.

3.   Extradition may not be granted when there is serious reason to believe that:

(i)   the person whose extradition has been requested will be subjected to torture or to inhuman or degrading treatment or punishment;

(ii)   the extradition request has been made for the purpose of prosecuting or punishing a person on account of his/her race, religion, nationality or political opinions, or that that person's position risks being prejudiced for any of these reasons.

4.   When the person whose extradition has been requested makes out an arguable case that he/she has suffered or risks suffering a flagrant denial of justice in the requesting State, the requested State must consider the well-foundedness of that argument before deciding whether to grant extradition.

XIV. Right to property

The use of the property of persons or organisations suspected of terrorist activities may be suspended or limited, notably by such measures as freezing orders or seizures, by the relevant authorities. The owners of the property have the possibility to challenge the lawfulness of such a decision before a court.

XV. Possible derogations

1.   When the fight against terrorism takes place in a situation of war or public emergency which threatens the life of the nation, a State may adopt measures temporarily derogating from certain obligations ensuing from the international instruments of protection of human rights, to the extent strictly required by the exigencies of the situation, as well as within the limits and under the conditions fixed by international law. The State must notify the competent authorities of the adoption of such measures in accordance with the relevant international instruments.

2.   States may never, however, and whatever the acts of the person suspected of terrorist activities, or convicted of such activities, derogate from the right to life as guaranteed by these international instruments, from the prohibition against torture or inhuman or degrading treatment or punishment, from the principle of legality of sentences and of measures, nor from the ban on the retrospective effect of criminal law.

3.   The circumstances which led to the adoption of such derogations need to be reassessed on a regular basis with the purpose of lifting these derogations as soon as these circumstances no longer exist.

XVI. Respect for peremptory norms of international law and for international humanitarian law

In their fight against terrorism, States may never act in breach of peremptory norms of international law nor in breach of international humanitarian law, where applicable.

XVII. Compensation for victims of terrorist acts

When compensation is not fully available from other sources, in particular through the confiscation of the property of the perpetrators, organisers and sponsors of terrorist acts, the State must contribute to the compensation of the victims of attacks that took place on its territory, as far as their person or their health is concerned.

Texts of reference
used for the preparation of the guidelines
on human rights and the fight against terrorism

Preliminary Note:

This document was prepared by the Secretariat, in co-operation with the Chairman of the Group of Specialists on Human Rights and the Fight against Terrorism (DH-S-TER). It is not meant to be taken as an explanatory report or memorandum of the guidelines.

Aim of the guidelines

1. The guidelines concentrate mainly on the limits to be considered and that States should not go beyond, under any circumstances, in their legitimate fight against terrorism.[1] [2] The main objective of these guidelines is not to deal with other important questions such as the causes and consequences of terrorism or measures which might prevent it, which are nevertheless mentioned in the Preamble to provide a background[3].

Legal basis

2. The specific situation of States parties to the European Convention on Human Rights ("the Convention") should be recalled: its Article 46 sets out the compulsory jurisdiction of the European Court of Human Rights ("the Court") and the supervision of the execution of its judgments by the Committee of Ministers). The Convention and the case-law of the Court are thus a primary source for defining guidelines for the fight against terrorism. Other sources such as the UN Covenant on Civil and Political Rights and the observations of the UN Human Rights Committee should however also be mentioned.

---

[1] The Group of Specialists on Democratic Strategies for dealing with Movements threatening Human Rights (DH-S-DEM) has not failed to confirm the well-foundedness of this approach : "*On the one hand, it is necessary for a democratic society to take certain measures of a preventative or repressive nature to protect itself against threats to the very values and principles on which that society is based. On the other hand, public authorities (the legislature, the courts, the administrative authorities) are under a legal obligation, also when taking measures in this area, to respect the human rights and fundamental freedoms set out in the European Convention on Human Rights and other instruments to which the member States are bound*". See document DH-S-DEM (99) 4 Addendum, para. 16.

[2] The European Court of Human Rights has also supported this approach: "*The Contracting States enjoy an unlimited discretion to subject persons within their jurisdiction to secret surveillance. The Court, being aware of the danger such a law poses of undermining or even destroying democracy on the ground of defending it, affirms that the Contracting States may not, in the name of the struggle against espionage and terrorism, adopt whatever measures they deem appropriate*", Klass and Others v. Germany, 6 September 1978, Series A n° 28, para. 49.

[3] See below paras. 8-12.

General considerations

3.   The Court underlined on several occasions the balance between, on one hand, the defence of the institutions and of democracy, for the common interest, and, on the other hand, the protection of individual rights: "*The Court agrees with the Commission that some compromise between the requirements for defending democratic society and individual rights is inherent in the system of the Convention*"[4].

4.   The Court also takes into account the specificities linked to an effective fight against terrorism: "*The Court is prepared to take into account the background to the cases submitted to it, particularly problems linked to the prevention of terrorism*"[5].

5.   Definition - Neither the Convention nor the case-law of the Court give a definition of terrorism. The Court always preferred to adopt a case by case approach. For its part, the Parliamentary Assembly "*considers an act of terrorism to be 'any offence committed by individuals or groups resorting to violence or threatening to use violence against a country, its institutions, its population in general or specific individuals which, being motivated by separatist aspirations, extremist ideological conceptions, fanaticism or irrational and subjective factors, is intended to create a climate of terror among official authorities, certain individuals or groups in society, or the general public*"[6].

6.   Article 1 of the European Council Common Position of 27 December 2001 on the application of specific measures to combat terrorism gives a very precise definition of "terrorist act" that states:

"3.   For the purposes of this Common Position, "terrorist act" shall mean one of the following intentional acts, which, given its nature or its context, may seriously damage a country or an international organisation, as defined as an offence under national law, where committed with the aims of:

i.   seriously intimidating a population, or

---

[4] *Klass and Others v. Germany*, 6 September 1978, A n° 28, para. 59. See also *Brogan and Others v. United Kingdom*, 29 November 1999, A n° 145-B, para. 48.

[5] *Incal v. Turkey*, 9 June 1998, para. 58. See also the cases *Ireland v. United Kingdom*, 18 January 1978, A n° 25, paras. 11 and following, *Aksoy v. Turkey*, 18 December 1996, paras. 70 and 84; *Zana v. Turkey*, 25 November 1997, paras. 59-60; and, *United Communist Party of Turkey and Others v. Turkey*, 30 November 1998, para. 59.

[6] Recommendation 1426 (1999), *European democracies facing up to terrorism* (23 September 1999), para. 5.

ii.   unduly compelling a government or an international organisation to perform or abstain from performing any act, or

iii.   seriously destabilising or destroying the fundamental political, constitutional, economic or social structures of a country or an international organisation:

   a.   attacks upon a person's life which may cause death;

   b.   attacks upon the physical integrity of a person;

   c.   kidnapping or hostage-taking;

   d.   causing extensive destruction to a government or public facility, a transport system, an infrastructure facility, including an information system, a fixed platform located on the continental shelf, a public place or private property, likely to endanger human life or result in major economic loss;

   e.   seizure of aircraft, ships or other means of public or goods transport;

   f.   manufacture, possession, acquisition, transport, supply or use of weapons, explosives or of nuclear, biological or chemical weapons, as well as research into, and development of, biological and chemical weapons;

   g.   release of dangerous substances, or causing fires, explosions or floods the effect of which is to endanger human life;

   h.   interfering with or disrupting the supply of water, power or any other fundamental natural resource, the effect of which is to endanger human life;

   i.   threatening to commit any of the acts listed under (a) to (h);

   j.   directing a terrorist group;

   k.   participating in the activities of a terrorist group, including by supplying information or material resources, or by funding its activities in any way, which knowledge of the fact that such participation will contribute to the criminal activities of the group.

For the purposes of this paragraph, "terrorist group" shall mean a structured group of more than two persons, established over a period of time and acting in concert to commit terrorist acts. "Structured group" means a group that is not randomly formed for the immediate commission of a terrorist act and that does not need to have formally defined roles for its members, continuity of its membership or a developed structure."

7.   The work in process within the United Nations on the draft general convention on international terrorism also seeks to define terrorism or a terrorist act.

*   *   *

Preamble

The Committee of Ministers,

[a.] Considering that terrorism seriously jeopardises human rights, threatens democracy, and aims notably to destabilise legitimately constituted governments and to undermine pluralistic civil society;

8.   The General Assembly of the United Nations recognises that terrorist acts are "*activities aimed at the destruction of human rights, fundamental freedoms and democracy, threatening the territorial integrity and security of States, destabilizing legitimately constituted Governments, undermining pluralistic civil society and having adverse consequences for the economic and social development of States*"[7].

[b.] Unequivocally condemning all acts, methods and practices of terrorism as criminal and unjustifiable, wherever and by whomever committed;

[c.] Recalling that a terrorist act can never be excused or justified by citing motives such as human rights and that the abuse of rights is never protected;

[d.] Recalling that it is not only possible, but also absolutely necessary, to fight terrorism while respecting human rights, the rule of law and, where applicable, international humanitarian law;

[e.] Recalling the need for States to do everything possible, and notably to co-operate, so that the suspected perpetrators, organisers and sponsors of terrorist acts are brought to justice to

---

[7] Resolution 54/164, *Human Rights and terrorism*, adopted by the General Assembly, 17 December 1999.

answer for all the consequences, in particular criminal and civil, of their acts;

9. The obligation to bring to justice suspected perpetrators, organisers and sponsors of terrorist acts is clearly indicated in different texts such as Resolution 1368 (2001) adopted by the Security Council at its 4370th meeting, on 12 September 2001 (extracts): *"The Security Council, (...) Reaffirming, the principles and purposes of the Charter of the United Nations, (...) 3. Calls on all States to work together urgently to bring to justice the perpetrators, organizers and sponsors of these terrorist attacks (...)"*. Resolution 56/1, *Condemnation of terrorist attacks in the United States of America*, adopted by the General Assembly, on 12 September 2001 (extracts): *"The General Assembly, Guided by the purposes and principles of the Charter of the United Nations, (...) 3. Urgently calls for international co-operation to bring to justice the perpetrators, organizers and sponsors of the outrages of 11 September"*.

[f.] Reaffirming the imperative duty of States to protect their populations against possible terrorist acts;

10. Committee of Ministers has stressed *"the duty of any democratic State to ensure effective protection against terrorism, respecting the rule of law and human rights (...)"*[8].

[g.] Recalling the necessity for States, notably for reasons of equity and social solidarity, to ensure that victims of terrorist acts can obtain compensation;

[h.] Keeping in mind that the fight against terrorism implies long-term measures with a view to preventing the causes of terrorism, by promoting, in particular, cohesion in our societies and a multicultural and inter-religious dialogue;

11. It is essential to fight against the causes of terrorism in order to prevent new terrorist acts. In this regard, one may recall Resolution 1258 (2001) of the Parliamentary Assembly, *Democracies facing terrorism* (26 September 2001), in which the Assembly calls upon States to *"renew and generously resource their commitment to pursue economic, social and political policies designed to secure democracy, justice, human rights and well-being for all people throughout the world"* (17 (viii)).

12. In order to fight against the causes of terrorism, it is also essential to promote multicultural and inter-religious dialogue. The Parliamentary Assembly has devoted a number of important documents to this issue, among which its Recommendations 1162 (1991) *Contribution of the Islamic*

---

[8] Interim resolution DH (99) 434, *Human Rights action of the security forces in Turkey: Measures of a general character.*

civilisation to European culture[9], 1202 (1993) *Religious tolerance in a democratic society*[10], 1396 (1999) *Religion and democracy*[11], 1426 (1999) *European democracies facing up terrorism*[12], as well as its Resolution 1258 (2001), *Democracies facing terrorism*[13]. The Secretary General of the Council of Europe has also highlighted the importance of multicultural and inter-religious dialogue in the long-term fight against terrorism[14].

[i.] Reaffirming States' obligation to respect, in their fight against terrorism, the international instruments for the protection of human rights and, for the member States in particular, the Convention for the Protection of Human Rights and Fundamental Freedoms and the case-law of the European Court of Human Rights;

---

[9] Adopted on 19 September 1991 (11th sitting). The Assembly, inter alia, proposed preventive measures in the field of education (such as the creation of an Euro-Arab University following Recommendation 1032 (1986)), the media (production and broadcasting of programmes on Islamic culture), culture (such as cultural exchanges, exhibitions, conferences etc.) and multilateral co-operation (seminars on Islamic fundamentalism, the democratisation of the Islamic world, the compatibility of different forms of Islam with modern European society etc.) as well as administrative questions and everyday life (such as the twinning of towns or the encouragement of dialogue between Islamic communities and the competent authorities on issues like holy days, dress, food etc.). See in particular paras. 10-12.

[10] Adopted on 2 February 1993 (23rd sitting). The Assembly, inter alia, proposed preventive measures in the field of legal guarantees and their observance (especially following the rights indicated in Recommendation 1086 (1988), paragraph 10), education and exchanges (such as the establishment of a "religious history school-book conference", exchange programmes for students and other young people), information and "sensibilisation" (like the access to fundamental religious texts and related literature in public libraries) and research (for instance, stimulation of academic work in European universities on questions concerning religious tolerance). See in particular paras. 12, 15-16.

[11] Adopted on 27 January 1999 (5th sitting). The Assembly, inter alia, recommended preventive measures to promote better relations with and between religions (through a more systematic dialogue with religious and humanist leaders, theologians, philosophers and historians) or the cultural and social expression of religions (including religious buildings or traditions). See in particular paras. 9-14.

[12] Adopted on 23 September 1999 (30th sitting). The Assembly underlined inter alia that "The prevention of terrorism also depends on education in democratic values and tolerance, with the eradication of the teaching of negative or hateful attitudes towards others and the development of a culture of peace in all individuals and social groups (para. 9).

[13] Adopted on 26 September 2001 (28th sitting). *"(…) the Assembly believes that long-term prevention of terrorism must include a proper understanding of its social, economic, political and religious roots and of the individual's capacity for hatred. If these issues are properly addressed, it will be possible to seriously undermine the grass roots support for terrorists and their recruitment networks"* (para. 9).

[14] See "The aftermath of September 11: Multicultural and Inter-religious Dialogue – Document of the Secretary General", Information Documents SG/Inf (2001) 40 Rev.2, 6 December 2001.

adopts the following guidelines and invites member States to ensure that they are widely disseminated among all authorities responsible for the fight against terrorism.

I.   States' obligation to protect everyone against terrorism

States are under the obligation to take the measures needed to protect the fundamental rights of everyone within their jurisdiction against terrorist acts, especially the right to life. This positive obligation fully justifies States' fight against terrorism in accordance with the present guidelines.

13.   The Court indicated that:

> "the first sentence of Article 2 para. 1 enjoins the State not only to refrain from the intentional and unlawful taking of life, but also to take appropriate steps to safeguard the lives of those within its jurisdiction (see the L.C.B. v. the United Kingdom judgment of 9 June 1998, Reports of Judgments and Decisions 1998-III, p. 1403, para. 36). This obligation (…) may also imply in certain well-defined circumstances a positive obligation on the authorities to take preventive operational measures to protect an individual whose life is at risk from the criminal acts of another individual (Osman v. the United Kingdom judgment of 28 October 1998, Reports 1998-VIII, para. 115; Kiliç v. Turkey, no. 22492/93, (Sect. 1) ECHR 2000-III, paras. 62 and 76)."[15]

II.   Prohibition of arbitrariness

All measures taken by States to fight terrorism must respect human rights and the principle of the rule of law, while excluding any form of arbitrariness, as well as any discriminatory or racist treatment, and must be subject to appropriate supervision.

14. The words "discriminatory treatment" are taken from the Political Declaration adopted by Ministers of Council of Europe member States on 13 October 2000 at the concluding session of the European Conference against Racism.

III.   Lawfulness of anti-terrorist measures

1.   All measures taken by States to combat terrorism must be lawful.

2.   When a measure restricts human rights, restrictions must be defined as precisely as possible and be necessary and proportionate to the aim pursued.

---

[15] Pretty v. United Kingdom, 29 April 2002, para. 38.

IV. *Absolute prohibition of torture*

The use of torture or of inhuman or degrading treatment or punishment, is absolutely prohibited, in all circumstances, and in particular during the arrest, questioning and detention of a person suspected of or convicted of terrorist activities, irrespective of the nature of the acts that the person is suspected of or for which he/she was convicted.

15. The Court has recalled the absolute prohibition to use torture or inhuman or degrading treatment or punishment (Article 3 of the Convention) on many occasions, for example:

> "*As the Court has stated on many occasions, Article 3 enshrines one of the most fundamental values of democratic societies. Even in the most difficult circumstances, such as the fight against terrorism and organised crime, the Convention prohibits in absolute terms torture and inhuman or degrading treatment or punishment. Unlike most of the substantive clauses of the Convention and of Protocols Nos. 1 and 4, Article 3 makes no provision for exceptions and no derogation from it is permissible under Article 15 para. 2 even in the event of a public emergency threatening the life of the nation (...). The Convention prohibits in absolute terms torture and inhuman or degrading treatment or punishment, irrespective of the victim's conduct (see the Chahal v. the United Kingdom judgment of 15 November 1996, Reports 1996-V, p. 1855, para. 79). The nature of the offence allegedly committed by the applicant was therefore irrelevant for the purposes of Article 3.*"[16].

> "*The requirements of the investigation and the undeniable difficulties inherent in the fight against crime, particularly with regard to terrorism, cannot result in limits being placed on the protection to be afforded in respect of the physical integrity of individuals.*"[17]

16. According to the case law of the Court, it is clear that the nature of the crime is not relevant: "*The Court is well aware of the immense difficulties faced by States in modern times in protecting their communities from terrorist violence. However, even in these circumstances, the Convention*

---

[16] *Labita v. Italy*, 6 April 2000, para. 119. See also *Ireland v. United Kingdom*, 18 January 1978, A n° 25, para. 163; *Soering v. United Kingdom*, 7 July 1989, A n° 161, para. 88; *Chahal v. United Kingdom*, 15 November 1996, para. 79; *Aksoy v. Turkey*, 18 December 1996, para. 62; *Aydin v. Turkey*, 25 September 1997, para. 81; *Assenov and Others v. Bulgaria*, 28 October 1998, para. 93; *Selmouni v. France*, 28 July 1999, para. 95.

[17] *Tomasi v. France*, 27 August 1992, para. 115. See also *Ribitsch v. Austria*, 4 December 1995, para. 38.

prohibits in absolute terms torture or inhuman or degrading treatment or punishment, irrespective of the victim's conduct."[18].

V.   Collection and processing of personal data by any competent authority in the field of State security

Within the context of the fight against terrorism, the collection and the processing of personal data by any competent authority in the field of State security may interfere with the respect for private life only if such collection and processing, in particular:

(i)   are governed by appropriate provisions of domestic law;

(ii)   are proportionate to the aim for which the collection and the processing were foreseen;

(iii)   may be subject to supervision by an external independent authority.

17.   As concerns the collection and processing of personal data, the Court stated for the first time that:

> *"No provision of domestic law, however, lays down any limits on the exercise of those powers. Thus, for instance, domestic law does not define the kind of information that may be recorded, the categories of people against whom surveillance measures such as gathering and keeping information may be taken, the circumstances in which such measures may be taken or the procedure to be followed. Similarly, the Law does not lay down limits on the age of information held or the length of time for which it may be kept.*
>
> *(...)*
>
> *The Court notes that this section contains no explicit, detailed provision concerning the persons authorised to consult the files, the nature of the files, the procedure to be followed or the use that may be made of the information thus obtained.*
>
> *(...) It also notes that although section 2 of the Law empowers the relevant authorities to permit interferences necessary to prevent and counteract threats to national security, the ground allowing such interferences is not laid down with sufficient precision"*[19].

---

[18]   *Chahal v. United Kingdom*, 15 November 1996, para. 79; see also *V. v. United Kingdom*, 16 December 1999, para. 69.

[19]   *Rotaru v. Romania*, 4 May 2000, paras. 57-58.

VI. *Measures which interfere with privacy*

1. Measures used in the fight against terrorism that interfere with privacy (in particular body searches, house searches, bugging, telephone tapping, surveillance of correspondence and use of undercover agents) must be provided for by law. It must be possible to challenge the lawfulness of these measures before a court.

18. The Court accepts that the fight against terrorism may allow the use of specific methods:

> "*Democratic societies nowadays find themselves threatened by highly sophisticated forms of espionage and by terrorism, with the result that the State must be able, in order effectively to counter such threats, to undertake the secret surveillance of subversive elements operating within its jurisdiction. The Court has therefore to accept that the existence of some legislation granting powers of secret surveillance over the mail, post and telecommunications is, under exceptional conditions, necessary in a democratic society in the interests of national security and/or for the prevention of disorder or crime.*"[20]

19. With regard to tapping, it must to be done in conformity with the provisions of Article 8 of the Convention, notably be done in accordance with the "law". The Court, thus, recalled that: "*tapping and other forms of interception of telephone conversations constitute a serious interference with private life and correspondence and must accordingly be based on a "law" that is particularly precise. It is essential to have clear, detailed rules on the subject, especially as the technology available for use is continually becoming more sophisticated (see the above-mentioned Kruslin and Huvig judgments, p. 23, para. 33, and p. 55, para. 32, respectively)*"[21].

20. The Court also accepted that the use of confidential information is essential in combating terrorist violence and the threat that it poses on citizens and to democratic society as a whole:

> "*The Court would firstly reiterate its recognition that the use of confidential information is essential in combating terrorist violence and the threat that organised terrorism poses to the lives of citizens and to democratic society as a whole (see also the Klass and Others v. Germany judgment of 6 September 1978, Series A no. 28, p. 23, para. 48). This does not mean, however, that the investigating authorities have carte blanche under Article 5 (art. 5) to arrest suspects for questioning, free from effective control by the domestic courts or by*

---

[20] *Klass and Others v. Germany*, 6 September 1978, A n° 28, para. 48.

[21] *Kopp v. Switzerland*, 25 March 1998, para. 72. See also *Huvig v. France*, 24 April 1990, paras. 34-35.

the Convention supervisory institutions, whenever they choose to assert that terrorism is involved (ibid., p. 23, para. 49).*[22]

2. Measures taken to fight terrorism must be planned and controlled by the authorities so as to minimise, to the greatest extent possible, recourse to lethal force and, within this framework, the use of arms by the security forces must be strictly proportionate to the aim of protecting persons against unlawful violence or to the necessity of carrying out a lawful arrest.

21. Article 2 of the Convention does not exclude the possibility that the deliberate use of a lethal solution can be justified when it is "absolutely necessary" to prevent some sorts of crimes. This must be done, however, in very strict conditions so as to respect human life as much as possible, even with regard to persons suspected of preparing a terrorist attack.

> *"Against this background, in determining whether the force used was compatible with Article 2 (art. 2), the Court must carefully scrutinise, as noted above, not only whether the force used by the soldiers was strictly proportionate to the aim of protecting persons against unlawful violence but also whether the anti-terrorist operation was planned and controlled by the authorities so as to minimise, to the greatest extent possible, recourse to lethal force."*[23]

VII. *Arrest and police custody*

1. A person suspected of terrorist activities may only be arrested if there are reasonable suspicions. He/she must be informed of the reasons for the arrest.

22. The Court acknowledges that "reasonable" suspicion needs to form the basis of the arrest of a suspect. It adds that this feature depends upon all the circumstances, with terrorist crime falling into a specific category:

> *"32. The "reasonableness" of the suspicion on which an arrest must be based forms an essential part of the safeguard against arbitrary arrest and detention which is laid down in Article 5 para. 1 (c) (art. 5-1-c). (…) [H]aving a "reasonable suspicion" presupposes the existence of facts or information which would satisfy an objective observer that the person concerned may have committed the offence. What may be regarded as "reasonable" will however depend upon all the circumstances. In this respect, terrorist crime falls into a special category. Because of the attendant risk of loss of life and human suffering, the police are obliged*

---

[22] *Murray v. United Kingdom*, 28 October 1994, para. 58.

[23] *McCann and Others v. United Kingdom*, 27 September 1995, para. 194. In this case, the Court, not convinced that the killing of three terrorists was a use of force not exceeding the aim of protecting persons against unlawful violence, considered that there had been a violation of article 2.

to act with utmost urgency in following up all information, including information from secret sources. Further, the police may frequently have to arrest a suspected terrorist on the basis of information which is reliable but which cannot, without putting in jeopardy the source of the information, be revealed to the suspect or produced in court to support a charge.

(...) [T]he exigencies of dealing with terrorist crime cannot justify stretching the notion of "reasonableness" to the point where the essence of the safeguard secured by Article 5 para. 1 (c) (art. 5-1-c) is impaired (...).

(...)

34. Certainly Article 5 para. 1 (c) (art. 5-1-c) of the Convention should not be applied in such a manner as to put disproportionate difficulties in the way of the police authorities of the Contracting States in taking effective measures to counter organised terrorism (...). It follows that the Contracting States cannot be asked to establish the reasonableness of the suspicion grounding the arrest of a suspected terrorist by disclosing the confidential sources of supporting information or even facts which would be susceptible of indicating such sources or their identity.

Nevertheless the Court must be enabled to ascertain whether the essence of the safeguard afforded by Article 5 para. 1 (c) (art. 5-1-c) has been secured. Consequently the respondent Government have to furnish at least some facts or information capable of satisfying the Court that the arrested person was reasonably suspected of having committed the alleged offence."[24]

2. **A person arrested or detained for terrorist activities shall be brought promptly before a judge. Police custody shall be of a reasonable period of time, the length of which must be provided for by law.**

3. **A person arrested or detained for terrorist activities must be able to challenge the lawfulness of his/her arrest and of his/her police custody before a court.**

23. The protection afforded by Article 5 of the Convention is also relevant here. There are limits linked to the arrest and detention of persons suspected of terrorist activities. The Court accepts that protecting the community against terrorism is a legitimate goal but that this cannot justify all measures. For instance, the fight against terrorism can justify the extension of police custody, but it cannot authorise that there is no judicial control at all over this custody, or, that judicial control is not prompt enough:

---

[24] *Fox, Campbell and Hartley v. United Kingdom*, 30 August 1990, paras. 32 and 34.

"The Court accepts that, subject to the existence of adequate safeguards, the context of terrorism in Northern Ireland has the effect of prolonging the period during which the authorities may, without violating Article 5 para. 3 (art. 5-3), keep a person suspected of serious terrorist offences in custody before bringing him before a judge or other judicial officer.

The difficulties, alluded to by the Government, of judicial control over decisions to arrest and detain suspected terrorists may affect the manner of implementation of Article 5 para. 3 (art. 5-3), for example in calling for appropriate procedural precautions in view of the nature of the suspected offences. However, they cannot justify, under Article 5 para. 3 (art. 5-3), dispensing altogether with "prompt" judicial control."[25]

"The undoubted fact that the arrest and detention of the applicants were inspired by the legitimate aim of protecting the community as a whole from terrorism is not on its own sufficient to ensure compliance with the specific requirements of Article 5 para. 3 (art. 5-3)."[26]

"The Court recalls its decision in the case of Brogan and Others v. the United Kingdom (judgment of 29 November 1988, Series A no. 145-B, p. 33, para. 62), that a period of detention without judicial control of four days and six hours fell outside the strict constraints as to time permitted by Article 5 para. 3 (art. 5-3). It clearly follows that the period of fourteen or more days during which Mr Aksoy was detained without being brought before a judge or other judicial officer did not satisfy the requirement of "promptness"."[27]

"The Court has already accepted on several occasions that the investigation of terrorist offences undoubtedly presents the authorities with special problems (see the Brogan and Others v. the United Kingdom judgment of 29 November 1988, Series A no. 145-B, p. 33, para. 61, the Murray v. the United Kingdom judgment of 28 October 1994, Series A no. 300-A, p. 27, para. 58, and the above-mentioned Aksoy judgment, p. 2282, para. 78). This does not mean, however, that the investigating authorities have carte blanche under Article 5 to arrest suspects for questioning, free from effective control by the domestic courts and, ultimately, by the Convention supervisory institutions, whenever they choose to assert that terrorism is involved (see, mutatis mutandis, the above-mentioned Murray judgment, p. 27, para. 58).

---

[25] *Brogan and Others v. United Kingdom*, 29 November 1998, A n° 145-B, para. 61.

[26] *Brogan and Others v. United Kingdom*, 29 November 1998, A n° 145-B, para. 62. See also *Brannigan and Mc Bride v. United Kingdom*, 26 May 1993, para. 58.

[27] *Aksoy v. Turkey*, 12 December 1996, para. 66.

What is at stake here is the importance of Article 5 in the Convention system: it enshrines a fundamental human right, namely the protection of the individual against arbitrary interferences by the State with his right to liberty. Judicial control of interferences by the executive is an essential feature of the guarantee embodied in Article 5 para. 3, which is intended to minimise the risk of arbitrariness and to secure the rule of law, "one of the fundamental principles of a democratic society ..., which is expressly referred to in the Preamble to the Convention" (see the above-mentioned Brogan and Others judgment, p. 32, para. 58, and the above-mentioned Aksoy judgment, p. 2282, para. 76)."[28]

VIII. *Regular supervision of pre-trial detention*

A person suspected of terrorist activities and detained pending trial is entitled to regular supervision of the lawfulness of his or her detention by a court.

IX. *Legal proceedings*

1. A person accused of terrorist activities has the right to a fair hearing, within a reasonable time, by an independent, impartial tribunal established by law.

24. The right to a fair trial is acknowledged, for everyone, by Article 6 of the Convention. The case-law of the Court states that the right to a fair trial is inherent to any democratic society.

25. Article 6 does not forbid the creation of special tribunals to judge terrorist acts if these special tribunals meet the criterions set out in this article (independent and impartial tribunals established by law):

"The Court reiterates that in order to establish whether a tribunal can be considered "independent" for the purposes of Article 6 para. 1, regard must be had, inter alia, to the manner of appointment of its members and their term of office, the existence of safeguards against outside pressures and the question whether it presents an appearance of independence (see, among many other authorities, the Findlay v. the United Kingdom judgment of 25 February 1997, Reports 1997-I, p. 281, para. 73).

As to the condition of "impartiality" within the meaning of that provision, there are two tests to be applied: the first consists in trying to determine the personal conviction of a particular judge in a given case and the second in ascertaining whether the judge offered guarantees sufficient to exclude any legitimate doubt in this respect. (...) (see, mutatis

---

[28] *Sakik and Others v. Turkey*, 26 November 1997, para. 44.

mutandis, *the Gautrin and Others v. France judgment of 20 May 1998, Reports 1998-III, pp. 1030–31, para. 58)."*[29]

"Its (the Court's) task is not to determine in abstracto *whether it was necessary to set up such courts (special courts) in a Contracting State or to review the relevant practice, but to ascertain whether the manner in which one of them functioned infringed the applicant's right to a fair trial. (...) In this respect even appearances may be of a certain importance. What is at stake is the confidence which the courts in a democratic society must inspire in the public and above all, as far as criminal proceedings are concerned, in the accused (see, among other authorities, the Hauschildt v. Denmark judgment of 24 May 1989, Series A no. 154, p. 21, para. 48, the Thorgeir Thorgeirson judgment cited above, p. 23, para. 51, and the Pullar v. the United Kingdom judgment of 10 June 1996, Reports 1996-III, p. 794, para. 38). In deciding whether there is a legitimate reason to fear that a particular court lacks independence or impartiality, the standpoint of the accused is important without being decisive. What is decisive is whether his doubts can be held to be objectively justified (see,* mutatis mutandis, *the Hauschildt judgment cited above, p. 21, para. 48, and the Gautrin and Others judgment cited above, pp. 1030–31, para. 58).*

(...) [T]he Court attaches great importance to the fact that a civilian had to appear before a court composed, even if only in part, of members of the armed forces. It follows that the applicant could legitimately fear that because one of the judges of the Izmir National Security Court was a military judge it might allow itself to be unduly influenced by considerations which had nothing to do with the nature of the case."[30]

2. A person accused of terrorist activities benefits from the presumption of innocence.

26. Presumption of innocence is specifically mentioned in Article 6, paragraph 2, of the European Convention on Human Rights that states: *"Everyone charged with a criminal offence shall be presumed innocent until proved guilty according to law"*. This article therefore applies also to persons suspected of terrorist activities.

27. Moreover, *"the Court considers that the presumption of innocence may be infringed not only by a judge or court but also by other public authorities"*[31]. Accordingly, the Court found that the public declaration made by a Minister of the Interior and by two high-ranking police officers referring to somebody as the accomplice in a murder before his judgment *"was clearly a declaration of the applicant's guilt which, firstly, encouraged the public to*

---

[29] *Incal v. Turkey*, 9 June 1998, para. 65.

[30] *Incal v. Turkey*, 9 June 1998, paras. 70-72.

[31] *Allenet de Ribemont v. France*, 10 February 1995, para. 36.

believe him guilty and, secondly, prejudged the assessment of the facts by the competent judicial authority. There has therefore been a breach of Article 6 para. 2"[32].

3.   The imperatives of the fight against terrorism may nevertheless justify certain restrictions to the right of defence, in particular with regard to:

(i)   the arrangements for access to and contacts with counsel;

(ii)   the arrangements for access to the case-file;

(iii)   the use of anonymous testimony.

4.   Such restrictions to the right of defence must be strictly proportionate to their purpose, and compensatory measures to protect the interests of the accused must be taken so as to maintain the fairness of the proceedings and to ensure that procedural rights are not drained of their substance.

28.   The Court recognises that an effective fight against terrorism requires that some of the guarantees of a fair trial may be interpreted with some flexibility. Confronted with the need to examine the conformity with the Convention of certain types of investigations and trials, the Court has, for example, recognised that the use of anonymous witnesses is not always incompatible with the Convention[33]. In certain cases, like those which are linked to terrorism, witnesses must be protected against any possible risk of retaliation against them which may put their lives, their freedom or their safety in danger.

> *"the Court has recognised in principle that, provided that the rights of the defence are respected, it may be legitimate for the police authorities to wish to preserve the anonymity of an agent deployed in undercover activities, for his own or his family's protection and so as not to impair his usefulness for future operations."*[34]

29.   The Court recognised that the interception of a letter between a prisoner – terrorist – and his lawyer is possible in certain circumstances:

> *"Il n'en demeure pas moins que la confidentialité de la correspondance entre un détenu et son défenseur constitue un droit fondamental pour un individu et touche directement les droits de la défense. C'est*

---

[32] *Id.*, para. 41.

[33] See *Doorson v. The Netherlands*, 26 March 1996, paras. 69-70. The Doorson case concerned the fight against drug trafficking. The concluding comments of the Court can nevertheless be extended to the fight against terrorism. See also *Van Mechelen and others v. The Netherlands*, 23 April 1997, para. 52.

[34] *Van Mechelen and others v. The Netherlands*, 23 April 1997, para. 57.

pourquoi, comme la Cour l'a énoncé plus haut, une dérogation à ce principe ne peut être autorisée que dans des cas exceptionnels et doit s'entourer de garanties adéquates et suffisantes contre les abus (voir aussi, mutatis mutandis, l'arrêt Klass précité, ibidem)." [35]

30. The case-law of the Court insists upon the compensatory mechanisms to avoid that measures taken in the fight against terrorism do not take away the substance of the right to a fair trial[36]. Therefore, if the possibility of non-disclosure of certain evidence to the defence exists, this needs to be counterbalanced by the procedures followed by the judicial authorities:

"*60. It is a fundamental aspect of the right to a fair trial that criminal proceedings, including the elements of such proceedings which relate to procedure, should be adversarial and that there should be equality of arms between the prosecution and defence. The right to an adversarial trial means, in a criminal case, that both prosecution and defence must be given the opportunity to have knowledge of and comment on the observations filed and the evidence adduced by the other party (see the Brandstetter v. Austria judgment of 28 August 1991, Series A no. 211, paras. 66, 67). In addition Article 6 para. 1 requires, as indeed does English law (see paragraph 34 above), that the prosecution authorities should disclose to the defence all material evidence in their possession for or against the accused (see the above-mentioned Edwards judgment, para. 36).*

61. However, as the applicants recognised (see paragraph 54 above), the entitlement to disclosure of relevant evidence is not an absolute right. In any criminal proceedings there may be competing interests, such as national security or the need to protect witnesses at risk of reprisals or keep secret police methods of investigation of crime, which must be weighed against the rights of the accused (see, for example, the Doorson v. the Netherlands judgment of 26 March 1996, Reports of Judgments and Decisions 1996-II, para. 70). In some cases it may be necessary to withhold certain evidence from the defence so as to preserve the fundamental rights of another individual or to safeguard an important public interest. However, only such measures restricting the rights of the defence which are strictly necessary are permissible under Article 6 para. 1 (see the Van Mechelen and Others v. the Netherlands judgment of 23 April 1997, Reports 1997-III, para. 58). Moreover, in order to ensure that the accused receives a fair trial, any difficulties caused to the defence by a limitation on its rights must be sufficiently counterbalanced by the procedures followed by the judicial authorities (see the above-mentioned Doorson judgment, para. 72 and the above-mentioned Van Mechelen and Others judgment, para. 54).

---

[35] *Erdem v. Germany*, 5 July 2001, para. 65, text only available in French.

[36] See notably, *Chahal v. United Kingdom*, 15 November 1996, paras. 131 and 144, and *Van Mechelen and others v. The Netherlands*, 23 April 1997, para. 54.

62. *In cases where evidence has been withheld from the defence on public interest grounds, it is not the role of this Court to decide whether or not such non-disclosure was strictly necessary since, as a general rule, it is for the national courts to assess the evidence before them (see the above-mentioned Edwards judgment, para. 34). Instead, the European Court's task is to ascertain whether the decision-making procedure applied in each case complied, as far as possible, with the requirements of adversarial proceedings and equality of arms and incorporated adequate safeguards to protect the interests of the accused."* [37].

X. *Penalties incurred*

1. The penalties incurred by a person accused of terrorist activities must be provided for by law for any action or omission which constituted a criminal offence at the time when it was committed; no heavier penalty may be imposed than the one that was applicable at the time when the criminal offence was committed.

31. This guideline takes up the elements contained in Article 7 of the European Convention on Human Rights. The Court recalled that:

"The guarantee enshrined in Article 7, which is an essential element of the rule of law, occupies a prominent place in the Convention system of protection, as is underlined by the fact that no derogation from it is permissible under Article 15 in time of war or other public emergency. It should be construed and applied, as follows from its object and purpose, in such a way as to provide effective safeguards against arbitrary prosecution, conviction and punishment (see the S.W. and C.R. v. the United Kingdom judgments of 22 November 1995, Series A nos. 335-B and 335-C, pp. 41-42, para. 35, and pp. 68-69, para. 33 respectively)." [38]

"The Court recalls that, according to its case-law, Article 7 embodies, inter alia, the principle that only the law can define a crime and prescribe a penalty (nullum crimen, nulla poena sine lege) and the principle that the criminal law must not be extensively construed to an accused's detriment, for instance by analogy. From these principles it follows that an offence and the sanctions provided for it must be clearly defined in the law. This requirement is satisfied where the individual can know from the wording of the relevant provision and, if need be, with the assistance of the courts' interpretation of it, what acts and omissions will make him criminally liable.

---

[37] *Rowe and Davies v. United Kingdom*, 16 February 2000, paras. 60-62.

[38] *Ecer and Zeyrek v. Turkey*, 27 February 2001, para. 29.

When speaking of "law" Article 7 alludes to the very same concept as that to which the Convention refers elsewhere when using that term, a concept which comprises statutory law as well as case-law and implies qualitative requirements, notably those of accessibility and foreseeability (see the Cantoni v. France judgment of 15 November 1996, Reports of Judgments and Decisions 1996-V, p. 1627, para. 29, and the S.W. and C.R. v. the United Kingdom judgments of 22 November 1995, Series A nos. 335-B and 335-C, pp. 41-42, para. 35, and pp. 68-69, para. 33, respectively)."[39]

2.   Under no circumstances may a person convicted of terrorist activities be sentenced to the death penalty; in the event of such a sentence being imposed, it may not be carried out.

32.   The present tendency in Europe is towards the general abolition of the death penalty, in all circumstances (Protocol No. 13 to the Convention). The Member States of the Council of Europe still having the death penalty within their legal arsenal have all agreed to a moratorium on the implementation of the penalty.

XI. *Detention*

1.   A person deprived of his/her liberty for terrorist activities must in all circumstances be treated with due respect for human dignity.

33.   According to the case law of the Court, it is clear that the nature of the crime is not relevant: "*The Court is well aware of the immense difficulties faced by States in modern times in protecting their communities from terrorist violence. However, even in these circumstances, the Convention prohibits in absolute terms torture or inhuman or degrading treatment or punishment, irrespective of the victim's conduct.*"[40].

34.   It is recalled that the practice of total sensory deprivation was condemned by the Court as being in violation with Article 3 of the Convention[41].

2.   The imperatives of the fight against terrorism may nevertheless require that a person deprived of his/her liberty for terrorist activities be submitted to more severe restrictions than those applied to other prisoners, in particular with regard to:

(i)   the regulations concerning communications and surveillance of correspondence, including that between counsel and his/her client;

---

[39] *Baskaya and Okçuoglu v. Turkey*, 8 July 1999, para. 36.

[40] *Chahal v. United Kingdom*, 15 November 1996, para. 79; see also *V. v. United Kingdom*, 16 December 1999, para. 69.

[41] See *Ireland v. United Kingdom*, 18 January 1978, notably paras. 165-168.

35. With regard to communication between a lawyer and his/her client, the case-law of the Court may be referred to, in particular a recent decision on inadmissibility in which the Court recalls the possibility for the State, in exceptional circumstances, to intercept correspondence between a lawyer and his/her client sentenced for terrorist acts. It is therefore possible to take measures which depart from ordinary law:

« 65. Il n'en demeure pas moins que la confidentialité de la correspondance entre un détenu et son défenseur constitue un droit fondamental pour un individu et touche directement les droits de la défense. C'est pourquoi, comme la Cour l'a énoncé plus haut, une dérogation à ce principe ne peut être autorisée que dans des cas exceptionnels et doit s'entourer de garanties adéquates et suffisantes contre les abus (voir aussi, mutatis mutandis, l'arrêt Klass précité, ibidem).

66. Or le procès contre des cadres du PKK se situe dans le contexte exceptionnel de la lutte contre le terrorisme sous toutes ses formes. Par ailleurs, il paraissait légitime pour les autorités allemandes de veiller à ce que le procès se déroule dans les meilleures conditions de sécurité, compte tenu de l'importante communauté turque, dont beaucoup de membres sont d'origine kurde, résidant en Allemagne.

67. La Cour relève ensuite que la disposition en question est rédigée de manière très précise, puisqu'elle spécifie la catégorie de personnes dont la correspondance doit être soumise à contrôle, à savoir les détenus soupçonnés d'appartenir à une organisation terroriste au sens de l'article 129a du code pénal. De plus, cette mesure, à caractère exceptionnel puisqu'elle déroge à la règle générale de la confidentialité de la correspondance entre un détenu et son défenseur, est assortie d'un certain nombre de garanties : contrairement à d'autres affaires devant la Cour, où l'ouverture du courrier était effectuée par les autorités pénitentiaires (voir notamment les arrêts Campbell, et Fell et Campbell précités), en l'espèce, le pouvoir de contrôle est exercé par un magistrat indépendant, qui ne doit avoir aucun lien avec l'instruction, et qui doit garder le secret sur les informations dont il prend ainsi connaissance. Enfin, il ne s'agit que d'un contrôle restreint, puisque le détenu peut librement s'entretenir oralement avec son défenseur ; certes, ce dernier ne peut lui remettre des pièce écrites ou d'autres objets, mais il peut porter à la connaissance du détenu les informations contenues dans les documents écrits.

68. Par ailleurs, la Cour rappelle qu'une certaine forme de conciliation entre les impératifs de la défense de la société démocratique et ceux de la sauvegarde des droits individuels est inhérente au système de la Convention (voir, mutatis mutandis, l'arrêt Klass précité, p. 28, para. 59).

69. Eu égard à la menace présentée par le terrorisme sous toutes ses formes (voir la décision de la Commission dans l'affaire Bader, Meins, Meinhof et Grundmann c. Allemagne du 30 mai 1975, n° 6166/75), des garanties dont est entouré le contrôle de la correspondance en l'espèce et de la marge d'appréciation dont dispose l'Etat, la Cour conclut que l'ingérence litigieuse n'était pas disproportionnée par rapport aux buts légitimes poursuivis. »[42]

(ii) placing persons deprived of their liberty for terrorist activities in specially secured quarters;

(iii) the separation of such persons within a prison or among different prisons,

36. With regard to the place of detention, the former European Commission of Human Rights indicated that:

"It must be recalled that the Convention does not grant prisoners the right to choose the place of detention and that the separation from their family are inevitable consequences of their detention".[43]

on condition that the measure taken is proportionate to the aim to be achieved.

" (…) the notion of necessity implies that the interference corresponds to a pressing social need and, in particular, that it is proportionate to the legitimate aim pursued. In determining whether an interference is "necessary in a democratic society" regard may be had to the State's margin of appreciation (see, amongst other authorities, The Sunday Times v. the United Kingdom (no. 2) judgment of 26 November 1991, Series A no. 217, pp. 28-29, para. 50)."[44]

XII. *Asylum, return ("refoulement") and expulsion*

1.   All requests for asylum must be dealt with on an individual basis. An effective remedy must lie against the decision taken. However, when the State has serious grounds to believe that the person who seeks to be granted asylum has participated in terrorist activities, refugee status must be refused to that person.

---

[42] *Erdem v. Germany*, 5 July 2001, paras. 65-69. The text of this judgment is available in French only. See also *Lüdi v. Switzerland*, 15 June 1992.

[43] Venetucci v. Italy (application n° 33830/96), Decision as to admissibility, 2 March 1998.

[44] *Campbell v. United Kingdom*, 25 March 1992, A n° 233, para. 44.

37. Article 14 of the Universal Declaration of Human Rights states: "*1. Everyone has the right to seek and enjoy in other countries asylum from persecution*".

38. Moreover, a concrete problem that States may have to confront is that of the competition between an asylum request and a demand for extradition. Article 7 of the draft General Convention on international terrorism must be noted in this respect: "*States Parties shall take appropriate measures, in conformity with the relevant provisions of national and international law, including international human rights law, for the purpose of ensuring that refugee status is not granted to any person in respect of whom there are serious reasons for considering that he or she has committed an offence referred to in article 2*".

39. It is also recalled that Article 1 F of the Convention on the Status of Refugees of 28 July 1951 provides : "*F. The provisions of this Convention shall not apply to any person with respect to whom there are serious reasons for considering that (a) He has committed a crime against peace, a war crime, or a crime against humanity, as defined in the international instruments drawn up to make provision in respect of such crimes; (b) He has committed a serious non-political crime outside the country of refuge prior to his admission to that country as a refugee; (c) He has been guilty of acts contrary to the purposes and principles of the United Nations*".

2. It is the duty of a State that has received a request for asylum to ensure that the possible return ("*refoulement*") of the applicant to his/her country of origin or to another country will not expose him/her to the death penalty, to torture or to inhuman or degrading treatment or punishment. The same applies to expulsion.

3. Collective expulsion of aliens is prohibited.

40. This guideline takes up word by word the content of Article 4 of Protocol No. 4 to the European Convention on Human Rights.

41. The Court thus recalled that:

"*collective expulsion, within the meaning of Article 4 of Protocol No. 4, is to be understood as any measure compelling aliens, as a group, to leave a country, except where such a measure is taken on the basis of a reasonable and objective examination of the particular case of each individual alien of the group (see Andric v. Sweden, cited above)*"[45].

4. In all cases, the enforcement of the expulsion or return ("*refoulement*") order must be carried out with respect for the physical integrity and for the dignity of the person concerned, avoiding any inhuman or degrading treatment.

---

[45] *Conka v. Belgium*, 5 February 2002, para. 59.

42. See the comments made in paragraph 15 above and the case-law references there mentionned.

XIII. *Extradition*

1. Extradition is an essential procedure for effective international co-operation in the fight against terrorism.

2. The extradition of a person to a country where he/she risks being sentenced to the death penalty may not be granted. A requested State may however grant an extradition if it has obtained adequate guarantees that:

(i) the person whose extradition has been requested will not be sentenced to death; or

(ii) in the event of such a sentence being imposed, it will not be carried out.

43. In relation to the death penalty, it can legitimately be deduced from the case-law of the Court that the extradition of someone to a State where he/she risks the death penalty is forbidden[46]. Accordingly, even if the judgment does not say *expressis verbis* that such an extradition is prohibited, this prohibition is drawn from the fact that the waiting for the execution of the sentence by the condemned person ("death row") constitutes an inhuman treatment, according to Article 3 of the Convention. It must also be recalled that the present tendency in Europe is towards the general abolition of the death penalty, in all circumstances (see guideline X, *Penalties incurred*).

3. Extradition may not be granted when there is serious reason to believe that:

(i) the person whose extradition has been requested will be subjected to torture or to inhuman or degrading treatment or punishment;

(ii) the extradition request has been made for the purpose of prosecuting or punishing a person on account of his/her race, religion, nationality or political opinions, or that that person's position risks being prejudiced for any of these reasons.

44. As concerns the absolute prohibition to extradite or return an individual to a State in which he risks torture or inhuman and degrading treatment or punishment see above para. 44.

---

[46] See *Soering v. United Kingdom*, 7 July 1989, A No. 161.

4. When the person whose extradition has been requested makes out an arguable case that he/she has suffered or risks suffering a flagrant denial of justice in the requesting State, the requested State must consider the well-foundedness of that argument before deciding whether to grant extradition.

45. The Court underlined that it *"does not exclude that an issue might exceptionally be raised under Article 6 (art. 6) by an extradition decision in circumstances where the fugitive has suffered or risks suffering a flagrant denial of a fair trial in the requesting country."[47]*.

46. Article 5 of the European Convention on the suppression of terrorism[48] states:

> *"Nothing in this Convention shall be interpreted as imposing an obligation to extradite if the requested State has substantial grounds for believing that the request for extradition for an offence mentioned in Article 1 or 2 has been made for the purpose of prosecuting or punishing a person on account of his race, religion, nationality or political opinion, or that that person's position may be prejudiced for any of these reasons."*

47. The explanatory report indicates:

> *"50. If, in a given case, the requested State has substantial grounds for believing that the real purpose of an extradition request, made for one of the offences mentioned in Article 1 or 2, is to enable the requesting State to prosecute or punish the person concerned for the political opinions he holds, the requested State may refuse extradition.*
> *The same applies where the requested State has substantial grounds for believing that the person's position may be prejudiced for political or any of the other reasons mentioned in Article 5.* ***This would be the case, for instance, if the person to be extradited would, in the***

---

[47] *Soering v. United Kingdom* (7 July 1989, A n° 161) para. 113. Position confirmed by the Court in its judgment in the case *Drozd and Janousek v. France and Spain*, 26 June 1992, A No. 240, para. 110 : *"As the Convention does not require the Contracting Parties to impose its standards on third States or territories, France was not obliged to verify whether the proceedings which resulted in the conviction were compatible with all the requirements of Article 6 (art. 6) of the Convention. To require such a review of the manner in which a court not bound by the Convention had applied the principles enshrined in Article 6 (art. 6) would also thwart the current trend towards strengthening international co-operation in the administration of justice, a trend which is in principle in the interests of the persons concerned. The Contracting States are, however, obliged to refuse their co-operation if it emerges that the conviction is the result of a flagrant denial of justice (see, mutatis mutandis, the Soering v. the United Kingdom judgment of 7 July 1989, Series A no. 161, p. 45, para. 113)."* and in its final decision on admissibility in the case *Einhorn v. France*, 16 October 2001, para. 32.

[48] ETS No 090, 27 January 1977.

requesting State, be deprived of the rights of defence as they are guaranteed by the European Convention on Human Rights."[49]

48. Moreover, it seems that extradition should be refused when the individual concerned runs the risk of being sentenced to life imprisonment without any possibility of early release, which may raise an issue under Article 3 of the European Convention on Human Rights. The Court underlined that *"it is (…) not to be excluded that the extradition of an individual to a State in which he runs the risk of being sentenced to life imprisonment without any possibility of early release may raise an issue under Article 3 of the Convention (see Nivette, cited above, and also the Weeks v. the United Kingdom judgment of 2 March 1987, Series A n° 114, and Sawoniuk v. the United Kingdom (dec.), n° 63716/00, 29 May 2001)"*[50].

XIV. *Right to property*

The use of the property of persons or organisations suspected of terrorist activities may be suspended or limited, notably by such measures as freezing orders or seizures, by the relevant authorities. The owners of the property have the possibility to challenge the lawfulness of such a decision before a court.

49. See notably Article 8 of the United Nations Convention for the Suppression of the Financing of Terrorism (New York, 9 December 1999):

"1.   Each State Party shall take appropriate measures, in accordance with its domestic legal principles, for the identification, detection and freezing or seizure of any funds used or allocated for the purpose of committing the offences set forth in article 2 as well as the proceeds derived from such offences, for purposes of possible forfeiture.

2.   Each State Party shall take appropriate measures, in accordance with its domestic legal principles, for the forfeiture of funds used or allocated for the purpose of committing the offences set forth in article 2 and the proceeds derived from such offences.

3.   Each State Party concerned may give consideration to concluding agreements on the sharing with other States Parties, on a regular or case-by-case basis, of the funds derived from the forfeitures referred to in this article.

4.   Each State Party shall consider establishing mechanisms whereby the funds derived from the forfeitures referred to in this article are utilized to compensate the victims of offences referred to in article 2, paragraph 1, subparagraph (a) or (b), or their families.

---

[49] Emphases added.

[50] *Einhorn v. France*, 16 October 2001, para. 27.

5. The provisions of this article shall be implemented without prejudice to the rights of third parties acting in good faith."

50. The confiscation of property following a condemnation for criminal activity has been admitted by the Court[51].

XV. *Possible derogations*

1. When the fight against terrorism takes place in a situation of war or public emergency which threatens the life of the nation, a State may adopt measures temporarily derogating from certain obligations ensuing from the international instruments of protection of human rights, to the extent strictly required by the exigencies of the situation, as well as within the limits and under the conditions fixed by international law. The State must notify the competent authorities of the adoption of such measures in accordance with the relevant international instruments.

2. States may never, however, and whatever the acts of the person suspected of terrorist activities, or convicted of such activities, derogate from the right to life as guaranteed by these international instruments, from the prohibition against torture or inhuman or degrading treatment or punishment, from the principle of legality of sentences and of measures, nor from the ban on the retrospective effect of criminal law.

3. The circumstances which led to the adoption of such derogations need to be reassessed on a regular basis with the purpose of lifting these derogations as soon as these circumstances no longer exist.

51. The Court has indicated some of the parameters that permit to say which are the situations of "public emergency threatening the life of the nation"[52].

52. The Court acknowledges a large power of appreciation to the State to determine whether the measures derogating from the obligations of the Convention are the most appropriate or expedient:

> *"It is not the Court's role to substitute its view as to what measures were most appropriate or expedient at the relevant time in dealing with an emergency situation for that of the Government which have direct responsibility for establishing the balance between the taking of effective measures to combat terrorism on the one hand, and respecting individual rights on the other (see the above-mentioned*

---

[51] See *Phillips v. United Kingdom*, 5 July 2001, in particular paras. 35 and 53.

[52] See *Lawless v. Ireland* (No 3), 1st July 1961.

Ireland v. the United Kingdom judgment, Series A no. 25, p. 82, para. 214, and the Klass and Others v. Germany judgment of 6 September 1978, Series A no. 28, p. 23, para. 49)".[53]

53. Article 15 of the Convention gives an authorisation to contracting States to derogate from the obligations set forth by the Convention "*in time of war or other public emergency threatening the life of the nation*".

54. Derogations are however limited by the text of Article 15 itself ("*No derogation from Article 2, except in respect of deaths resulting from lawful acts of war, or from Articles 3, 4 (paragraph 1) and 7*" and "*to the extent strictly required by the exigencies of the situation*").

> "*As the Court has stated on many occasions, Article 3 enshrines one of the most fundamental values of democratic societies. Even in the most difficult circumstances, such as the fight against terrorism and organised crime, the Convention prohibits in absolute terms torture and inhuman or degrading treatment or punishment. Unlike most of the substantive clauses of the Convention and of Protocols Nos. 1 and 4, Article 3 makes no provision for exceptions and no derogation from it is permissible under Article 15 para. 2 even in the event of a public emergency threatening the life of the nation (...).*"[54]

55. The Court was led to judge cases in which Article 15 was referred to by the defendant State. The Court affirmed therefore its jurisdiction to control the existence of a public emergency threatening the life of the nation: "*whereas it is for the Court to determine whether the conditions laid down in Article 15 (art. 15) for the exercise of the exceptional right of derogation have been fulfilled in the present case*"[55].

56. Examining a derogation on the basis of Article 15, the Court agreed that this derogation was justified by the reinforcement and the impact of terrorism and that, when deciding to put someone in custody, against the opinion of the judicial authority, the Government did not exceed its margin of appreciation. It is not up to the Court to say what measures would best fit the emergency situations since it is the direct responsibility of the governments to weigh up the situation and to decide between towards efficient measures to fight against terrorism or the respect of individual rights:

---

[53] *Brannigan and McBride v. United Kingdom*, 26 May 1993, para. 59.

[54] *Labita v. Italy*, 6 April 2000, para. 119. See also *Ireland v. United Kingdom*, 18 January 1978, A n° 25, para. 163; *Soering v. United Kingdom*, 7 July 1989, A n° 161, para. 88; *Chahal v. United Kingdom*, 15 November 1996, para. 79; *Aksoy v. Turkey*, 18 December 1996, para. 62; *Aydin v. Turkey*, 25 September 1997, para. 81; *Assenov and Others v. Bulgaria*, 28 October 1998, para. 93; *Selmouni v. France*, 28 July 1999, para. 95.

[55] *Lawless v. Ireland*, 1 July 1961, A n° 3, para. 22.

"The Court recalls that it falls to each Contracting State, with its responsibility for "the life of [its] nation", to determine whether that life is threatened by a "public emergency" and, if so, how far it is necessary to go in attempting to overcome the emergency. By reason of their direct and continuous contact with the pressing needs of the moment, the national authorities are in principle in a better position than the international judge to decide both on the presence of such an emergency and on the nature and scope of derogations necessary to avert it. Accordingly, in this matter a wide margin of appreciation should be left to the national authorities (see the Ireland v. the United Kingdom judgment of 18 January 1978, Series A no. 25, pp. 78-79, para. 207).

Nevertheless, Contracting Parties do not enjoy an unlimited power of appreciation. It is for the Court to rule on whether inter alia the States have gone beyond the "extent strictly required by the exigencies" of the crisis. The domestic margin of appreciation is thus accompanied by a European supervision (ibid.). At the same time, in exercising its supervision the Court must give appropriate weight to such relevant factors as the nature of the rights affected by the derogation, the circumstances leading to, and the duration of, the emergency situation."[56]

57. Concerning the length of the custody after arrest, and even if the Court recognizes the existence of a situation that authorises the use of Article 15, 7 days seem to be a length that satisfies the State obligations given the circumstances[57], but 30 days seem to be too long[58].

58. The General comment n° 29 of the UN Human Rights Committee[59] on Article 4 of the International Covenant on Civil and Political Rights (16 December 1966) need also to be taken into consideration. This general observation tends to limit the authorised derogation to this Covenant, even in cases of exceptional circumstances.

XVI. *Respect for peremptory norms of international law and for international humanitarian law*

In their fight against terrorism, States may never act in breach of peremptory norms of international law nor in breach international humanitarian law, where applicable.

---

[56] *Brannigan and Mc Bride v. United Kingdom*, 26 May 1993, para. 43.

[57] See *Brannigan and Mc Bride v. United Kingdom*, 26 May 1993, paras. 58-60.

[58] See *Aksoy v. Turkey*, 18 December 1996, paras. 71-84.

[59] Adopted on 24 July 2001 at its 1950th meeting, see document CCPR/C/21/Rev.1/Add.11.

XVII. *Compensation for victims of terrorist acts*

When compensation is not fully available from other sources, in particular through the confiscation of the property of the perpetrators, organisers and sponsors of terrorist acts, the State must contribute to the compensation of the victims of attacks that took place on its territory, as far as their person or their health is concerned.

59. First, see Article 2 of the European Convention on Compensation of Victims of Violent Crimes (Strasbourg, 24 November 1983, ETS No. 116):

> *"1. When compensation is not fully available from other sources the State shall contribute to compensate:*
> > *a. those who have sustained serious bodily injury or impairment of health directly attributable to an intentional crime of violence;*
> > *b. the dependants of persons who have died as a result of such crime.*
> *2. Compensation shall be awarded in the above cases even if the offender cannot be prosecuted or punished."*

60. See also Article 8, para.4, of the International Convention for the Suppression of the Financing of Terrorism (New York, 8 December 1999):

> *"Each State Party shall consider establishing mechanisms whereby the funds derived from the forfeitures referred to in this article are utilized to compensate the victims of offences referred to in article 2, paragraph 1, sub paragraph (a) or (b), or their families."*

Guidelines on the Protection of Victims of Terrorist Acts (2005)

adopted by the Committee of Ministers on 2 March 2005 at the 917th meeting of the Ministers' Deputies

Preamble

The Committee of Ministers,

[a] Considering that terrorism seriously jeopardises human rights, threatens democracy, aims notably to destabilise legitimately constituted governments and to undermine pluralistic civil society and challenges the ideals of everyone to live free from fear;

[b] Unequivocally condemning all acts of terrorism as criminal and unjustifiable, wherever and by whomever committed;

[c] Recognising the suffering endured by the victims of terrorist acts and their close family and considering that these persons must be shown national and international solidarity and support;

[d] Recognising in that respect the important role of associations for the protection of victims of terrorist acts;

[e] Reaffirming the Guidelines on Human Rights and the Fight against Terrorism, adopted on 11 July 2002 at the 804th meeting of the Ministers' Deputies, as a permanent and universal reference;

[f] Underlining in particular the States' obligation to take the measures needed to protect the fundamental rights of everyone within their jurisdiction against terrorist acts, especially the right to life;

[g] Recalling also that all measures taken by States to fight terrorism must respect human rights and the principle of the rule of law, while excluding any form of arbitrariness, as well as any discriminatory or racist treatment, and must be subject to appropriate supervision;

[h] Considering that the present Guidelines aim at addressing the needs and concerns of the victims of terrorist acts in identifying the means to be implemented to help them and to protect their fundamental rights while excluding any form of arbitrariness, as well as any discriminatory or racist treatment;

[i] Considering that the present Guidelines should not, under any circumstances, be construed as restricting in any way the Guidelines of 11 July 2002;

adopts the following guidelines and invites member States to implement them and ensure that they are widely disseminated among all authorities responsible for the fight against terrorism and for the protection of the victims of terrorist acts, as well as among representatives of civil society.

I. Principles

1. States should ensure that any person who has suffered direct physical or psychological harm as a result of a terrorist act as well as, in appropriate circumstances, their close family can benefit from the services and measures prescribed by these Guidelines. These persons are considered victims for the purposes of these Guidelines.

2. The granting of these services and measures should not depend on the identification, arrest, prosecution or conviction of the perpetrator of the terrorist act.

3. States must respect the dignity, private and family life of victims of terrorist acts in their treatment.

II. Emergency assistance

In order to cover the immediate needs of the victims, States should ensure that appropriate (medical, psychological, social and material) emergency assistance is available free of charge to victims of terrorist acts; they should also facilitate access to spiritual assistance for victims at their request.

III. Continuing assistance

1. States should provide for appropriate continuing medical, psychological, social and material assistance for victims of terrorist acts.

2. If the victim does not normally reside on the territory of the State where the terrorist act occurred, that State should co-operate with the State of residence in ensuring that the victim receives such assistance.

IV. Investigation and prosecution

1. Where there have been victims of terrorist acts, States must launch an effective official investigation into those acts.

2. In this framework, special attention must be paid to victims without it being necessary for them to have made a formal complaint.

3. In cases where, as a result of an investigation, it is decided not to take action to prosecute a suspected perpetrator of a terrorist act, States should allow victims to ask for this decision to be re-examined by a competent authority.

V. Effective access to the law and to justice

States should provide effective access to the law and to justice for victims of terrorist acts by providing:

(i)   the right of access to competent courts in order to bring a civil action in support of their rights, and

(ii) legal aid in appropriate cases.

VI. Administration of justice

1.   States should, in accordance with their national legislation, strive to bring individuals suspected of terrorist acts to justice and obtain a decision from a competent tribunal within a reasonable time.

2.   States should ensure that the position of victims of terrorist acts is adequately recognised in criminal proceedings.

VII. Compensation

1.   Victims of terrorist acts should receive fair, appropriate and timely compensation for the damages which they suffered. When compensation is not available from other sources, in particular through the confiscation of the property of the perpetrators, organisers and sponsors of terrorist acts, the State on the territory of which the terrorist act happened must contribute to the compensation of victims for direct physical or psychological harm, irrespective of their nationality.

2.   Compensation should be easily accessible to victims, irrespective of nationality. To this end, the State on the territory of which the terrorist act happened should introduce a mechanism allowing for a fair and appropriate compensation, after a simple procedure and within a reasonable time.

3.   States whose nationals were victims of a terrorist act on the territory of another State should also encourage administrative co-operation with the competent authorities of that State to facilitate access to compensation for their nationals.

4.   Apart from the payment of pecuniary compensation, States are encouraged to consider, depending on the circumstances, taking other measures to mitigate the negative effects of the terrorist act suffered by the victims.

VIII. Protection of the private and family life of victims of terrorist acts

1.   States should take appropriate steps to avoid as far as possible undermining respect for the private and family life of victims of terrorist

acts, in particular when carrying out investigations or providing assistance after the terrorist act as well as within the framework of proceedings initiated by victims.

2. States should, where appropriate, in full compliance with the principle of freedom of expression, encourage the media and journalists to adopt self-regulatory measures in order to ensure the protection of the private and family life of victims of terrorist acts in the framework of their information activities.

3. States must ensure that victims of terrorist acts have an effective remedy where they raise an arguable claim that their right to respect for their private and family life has been violated.

IX. Protection of the dignity and security of victims of terrorist acts

1. At all stages of the proceedings, victims of terrorist acts should be treated in a manner which gives due consideration to their personal situation, their rights and their dignity.

2. States must ensure the protection and security of victims of terrorist acts and should take measures, where appropriate, to protect their identity, in particular where they intervene as witnesses.

X. Information for victims of terrorist acts

States should give information, in an appropriate way, to victims of terrorist acts about the act of which they suffered, except where victims indicate that they do not wish to receive such information. For this purpose, States should:

(i) set up appropriate information contact points for the victims, concerning in particular their rights, the existence of victim support bodies, and the possibility of obtaining assistance, practical and legal advice as well as redress or compensation;

(ii) ensure the provision to the victims of appropriate information in particular about the investigations, the final decision concerning prosecution, the date and place of the hearings and the conditions under which they may acquaint themselves with the decisions handed down.

XI. Specific training for persons responsible for assisting victims of terrorist acts

States should encourage specific training for persons responsible for assisting victims of terrorist acts, as well as granting the necessary resources to that effect.

XII. Increased protection

Nothing in these Guidelines restrains States from adopting more favourable services and measures than described in these Guidelines.

Texts of reference

Used for the preparation of the
Guidelines on the protection of victims of terrorist acts

Preliminary note

This document was prepared by the Secretariat, in co-operation with the Chairman of the Group of Specialists on Human Rights and the Fight against Terrorism (DH-S-TER). **It is not meant to be taken as an explanatory report or memorandum of the Guidelines.**

Preamble

The Committee of Ministers,

[a] Considering that terrorism seriously jeopardises human rights, threatens democracy, aims notably to destabilise legitimately constituted governments and to undermine pluralistic civil society and challenges the ideals of everyone to live free from fear;

1.   The first part of this paragraph repeats paragraph [a] of the Preamble of the Guidelines adopted in July 2002. The phrase "free from fear" finds its origin in the second paragraph of the Preamble of the Universal Declaration of Human Rights adopted by the General Assembly of the United Nations in its resolution 217 A (III) of 10 December 1948.

[b] Unequivocally condemning all acts of terrorism as criminal and unjustifiable, wherever and by whomever committed;

2.   The wording repeats that of paragraph [b] of the Preamble of the July 2002 Guidelines.

[c] Recognising the suffering endured by the victims of terrorist acts and their close family and considering that these persons must be shown national and international solidarity and support;

[d] Recognising in that respect the important role of associations for the protection of victims of terrorist acts;

[e] Reaffirming the Guidelines on Human Rights and the Fight against Terrorism, adopted on 11 July 2002 at the 804th meeting of the Ministers' Deputies, as a permanent and universal reference;

[f] Underlining in particular the States' obligation to take the measures needed to protect the fundamental rights of everyone within their jurisdiction against terrorist acts, especially the right to life;

[g] Recalling also that all measures taken by States to fight terrorism must respect human rights and the principle of the rule of law, while excluding any form of arbitrariness, as well as any discriminatory or racist treatment, and must be subject to appropriate supervision;

3. This paragraph repeats Guideline II of July 2002.

4. In this context, *the European Commission against Racism and Intolerance (ECRI) General Policy Recommendation No. 8 on Combating Racism while Fighting Terrorism* of 17 March 2004 should be recalled.

[h] Considering that the present Guidelines aim at addressing the needs and concerns of the victims of terrorist acts in identifying the means to be implemented to help them and to protect their fundamental rights while excluding any form of arbitrariness, as well as any discriminatory or racist treatment;

5. *Recommendation 1426 (1999)* of the Parliamentary Assembly of the Council of Europe on *European democracies facing up to terrorism* of 23 September 1999, asks that the Committee of Ministers consider "the incorporation of the principle of fuller protection for victims of terrorist acts at both national and international level";

6. More recently, *Recommendation 1677 (2004)* and *Resolution 1677 (2004)* of the Parliamentary Assembly on the *Challenge of terrorism in Council of Europe member States* of 6 October 2004 should be recalled. The first one asks the Committee of Ministers to "finalise as soon as possible the elaboration of guidelines on the rights of victims and the corresponding duties of member States to provide all necessary assistance and to create a forum for the exchange of good practice and training experiences between member States". The second one "calls on national parliaments to (i.) adopt an integrated and co-ordinated approach to countering terrorism at all its stages, including drawing up a legislative framework aimed at: (...) (d.) protecting, rehabilitating and compensating victims of terrorist acts".

7. Moreover, *Resolution No. 1 on Combating international terrorism*, adopted by the Ministers at the 24th Conference of European Ministers of Justice (Moscow, 4-5 October 2001) invites the Committee of Ministers to "c) (review) existing or, where necessary, (adopt) new rules concerning: (...) iv. the improvement of the protection, support and compensation of victims of terrorist acts and their families". *Resolution No. 1 on Combating terrorism* adopted by the Ministers at the 25th Conference of European Ministers of Justice (Sofia, 9-10 October 2003) reiterates this invitation.

8. Finally, paragraph 1 of *the European Commission against Racism and Intolerance (ECRI) General Policy Recommendation No. 8 on Combating Racism while Fighting Terrorism* of 17 March 2004 recommends to governments of member States "to take all adequate measures, especially

through international co-operation, (...) to support the victims of terrorism (...)".

[i] **Considering that the present Guidelines should not, under any circumstances, be construed as restricting in any way the Guidelines of 11 July 2002;**

adopts the following guidelines and invites member States to implement them and ensure that they are widely disseminated among all authorities responsible for the fight against terrorism and for the protection of the victims of terrorist acts, as well as among representatives of civil society.

9.   The terms "invites member States to implement them and ensure that they are widely disseminated among all authorities responsible for the fight against terrorism" are taken from the last sentence of the Preamble to the Guidelines of July 2002.

I.   Principles

1.   **States should ensure that any person who has suffered direct physical or psychological harm as a result of a terrorist act as well as, in appropriate circumstances, their close family can benefit from the services and measures prescribed by these Guidelines. These persons are considered victims for the purposes of these Guidelines.**

10. *Definition.* Neither the European Convention on Human Rights nor the case-law of the Court gives a definition of what a victim of a terrorist act is, nor even of the word "victim". The Court always preferred to adopt a case by case approach.

11. In the framework of the United Nations, the Declaration of Basic Principles of Justice for Victims of Crime and Abuse of Power adopted on 29 November 1985 by the General Assembly (A/RES/40/34) gives the following definition:

"A.   Victims of Crime

1.   "Victims" means persons who, individually or collectively, have suffered harm, including physical or mental injury, emotional suffering, economic loss or substantial impairment of their fundamental rights, through acts or omissions that are in violation of criminal laws operative within Member States, including those laws proscribing criminal abuse of power.

2.   A person may be considered a victim, under this Declaration, regardless of whether the perpetrator is identified, apprehended, prosecuted or convicted and regardless of the familial relationship between the perpetrator and the victim.   The term "victim" also includes, where appropriate, the immediate family or dependants of the direct victim and

persons who have suffered harm in intervening to assist victims in distress or to prevent victimization.

3.   The provisions contained herein shall be applicable to all, without distinction of any kind, such as race, colour, sex, age, language, religion, nationality, political or other opinion, cultural beliefs or practices, property, birth or family status, ethnic or social origin, and disability."

12. For its part, Article 1 of the Council of the European Union Framework Decision of 15 March 2001 on the standing of victims in criminal proceedings (2001/220/JHA) states that for the purposes of the Framework Decision:

"(a) "victim" shall mean a natural person who has suffered harm, including physical or mental injury, emotional suffering or economic loss, directly caused by acts or omissions that are in violation of the criminal law of a Member State;"

13. Moreover, the Court recognises that the family of a victim can, in certain cases, be considered as a victim:

-    *Cyprus v. Turkey*, 10 May 2001, § 156:

     "The Court recalls that the question whether a family member of a "disappeared person" is a victim of treatment contrary to Article 3 will depend on the existence of special factors which give the suffering of the person concerned a dimension and character distinct from the emotional distress which may be regarded as inevitably caused to relatives of a victim of a serious human-rights violation. Relevant elements will include the proximity of the family tie – in that context, a certain weight will attach to the parent-child bond –, the particular circumstances of the relationship, the extent to which the family member witnessed the events in question, the involvement of the family member in the attempts to obtain information about the disappeared person and the way in which the authorities responded to those enquiries. The Court further recalls that the essence of such a violation does not so much lie in the fact of the "disappearance" of the family member but rather in the authorities' reactions and attitudes to the situation when it is brought to their attention. It is especially in respect of the latter that a relative may claim directly to be a victim of the authorities' conduct (see Çakici v. Turkey [GC], no. 23657/94, § 98, ECHR 1999-IV)."

2.   The granting of these services and measures should not depend on the identification, arrest, prosecution or conviction of the perpetrator of the terrorist act.

14. Paragraph 2 of the Declaration of Basic Principles of Justice for Victims of Crime and Abuse of Power adopted on 29 November 1985 by the General Assembly of the United Nations (A/RES/40/34) states that: "A person may be

considered a victim, under this Declaration, regardless of whether the perpetrator is identified, apprehended, prosecuted or convicted (...)".

3. States must respect the dignity, private and family life of victims of terrorist acts in their treatment.

15. Paragraph 4 of the Declaration of Basic Principles of Justice for Victims of Crime and Abuse of Power adopted on 29 November 1985 by the General Assembly of the United Nations (A/RES/40/34) specifies that: "Victims should be treated with compassion and respect for their dignity. (...)".

16. Article 2, paragraph 1, of the Council of the European Union Framework Decision of 15 March 2001 on the standing of victims in criminal proceedings (2001/220/JHA) states that: "Each Member State (...) shall continue to make every effort to ensure that victims are treated with due respect for the dignity of the individual during proceedings and shall recognise the rights and legitimate interests of victims with particular reference to criminal proceedings.".

II. Emergency assistance

In order to cover the immediate needs of the victims, States should ensure that appropriate (medical, psychological, social and material) emergency assistance is available free of charge to victims of terrorist acts; they should also facilitate access to spiritual assistance for victims at their request.

17. Paragraph 4 of Recommendation No. R (87) 21 of the Committee of Ministers to member States on assistance to victims and the prevention of victimisation recommends that the governments of member States "ensure that victims and their families, especially those who are most vulnerable, receive in particular (...) emergency help to meet immediate needs (...)".

18. The word "assistance" was preferred to the word "help" in particular because it is used in several articles of the European Social Charter (Revised) (CETS No. 163, of 3 May 1996): see for example Article 13 "Right to social and medical assistance".

19. Even if the text of the European Convention of Human Rights does not expressly mention the right to health care nor the right to medical assistance, the Court has clearly indicated that, in certain cases, the State can have an obligation to provide appropriate medical assistance so as not to risk violation of Article 2 of the Convention (Right to life) or Article 3 (Prohibition of torture).

20. In its decision *Cyprus v. Turkey* of 10 May 2001, para 219, the Court indicates that:

"The Court observes that an issue may arise under Article 2 of the Convention where it is shown that the authorities of a Contracting State put an individual's life at risk through the denial of health care which they have undertaken to make available to the population generally. It notes in this connection that Article 2 § 1 of the Convention enjoins the State not only to refrain from the intentional and unlawful taking of life, but also to take appropriate steps to safeguard the lives of those within its jurisdiction (see the L.C.B. v. the United Kingdom judgment of 9 June 1998, Reports 1998-III, p. 1403, § 36)."

21. In its decision *Ilhan v. Turkey* of 27 June 2000, para 76:

"The Court observes that these three cases[1] concerned the positive obligation on the State to protect the life of the individual from third parties or from the risk of illness under the first sentence of Article 2 § 1."

22. The Court reiterated its position in its decision *Berktay v. Turkey* of 1 March 2001, para 154.

23. In its decision on admissibility no. 65653/01 in the case *Nitecki v. Poland* of 21 March 2002, the Court recalled that:

"The Court recalls that the first sentence of Article 2 enjoins the State not only to refrain from the intentional and unlawful taking of life, but also to take appropriate steps to safeguard the lives of those within its jurisdiction. It cannot be excluded that the acts and omissions of the authorities in the field of health care policy may in certain circumstances engage their responsibility under Article 2 (see Powell v. the United Kingdom [decision], no. 45305/99, 4.5.2000).

The Court has held in cases involving allegations of medical malpractice that the State's positive obligations under Article 2 to protect life include the requirement for hospitals to have regulations for the protection of their patients' lives and also the obligation to establish an effective judicial system for establishing the cause of a death which occurs in hospital and any liability on the part of the medical practitioners concerned (see, among other authorities, Erikson v. Italy, [decision], no. 37900/97, 26.10.1999; Calvelli and Ciglio v. Italy [GC], no. 32967/96, § 49, ECHR 2002).

Furthermore, with respect to the scope of the State's positive obligations in the provision of health care, the Court has stated that an issue may arise under Article 2 where it is shown that the authorities of a Contracting State put an individual's life at risk through the denial of

---

[1] Note from the Secretariat: These are *Osman v. United Kingdom* (decision of 28 October 1998), *Yaşa v. Turkey* (Decision of 2 September 1998) and *L.C.B. v. United Kingdom* (decision of 9 June 1998).

health care which they have undertaken to make available to the population generally (see Cyprus v. Turkey [GC], no. 25781/94, § 219, ECHR 2001-IV)."

24. The European Commission of Human Rights recognised that, in certain specific circumstances, States had a positive obligation drawn from Article 3 of the Convention, to provide immediate medical care. In this regard, see, as concerns a detained person, in the case *Hurtado v Switzerland*, the report of the Commission in which it considered, unanimously, that the applicant had suffered violation of Article 3 by not having received immediate medical care. This case was concluded by a friendly settlement (judgment dated 28 January 1994 striking out the case). Also see the case *McGlinchey v. United Kingdom* of 29 April 2003, paragraph 46:

"Under this provision the State must ensure that a person is detained in conditions which are compatible with respect for her human dignity, that the manner and method of the execution of the measure do not subject her to distress or hardship of an intensity exceeding the unavoidable level of suffering inherent in detention and that, given the practical demands of imprisonment, her health and well-being are adequately secured by, among other things, providing her with the requisite medical assistance (see, mutatis mutandis, Aerts v. Belgium, judgment of 30 July 1998, Reports 1998-V, p. 1966, §§ 64 et seq., and Kudła v. Poland [GC], no. 30210/96, § 94, ECHR 2000-XI)."

III. Continuing assistance

1. States should provide for appropriate continuing medical, psychological, social and material assistance for victims of terrorist acts.

2. If the victim does not normally reside on the territory of the State where the terrorist act occurred, that State should co-operate with the State of residence in ensuring that the victim receives such assistance.

25. As concerns social assistance, the Court noted that a violation of Article 3 could be acknowledged, in certain specific circumstances, if a pension and the other social benefits were wholly insufficient. In this regard, see the inadmissiblity decision taken by the Court in the case *Larioshina v. Russian Federation*, of 23 April 2002:

"(…) the Court considers that a complaint about a wholly insufficient amount of pension and the other social benefits may, in principle, raise an issue under Article 3 of the Convention which prohibits inhuman or degrading treatment."

26. Paragraph 4 of Committee of Ministers Recommendation No. R (87) 21 to member States on assistance to victims and the prevention of victimisation recommends that governments of member States "ensure that

victims and their families, especially those who are most vulnerable, receive in particular (...) continuing medical, psychological, social and material help".

27. As concerns the case-law of the Court, see the extracts quoted above illustrating Guideline II (Emergency Assistance) which can be applied, *mutadis mutandis*, to continuing assistance.

28. As for the European Social Charter (Revised) (CETS No. 163, of 3 May 1996) its Articles 11 and 14, provides in particular that:

Article 11 –The right to protection of health

"With a view to ensuring the effective exercise of the right to protection of health, the Parties undertake, either directly or in co-operation with public or private organisations, to take appropriate measures designed inter alia:

1   to remove as far as possible the causes of ill health;

2   to provide advisory and educational facilities for the promotion of health and the encouragement of individual responsibility in matters of health;

3   to prevent as far as possible epidemic, endemic and other diseases, as well as accidents."

Article 14 – The right to benefit from social welfare services

"With a view to ensuring the effective exercise of the right to benefit from social welfare services, the Parties undertake:

1   to promote or provide services which, by using methods of social work, would contribute to the welfare and development of both individuals and groups in the community, and to their adjustment to the social environment;

2   to encourage the participation of individuals and voluntary or other organisations in the establishment and maintenance of such services."

29. Finally, Paragraph 14 of the Declaration of Basic Principles of Justice for Victims of Crime and Abuse of Power adopted on 29 November 1985 by the General Assembly of the United Nations (A/RES/40/34), states that:

"Victims should receive the necessary material, medical, psychological and social assistance through governmental, voluntary, community-based and indigenous means."

IV. Investigation and prosecution

1. Where there have been victims of terrorist acts, States must launch an effective official investigation into those acts.

30. The Court recognises that there should be an official investigation when individuals have been killed as a result of the use of force and that this obligation is not confined to cases where it has been established that the killing was caused by an agent of the State:

- *Ulku Ekinci v. Turkey*, 16 July 2002, § 144:

   "The Court recalls that, according to its case-law, the obligation to protect the right to life under Article 2, read in conjunction with the State's general duty under Article 1 to "secure to everyone within [its] jurisdiction the rights and freedoms defined in [the] Convention", requires by implication that there should be some form of effective official investigation when individuals have been killed as a result of the use of force. This obligation is not confined to cases where it has been established that the killing was caused by an agent of the State. Nor is it decisive whether members of the deceased's family or others have lodged a formal complaint about the killing with the competent investigation authority. The mere fact that the authorities were informed of the killing of the applicant's husband gave rise ipso facto to an obligation under Article 2 of the Convention to carry out an effective investigation into the circumstances surrounding the death (cf. Tanrikulu v. Turkey [GC], no. 23763/94, §§ 101 and 103, ECHR 1999-IV). The nature and degree of scrutiny which satisfies the minimum threshold of an investigation's effectiveness depends on the circumstances of each particular case. It must be assessed on the basis of all relevant facts and with regard to the practical realities of investigation work (cf. Velikova v. Bulgaria, no. 41488/98, § 80, ECHR 2000-VI)."

- *Tepe v. Turkey*, 9 May 2003, § 195:

   "Given the fundamental importance of the right to protection of life, Article 13 requires, in addition to the payment of compensation where appropriate, a thorough and effective investigation capable of leading to the identification and punishment of those responsible for the deprivation of life and including effective access for the complainant to the investigation procedure (see Kaya, cited above, pp. 330-31, § 107)."

31. Moreover, the Court recognises that the investigation must be led with promptness and reasonable expedition:

- *Finucane v. United Kingdom*, of 1 July 2003, para. 71

   "70. A requirement of promptness and reasonable expedition is implicit in this context (see Yaşa v. Turkey, judgment of 2 September 1998,

Reports 1998-IV, pp. 2439-2440, §§ 102-104; Cakıcı v. Turkey [GC], no. 23657/94, ECHR 1999-IV, §§ 80, 87 and 106; Tanrıkulu v. Turkey, cited above, § 109; Mahmut Kaya v. Turkey, no. 22535/93, ECHR 2000-III, §§ 106-107). While there may be obstacles or difficulties which prevent progress in an investigation in a particular situation, a prompt response by the authorities in investigating a use of lethal force may generally be regarded as essential in maintaining public confidence in their adherence to the rule of law and in preventing any appearance of collusion in or tolerance of unlawful acts (see, for example, Hugh Jordan v. the United Kingdom, cited above, §§ 108, 136 140)."

2. In this framework, special attention must be paid to victims without it being necessary for them to have made a formal complaint.

32. The Court recognises that the close family of a deceased victim must be involved in the investigation to the extent necessary to safeguard his or her legitimate interests, failing which this investigation could not be considered "effective":

33. *Slimani v. France*, 27 July 2004, para. 32 and 47:

[The text of this judgment is available in French only]

"32. (...) Dans le même type d'affaires, la Cour a souligné qu'il doit y avoir un élément suffisant de contrôle public de l'enquête ou de ses résultats pour garantir que les responsables aient à rendre des comptes, tant en pratique qu'en théorie. Elle a précisé que, si le degré de contrôle public requis peut varier d'une affaire à l'autre, les proches de la victime doivent, dans tous les cas, être associés à la procédure dans la mesure nécessaire à la sauvegarde de leurs intérêts légitimes (voir, notamment, l'arrêt *Hugh Jordan c. Royaume-Uni* du 4 mai 2001, no 24746/94, § 109 et les arrêts, précités, McKerr, § 115 et Edwards, § 73) ; elle estime qu'il doit en aller ainsi dès lorsqu'une personne décède entre les mains d'autorités."

"47. Il n'en reste pas moins que, comme la Cour l'a précédemment souligné, dans tous les cas où un détenu décède dans des conditions suspectes, l'article 2 met à la charge des autorités l'obligation de conduire d'office, dès que l'affaire est portée à leur attention, une « enquête officielle et effective » de nature à permettre d'établir les causes de la mort et d'identifier les éventuels responsables de celle-ci et d'aboutir à leur punition : les autorités ne sauraient laisser aux proches du défunt l'initiative de déposer une plainte formelle ou d'assumer la responsabilité d'une procédure d'enquête. Or à cela il faut ajouter qu'une telle enquête ne saurait être qualifiée d'« effective » que si, notamment, les proches de la victime sont impliqués dans la procédure de manière propre à permettre la sauvegarde de leurs intérêts légitimes (paragraphes 29-32 ci-dessus).

Selon la Cour, exiger que les proches du défunt déposent une plainte avec constitution de partie civile pour pouvoir être impliqués dans la procédure d'enquête contredirait ces principes. Elle estime que, dès lors qu'elles ont connaissance d'un décès intervenu dans des conditions suspectes, les autorités doivent, d'office, mener une enquête, à laquelle les proches du défunt doivent, d'office également, être associés."

34. *McKerr v. United Kingdom* of 4 May 2001, para 148 and 159-160:

"148. (...) The Court considers that the right of the family of the deceased whose death is under investigation to participate in the proceedings requires that the procedures adopted ensure the requisite protection of their interests, which may be in direct conflict with those of the police or security forces implicated in the events. The Court is not persuaded that the applicant's interests as next-of-kin were fairly or adequately protected in this respect."

"159. (...) the Court considers that the requirements of Article 2 may nonetheless be satisfied if, while seeking to take into account other legitimate interests such as national security or the protection of material relevant to other investigations, the various procedures provide for the necessary safeguards in an accessible and effective manner. In the present case, the available procedures have not struck the right balance.

160. The Court would observe that the shortcomings in transparency and effectiveness identified above run counter to the purpose identified by the domestic courts of allaying suspicions and rumour. Proper procedures for ensuring the accountability of agents of the State are indispensable in maintaining public confidence and meeting the legitimate concerns that might arise from the use of lethal force. A lack of such procedures will only add fuel to fears of sinister motivations, as is illustrated, inter alia, by the submissions made by the applicant concerning the alleged shoot-to-kill policy."

35. Finally, with regard to the European Union, Article 10, paragraph 1, of the Council Framework Decision of 13 June 2002 on combating terrorism specifies that:

"Member States shall ensure that investigation into, or prosecution of, offences covered by this Framework Decision are not dependent on a report or accusation made by a person subjected to the offence, at least if the acts were committed on the territory of the Member State."

3. In cases where, as a result of an investigation, it is decided not to take action to prosecute a suspected perpetrator of a terrorist act, States should allow victims to ask for this decision to be re-examined by a competent authority.

36. Moreover, the Court recognises the need for public scrutiny of investigation or their results:

- *Finucane v. United Kingdom*, of 1 July 2003, para. 71:

"71. For the same reasons, there must be a sufficient element of public scrutiny of the investigation or its results to secure accountability in practice as well as in theory. The degree of public scrutiny required may well vary from case to case. In all cases, however, the next-of-kin of the victim must be involved in the procedure to the extent necessary to safeguard his or her legitimate interests (see Güleç v. Turkey, cited above, p. 1733, § 82; Oğur v. Turkey, cited above, § 92; Gül v. Turkey, cited above, § 93; and recent Northern Irish cases, for example, McKerr v. the United Kingdom, cited above, § 148)."

37. With regard to a case where the State's authorities decide not to bring to justice the presumed author of a terrorist act, for example through lack of evidence, Paragraph 7 of Recommendation No. R (85) 11 of the Committee of Ministers to member States on the position of the victim in the framework of criminal law and procedure specifies that "the victim should have the right to ask for a review by a competent authority of a decision not to prosecute, or the right to institute private proceedings".

V. Effective access to the law and to justice

States should provide effective access to the law and to justice for victims of terrorist acts by providing:

(i)   the right of access to competent courts in order to bring a civil action in support of their rights, and

(ii)   legal aid in appropriate cases.

38. The expression "effective access to the law and to justice" has been taken from Recommendation No. R (93) 1 of the Committee of Ministers to member States on effective access to the law and to justice for the very poor.

39. Principles laid down in Recommendation No. R (81) 7 of the Committee of Ministers on measures facilitating access to justice are applicable, *mutadis mutandis*, to victims of terrorist acts and should be implemented by all member States.

40. Finally, Paragraph 6 of the Declaration of Basic Principles of Justice for Victims of Crime and Abuse of Power (A/RES/40/34) adopted on 29 November 1985 by the General Assembly of the United Nations, states that:

"6. The responsiveness of judicial and administrative processes to the needs of victims should be facilitated by:

(a) Informing victims of their role and the scope, timing and progress of the proceedings and of the disposition of their cases, especially where serious crimes are involved and where they have requested such information;

(b) Allowing the views and concerns of victims to be presented and considered at appropriate stages of the proceedings where their personal interests are affected, without prejudice to the accused and consistent with the relevant national criminal justice system;

(c) Providing proper assistance to victims throughout the legal process;

(d) Taking measures to minimize inconvenience to victims, protect their privacy, when necessary, and ensure their safety, as well as that of their families and witnesses on their behalf, from intimidation and retaliation;

(e) Avoiding unnecessary delay in the disposition of cases and the execution of orders or decrees granting awards to victims."

VI. Administration of justice

1. States should, in accordance with their national legislation, strive to bring individuals suspected of terrorist acts to justice and obtain a decision from a competent tribunal within a reasonable time.

41. The Court also recognises that suspects must be judged within a reasonable time. See in particular:

- *Mutimara v. France,* 8 June 2004, §§ 69-74:

In this case, the Court found a breach of the Convention in respect of the length of proceedings concerning the examination of a complaint against a person who allegedly was involved in the genocide that took place in Rwanda.

[The text of this judgment is available in French only]

"69. La Cour rappelle que le caractère raisonnable de la durée d'une procédure s'apprécie eu égard aux critères consacrés par sa jurisprudence, en particulier la complexité de l'affaire, le comportement du requérant et celui des autorités compétentes (voir, parmi beaucoup d'autres, Doustaly c. France arrêt du 22 avril 1998, Recueil des arrêts et décisions 1998 II, p. 857, § 39 ; Slimane-Kaïd c. France (no 3), no 45130/98, § 38, 6 avril 2004) et suivant les circonstances de la cause, lesquelles commandent en l'occurrence une évaluation globale (Versini c. France, arrêt du 10 juillet 2001, no 40096/98, § 26 ; Slimane-Kaïd, précité).

70. En l'espèce, la Cour constate que la procédure, qui a débuté le 1er août 1995 (plainte avec constitution de partie civile de la requérante) est actuellement toujours pendante devant le juge d'instruction, soit une durée de huit ans et plus de huit mois à ce jour.

71. La Cour estime que l'affaire présentait une certaine complexité, ce dont atteste notamment la délivrance de nombreuses commissions rogatoires internationales. Cependant, cela ne saurait suffire, en soi, à justifier la durée de la procédure.

[...]

74. Compte tenu des circonstances de l'espèce et en dépit de leur particularité, la Cour estime que l'on ne saurait considérer comme « raisonnable » une durée globale de presque neuf ans pour une information pénale au demeurant toujours en cours."

2. States should ensure that the position of victims of terrorist acts is adequately recognised in criminal proceedings.

42. The Court recognises that victims should be taken into consideration in criminal proceedings, in addition to their right to bring civil proceedings in order to secure at least symbolic reparation or to protect a civil right:

- *Perez v. France*, 12 February 2004 (Grand Chamber), §§ 70-72:

"70. The Court (...) notes that the Convention does not confer any right, as demanded by the applicant, to "private revenge" or to an actio popularis. Thus, the right to have third parties prosecuted or sentenced for a criminal offence cannot be asserted independently: it must be indissociable from the victim's exercise of a right to bring civil proceedings in domestic law, even if only to secure symbolic reparation or to protect a civil right such as the right to a "good reputation" (see Golder v. the United Kingdom, judgment of 21 February 1975, Series A no. 18, p.13, § 27; Helmers, cited above, p. 14, § 27; and Tolstoy Miloslavsky v. the United Kingdom, judgment of 13 July 1995, Series A no. 316-B, p. 78, § 58).

[...]

72. (In addition, the Court notes) the need to safeguard victims' rights and their proper place in criminal proceedings. Simply because the requirements inherent in the concept of a "fair trial" are not necessarily the same in disputes about civil rights and obligations as they are in cases involving criminal trials, as evidenced by the fact that for civil

disputes there are no detailed provisions similar to those in Article 6 §§ 2 and 3 (see Dombo Beheer B.V. v. the Netherlands, judgment of 27 October 1993, Series A no. 274, p. 19, § 32) does not mean that the Court can ignore the plight of victims and downgrade their rights. [...] Lastly, the Court draws attention for information to the text of Recommendations R (83) 7, R (85) 11 and R (87) 21 of the Committee of Ministers (see paragraphs 26-28 above), which clearly specify the rights which victims may assert in the context of criminal law and procedure."

43. As indicated above by the Court, Recommendations Nos. R (83) 7, R (85) 11 and R (87) 21 of the Committee of Ministers recognise a number of rights that victims may claim under criminal law and in criminal proceedings. In particular, paragraph 29 of Recommendation No R (83) 7 of the Committee of Ministers to member States on participation of the public in crime policy provides that the governments of member States should assist victims by "establishing an efficient system of legal aid for victims so that they may have access to justice in all circumstances". Furthermore, paragraph 4 of Recommendation No. R (87) 21 of the Committee of Ministers to member States on assistance to victims and the prevention of victimisation states that the governments of member States "ensure that victims and their families, especially those who are most vulnerable, receive in particular (...) assistance during the criminal process, with due respect to the defence".

44. Article 6 (Specific assistance to the victim) of the Council of the European Union Framework Decision of 15 March 2001 on the standing of victims in criminal proceedings (2001/220/JHA) specifies: "Each Member State shall ensure that victims have access to advice as referred to in Article 4(1)(f)(iii), provided free of charge where warranted, concerning their role in the proceedings and, where appropriate, legal aid as referred to in Article 4(1)(f)(ii), when it is possible for them to have the status of parties to criminal proceedings".

45. Paragraph 6 of the Declaration of Basic Principles of Justice for Victims of Crime and Abuse of Power adopted on 29 November 1985 by the General Assembly of the United Nations (A/RES/40/34) mentions that:

"The responsiveness of judicial and administrative processes to the needs of victims should be facilitated by:

(a) Informing victims of their role and the scope, timing and progress of the proceedings and of the disposition of their cases, especially where serious crimes are involved and where they have requested such information;

(b) Allowing the views and concerns of victims to be presented and considered at appropriate stages of the proceedings where their personal interests are affected, without prejudice to the accused and consistent with the relevant national criminal justice system;

(c) Providing proper assistance to victims throughout the legal process;

(d) Taking measures to minimize inconvenience to victims, protect their privacy, when necessary, and ensure their safety, as well as that of their families and witnesses on their behalf, from intimidation and retaliation;

(e) Avoiding unnecessary delay in the disposition of cases and the execution of orders or decrees granting awards to victims."

VII. Compensation

1. Victims of terrorist acts should receive fair, appropriate and timely compensation for the damages which they suffered. When compensation is not available from other sources, in particular through the confiscation of the property of the perpetrators, organisers and sponsors of terrorist acts, the State on the territory of which the terrorist act happened must contribute to the compensation of victims for direct physical or psychological harm, irrespective of their nationality.

46. Guideline No. XVII of July 2002 (Compensation for victims of terrorist acts) recalls that: "When compensation is not fully available from other sources, in particular through the confiscation of the property of the perpetrators, organisers and sponsors of terrorist acts, the State must contribute to the compensation of the victims of attacks that took place on its territory, as far as their person or their health is concerned."

47. Resolution 2002/35 of the United Nations Commission on Human Rights entitled Human rights and terrorism, "welcomes the report of the Secretary-General (A/56/190), and invites him to continue to seek the views of Member States on the implications of terrorism in all its forms and manifestations for the full enjoyment of all human rights and fundamental freedoms and on how the needs and concerns of victims of terrorism might be addressed, including through the possible establishment of a voluntary fund for the victims of terrorism, as well as on ways and means to rehabilitate the victims of terrorism and to reintegrate them into society, with a view to incorporating his findings in his reports to the Commission and the General Assembly".

48. Moreover, in its Resolution 1566(2004) adopted at its 5053rd meeting on 8 October 2004, the United Nations Security Council:

"10. Requests further the working group, established under paragraph 9 to consider the possibility of establishing an international fund to compensate victims of terrorist acts and their families, which might be financed through voluntary contributions, which could consist in part of assets seized from terrorist organizations, their members and sponsors, and submit its recommendations to the Council".

49. Finally, with regard to compensation, it is useful to recall Article 75 of the Statute of the International Criminal Court:

Article 75 – Reparations to victims

"1. The Court shall establish principles relating to reparations to, or in respect of, victims, including restitution, compensation and rehabilitation. On this basis, in its decision the Court may, either upon request or on its own motion in exceptional circumstances, determine the scope and extent of any damage, loss and injury to, or in respect of, victims and will state the principles on which it is acting.

2. The Court may make an order directly against a convicted person specifying appropriate reparations to, or in respect of, victims, including restitution, compensation and rehabilitation. Where appropriate, the Court may order that the award for reparations be made through the Trust Fund provided for in article 79.

3. Before making an order under this article, the Court may invite and shall take account of representations from or on behalf of the convicted person, victims, other interested persons or interested States.

4. In exercising its power under this article, the Court may, after a person is convicted of a crime within the jurisdiction of the Court, determine whether, in order to give effect to an order which it may make under this article, it is necessary to seek measures under article 93, paragraph 1.

5. A State Party shall give effect to a decision under this article as if the provisions of article 109 were applicable to this article.

6. Nothing in this article shall be interpreted as prejudicing the rights of victims under national or international law."

2.   Compensation should be easily accessible to victims, irrespective of nationality. To this end, the State on the territory of which the terrorist act happened should introduce a mechanism allowing for a fair and appropriate compensation, after a simple procedure and within a reasonable time.

3.   States whose nationals were victims of a terrorist act on the territory of another State should also encourage administrative co-operation with the competent authorities of that State to facilitate access to compensation for their nationals.

4. Apart from the payment of pecuniary compensation, States are encouraged to consider, depending on the circumstances, taking other measures to mitigate the negative effects of the terrorist act suffered by the victims.

50. Paragraph 11 of the European Union Council Directive 2004/80/CE of 29 April 2004 relating to compensation to crime victims states that: "A system of co-operation between authorities of the Member States should be introduced to facilitate access to compensation in cases where the crime was committed in a Member State other than that of the victim's residence".

VIII. Protection of the private and family life of victims of terrorist acts

1. States should take appropriate steps to avoid as far as possible undermining respect for the private and family life of victims of terrorist acts, in particular when carrying out investigations or providing assistance after the terrorist act as well as within the framework of proceedings initiated by victims.

51. Paragraph 8 of Recommendation No. R (85) 11 of the Committee of Ministers to member States on the position of the victim in the framework of criminal law and procedure specifies that "at all stages of the procedure, the victim should be questioned in a manner which gives due consideration to his personal situation, his rights and his dignity".

52. Paragraph 9 of Recommendation No. R (87) 21 of the Committee of Ministers to member States on assistance to victims and the prevention of victimisation calls on the governments of member States to "take steps to prevent victim assistance services from disclosing personal information regarding victims, without their consent, to third parties".

53. In the context of the United Nations, paragraph 6, d) of the Declaration of Basic Principles of Justice for Victims of Crime and Abuse of Power adopted on 29 November 1985 by the General Assembly (A/RES/40/34) states that:

"The responsiveness of judicial and administrative processes to the needs of victims should be facilitated by: (...)

(d) Taking measures to minimize inconvenience to victims, protect their privacy, when necessary, and ensure their safety, as well as that of their families and witnesses on their behalf, from intimidation and retaliation;"

2. States should, where appropriate, in full compliance with the principle of freedom of expression, encourage the media and journalists to adopt self-regulatory measures in order to ensure the

protection of the private and family life of victims of terrorist acts in the framework of their information activities.

3. States must ensure that victims of terrorist acts have an effective remedy where they raise an arguable claim that their right to respect for their private and family life has been violated.

54. Recommendation No. (97) 19 of the Committee of Ministers to member States on the portrayal of violence in the electronic media and Recommendation No. (99) 5 on the protection of privacy on the Internet should be mentioned in this context.

IX. Protection of the dignity and security of victims of terrorist acts

1. At all stages of the proceedings, victims of terrorist acts should be treated in a manner which gives due consideration to their personal situation, their rights and their dignity.

55. The first paragraph is partly inspired by paragraph 8 of Recommendation No. R (85) 11 of the Committee of Ministers to member States on the position of the victim in the framework of criminal law and procedure which specifies that "at all stages of the procedure, the victim should be questioned in a manner which gives due consideration to his personal situation, his rights and his dignity".

2. States must ensure the protection and security of victims of terrorist acts and should take measures, where appropriate, to protect their identity, in particular where they intervene as witnesses.

56. Paragraph 6, d) of the Declaration of Basic Principles of Justice for Victims of Crime and Abuse of Power adopted on 29 November 1985 by the General Assembly of the United Nations (A/RES/40/34) states that:

> "The responsiveness of judicial and administrative processes to the needs of victims should be facilitated by: (…)
>
> (d) Taking measures to minimize inconvenience to victims, protect their privacy, when necessary, and ensure their safety, as well as that of their families and witnesses on their behalf, from intimidation and retaliation;"

X. Information for victims of terrorist acts

States should give information, in an appropriate way, to victims of terrorist acts about the act of which they suffered, except where victims indicate that they do not wish to receive such information. For this purpose, States should:

57. The Court recognises that, in certain circumstances, a family member of a "disappeared person" may suffer inhuman treatment, within the meaning of Article 3 of the Convention, if the State authorities remain silent despite attempts to obtain information about the disappeared person.

-   *Cyprus v. Turkey*, 10 May 2001, §§ 156-157:

> "156. [...] The Court recalls that the question whether a family member of a "disappeared person" is a victim of treatment contrary to Article 3 will depend on the existence of special factors which give the suffering of the person concerned a dimension and character distinct from the emotional distress which may be regarded as inevitably caused to relatives of a victim of a serious human-rights violation. Relevant elements will include [...] the involvement of the family member in the attempts to obtain information about the disappeared person and the way in which the authorities responded to those enquiries. [...]
>
> 157. [...] For the Court, the silence of the authorities of the respondent State in the face of the real concerns of the relatives of the missing persons attains a level of severity which can only be categorised as inhuman treatment within the meaning of Article 3."

(i) set up appropriate information contact points for the victims, concerning in particular their rights, the existence of victim support bodies, and the possibility of obtaining assistance, practical and legal advice as well as redress or compensation;

58. Paragraph 2 of Recommendation No. R (85) 11 of the Committee of Ministers to member States on the position of the victim in the framework of criminal law and procedure states that "the police should inform the victim about the possibilities of obtaining assistance, practical and legal advice, compensation from the offender and State compensation".

59. Paragraph 4 of Recommendation No. R (87) 21 of the Committee of Ministers to member States on assistance to victims and the prevention of victimisation provides that the governments of member States "ensure that victims and their families, especially those who are most vulnerable, receive in particular (...) information on the victim's rights".

(ii) ensure the provision to the victims of appropriate information in particular about the investigations, the final decision concerning prosecution, the date and place of the hearings and the conditions under which they may acquaint themselves with the decisions handed down.

60. Paragraph 3 of Committee of Ministers Recommendation No. R (85) 11 to member States on the position of the victim in the framework of criminal law and procedure states that "the victim should be able to obtain information on the outcome of the police investigation".

61. Paragraph 6 of this same Recommendation adds that "the victim should be informed of the final decision concerning prosecution, unless he indicates that he does not want this information".

62. Finally, paragraph 9 of Recommendation No. R (85) 11 to member States on the position of the victim in the framework of criminal law and procedure states that "the victim should be informed of: the date and place of a hearing concerning an offence which caused him suffering; his opportunities of obtaining restitution and compensation within the criminal justice process, legal assistance and advice; how he can find out the outcome of the case".

63. Article 4 of the Council of the European Union Framework Decision of 15 March 2001 on the standing of victims in criminal proceedings (2001/220/JHA) on the "Right to receive information" specifies in particular that "Member States shall take the necessary measures to ensure that, at least in cases where there might be danger to the victims, when the person prosecuted or sentenced for an offence is released, a decision may be taken to notify the victim if necessary".

XI. Specific training for persons responsible for assisting victims of terrorist acts

States should encourage specific training for persons responsible for assisting victims of terrorist acts, as well as granting the necessary resources to that effect.

64. Paragraph 11 of the preamble of the Council of the European Union Framework Decision of 15 March 2001 on the standing of victims in criminal proceedings (2001/220/JHA) provides that "suitable and adequate training should be given to persons coming into contact with victims, as this is essential both for victims and for achieving the purposes of proceedings". Article 14 of this same framework decision specifies:

Article 14 – Training for personnel involved in proceedings or otherwise in contact with victims

"1. Through its public services or by funding victim support organisations, each Member State shall encourage initiatives enabling personnel involved in proceedings or otherwise in contact with victims to receive suitable training with particular reference to the needs of the most vulnerable groups.

2. Paragraph 1 shall apply in particular to police officers and legal practitioners."

65. Paragraph 16 of the Declaration of Basic Principles of Justice for Victims of Crime and Abuse of Power adopted on 29 November 1985

by the General Assembly of the United Nations (A/RES/40/34) states that: "Police, justice, health, social service and other personnel concerned should receive training to sensitize them to the needs of victims, and guidelines to ensure proper and prompt aid."

XII. Increased protection

Nothing in these Guidelines restrains States from adopting more favourable services and measures than described in these Guidelines.

Declaration on freedom of expression and information in the media in the context of the fight against terrorism (2005)

(Adopted by the Committee of Ministers on 2 March 2005 at the 917th meeting of the Ministers' Deputies)

The Committee of Ministers of the Council of Europe,

Considering that the aim of the Council of Europe is to achieve a greater unity between its members for the purpose of safeguarding and promoting the ideals and principles which are their common heritage;

Considering the dramatic effect of terrorism on the full enjoyment of human rights, in particular the right to life, its threat to democracy, its aim notably to destabilise legitimately constituted governments and to undermine pluralistic civil society and its challenge to the ideals of everyone to live free from fear;

Unequivocally condemning all acts of terrorism as criminal and unjustifiable, wherever and by whomever committed;

Noting that every state has the duty to protect human rights and fundamental freedoms of all persons;

Recalling its firm attachment to the principles of freedom of expression and information as a basic element of democratic and pluralist society and a prerequisite for the progress of society and for the development of human beings, as underlined in the case-law of the European Court of Human Rights under Article 10 of the European Convention on Human Rights as well as in the Committee of Ministers' Declaration on the freedom of expression and information of 1982;

Considering that the free and unhindered dissemination of information and ideas is one of the most effective means of promoting understanding and tolerance, which can help prevent or combat terrorism;

Recalling that states cannot adopt measures which would impose restrictions on freedom of expression and information going beyond what is permitted by Article 10 of the European Convention on Human Rights, unless under the strict conditions laid down in Article 15 of the Convention;

Recalling furthermore that in their fight against terrorism, states must take care not to adopt measures that are contrary to human rights and fundamental freedoms, including the freedom of expression, which is one of the very pillars of the democratic societies that terrorists seek to destroy;

Noting the value which self-regulatory measures taken by the media may have in the particular context of the fight against terrorism;

Recalling Article 10 of the European Convention on Human Rights, the Committee of Ministers' Declarations on the freedom of expression and information adopted on 29 April 1982, on the protection of journalists in situations of conflict and tension adopted on 3 May 1996, and its Recommendations No. R (97) 20 on hate speech, No. R (97) 21 on the media and the promotion of a culture of tolerance, No. R (2000) 7 on the right of journalists not to disclose their sources of information and Rec(2003)13 on the provision of information through the media in relation to criminal proceedings;

Bearing in mind the Resolutions and Recommendations of the Parliamentary Assembly on terrorism;

Recalling the Guidelines on Human Rights and the Fight against Terrorism which it adopted on 11 July 2002,

Calls on public authorities in member states:

- not to introduce any new restrictions on freedom of expression and information in the media unless strictly necessary and proportionate in a democratic society and after examining carefully whether existing laws or other measures are not already sufficient;

- to refrain from adopting measures equating media reporting on terrorism with support for terrorism;

- to ensure access by journalists to information regularly updated, in particular by appointing spokespersons and organising press conferences, in accordance with national legislation;

- to provide appropriate information to the media with due respect for the principle of the presumption of innocence and the right to respect for private life;

- to refrain from creating obstacles for media professionals in having access to scenes of terrorist acts that are not imposed by the need to protect the safety of victims of terrorism or of law enforcement forces involved in an ongoing anti-terrorist operation, of the investigation or the effectiveness of safety or security measures; in all cases where the authorities decide to restrict such access, they should explain the reasons for the restriction and its duration should be proportionate to the circumstances and a person authorised by the authorities should provide information to journalists until the restriction has been lifted;

- to guarantee the right of the media to know the charges brought by the judicial authorities against persons who are the subject of anti-terrorist judicial proceedings, as well as the right to follow these proceedings and to report on them, in accordance with national legislation and with due respect for the presumption of innocence and for private life; these rights may only be restricted when prescribed by law where their exercise is likely to prejudice the secrecy of investigations and police inquiries or to delay or impede the outcome of the proceedings and without prejudice to the exceptions mentioned in Article 6 paragraph 1 of the European Convention on Human Rights;

- to guarantee the right of the media to report on the enforcement of sentences, without prejudice to the right to respect for private life;

- to respect, in accordance with Article 10 of the European Convention on Human Rights and with Recommendation No. R (2000) 7, the right of journalists not to disclose their sources of information; the fight against terrorism does not allow the authorities to circumvent this right by going beyond what is permitted by these texts;

- to respect strictly the editorial independence of the media, and accordingly, to refrain from any kind of pressure on them;

- to encourage the training of journalists and other media professionals regarding their protection and safety and to take, where appropriate and, if circumstances permit, with their agreement, measures to protect journalists or other media professionals who are threatened by terrorists;

Invites the media and journalists to consider the following suggestions:

- to bear in mind their particular responsibilities in the context of terrorism in order not to contribute to the aims of terrorists; they should, in particular, take care not to add to the feeling of fear that terrorist acts can create, and not to offer a platform to terrorists by giving them disproportionate attention;

- to adopt self-regulatory measures, where they do not exist, or adapt existing measures so that they can effectively respond to ethical issues raised by media reporting on terrorism, and implement them;

- to refrain from any self-censorship, the effect of which would be to deprive the public of information necessary for the formation of its opinion;

- to bear in mind the significant role which they can play in preventing "hate speech" and incitement to violence, as well as in promoting mutual understanding;

- to be aware of the risk that the media and journalists can unintentionally serve as a vehicle for the expression of racist or xenophobic feelings or hatred;

- to refrain from jeopardising the safety of persons and the conduct of antiterrorist operations or judicial investigations of terrorism through the information they disseminate;

-    to respect the dignity, the safety and the anonymity of victims of terrorist acts and of their families, as well as their right to respect for private life, as guaranteed by Article 8 of the European Convention on Human Rights;

-    to respect the right to the presumption of innocence of persons who are prosecuted in the context of the fight against terrorism;

-    to bear in mind the importance of distinguishing between suspected or convicted terrorists and the group (national, ethnic, religious or ideological) to which they belong or to which they claim to subscribe;

-    to assess the way in which they inform the public of questions concerning terrorism, in particular by consulting the public, by analytical broadcasts, articles and colloquies, and to inform the public of the results of this assessment;

-    to set up training courses, in collaboration with their professional organisations, for journalists and other media professionals who report on terrorism, on their safety and the historical, cultural, religious and geopolitical context of the scenes they cover, and to invite journalists to follow these courses.

The Committee of Ministers agrees to monitor, within the framework of the existing procedures, the initiatives taken by governments of member states aiming at reinforcing measures, in particular in the legal field, to fight terrorism as far as they could affect the freedom of the media, and invites the Parliamentary Assembly to do alike.

Recommendation Rec (2005) 7
of the Committee of Ministers to member states concerning identity
and travel documents and the fight against terrorism

Adopted by the Committee of Ministers on 30 March 2005, at the
921st meeting of the Ministers' Deputies

The Committee of Ministers, under the terms of Article 15.*b* of the Statute of
the Council of Europe,

Considering that the aim of the Council of Europe is to achieve greater unity
between its members;

Bearing in mind Resolution No.1 on combating international terrorism
approved at the 24th Conference of European Ministers of Justice (Moscow,
4-5 October 2001) and Resolution No.1 on combating terrorism approved at
the 25th Conference of European Ministers of Justice, (Sofia,
9-10 October 2003);

Considering that the Final Report of the Multidisciplinary Group on
International Action against Terrorism (GMT) and the subsequent decisions
of the Committee of Ministers recognise the field of identity and identity and
travel documents as a priority area for the Council of Europe's legal action
against terrorism;

Bearing in mind the Final Activity Report of the Group of Specialists on
Identity and Terrorism (CJ-S-IT) of 23 April 2004 and the opinion of the
Committee of Experts on Terrorism (CODEXTER) thereon;

Taking into account the Convention for the Protection of Individuals with
regard to Automatic Processing of Personal Data (ETS No. 108) and its
Additional Protocol, regarding supervisory authorities and transborder data
flows (ETS No. 181);

Taking into account the European Convention on Nationality (ETS No. 166);

Bearing in mind the provisions of the European Convention on Human
Rights, in particular Articles 8, 13, 14 and 15, and the relevant case-law of
the European Court of Human Rights;

Mindful of the Guidelines on human rights and the fight against terrorism,
adopted by the Committee of Ministers on 11 July 2002;

Bearing in mind the work of the International Civil Aviation Organisation
(ICAO) in the field of standard-setting for travel documents, and in particular
the ICAO standards for machine-readable travel documents and current
developments concerning the introduction of globally interoperable
biometrics;

Bearing in mind the work of the International Commission on Civil Status (ICCS) and its Convention No. 26 on the international exchange of information relating to civil status (12 September 1997);

Acknowledging that the overwhelming majority of persons applying for or using identity and travel documents do so for lawful purposes;

Considering, however, that proper, rapid and reliable identification of individuals is of the utmost importance in order to fight terrorism and facilitate secure international travel, in particular as regards the issuing of identity and travel documents,

Recommends that governments of member states:

i.   be guided, when formulating their internal legislation and reviewing their policy and practice relating to identity and travel documents, by the principles appended to this Recommendation, in order to combat fraud and other forms of abuse in the context of the fight against terrorism;

ii.   ensure that these principles are disseminated as broadly as possible to their competent authorities and in particular to those involved in the issuing and control of identity and travel documents.

Appendix to Recommendation Rec(2005)7 of the Committee of Ministers to member states on identity and travel documents and the fight against terrorism

I. Definitions

For the purposes of this Recommendation:

- "identity" means a unique combination of characteristics relating to every natural person – such as last name, first name, date and place of birth, gender and physical characteristics – that, in accordance with national law, or international law where appropriate, permits his or her identification by the competent authorities;

- "identity document" means any document that is issued by the competent authorities according to national law in order to confirm the identity of the document holder;

- "travel document" means any official document issued by a state or competent organisation that is used by the document holder for international travel (for example passport, visa or identity document) and contains mandatory visual (eye-readable) data and, generally, an image of the holder.

II. Security of identity and travel documents

1. Member states should take all legislative and other appropriate measures, including technical and organisational measures, to strengthen the physical security of identity and travel documents and the integrity of application and issuing procedures, especially with regard to verifying the identity of applicants.

2. Member states should take all appropriate measures to ensure that records of issued identity and travel documents, including all relevant personal data, and biometric data where appropriate, are secure and accessible for verification by their competent authorities.

3. Member states, if they do not already, should comply with ICAO standard 9303 on machine-readable travel documents, for all documents confirming identity and nationality that are used for crossing borders by all categories of travellers, including sea-farers. In particular, member states are encouraged to develop biometric standards in their travel documents to the highest possible level, in line with the globally interoperable standards developed by ICAO.

4. Member states should take all appropriate measures to ensure that the loss or theft of identity and travel documents is reported as soon as possible to the competent authorities by their rightful holders. Member states should

refrain from issuing replacement documents unless this procedure is followed.

5.   Member states should take all appropriate measures to ensure that identity and travel documents reported lost or stolen are automatically considered null and void. If such documents are recovered after new documents have been issued, member states should ensure that the lost or stolen documents are not reactivated.

6.   Member states are encouraged to consider appropriate measures covering the use of identity and travel documents, including measures to prevent unauthorised copying of these documents, and to issue guidance on the rights and responsibilities of private and public bodies, as well as those of the holder of the document.

7.   Member states should take all appropriate measures to ensure that information is collected on the issuance and serial numbers of lost or stolen identity and travel documents, whether issued or blank.

III. Proof of identity

8.   Member states should take all appropriate measures to promote the creation and development of systems that allow for rapid and reliable identity checks to be carried out with reference to civil-status records and, where appropriate, nationality records and population registers, in accordance with national legislation and international instruments, in particular the Convention for the Protection of Individuals with regard to the Automatic Processing of Personal Data (ETS No. 108). Such systems should, in particular, include provisions enabling cross-referencing between birth and death records and marriage registers, as appropriate.

9.   Member states should take all appropriate measures to ensure that competent authorities, when presented with a birth certificate or another document in connection with an application for an identity or travel document, carry out checks using all relevant records and registers (of civil status and, where appropriate, population and nationality) and instigate other enquiries, where appropriate, in accordance with national legislation and international instruments.

IV. Registration of births and birth certificates

10.   Member states should take all appropriate measures in order to avoid abuse in the framework of the registration of births and the issuing of birth certificates, as they are key documents that are necessary to obtain identity and travel documents. In particular, they should:

    a.   ensure that births are registered in civil-status records as soon after birth as possible;

b. take all appropriate measures to ensure that information provided to registrars is checked as far as possible, for example with medical personnel supervising the birth;

c. keep the conditions and procedures for issuing birth certificates under review;

d. if appropriate, consider the introduction of a national personal identification number allocated at the time of registration of birth, in accordance with national legislation and international instruments. If member states decide to use a national personal identification number, or any other unique identifier of general application, they should determine the conditions under which this number may be processed, in accordance with the Convention for the Protection of Individuals with regard to the Automatic Processing of Personal Data.

V. International co-operation

11. Member states are encouraged to co-operate with other member states regarding the identity of applicants and, where appropriate, with international law-enforcement bodies such as, Europol and Interpol, with regard to the rapid dissemination of information on trends and developments in the area of identity and travel documents. In particular, member states are encouraged to make information concerning lost or stolen identity and travel documents, whether issued or blank, available to other member states, as well as to Europol and Interpol.

12. Member states should try, as far as possible, to adopt or develop systems of updating all relevant records and registers (civil-status and, if appropriate, population and nationality) in order to be able to integrate events affecting their nationals or residents that occur in other countries, concerning nationality, marriage, divorce, death and change of name. To this end, they may consider the possibility of:

- adopting or developing effective systems of registration of modifications resulting from events occurring abroad;

- adopting or developing effective systems to notify those member states holding a person's civil-status records of events concerning that person which have occurred in another member state;

- ratify the ICCS Convention No. 26 on the international exchange of information relating to civil status (signed at Neuchâtel on 12 September 1997).

13. Member states are invited to consider ratifying the European Convention on Nationality (ETS No. 166). Having due regard to this instrument and the problems that might arise in the context of terrorism, they

are encouraged to exchange information in the area of nationality in order to deal with matters of common interest and thereby contribute to the prevention of the misuse of nationality laws.

Recommendation Rec (2005) 9
of the Committee of Ministers to member states
on the protection of witnesses and collaborators of justice

(Adopted by the Committee of Ministers on 20 April 2005 at the 924th meeting of the Ministers' Deputies)

The Committee of Ministers, under the terms of Article 15.*b* of the Statute of the Council of Europe,

Recalling that the aim of the Council of Europe is to achieve greater unity among its members;

Aware of the need for member states to develop a common crime policy in relation to witness protection;

Noting that there is growing recognition of the special role of witnesses in criminal proceedings and that their evidence is often crucial to securing the conviction of offenders, especially in respect of serious crime;

Considering that in some areas of criminality, such as organised crime and terrorism, there is an increasing risk that witnesses will be subjected to intimidation;

Considering that the final report of the Multidisciplinary Group on International Action against Terrorism (GMT) and the subsequent decisions of the Committee of Ministers recognise the protection of witnesses and collaborators of justice as a priority area of the Council of Europe's legal action against terrorism;

Recalling that in Resolution No. 1 on Combating International Terrorism approved at the 24th Conference of European Ministers of Justice (Moscow, 4-5 October 2001), the Committee of Ministers was invited to adopt urgently all normative measures considered necessary for assisting states to prevent, detect, prosecute and punish acts of terrorism, such as the improvement of the protection of witnesses and other persons participating in proceedings involving persons accused of terrorist crimes;

Recalling that in Resolution No. 1 on Combating Terrorism approved at the 25th Conference of European Ministers of Justice (Sofia, 9-10 October 2003), the Committee of Ministers was invited to, *inter alia*, pursue without delay the work with a view to adopting relevant international instruments on the protection of witnesses and collaborators of justice;

Convinced that, while all persons have a civic duty to give sincere testimony as witnesses if so required by the criminal justice system, there should also be greater recognition given to their rights and needs, including the right not to be subject to any undue interference or be placed at personal risk;

Considering that member states have a duty to protect witnesses against such interference by providing them with specific protection measures aimed at effectively ensuring their safety;

Considering that it is unacceptable for the criminal justice system to fail to bring defendants to trial and obtain a judgment because witnesses have been effectively discouraged from testifying freely and truthfully;

Aware that the protection of witnesses and collaborators of justice requires confidentiality and that efforts should be made to ensure that effective measures are taken to thwart attempts to trace witnesses and collaborators of justice, in particular by criminal organisations, including terrorist organisations;

Bearing in mind the provisions of the European Convention on Human Rights (ETS No. 5) and the case-law of its organs, which recognise the rights of the defence to examine the witness and to challenge his/her testimony;

Taking into account Recommendation No. R (97) 13 concerning intimidation of witnesses and the rights of the defence, in particular with respect to the measures to be taken in relation to vulnerable witnesses, especially in cases of crime within the family; Recommendation No. R (85) 4 on violence in the family, Recommendation No. R (85) 11 on the position of the victim in the framework of criminal law and procedure, Recommendation No. R (87) 21 on assistance to victims and the prevention of victimisation, Recommendation No. R (91) 11 concerning sexual exploitation, pornography and prostitution of, and trafficking in, children and young adults and Recommendation No. R (96) 8 on crime policy in Europe in a time of change,

Recommends that governments of member states:

i.   be guided, when formulating their internal legislation and reviewing their criminal policy and practice, by the principles and measures appended to this Recommendation;

ii.   ensure that all the necessary publicity for these principles and measures is distributed to all interested bodies, such as judicial organs, investigating and prosecuting authorities, bar associations, and relevant social institutions.

Appendix to Recommendation Rec(2005)9

1. Definitions

For the purposes of this Recommendation, the term:

- "witness" means any person who possesses information relevant to criminal proceedings about which he/she has given and/or is able to give testimony (irrespective of his/her status and of the direct or indirect, oral or written form of the testimony, in accordance with national law), who is not included in the definition of "collaborator of justice";

- "collaborator of justice" means any person who faces criminal charges, or has been convicted of taking part in a criminal association or other criminal organisation of any kind, or in offences of organised crime, but who agrees to co-operate with criminal justice authorities, particularly by giving testimony about a criminal association or organisation, or about any offence connected with organised crime or other serious crimes;

- "intimidation" means any direct or indirect threat carried out or likely to be carried out to a witness or collaborator of justice, which may lead to interference with his/her willingness to give testimony free from undue interference, or which is a consequence of his/her testimony;

- "anonymity" means that the identifying particulars of the witness are not generally divulged to the opposing party or to the public in general;

- "people close to witnesses and collaborators of justice" includes the relatives and other persons in a close relationship to the witnesses and the collaborators of justice, such as the partner, (grand)children, parents and siblings;

- "protection measures" are all individual procedural or non-procedural measures aimed at protecting the witness or collaborator of justice from any intimidation and/or any dangerous consequences of the decision itself to co-operate with justice;

- "protection programme" means a standard or tailor-made set of individual protection measures which are, for example, described in a memorandum of understanding, signed by the responsible authorities and the protected witness or collaborator of justice.

II. General Principles

1. Appropriate legislative and practical measures should be taken to ensure that witnesses and collaborators of justice may testify freely and without being subjected to any act of intimidation.

2.   While respecting the rights of the defence, the protection of witnesses, collaborators of justice and people close to them should be organised, where necessary, before, during and after the trial.

3.   Acts of intimidation of witnesses, collaborators of justice and people close to them should, where necessary, be made punishable either as separate criminal offences or as part of the offence of using illegal threats.

4.   Subject to legal privileges providing the right of some persons to refuse to give testimony, witnesses and collaborators of justice should be encouraged to report any relevant information regarding criminal offences to the competent authorities and thereafter agree to give testimony in court.

5.   While taking into account the principle of free assessment of evidence by courts and the respect of the rights of the defence, procedural law should enable the impact of intimidation on testimonies to be taken into consideration and statements made during the preliminary phase of the procedure to be allowed (and/or used) in court.

6.   While respecting the rights of the defence, alternative methods of giving evidence which protect witnesses and collaborators of justice from intimidation resulting from face-to-face confrontation with the accused should be considered.

7.   Criminal justice personnel should have adequate training and guidelines to deal with cases where witnesses might require protection measures or programmes.

8.   All the stages of the procedure related to the adoption, implementation, modification and revocation of protection measures or programmes should be kept confidential; the unauthorised disclosure of this information should be made punishable as a criminal offence where appropriate, especially to ensure the security of a protected person.

9.   The adoption of protection measures or programmes should also take into account the need to strike an adequate balance with the principle of safeguarding the rights and expectations of victims.

III.   Protection measures and programmes

10.   When designing a framework of measures to combat serious offences, including those related to organised crime and terrorism, and violations of international humanitarian law, appropriate measures should be adopted to protect witnesses and collaborators of justice against intimidation.

11.   No terrorism-related crimes should be excluded from the offences for which specific witness protection measures/programmes are envisaged.

12. The following criteria should, *inter alia*, be taken into consideration when deciding upon the entitlement of a witness/collaborator of justice to protection measures or programmes:

- involvement of the person to be protected (as a victim, witness, co-perpetrator, accomplice or aider and abetter) in the investigation and/or in the case;

- relevance of the contribution;

- seriousness of the intimidation;

- willingness and suitability to being subject to protection measures or programmes

13. When deciding upon the adoption of protection measures it should also be considered, in addition to the criteria mentioned in paragraph 12, whether there is no other evidence available that could be deemed sufficient to establish a case related to serious offences.

14. Proportionality between the nature of the protection measures and the seriousness of the intimidation of the witness/collaborator of justice should be ensured.

15. Witnesses/collaborators of justice being subjected to the same kind of intimidation should be entitled to similar protection. However, any protection measures/programmes adopted will need to take into account the particular characteristics of the matter and the individual needs of the person(s) to be protected.

16. Procedural rules aimed at the protection of witnesses and collaborators of justice should ensure that the balance necessary in a democratic society is maintained between the prevention of crime, the needs of the victims and witnesses and the safeguarding of the right to a fair trial.

17. While ensuring that the parties have adequate opportunity to challenge the evidence given by a witness/collaborator of justice, the following measures aimed at preventing identification of the witness may, *inter alia*, be considered:

- audiovisual recording of statements made by witnesses/collaborators of justice during the preliminary phase of the procedure;

- using statements given during the preliminary phase of the procedure as evidence in court when it is not possible for witnesses to appear before the court or when appearing in court might result in great and actual danger to the witnesses/collaborators of justice or to people close to them; pre-trial statements should be regarded as valid evidence if the parties have, or have had, the chance to participate in the examination and interrogate and/or cross-examine the witness and to discuss the contents of the statement during the procedure;

- disclosing information which enables the witness to be identified at the latest possible stage of the proceedings and/or releasing only selected details;

- excluding or restricting the media and/or the public from all or part of the trial;

- using devices preventing the physical identification of witnesses and collaborators of justice, such as using screens or curtains, disguising the face of the witness or distorting his/her voice;

- using video-conferencing.

18. Any decision to grant anonymity to a witness in criminal proceedings will be made in accordance with domestic law and European human rights law.

19. Where available, and in accordance with domestic law, anonymity of persons who might give evidence should be an exceptional measure. Where the guarantee of anonymity has been requested by such persons and/or temporarily granted by the competent authorities, criminal procedural law should provide for a verification procedure to maintain a fair balance between the needs of criminal justice and the rights of the parties. The parties should, through this procedure, have the opportunity to challenge the alleged need for anonymity of the witness, his/her credibility and the origin of his/her knowledge.

20. Any decision to grant anonymity should only be taken when the competent judicial authority finds that the life or freedom of the person involved, or of the persons close to him or her, is seriously threatened, the evidence appears to be significant and the person appears to be credible.

21. When anonymity has been granted, the conviction should not be based solely, or to a decisive extent, on the evidence provided by anonymous witnesses.

22. Where appropriate, witness protection programmes should be set up and made available to witnesses and collaborators of justice who need protection. The main objective of these programmes should be to safeguard the life and personal security of witnesses/collaborators of justice, and people close to them, aiming in particular at providing the appropriate physical, psychological, social and financial protection and support.

23. Protection programmes implying dramatic changes in the life/privacy of the protected person (such as relocation and change of identity) should be applied to witnesses and collaborators of justice who need protection beyond the duration of the criminal trials where they give testimony. Such programmes, which may last for a limited period or for life, should be adopted only if no other measures are deemed sufficient to protect the witness/collaborator of justice and persons close to them.

24. The adoption of such programmes requires the informed consent of the person(s) to be protected and an adequate legal framework, including appropriate safeguards for the rights of the witnesses or collaborators of justice according to national law.

25. Where appropriate, protection measures could be adopted on an urgent and provisional basis before a protection programme is formally adopted.

26. Given the essential role that collaborators of justice may play in the fight against serious offences, they should be given adequate consideration. Where necessary, protection programmes applicable to collaborators of justice serving a prison sentence may also include specific arrangements such as special penitentiary regimes.

27. Protection of collaborators of justice should also be aimed at preserving their credibility and public security. Adequate measures should be undertaken to protect against the risk of the collaborators of justice committing further crimes while under protection and therefore, even involuntarily, jeopardising the case in court. The intentional perpetration of an offence by a collaborator of justice under protection should, according to the relevant circumstances, imply the revocation of protection measures.

28. While respecting the fundamental principles of administrative organisation of each state, staff dealing with the implementation of protection measures should be afforded operational autonomy and should not be involved either in the investigation or in the preparation of the case where the witness/collaborator of justice is to give evidence. Therefore, an organisational separation between these functions should be provided for. However, an adequate level of co-operation/contact with or between law-enforcement agencies should be ensured in order to successfully adopt and implement protection measures and programmes.

IV. International co-operation

29. While respecting the different legal systems and the fundamental principles of administrative organisation of each state, a common approach in international issues related to the protection of witnesses and collaborators of justice should be followed. Such a common approach should aim at ensuring proper professional standards, at least in the crucial aspects of confidentiality, integrity and training. Member states should ensure

sufficient exchange of information and co-operation between the authorities responsible for protection programmes.

30. Measures aimed at fostering international co-operation should be adopted and implemented in order to facilitate the examination of protected witnesses and collaborators of justice and to allow protection programmes to be implemented across borders.

31. The scope and the effective and rapid implementation of international co-operation in matters related to the protection of witnesses and collaborators of justice, including with relevant international jurisdictions, should be improved.

32. The following objectives should, for example, be considered:

- to provide assistance in relocating abroad protected witnesses, collaborators of justice and persons close to them and ensuring their protection, in particular in those cases where no other solution can be found for their protection;

- to facilitate and improve the use of modern means of telecommunication such as video-links, and the security thereof, while safeguarding the rights of the parties;

- to co-operate and exchange best practices through the use of already existing networks of national experts;

- to contribute to the protection of witnesses and collaborators of justice within the context of co-operation with international criminal courts.

**Recommendation Rec (2005) 10
of the Committee of Ministers to member states on "special
investigation techniques" in relation to serious crimes including acts
of terrorism**

*(Adopted by the Committee of Ministers on 20 April 2005 at the
924th meeting of the Ministers' Deputies)*

The Committee of Ministers, under the terms of Article 15.*b* of the Statute of
the Council of Europe,

Recalling that the aim of the Council of Europe is to achieve a greater unity
among its members;

Recalling that in Resolution No. 1 on combating international terrorism
adopted at the 24th Conference of European Ministers of Justice (Moscow,
4-5 October 2001), the Committee of Ministers was invited to adopt urgently
all normative measures considered necessary for assisting states to prevent,
detect, prosecute and punish acts of terrorism;

Considering that the final report of the Multidisciplinary Group on
International Action against Terrorism (GMT) and the subsequent decisions
of the Committee of Ministers recognise the use of special investigation
techniques as a priority area of the Council of Europe's legal action against
terrorism;

Recalling that in Resolution No. 1 on combating terrorism, adopted at the
25th Conference of European Ministers of Justice (Sofia,
9-10 October 2003), the Committee of Ministers was invited, *inter alia*, to
pursue without delay work with a view to adopting relevant international
instruments on the use of special investigation techniques;

Bearing in mind the final report on special investigation techniques in relation
to acts of terrorism prepared by the Committee of Experts on Special
Investigation Techniques in relation to Acts of Terrorism (PC-TI) and the
opinions of the Committee of Experts on Terrorism (CODEXTER) and of the
European Committee on Crime Problems (CDPC) thereon;

Bearing in mind the surveys on "best practices" against organised crime
carried out by the Group of Specialists on Criminal Law and Criminological
Aspects of Organised Crime (PC-S-CO), as well as the reports adopted in
the framework of the Council of Europe's technical co-operation programmes
for the fight against corruption and organised crime;

Taking into account Recommendation No. R (96) 8 on crime policy in Europe
in a time of change and Recommendation Rec(2001)11 concerning guiding
principles in the fight against organised crime;

Taking into account the Convention for the Protection of Individuals with regard to Automatic Processing of Personal Data (ETS No. 108, 28 January 1981) and its Additional Protocol on Supervisory Authorities and Transborder Data Flows (ETS No. 181, 8 November 2001); Recommendation No. R (87) 15 regulating the use of personal data in the police sector; and Recommendation No. R (95) 4 on the protection of personal data in the area of telecommunication services, with particular reference to telephone services;

Taking into account the existing Council of Europe conventions on co-operation in the penal field, as well as similar treaties which exist between Council of Europe member states and other states;

Mindful of the Guidelines on human rights and the fight against terrorism, adopted by the Committee of Ministers of the Council of Europe on 11 July 2002;

Mindful of the obligation on member states to maintain a fair balance between ensuring public safety through law enforcement measures and securing the rights of individuals, as enshrined in the provisions of the European Convention on Human Rights and the case-law of the European Court of Human Rights in particular;

Considering that special investigation techniques are numerous, varied and constantly evolving and that their common characteristics are their secret nature and the fact that their application could interfere with fundamental rights and freedoms;

Recognising that the use of special investigation techniques is a vital tool for the fight against the most serious forms of crime, including acts of terrorism;

Aware that the use of special investigation techniques in criminal investigations requires confidentiality and that any efforts to pursue the commission of serious crime, including acts of terrorism, should where appropriate be thwarted with secured covert means of operation;

Aware of the need to reinforce the effectiveness of special investigation techniques by developing common standards governing their proper use and the improvement of international co-operation in matters related to them;

Recognising that the development of such standards would contribute to further build public confidence as well as confidence amongst relevant competent authorities of the member states in the use of special investigation techniques,

Recommends that governments of member states:

i.   be guided, when formulating their internal legislation and reviewing their criminal policy and practice, and when using special investigation techniques, by the principles and measures appended to this Recommendation;

ii. ensure that all the necessary publicity for these principles and measures is distributed to competent authorities involved in the use of special investigation techniques.

Appendix to Recommendation Rec(2005)10

Chapter I – Definitions and scope

For the purpose of this Recommendation, "special investigation techniques" means techniques applied by the competent authorities in the context of criminal investigations for the purpose of detecting and investigating serious crimes and suspects, aiming at gathering information in such a way as not to alert the target persons.

For the purpose of this Recommendation, "competent authorities" means judicial, prosecuting and investigating authorities involved in deciding, supervising or using special investigation techniques in accordance with national legislation.

Chapter II – Use of special investigation techniques at national level

a. General principles

1.   Member states should, in accordance with the requirements of the European Convention on Human Rights (ETS No. 5), define in their national legislation the circumstances in which, and the conditions under which, the competent authorities are empowered to resort to the use of special investigation techniques.

2.   Member states should take appropriate legislative measures to allow, in accordance with paragraph 1, the use of special investigation techniques with a view to making them available to their competent authorities to the extent that this is necessary in a democratic society and is considered appropriate for efficient criminal investigation and prosecution.

3.   Member states should take appropriate legislative measures to ensure adequate control of the implementation of special investigation techniques by judicial authorities or other independent bodies through prior authorisation, supervision during the investigation or ex post facto review.

b. Conditions of use

4.   Special investigation techniques should only be used where there is sufficient reason to believe that a serious crime has been committed or prepared, or is being prepared, by one or more particular persons or an as-yet-unidentified individual or group of individuals.

5.   Proportionality between the effects of the use of special investigation techniques and the objective that has been identified should be ensured. In this respect, when deciding on their use, an evaluation in the light of the seriousness of the offence and taking account of the intrusive nature of the specific special investigation technique used should be made.

6. Member states should ensure that competent authorities apply less intrusive investigation methods than special investigation techniques if such methods enable the offence to be detected, prevented or prosecuted with adequate effectiveness.

7. Member states should, in principle, take appropriate legislative measures to permit the production of evidence gained from the use of special investigation techniques before courts. Procedural rules governing the production and admissibility of such evidence shall safeguard the rights of the accused to a fair trial.

c. **Operational guidelines**

8. Member states should provide the competent authorities with the required technology, human and financial resources with a view to facilitating the use of special investigation techniques.

9. Member states should ensure that, with respect to those special investigation techniques involving technical equipment, laws and procedures take account of the new technologies. For this purpose, they should work closely with the private sector to obtain their assistance in order to ensure the most effective use of existing technologies used in special investigation techniques and to maintain effectiveness in the use of new technologies.

10. Member states should ensure, to an appropriate extent, retention and preservation of traffic and location data by communication companies, such as telephone and Internet service providers, in accordance with national legislation and international instruments, especially the European Convention on Human Rights and the Convention for the Protection of Individuals with regard to Automatic Processing of Personal Data (ETS No. 108).

11. Member states should take appropriate measures to ensure that the technology required for special investigation techniques, in particular with respect to interception of communications, meets minimum requirements of confidentiality, integrity and availability.

d. **Training and coordination**

12. Member states should ensure adequate training of competent authorities in charge of deciding to use, supervising and using special investigation techniques. Such training should comprise training on technical and operational aspects of special investigation techniques, training on criminal procedural legislation in connection with them and relevant training in human rights.

13. Member states should consider the provision of specialised advice at national level with a view to assisting or advising competent authorities in the use of special investigation techniques.

Chapter III – International co-operation

14. Member states should make use to the greatest extent possible of existing international arrangements for judicial or police co-operation in relation to the use of special investigation techniques. Where appropriate member states should also identify and develop additional arrangements for such co-operation.

15. Member states are encouraged to sign, to ratify and to implement existing conventions or instruments in the field of international co-operation in criminal matters in areas such as exchange of information, controlled delivery, covert investigations, joint investigation teams, cross-border operations and training.

Relevant instruments include, *inter alia*:

- the United Nations Convention against Illicit Traffic in Narcotic Drugs and Psychotropic Substances of 20 December 1988;

- the Convention on Laundering, Search, Seizure and Confiscation of the Proceeds from Crime of 8 November 1990 (ETS No. 141);

- the Criminal Law Convention on Corruption of 27 January 1999 (ETS No. 173);

- the Second Additional Protocol to the European Convention on Mutual Assistance in Criminal Matters of 8 November 2001 (ETS No. 182);

- the Convention on Cybercrime of 23 November 2001 (ETS No. 185);

- the United Nations Convention against Transnational Organised Crime of 15 November 2000 and the Protocols thereto;

- the United Nations Convention on Corruption of 31 October 2003.

16. Member states are encouraged to make better use of existing relevant international bodies, such as the Council of Europe, the European Judicial Network, Europol, Eurojust, the International Criminal Police Organisation (Interpol) and the International Criminal Court, with a view to exchanging experience, further improving international co-operation and conducting best practice analysis in the use of special investigation techniques.

17. Member states should encourage their competent authorities to make better use of their international networks of contacts in order to exchange information on national regulations and operational experience with a view to

facilitating the use of special investigation techniques in an international context. If needed, new networks should be developed.

18. Member states should promote compliance of technical equipment with internationally agreed standards with a view to overcoming technical obstacles in the use of special investigation techniques in an international context, including those connected with interceptions of mobile telecommunications.

19. Member states are encouraged to take appropriate measures to promote confidence between their respective competent authorities in charge of deciding to use, supervising or using special investigation techniques with a view to improving their efficiency in an international context, while ensuring full respect for human rights.

Parliamentary Assembly

**Recommendation 684 (1972)[1]
on international terrorism**

The Assembly,

1.   Denouncing the increase in Europe and throughout the world of terrorist activities of which the Munich tragedy is a particularly horrifying example;

2.   Noting that such acts, which are in utter conflict with the traditions and practices governing international relations, raise, in entirely new terms, the question of the responsibility of governments to put an end to them;

3.   Noting with satisfaction that when the Foreign Ministers of the enlarged Community met in Rome on 11 September 1972, they also recognised Europe's responsibility in this undertaking of vital importance to our society;

4.   Stressing that, although responsibility in this matter is universal, the forces involved in the conflict on either side make it logical for a practical orientation at European level to be found under the political guidance of the Committee of Ministers of the Council of Europe, this being the body composed of the greatest number of European States resolved to exert their efforts in the same direction;

5.   Recalling Resolution (54) 16 of the Committee of Ministers, urging the governments of the member States of the Council of Europe to harmonise the attitudes adopted by the European countries within the United Nations and other international organisations;

6.   Deploring the fact that the political and material support of a certain number of governments and organisations permits, or facilitates directly or indirectly, the preparation of terrorist outbreaks, or offers refuge to their authors or instigators,

7.   Recommends that the Committee of Ministers:

(a)   work out, in close co-operation, a joint European front to combat terrorism, and make this a permanent item on its agenda as from its 51st Session in December 1972;

(b)   invite, without delay, the governments of the member States to prevent the use of diplomatic missions or agencies for the preparation of, or as cover for, terrorist activity;

---

[1] *Assembly debate* on 21 and 23 October 1972 (14th and 16th Sittings) (see Doc. 3201, report of the Political Affairs Committee).

Text adopted by the Assembly on 23 October 1972 (16th Sitting).

(c)   invite the governments of member States to use all their political and economic influence to dissuade the States concerned from pursuing a policy which allows terrorists to prepare their acts or to reside or find asylum on their territory ;

(d)   invite governments of member States which have not yet done so to sign and/or ratify most urgently the three conventions (the Convention on Offences and certain other Acts on Board Aircraft, Tokyo 1963 ; the Convention for the Suppression of Unlawful Seizure of Aircraft, The Hague, 1970 ; and the Convention for the Suppression, of Unlawful Acts against the Safety of Civil Aviation, Montreal 1971) against hijacking of aircraft and securing international air transport;

(e)   invite the organs of the Council of Europe not to maintain relations with organisations that consider terrorism as a legitimate method of action.

**Recommendation 703 (1973)[1]
on international terrorism**

The Assembly,

1.   Condemning international terrorist acts which, regardless of their cause, should be punished as serious criminal offences involving the killing, kidnapping or endangering of the lives of innocent people,

2.   Considers that the disappointing response of the international community makes joint action among member States of the Council of Europe all the more necessary and urgent ;

3.   Deplores the fact that the political and material support of a certain number of governments and organisations permits acts of international terrorism ;

4.   Appreciates the good intentions of the Committee of Ministers in response to its Recommendation 684 (1972) in setting up an ad hoc Committee of Senior Officials to study the legal aspects of international terrorism, but considers that this will not in itself contribute in the immediate future towards a reduction of terrorist acts ;

5.   Realises and shares the deep concern of airline pilots and international transport workers, and their manifest desire for effective sanctions against terrorism ;

6.   Recommends that the Committee of Ministers :

   (i)   invite the governments of member States :

      (a)   to ratify most urgently the Tokyo, Hague and Montreal Conventions against hijacking and unlawful interference with civil aviation ;

      (b)   to use all their political and economic influence to dissuade the States concerned from pursuing a policy which allows terrorists to prepare their acts or to reside or find asylum on their territory ;

      (c)   in accordance with paragraph 1 of this recommendation to establish a common definition for the notion of "political offence", in order to be able to refute any "political" justification

---

[1]   *Assembly debate* on 15 and 16 May 1973 (2nd and 4th Sittings) (see Doc. 3285, report of the Political Committee).

Text adopted by the Assembly on 16 May 1973 (4th Sitting).

whenever an act of terrorism endangers the life of innocent persons ;

(ii) work out a joint European front to combat international terrorism, and in particular :

    (a) co-ordinate their proposals for action at United Nations level, both in the follow-up to Resolution 3034 and in ICAO on the basis of recommendations which should be made by the ad hoc Committee of Senior Officials ;

    (b) urgently convene a special conference of the Ministers of Interior of member States or other Ministers who are responsible for the police and home security, in order to work out proposals and co-ordinate measures aiming at the prevention of acts of terrorism on the regional basis of the member States of the Council of Europe ;

(iii) take seriously into account the fact that, failing effective and urgent European governmental action, parliamentary and public opinion will openly support retaliatory measures by the airline pilots and international transport workers against services to and from offending States.

Recommendation 852 (1979)[1]
on terrorism in Europe

The Assembly,

1.   Recalling Recommendation 703 (1973), on international terrorism, and Resolution 648 (1977), on the European Convention on the Suppression of Terrorism;

2.   Concerned at the fact that terrorism represents a threat to which no European country can claim to be entirely immune;

3.   Condemning all terrorist acts, which regardless of their cause, consist of calculated violence against innocent people;

4.   Convinced that there is no justification for politically motivated violence in a democratic society where legal provision is made for change, improvement and development by means of political persuasion, and that, consequently, terrorism is an attack against the constitution and the democratic stability of the state;

5.   Accepting and emphasising that it is the responsibility of the state to remove the sociological conditions that may lie at the roots of certain forms of violence, and stressing the need for the member states of the Council of Europe, individually and collectively, to work out comprehensive policies aimed at safeguarding and strengthening their democratic structures;

6.   Convinced that resistance to terrorist blackmail should be a basic duty of democratic governments;

7.   Appreciating that, within member states, legislative and administrative measures have been taken, but more needs to be done to strengthen and co-ordinate police forces, to improve the gathering of intelligence, to ensure more thorough protection of persons and installations, especially nuclear installations, and to adapt criminal and procedural laws to this new form of crime;

8.   Stressing, however, that anti-terrorist strategies, if they are vital for the preservation of democratic institutions, must also be compatible with them, and must always be subject to national constitutions and the European Convention on Human Rights;

---

[1]   *Assembly debate* on 31 January 1979 (22nd Sitting) *(see* Doc. 4258, report of the Political Affairs Committee).

Text adopted by the Assembly on 31 January 1979 (22nd Sitting).

9.   Believing that a comprehensive counter-terrorist strategy at national level must also include popular awareness and popular mobilisation in support of democratic institutions and the isolation of terrorists;

10.   Considering that the media, when reporting on terrorist incidents, should accept the self-restraint required to balance the public's right to be informed with the duty to avoid giving help to the terrorists by publicising unduly their activities;

11.   Concerned at the international dimension of present-day terrorism, not only through operational or ideological links between terrorist groups active in different countries, but also through the involvement of certain states which aid or abet terrorists;

12.   Calling upon the Council of Europe member states and all other states to co-operate with one another in implementing the guiding principles of the European Convention on the Suppression of Terrorism and increasing its effectiveness by mutual assistance in the fight against international terror;

13.   Mindful of the role of the Council of Europe in organising the response of its member states to national and international terrorism;

14.   Noting that the Committee of Ministers adopted a Declaration on Terrorism on 23 November 1978,

15.   Recommends that the Committee of Ministers:

    i.   in the context of their exchanges of views on UN activities, co-ordinate the positions of member states on:

        a.   the draft international convention on hostage-taking;

        b.   the advisability of promoting an international convention to sanction breaches of the 1963 Tokyo Convention, the 1970 Hague Convention and the 1971 Montreal Convention, on Air Piracy; and

        c.   the advisability of promoting other conventions prosecuting specific terrorist activities;

    ii.   co-ordinate the positions of member states in respect of the implementation of all the clauses of the 1961 Vienna Convention on Diplomatic Relations, and examine the advisability of negotiating appropriate amendments to it;

    iii.   invite the governments of member states which have not yet done so to join the agreement on sanctions against air piracy reached in Bonn on 17 July 1978 between the heads of state and government of the seven most industrialised Western nations;

iv.   invite the governments of member states to use all their political and economic influence to dissuade those states which aid or abet terrorists from doing so;

v.   encourage judiciary, police and intelligence co-operation against terrorism among member states, and use the intergovernmental mechanisms of the Council of Europe to promote such co-operation;

vi.   invite the governments of member states to take all the action necessary to prevent the presence on their territory of persons linked with terrorist groups, who are active on the territory of other member states;

vii. invite the governments of member states which have not yet done so to sign and ratify most urgently the European Convention on the Suppression of Terrorism, which should become fully operative over the widest possible area of European democratic states;

viii. take action to establish a juridical area common to all member states of the Council of Europe and prevent the territory of one member state from being used as a base for the preparation of terrorist activities in another member state;

ix.   and invite the governments of member states to promote, in pursuit of police co-operation, the exchange of topical information on the daily situation, with special regard to transfrontier movements of members of terrorist circles, to harmonise the methods of search for objects like weapons, passports, etc., in order to enable their transfrontier application, and to establish secure telex lines between national police centres;

x.   invite the governments of member states to hold meetings periodically of Ministers of the Interior and other ministers responsible for public security, in order to exchange views and co-ordinate their national policies against terrorism.

Recommendation 916 (1981)[1]
on the Conference on "Defence of Democracy against Terrorism in Europe – Tasks and Problems"
(Strasbourg, 12-14 November 1980)

The Assembly,

1. Having taken note of the report of its Political Affairs Committee on the Conference on "Defence of Democracy against Terrorism in Europe: Tasks and Problems", held in Strasbourg from 12 to 14 November 1980 (Doc. 4688);[2]

2. Having regard to its Recommendation 852 (1979) on terrorism in Europe;

3. Considering that the General Assembly of the United Nations recommended in its Resolution 34/145 (paragraph I0), of 17 December 1979, to the appropriate specialised agencies and regional organisations that they consider measures to prevent and combat international terrorism within their respective spheres of responsibility and regions;

4. Considering that the Strasbourg Conference was the first occasion on which the problem of protecting democracy against terrorism had been discussed in such a broad framework;

5. Noting that it was generally agreed at the conference that in Council of Europe member countries the aim of terrorist movements, whatever their names or origins, is to overthrow and destroy democracy and parliamentary institutions, as well as stifle the free political, economic and social development that only a democratic system permits;

6. Noting that the participants in the conference emphasised that democracy could react against terrorism in member countries with efficiency and coherence only while respecting democratic principles and fundamental rights and freedoms, and in full respect for the constitutional laws in force in member states, as well as the European Convention on Human Rights and the Statute of the Council of Europe, and on the basis of a broad popular consensus, which is essential for ensuring the confidence of citizens in democratic institutions;

7. Noting that the conference recognised the courageous contribution of the press to efforts aimed at isolating and condemning terrorists, and at the same time called upon the mass media to be firm in their refusal to act or to appear to act as the instrument of terrorism;

---

[1] *Text adopted by the Standing Committee,* acting on behalf of the Assembly, on 26 March 1981.
See Doc. 4688, report of the Political Affairs Committee.

[2] Document reproduced in Appendix.

8.   Noting the special attention paid by the conference to the role of culture and education in the achievement of a consensus regarding the suppression of terrorism, particularly through the outlawing of the various forms of violence in society;

9.   Considering that only ten member states have so far ratified the European Convention on the Suppression of Terrorism, which came into force on 4 August 1978, and that only five of them apply the extradition clauses without reservation;

10.   Believing that active and continuous co-operation between the police forces of member countries, especially those with a common frontier, is a prerequisite for the establishment of a genuine European judicial area;

11.   Sharing the view expressed by the participants in the conference that the Council of Europe should make a major contribution to the discussion and solution of problems concerning the protection of democracy against terrorism;

12.   Considering that no support, even of a moral nature, can be given to any political organisation which advocates violence as a method of solving political, economic and social problems in member countries,

13.   Recommends that the Committee of Ministers:

   a.   hold an exchange of views, possibly with the participation of government-appointed experts, on prospects for rapid ratification of the European Convention on the Suppression of Terrorism by all member states of the Council of Europe;

   b.   consider the application and effects of the European Convention on the Suppression of Terrorism in actual cases occurring since its entry into force;

   c.   study the legislative measures that may be regarded as acceptable in a democratic system for dealing with terrorism;

   d.   promote a uniform legal definition of terrorism as an offence at both national and international level, when appropriate in consultation with the Assembly;

   e.   have a study made, in the framework of intergovernmental co-operation, of the role of culture and education and of the mass media in preventing and suppressing terrorism, and request the European Youth Centre to pay special attention thereto;

   f.   invite member states to intensify or, if appropriate, establish frontier co-operation between neighbouring countries on the basis of bilateral agreements;

g.   encourage member states to use the intergovernmental machinery of the Council of Europe for the purpose of ensuring co-operation between the judiciary, police and intelligence services of member states in the combating of terrorism;

h.   create — in response to the wish widely expressed by the Strasbourg Conference and as a contribution to the measures called for by the General Assembly of the United Nations (see paragraph 3 above) — a study and documentation centre on the causes, prevention and suppression of terrorism, with governmental and parliamentary support, and a contribution from non-governmental organisations;

i.   invite the governments of member states to ratify as soon as possible the European Convention on the control of the acquisition and possession of firearms by individuals;

j.   expedite the framing of European agreements to harmonise regulations concerning firearms.

Appendix

Parliamentary Assembly Document 4688 of 19 February 1981: Report on the Conference on "Defence of Democracy against Terrorism in Europe — Tasks and Problems"[1]
(Strasbourg, 12—14 November 1980)

**Explanatory Memorandum
by Mr Calamandrei**

General remarks

1.   This report is devoted to the examination of the results attained by the Conference on "Defence of Democracy against Terrorism in Europe –Tasks and Problems" held in Strasbourg from 12 to 14 November 1980, and to the conclusions which should, even if provisionally, be drawn in the form of a programme to be followed by the Assembly and its organs and of recommendations to be addressed to the Committee of Ministers.

The first part of the report is a review of the results of the conference, where an attempt is made to assess its proceedings (which, I think, can be judged favourably) and, at the same time, identify the points on which there was some convergence of views among the participants I shall therefore go through the various sets of questions discussed (political issues, security matters, role of the mass media, role of culture and education, international co-operation) and try to establish in respect of each one what the inclinations and conclusions of the majority of participants were. In the second part, I shall consider what proposals the Assembly might make to the Committee of Ministers to ensure that the conference's proceedings as well as the preceding and subsequent activities of the Assembly lead to practical results in the interests of the Council of Europe and all our member states. I shall bear in mind that the report is to be submitted to the Legal Affairs Committee for an opinion and that the Committee on Culture and Education will also be expressing its views thereon; I shall not, therefore, dwell either on the legal issues or on questions concerning the role of culture and education, except to stress the points on which participants were in agreement.

2.   I should first and foremost like to emphasise that both I and the participants I consulted feel that the conference was a considerable success. It was the first time the problem of protecting democracy against terrorism had been discussed in such a wide forum. Suffice it to recall in this connection that, in addition to the Permanent Representatives to the Council of Europe and our Assembly's parliamentarians, sixteen member countries delegated government experts and nine sent representatives of their parliaments. Moreover, the European Parliament sent a big delegation led by the Chairman of its Legal Affairs Committee, Observers and experts also came from four non-member countries (Yugoslavia, the United States, Israel

---

[1] Rapporteur: Mr Calamandrei. See Orders Nos. 374 (1978) and 376 (1979).

and Canada). The considerable attention given by the press in our member countries to the conference's work constitutes another positive aspect.

3.   Lastly, I should like to point out that both the conference itself and this report should be regarded as but a stage in the Assembly's work on the subject. In other words, we cannot claim to be saying the last word on the phenomenon of terrorist violence, which is unfortunately still rife. We can, however, try to define more precisely the criteria and instruments that should guide democracy's response to terrorism. What is needed above all in an organisation such as the Council of Europe is an effort to make our member states aware of the need for co-ordination at all levels so as to achieve a common attitude to both the prevention and the suppression of terrorism.

A.   Results of the conference

1.   *Political issues*

4.   The problem of combating terrorism is primarily a political one, as the answers found for the political questions inherent in the need for firm action against terrorism and the means to be used for the purpose condition the answers that may be given to the questions arising on various technical levels, such as in the legal field or in the matter of international co-operation. It should first of all be observed that a very broad consensus emerged from the conference in support of the basic premise of its proceedings; namely that the aim of terrorism, under whatever name it passes and irrespective of its origins, is to overthrow and destroy democracy in our countries, together with the parliamentary and pluralistic connotations it has acquired in the course of western European history, and to stifle the scope for free, political, economic and social development which democracy offers. This fundamental idea, first expressed in the Assembly's January 1979 debate on the Tabone report (Doe. 4258) and in the Recommendation 852 adopted at the end of the debate, may rightly be regarded as the guiding thread of the Assembly's work on the subject. It implies several corollaries of the greatest importance which it is as well to specify here. The first one is that democracy's response to terrorism should be accompanied by strict observance of democratic principles as well as of the various rights and fundamental freedoms laid down in our member countries' constitutions and in the European Convention on Human Rights.

If the purpose of terrorism is to destroy democracy, there can be no more effective response than the strengthening of democracy itself in the sense that the reinforcement and development of democracy is a condition for the effectiveness of the counter-offensive of the state against terrorism. This means—the second corollary—that if the response to terrorism necessitates a wide popular consensus, every step must be taken to build up and consolidate the public's confidence in democratic institutions. This can be done only by strengthening the institutions themselves and providing machinery for citizen participation. This requirement was emphasised in many of the reports and speeches at the conference. However, for an understanding of the criteria just mentioned, the importance of a realistic attitude in the matter should be stressed, as terrorism has already inflicted many losses on our democracies—losses not only of human lives but also in terms of our countries' democratic and social progress. Before the outbreak of terrorism and the resultant wave of criminal violence, our societies had made considerable advances in extending citizens' rights and freedoms. In many countries, moreover, there had been an increase in spontaneous participation by citizens in the various political and ideological movements that had arisen within society.

5.   The outbreak of terrorism had a twofold implication. In the first place, the need to counter terrorism on a legal level and prevent criminals from availing themselves of rights guaranteed to every citizen, has somewhat complicated the process of extending individual freedoms. Many examples of this may be given, but suffice it to refer to the Italian act which, in 1972, reduced the maximum periods of pre-trial custody and provided for the automatic release of unconvicted prisoners after a certain time. The worsening of the law-and-order situation in Italy, especially as far as terrorism was concerned, necessitated an act that restored much longer maximum periods of custody on remand so as to prevent terrorists who had not been tried from being released and thus evading justice. Secondly, terrorist violence is no doubt responsible, because of its intimidatory effects, for causing many people to turn away from public affairs. There is talk nowadays of a withdrawal to the private sphere after years of increasing involvement in public life. Terrorism is very probably one of the main causes of this trend. As regards the slowing down of the process of widening involvement in public life. Terrorism is very probably one of the main causes of this trend. As regards the slowing down of the process of widening and extending individual rights, it has to be acknowledged that a more vigilant and cautious attitude to certain areas of human rights and fundamental freedoms has been made inevitable by the upsurge of terrorism. Some distinctions should be drawn, however, as there are certain sectors where a widening of the scope of guaranteed rights is fully compatible with the combating of terrorism with the intention of eliminating at source an argument which could be invoked by the terrorists as a pretext to justify their criminal action. This is the case, for example, with economic and social rights. The Assembly concerned itself with this problem on a previous occasion, when it recommended studying the possibility of including this category of rights in the European Convention on Human Rights. Clearly, a speeding up of intergovernmental work aimed at supplementing the European Convention on Human Rights would provide a suitable answer to the terrorist menace by contributing to more effective protection of certain rights which are now part of our heritage. As regards citizen participation. attention was drawn at the conference to the need to make the public aware that the primary aim of terrorism is to destroy personal freedom and undermine the democratic system.

6.   It may be seen from the foregoing observations that society's response to terrorism cannot be effective without far-reaching public involvement

covering several aspects and areas of public life. It should be acknowledged here that our societies have shown remarkable democratic vitality for, despite the crisis caused by terrorism, they have succeeded in remaining true to their principles and values. It is evident that the situation which has arisen in Turkey constitutes a special case. I should like here to express my appreciation for the constructive contribution to the work of the conference by Turkish parliamentarians and experts.

7.   The conference made it clear that the problem of terrorism in our democratic societies raises questions of a completely new and special kind. In particular, it was asserted that violence in a democratic society constitutes a criminal act. Moreover, the definition of the aim of terrorism which formed the basic premise of the conference's proceedings can be understood only in terms of a democratic society. In other words, as Mr Günes pointed out in the discussion, the terrorism now being experienced can be defined only in relation to democracy. Hence the need to consider terrorism in its specific western European context.

2.   *Legal issues*

8.   The question that was perhaps the one most extensively discussed at the conference was to what class of offences terrorism should be assigned. Most of the lawyers attending the conference were in favour of terrorism being downgraded within the class of political offences in view of the hideous and despicable methods it employs. This differed from what I myself originally proposed, which was that terrorism should be classified as an ordinary offence. The solution envisaged by the conference would result in terrorists being deprived of the privileges traditionally accorded to political offenders and indeed becoming liable to be treated more severely than ordinary offenders. Another requirement emphasised at the conference was the harmonisation of definitions of the offence of terrorism in member countries' legislation, as well as at international level: in other words, what is needed is a fundamental or outline definition of the offence in place of the somewhat fragmentary list of cases in the European Convention on the Suppression of Terrorism.

9.   Lastly, the participants were firmly agreed that a democratic state should not enter into negotiations with terrorist gangs or organisations. There are both legal and political arguments to support this view. Suffice it to refer here to what Professor Grevi said in his address: by agreeing to negotiate with terrorists, a democratic state would be embarking on a path leading to the "negation of the constitutional state".

The arguments in favour of the inadmissibility of negotiations between the institutions of a democratic state and terrorists were well presented by Professor Wilkinson in his report to the conference on this subject.

In brief, Professor Wilkinson noted first that negotiations between the state and terrorists represented for the latter a major symbolic victory which, by boosting their morale and their credibility, would increase their capacity to terrorise society as a whole. Secondly, Professor Wilkinson noted that such negotiation would ridicule the system of parliamentary democracy. The latter would thereby be according an implicit status and power to a violent minority as a direct "reward" for criminal violence. Thirdly, the fact of negotiating would implicitly place the terrorist above the law, thereby sapping the authority and the credibility of the judiciary and police. This would seriously and perhaps irremediably undermine confidence in democratic government and the rule of law. Finally "deals" with a terrorist group would inevitably encourage a wave of attacks by other extremist groups who would seek to bomb their way to the conference table.

10. Other legal issues on the conference's agenda, such as the independence of the judiciary, professional secrecy in the case of lawyers and, the question of state secrecy, did not make the same impact. This does not mean, however, that such matters are secondary or that the Assembly should not in future give close consideration 10 the various complex and difficult problems they raise.

3.   *Security issues*

11. Above all, the conference considered the international co-operation aspects of security questions. In this report, I shall give an account of the discussion on this subject in the section on international co-operation. Once again, emphasis should be placed here on the importance of the problem of adapting police forces and security services to the fight against terrorism. This raises problems concerning the selection and training, at different grades, of forces responsible for upholding law and order and state security as well as their ability to inspire confidence and behave in a democratic manner. On the one hand, security forces need to be able to deal with new tasks and, on the other, their duties should be performed in close collaboration with the public.

12. A particular point was highlighted by General Clutterbuck, namely the supervision of professional security institutions, both national and international. The General rightly pointed out that, unlike other professions such as doctors or lawyers, security personnel are not required to prove their ability to do their work or to adhere to a professional code or any general rules of behaviour. It would, I think, be desirable to follow up General Clutterbuck's proposal that the Council of Europe should encourage member states to draw up international standards for private security firms and, In due course, impose such standards by at least compelling those responsible for these firms to join approved professional bodies, as is the case with physicians and surgeons.

4.   *Role of culture and education*

13. The participants in the conference paid particular attention to the role of culture and education in producing a popular consensus on terrorism (to use

Mr Hamon's expression) and, more generally, in creating conditions for the outlawing of the various forms of violence in society. Some interesting practical proposals were put forward at the conference. I have in mind, in particular, Mr Hamon's report which, first of all, referred to the various efforts already made which have met with some success and could therefore serve as an example for future action and, secondly, suggested a new design for school and university curricula. As regards the first point, Mr Hamon mentioned as a noteworthy example the effort made since the First World War to discredit the very idea of war. As regards the second point, it is unnecessary here to recapitulate all the proposals in Mr Hamon's report, which were widely supported during the discussion. I should like to emphasise the vital need for university and school curricula to be pluralistic and anti-dogmatic. Education should be designed to provide an initiation in reality, where "being different" is considered an asset or an enriching feature rather than a negative factor which should be eliminated. I do not, however, think that discussion of the subject has yet reached the stage where the Assembly can make specific proposals on the harmonisation of curricula. Because of its complexity, the whole question needs to be studied in full detail. For that reason it should be recommended that the Committee of Ministers assign precise study functions to the Council of Europe's intergovernmental sector regarding, in general, the role of culture and education in the prevention and suppression of terrorism and, in particular, the drawing up of proposals for school and university curricula which will help to remove the seeds and roots of violence from hearts and minds. Similarly, the European Youth Centre might be asked to organise activities and discussions on the problem of the relationship between young people and terrorism and the role of youth organisations in encouraging young people to condemn terrorist violence. Clearly, the Assembly's Committee on Culture and Education should be consulted on this whole subject and asked to evaluate and supplement the above proposals.

14. The role of the cultural sector, on the other hand, in forming public opinion and in contributing to the efficiency of the institutions in the struggle against terrorism was not examined by the conference as it should have been. This is a subject which the Assembly should include in its work programme for the future. I will limit myself here to recalling that some intellectuals have shown remarkable courage in countries where subversive violence is a serious problem. It is sufficient to think of political activists, magistrates, journalists and also university teachers and members of the liberal professions, many of whom have fallen victim to terrorism.

On the other hand certain intellectual circles, out of a sincere sensibility to the real risks which society runs in the suppression of terrorism, have shown a tendency to find in this a reason to oppose and thereby to prejudice anti-terrorist measures.

Particularly where jurisprudence is concerned, a consequence of this attitude has been to slow down research aimed at drawing up new and more appropriate democratic legislation against terrorism.

5.   Role of information

15.   That freedom of information is the target of terrorist violence has been demonstrated by the many cases of journalists being murdered or savagely injured by terrorists. In all these cases, the journalists concerned had acted as spokesmen for courageous campaigns against violence or as the representatives of parties and ideologies at which terrorists wanted to strike, or else their investigations into terrorist organisations had led to discoveries which the organisations wanted to hush up. This attitude towards press freedom is accompanied by attempts to use the press as a means of achieving terrorism's subversive goals. A fairly positive assessment of the situation in this field was made by the conference, as it was acknowledged that the press had succeeded in resisting terrorist blackmail, even though lives had been lost. It was also acknowledged that mere press neutrality did not seem the best means of dealing with terrorism (see the De Salas report). The participants seemed to support the view I expressed in my general introduction to the conference that striking a balance between two opposing needs (the need to inform and the need to combat terrorism) was what the Federal Republic of Germany and Great Britain had to some extent achieved by pursuing an anti-terrorist information policy involving a form of co-operation between state institutions and the press.

16.   It should also be noted that certain questions were not examined during the conference. These include in particular problems connected with journalists' right not to disclose their sources and the relationship between the confidentiality of judicial investigations and the publicity given by the mass media to elements and phases of investigation into terrorist operations. Further, I consider that the intelligent and frank report of Mr de Salas should have found a wider echo in the discussions. It should not be forgotten that, in societies such as ours, this problem is really crucial in view of the enormous influence of the mass media; I would thus tend to draw the conclusion that, beyond laws and institutions, the democratic discussion in our member countries has not achieved the level of maturity necessary to sustain the mass media in the effort not to yield to "the frantic desire for sco-ops" (see the intervention of Professor Vassalli) and to become, without imbalance and negative consequences, a reliable instrument in the struggle against terrorism.

6.   International co-operation

17.   Questions concerning international co-operation may be approached in different ways, according to whether the co-operation is of a formal kind (i.e. inter-state co-operation based on international legal instruments) or an informal kind. I propose to consider these two aspects of international co-operation separately.

18.   With regard to the first aspect, the participants in the conference took stock of the results of the implementation of the European Convention on the

Suppression of Terrorism, which came into force on 4 August 1978. The operation of this convention has been hampered by a series of political difficulties. The convention's authors were themselves aware of these difficulties, as they included stipulations to the effect that, despite the various general obligations provided for, states could reserve the right to treat individual cases as "political" ones and refuse extradition. Only five of the ten states which have ratified the convention apply the extradition clauses between themselves without reservation. Moreover, the very fact that only ten states have ratified the convention—in other words, that most of the states which signed it have not yet ratified it—shows that there is a certain amount of hesitation, probably for political and constitutional reasons.

In my view, the time has come for the Committee of Ministers to make a detailed political examination of the situation regarding ratification of the European Convention on the Suppression of Terrorism. Only in the light of such an examination will it be possible to decide what efforts should be made to enable a generally acceptable legal system for the suppression of terrorism to be established. In this connection, note should also be taken of the failure of international efforts to establish a joint system for suppressing terrorism within the European Community.

The major problem lies in the failure to introduce a mechanism for extradition which is able to function both flexibly and rapidly.

19. Two other questions were highlighted at the conference. One was the negative effects which the existence of capital punishment in some member countries has on the chances of international co-operation. Here it may be said that the abolition of the death penalty in all member countries – as recommended in Resolution 727, which our Assembly adopted on 22 May 1980 – would not only facilitate joint action, other than that of a constitutional order, against subversive violence but would also help to protect and strengthen human rights in the geographical area of the Council of Europe.

20. The other question dwelt upon was the desirability of, indeed the need for, a relationship between the European Convention on the Suppression of Terrorism and the European Convention on Human Rights in the sense that the fulfilment of any obligation under the former would have to take account of the need to observe the provisions of the latter. My own opinion, which was supported by several speakers at the conference, is that the relationship should be a two-way one, that is to say, the European Convention on Human Rights should be amended by the inclusion of terrorism among the most serious violations of the rights it guarantees.

21. Another very noteworthy proposal is that neighbouring states might be requested to intensify or, where necessary, establish frontier co-operation on the basis of bilateral agreements. This idea might, I suggest, be included in the text which the Political Affairs Committee is to submit to the plenary Assembly.

22. The informal co-operation between member states to which I referred earlier mainly involves co-operation between national police forces, especially in the exchange of data and information. Several reservations were expressed at the conference regarding the setting up of a "data bank". Suffice it to mention here the objection that states could hardly be expected to "internationalise" information of the more sensitive kind by entrusting it to such a bank. Moreover, as pointed out by Dr Matzka, any internationalisation of the information network among the Council of Europe member countries should take account of the fact that some states belong to a military alliance, others are constitutionally neutral and yet others are non-aligned. However, even allowing for these reservations, I suggest reiterating the proposal in Recommendation 852 that the Committee of Ministers encourage judiciary, police and intelligence co-operation against terrorism among member states and the use of the intergovernmental mechanisms of the Council of Europe to promote such co-operation. Close and continuous co-operation between member states' police forces is in itself a condition for the creation of the climate of confidence that is essential for the functioning of a genuine "European judicial area".

B.   Proposals to be made to the Committee of Ministers

23.   The present outline of the proposals to be made to the Committee of Ministers is liable, like the other sections of this report, to be supplemented and revised in the light of discussions in the sub-committees and the Political Affairs Committee. The following three proposals, it will be remembered, were suggested in the previous sections:

-   The Assembly should invite the Committee of Ministers to make a detailed political examination of the situation regarding ratification of the European Convention on the Suppression of Terrorism in order to determine the deep-seated political and constitutional reasons why this convention must now be regarded as a semi-failure, contrary to the wish expressed by the Assembly in paragraph 15.x of its above-mentioned Recommendation 852 ("Recommends that the Committee of Ministers: ... invite the governments of member states to hold meetings periodically of the Ministers of the Interior and other ministers responsible for public security, in order to exchange views and co-ordinate their national policies against terrorism").

-   The Assembly might propose that the Committee of Ministers arrange for international standards to be drawn up for private security firms, laying down stringent criteria of competence and professional conduct and requiring the managers and advisers of security firms to join a professional body.

-   The Assembly might recommend that the Committee of Ministers assign to the Council of Europe's intergovernmental sector responsible for cultural matters some study functions regarding the role of culture and education in the prevention and suppression of terrorism. As already explained, the aim would be to propose secondary school curricula and permanent education programmes capable of providing an insight into the nature of the threat posed by terrorists to the very existence of the democratic and pluralistic societies in which we live.

24. A further proposal, to which several contributions have already alluded, would be to recommend that the Committee of Ministers set up a Council of Europe documentation centre for terrorism problems. The centre's primary function would be to collect precise information on every thing being done in the Council of Europe on the subject of terrorism : this would involve taking stock of, first, the activities of the various governmental committees dealing with terrorist problems in both the legal and the cultural fields, secondly, the discussions on the subject in the European Youth Centre and, thirdly, all the work being done on terrorism by the Assembly and its responsible committees. Member states should also be invited to provide the centre, on a voluntary basis, with precise, up-to-date documentation on their legislative work concerning terrorism. This material might be supplemented by any information member states considered necessary for an under standing of the terrorism problem in their territories. The centre could accordingly issue an annual report on the Council of Europe's activities, on the one hand, and on member states' activities, on the other. The implementation of this sector of activities of the centre, which would entail minimal expenditure by the Council of Europe, could be of great value for the organisation itself and for member states as well as for anyone wishing to obtain as clear a picture as possible of the phenomenon of terrorism and the way in which democratic societies are dealing with it. Participants in the conference also mentioned the need for an agency which would be not only responsible for documentation on terrorism but also serves as a study and discussion centre. This would, of course, entail greater expenditure.

I shall restrict myself here to resuming the ideas which could be drawn from the conference. There is first of all the requirement that the centre should constitute a permanent forum for discussion on the problem of the democratic response to terrorism. In the first place it would have the task of maintaining the contacts between the participants in the conference, including those outside the Council of Europe. Secondly, it should establish links with other centres engaged in studies on the problem of terrorism as a whole, or of specific aspects of it. Thirdly, it could set up expert groups with the task of considering the various problems falling within its competence.

Recommendation 941 (1982)[1]
**on the defence of democracy against terrorism
in Europe**

The Assembly,

1.   Having taken note of the report on the defence of democracy against terrorism in Europe, submitted by its Political Affairs Committee (Doc. 4878);

2.   Having regard to its Recommendations 852 (1979) and 916 (1981);

3.   Observing that, far from abating, the assault by terrorism on the values and institutions of pluralist, parliamentary democracy and on human rights is spreading to other Council of Europe member countries, affecting further sectors of domestic life in our societies and seeking to impair relations between the Western countries;

4.   Also observing the development of links between the various terrorist movements both in individual countries and throughout Western Europe, as well as the emergence of links between subversive forces in our region and similar forces in other regions and continents;

5.   Aware of the need for closer and more effective understanding between member states in combating and repelling, with democracy's full resources, the increasingly intensive and concerted assault by terrorism;

6.   Welcoming Committee of Ministers' Recommendation No. R (82) 1 of 26 January 1982 as an important step towards solving problems concerning co-operation between member states for the purpose of suppressing terrorism;

7.   Hoping that further progress will be made in the co-ordination of joint efforts to defend democracy against terrorism, in particular by a legal, judicial and legislative approach more suited to the nature of the problem, a more resolute, cultural and moral condemnation of subversive violence, a more incisive campaign by the mass media, and extensive mobilisation of public opinion, especially among young people;

8.   Noting that two member states of the Council of Europe (Ireland and Malta) have not signed the European Convention on the Suppression of Terrorism, and that six among the signatory states (Belgium, France, Greece, Italy, the Netherlands and Switzerland) have not yet ratified it,

---

[1] *Assembly debate* on 28 April 1982 (4th Sitting) (see Doc. 4878, report of the Political Affairs Committee).
Text adopted by the Assembly on 28 April 1982 (4th Sitting).

9.   Recommends that the Committee of Ministers:

   a.   devote all due attention to the question of the entry into force of the European Convention on the Suppression of Terrorism, and hence carry out a survey, as advocated in paragraph 13.*a* of Recommendation 916, of prospects for ratification of the convention by all member states;

   b.   examine the situation regarding ratification by both member and non-member states of the Vienna Conventions on Diplomatic and Consular Relations and the United Nations Convention on Internationally Protected Persons;

   c.   study, in consultation with the Assembly and in conjunction with such initiatives as it may take, the most appropriate ways of developing joint action by member states, the United States and Canada against terrorism in countries with a system of pluralist, parliamentary democracy;

   d.   support the proposal made by several member states at the CSCE meeting in Madrid for an undertaking by all signatory countries of the Helsinki Final Act to co-operate positively in the suppression of terrorism;

   e.   carry out the proposal in paragraph 13.*h* of Recommendation 916 for the setting up of a Study and Documentation Centre on the causes, prevention and suppression of terrorism, with governmental and parliamentary support and a contribution from non-governmental organisations.

Recommendation 982 (1984)[1]
on the defence of democracy against terrorism in Europe

The Assembly,

1.   Having taken note of the report on the defence of democracy against terrorism in Europe, presented by its Political Affairs Committee (Doc. 5187);

2.   Recalling its earlier pronouncements on the matter, in particular Recommendation 941 (1982);

3.   Recalling that it condemns terrorism essentially for its totalitarian character, and because it violates human rights and threatens democracy, and stressing that those defending democracy can never resort to the contradiction of using methods which are antidemocratic or themselves violate human rights, since the fight against terrorism cannot justify the establishment of regimes—or the adoption of measures—of a fascist nature, which are as hateful as terrorism itself and for the same reasons;

4.   Deeply concerned at the scale of the terrorist assault against democratic values and institutions and human rights in member countries;

5.   Outraged by the succession of massacres and murders by terrorist organisations in several member countries;

6.   Indignant at the terrorist acts recently perpetrated by the agents of certain states abusing diplomatic immunity with shameful impunity;

7.   Convinced that the Council of Europe can and must, in view of the principles embodied in its Statute and its experience and aims, play a cardinal role in the establishment of a genuine European juridical area;

8.   Noting that two member states of the Council of Europe have not signed the European Convention on the Suppression of Terrorism, and that five of the signatory states have not yet ratified it;

9.   Noting that in some member countries there are legal, legislative or constitutional obstacles to the ratification of the convention;

10.   Having studied with interest the Spanish Government's suggestion that a conference of heads of state or government be convened to consider the problems posed by international anti-terrorist co-operation;

---

[1]   *Assembly debate* on 8 and 9 May 1984 (3rd, 4th and 5th Sittings) (see Doc. 5187, report of the Political Affairs Committee, and Doc. 5199, opinion of the Legal Affairs Committee).

Text adopted by the Assembly on 9 May 1984 (5th Sitting).

11.   Noting with satisfaction that the final communiqué of the CSCE meeting in Madrid contained a formal undertaking by the participating states to condemn and prevent all forms of international terrorism;

12.   Concerned, however, at the ease with which international terrorists and their weapons and financial resources cross the frontiers of member countries, and at the numerous signs of further collusion in non-member countries;

13.   Emphasising the fundamental importance of culture and education in maintaining a broad popular consensus, which is a prerequisite for combating terrorism by ensuring public confidence in democratic institutions;

14.   Aware that the press and the mass media have a moral duty to avoid unconsciously serving the aims of terrorist subversion;

15.   Welcoming the opening of the Convention on the Compensation of Victims of Violent Crimes for ratification, but disappointed that so few member states have become parties to a number of the Council of Europe's highly important legal instruments in the field of penal law and criminology,

16.   Recommends that the Committee of Ministers:

    i.   ask the governments of the member states to support the Spanish proposal that a conference of heads of state or government be convened to examine the problems posed by international anti-terrorist co-operation;

    ii.   invite the governments of member states, insofar as they have not yet done so, to sign and ratify the following Council of Europe instruments:

- European Convention on Extradition and its additional protocols,

- European Convention on Mutual Assistance in Criminal Matters and its additional protocols,

- European Convention on the Supervision of Conditionally Sentenced or Conditionally Released Offenders,

- European Convention on the International Validity of Criminal Judgments,

- European Convention on the Control of the Acquisition and Possession of Firearms by Individuals,

- Convention on the Transfer of Sentenced Persons;

iii. speedily conduct a political examination of the prospects for ratification of the European Convention on the Suppression of Terrorism and, if it proves negative, undertake a search for alternative legal solutions with a view to devising machinery common to all member states in international anti-terrorist co-operation;

iv. hold informal consultations and talks with government officials in charge of the suppression of terrorism in order to stimulate co-ordination of national policies in the matter and encourage co-operation between the judiciary, the police and the intelligence services of the member states;

v. ensure that the booklet commissioned by the Secretary General for the information of the general public on human rights in a democratic society specifically and exhaustively discusses problems associated with terrorist violence;

vi. while having full respect for the freedom of the press, invite representative professional organisations to work out a code of ethics for the media in order to define their role and responsibilities in the defence of democracy, particularly against terrorism.

Recommendation 1010 (1985)[1]
on aviation security

The Assembly,

1.   Outraged by the recent acts of terrorism perpetrated against innocent passengers and crew of civil aircraft, causing the loss of hundreds of lives, or else keeping them as hostages under savage conditions;

2.   Recalling its resolutions and recommendations on air piracy, on air safety and the unlawful seizure of aircraft, and on the suppression of terrorism, but noting that the proposals formulated in these texts have not yet been implemented fully;

3.   Deploring the continuing epidemic of terrorism in the air and stressing that it calls for strengthened national and international co-operation against terrorism;

4.   Welcoming in this connection the adoption by the European Civil Aviation Conference on 21 June 1985 in Strasbourg of a resolution and statement of policy in the field of aviation security which constitutes a comprehensive and updated manual of security measures embodied in all existing ECAC recommendations and resolutions in the security field;

5.   Deploring also that some countries do not implement fully the relevant international ICAO conventions and recommendations on the unlawful seizure of aircraft and on safety in the air;

6.   Recalling, in particular, its Recommendation 982 (1984) on the defence of democracy against terrorism in Europe and urging the Committee of Ministers to take speedier action on the proposals formulated therein;

7.   Considering that the European Ministers of Justice, at their 1984 meeting in Madrid and again at their recent meeting on 14 June 1985 in Edinburgh, requested that the Committee of Ministers set up, as a matter of urgency, an ad hoc body open to all Ministers who in their respective governments are competent in matters relating to terrorism, and that this body be entrusted with carrying out concrete and relentless action,

8.   Recommends that the Committee of Ministers:

    a.   invite the governments of member states as a matter of urgency:

        i.   insofar as they have not yet done so, to sign and ratify

---

[1] *Text adopted by the Standing Committee,* acting on behalf of the Assembly, on 4 July 1985.
See Doc. 5429, report of the Committee on Economic Affairs and Development.

- the European Convention on the suppression of terrorism of 1977, notwithstanding paragraph 8. *b* below;

- the ICAO Convention on offences and certain other acts committed on board aircraft (1963);

- the ICAO Convention for the suppression of unlawful seizure of aircraft (1970); and

- the ICAO Convention for the suppression of unlawful acts against the safety of civil aviation (1971);

ii. to implement fully the resolution and statement on the ECAC policy in the field of aviation security, adopted in Strasbourg on 21 June 1985;

iii. to strengthen international co-operation against terrorism, and to envisage special measures and/or sanctions-without excluding boycott measures-against countries whose authorities show themselves tolerant towards international acts of terrorism or breach the international conventions on air piracy;

b. give urgent consideration to the recommendation of the Colombo Commission that the Council of Europe draw up a new convention on the combating of terrorism, to which all member states will be able to accede;

c. set up a special working party to work out proposals on the best ways and means of implementing the above proposals.

Recommendation 1024 (1986)[1]
on the European response to international terrorism

The Assembly,

1.   Outraged by the wave of murders and massacres perpetrated by various terrorist organisations in several countries, in particular the simultaneous attacks carried out at the airports of Rome and Vienna on 27 December 1985;

2.   Recalling its unqualified condemnation of terrorism, which denies democratic values and human rights;

3.   Emphasising again that democratic states must combat terrorism while respecting democratic principles and the rights and freedoms guaranteed in their constitutions as well as in the Statute of the Council of Europe and the European Convention on Human Rights;

4.   Noting with concern the growing evidence that terrorist organisations receive substantial logistic, political and financial support, relayed, in particular, by certain states - Libya, Syria and Iran, among others - in open contradiction with the obligations resulting from membership of the international community;

5.   Convinced that co-operation between the member states and the world's other pluralist democracies is the primary condition for effective prevention and suppression of all forms of terrorism;

6.   Anxious for a speedy and successful conclusion to the efforts being made at intergovernmental level to set up within the Council of Europe framework an *ad hoc* political body open to all ministers who in their national governments are responsible for matters relating to the problems of terrorism and international organised crime;

7.   Urging all member states of the Council of Europe to fully implement existing international agreements and, insofar as they have not yet done so, to ratify such important conventions as:

-   the European Convention on Extradition,
-   the European Convention on the Suppression of Terrorism,
-   the European Convention on the Control of the Acquisition and Possession of Firearms by Individuals,
-   the European Convention on Mutual Assistance in Criminal Matters, and others,

---

[1] *Assembly debate* on 28 and 29 January 1986 (22nd, 23rd, 24th and 25th Sittings) (see Doc. 5518, report of the Political Affairs Committee).

Text adopted by the Assembly on 29 January 1986 (25th Sitting).

8.   Having decided to consider in greater detail, at its next part-session, the Council of Europe action to improve co-operation between member states on the lines of this recommendation,

9.   Recommends that the Committee of Ministers:

   a.   introduce as a matter of urgency new forms of co-operation between their relevant authorities, and especially between police forces and intelligence services:

      i.   to expose and publicly denounce states which assist terrorism in any way;

      ii.   to forestall any attack by stepping up checks and circulating information;

      iii. to reinforce penal sanctions for all those responsible for terrorist acts;

   b.   take action in all international forums, particularly in the United Nations, within the CSCE framework and through more intensive Euro-Arab dialogue, in the light of the proposal made by President Mubarak to the Assembly on 28 January 1986, in order to secure the participation of as many states as possible in the battle against terrorism, and in the political and economic isolation and moral condemnation of states which support it;

   c.   consider together and, where possible, take all measures whether diplomatic, political or economic to deter and punish states recognised as being responsible directly or indirectly for assistance to terrorism.

Resolution 863 (1986)[1]
on the European response to international terrorism

The Assembly,

1.   Recalling its various appeals for the defence of democracy against terrorism in Europe, in particular Recommendation 1024 (1986) on the European response to international terrorism ;

2.   Renewing its unreserved condemnation of terrorism, which denies democratic values and human rights, and reiterating its conviction that the response of the European democracies to terrorism must be founded on respect for the principles enshrined in their constitutions, in the European Convention on Human Rights and in international law ;

3.   Regretting the procrastination of European states in reacting multilaterally to the terrorist threat, and the absence up to the present time of a coherent and binding set of co-ordinated measures adopted by common consent ;

4.   Deeply concerned at the link between terrorism and trafficking in weapons and drugs ;

5.   Convinced that those states that directly or indirectly support terrorism - particularly Libya, Syria and Iran - must be politically and morally isolated in all international forums ;

6.   Welcoming, as a first step in the right direction, the measures set out in the Declaration on International Terrorism adopted in Tokyo on 5 May 1986 by the heads of state or government of the seven major democracies and by the representatives of the European Community ;

7.   Convinced that the Council of Europe is called upon, by virtue of the wide geographical area it covers, its composition and democratic basis, to define and co-ordinate European action against international terrorism ;

8.   Welcoming the decision by the Committee of Ministers to convene, on 4 and 5 November 1986, a European Conference of Ministers responsible for Combating Terrorism;

9.   Invites the member states of the Council of Europe :

    a.   to join in imposing on any state they regard as directly or indirectly responsible for abetting terrorism, political and economic sanctions, including :

---

[1] *Assembly debate* on 18 September 1986 (10th and 11th Sittings) (see Doc. 5601, report of the Political Affairs Committee).

Text adopted by the Assembly on 18 September 1986 (11th Sitting).

i.   diplomatic measures against the government of that state, involving reduction and eventually severing of diplomatic relations ;

ii.   suspension of international flights to and from that country ;

iii.   suspension of trade in military materials ;

iv.   suspension of all training of military personnel ;

v.   curtailment of investment ;

vi.   in appropriate cases, gradual termination of purchases of raw materials and energy products ;

b.   to reconsider and reduce arms trade with some countries of Africa and the Middle East, since it is in those regions that terrorist groups and the governments that support them procure the means with which to carry out their activities ;

10. Urges the governments of the member states of the Council of Europe, which have not yet done so, to ratify the European Convention on the Suppression of Terrorism, and calls upon them, pending this necessary ratification, to co-operate as effectively as possible with the other member states in combating terrorism ;

11. Invites the governments of the member states to review and, where possible, to withdraw any reservations made to that convention at the time of signature or ratification ;

12. Invites the European Conference of Ministers responsible for Combating Terrorism to consider :

a.   inviting member states to reach an agreement, in consultation, on defining terrorism as a crime against humanity ;

b.   setting up within the Council of Europe, by means of a partial agreement, a co-operation group for combating terrorism, composed of the ministers in the national governments with responsibility in this field, membership of which might be open to other European and non-European democratic states ;

c.   drawing up criteria on the basis of which Council of Europe member states could define their attitude to states that abuse, in one way or another, their diplomatic immunity in order to promote terrorist acts ;

d.   encouraging where necessary, while having full respect for the freedom of the press, the representative professional organisations to work out a code of ethics for the media, in order to define their role and responsibilities in the defence of democracy, particularly against terrorism ;

e. setting up, in the Council of Europe, a study and documentation centre for the prevention and suppression of terrorism, benefiting from the fullest possible governmental and parliamentary support, with the participation of non-governmental organisations.

Recommendation 1170 (1991)[1]
on the European Convention on the Suppression of Terrorism

1.   The Assembly has repeatedly condemned terrorism in the most vigorous of terms and urged strong action against what may be considered as one of the great scourges of our time.

2.   In this respect the Assembly wishes to recall the many texts on terrorism which it has adopted since 1972.

3.   In addition, it is useful to recall the action undertaken by the Committee of Ministers, in particular the elaboration of the European Convention on the Suppression of Terrorism which was opened for signature and ratification by Council of Europe member states in 1977.

4.   This convention, the aim of which is to facilitate extradition of terrorists, entered into force in 1978 and has been ratified by twenty-one of the twenty-five member states of the Council of Europe.

5.   Unfortunately, the convention has some obvious weaknesses, the most important of which are :

   i.   the omission of certain crimes among those listed in Article 1, such as for instance the use of non-automatic firearms ;

   ii.   the wording of Article 2 which provides that Contracting States may consider certain offences as terrorist crimes but that they have no obligation to do so and that, consequently, in such cases political motives may be involved and extradition refused ;

   iii. Article 13 of the convention, in accordance with which a Contracting State is entitled to make a reservation which may practically render the convention powerless in respect of that state.

6.   In conclusion, the Assembly urges those member states which have not yet ratified the convention to do so, whereas those member states which made the reservation provided for by Article 13 are urged to withdraw it.

7.   In addition, it would be desirable if the weak spots were to be eliminated from the convention. For that reason the Assembly recommends that the Committee of Ministers of the Council of Europe instruct the European Committee on Crime Problems (CDPC), as a matter of urgency, to study how the convention may be modified in order to strengthen it.

---

[1] *Text adopted by the Standing Committee*, acting on behalf of the Assembly, on 25 November 1991.

See Doc. 6445, report of the Committee on Legal Affairs and Human Rights, Rapporteur: Sir Dudley Smith ; and Doc. 6460, opinion of the Political Affairs Committee, Rapporteur: Sir Geoffrey Finsberg.

8. It reiterates the proposal made in its Resolution 863 (1986) to reach an agreement on defining terrorism as a crime against humanity.

9. Finally, the Parliamentary Assembly recommends that action be taken to outlaw all crimes involving violence, to remove from such offences the label "political" and to ensure that effective extradition arrangements are in place in relation to all such crimes.

Recommendation 1199 (1992)[1]
on the fight against international terrorism in Europe

1.   Since 1986, when the Assembly last dealt with the issue, terrorist incidents have continued to take place in Council of Europe member states.

2.   The Assembly unreservedly condemns these criminal acts which have claimed hundreds of innocent lives and caused great human suffering. In addition, terrorism has entailed considerable economic cost and disrupted the daily lives of millions.

3.   While most incidents in Europe were the result of domestic extremists, some of the most gruesome attacks were carried out by international terrorist groups, with the backing of certain Middle Eastern states, in particular Libya.

4.   The Assembly therefore welcomes and supports United Nations Security Council Resolution 748 imposing sanctions on Libya for its failure to comply with earlier demands by the Security Council, including handing over the individuals held responsible for the bombing of flight Pan Am 103 over Lockerbie, and full co-operation with the French authorities' investigations regarding the bombing of UTA flight 772.

5.   The Assembly further welcomes the efforts of the TREVI Group which brings together the ministers of the member states of the European Community, responsible for counter-terrorism and other police matters, and which through regular meetings at various levels ensures practical co-operation in the fight against terrorism.

6.   In addition, the Assembly considers that co-operation in the Schengen Group, shortly to consist of nine states, can make a useful contribution to reducing the terrorist threat in Europe.

7.   The Assembly notes the concern expressed by the authorities of the Council of Europe's new member states from central and eastern Europe that they face a particular terrorist threat. It also notes the request by these member states for close co-operation with those countries which have already acquired considerable experience in combating terrorism.

8.   Given the limited geographical scope of the Schengen and TREVI Groups, the Assembly considers that the Council of Europe, as a pan-European organisation, is best placed to offer the co-operation sought by the new central and east European countries.

---

[1] *Text adopted by the Standing Committee*, acting on behalf of the Assembly on 5 November 1992.
See Doc. 6669, report of the Political Affairs Committee, Rapporteur : Mr Hardy.

9.   Consequently, the Assembly recommends that the Committee of Ministers make provision for renewed activity in the field of combating terrorism, with particular emphasis on co-operation with central and eastern Europe.

Resolution 1132 (1997)[1]
on the organisation of a parliamentary conference to reinforce democratic systems in Europe and co-operation in the fight against terrorism

1.   Over the past two years there has been a resurgence of terrorist activities in Europe, and almost all European countries have recently been affected, either directly or indirectly, by these acts of violence. They are indicative of a profound change in the nature of terrorism in Europe, and reveal the inadequacy of standard methods for judicial and police co-operation in combating it.

2.   This new type of terrorism stems from the activity of internationally organised networks which are established in several countries, sometimes even in Council of Europe member states, playing on the legal flaws of the territoriality of proceedings and in some cases enjoying powerful logistical and financial support.

3.   In the past, the Parliamentary Assembly has emphasised that it considers terrorism a matter for serious concern, and, in particular, in Recommendation 1199 (1992) on the fight against international terrorism in Europe, it insisted on the need for close international co-operation between the Council of Europe member states.

4.   The 1977 European Convention on the Suppression of Terrorism, currently in force in twenty-nine member states, contains some flaws and now seems outdated. Firstly, terrorism has assumed new forms that were inconceivable when the convention was drafted, and secondly, terrorism has emerged in some central and east European countries since the collapse of communism.

5.   In its Recommendation 1324 (1997), the Parliamentary Assembly proposed that further means of countering terrorism, corruption and organised crime should be discussed at the 2nd Summit of Heads of State and Government of the Council of Europe to be held in Strasbourg on 10 and 11 October 1997, and called, in particular, for steps to be taken to "increase the effectiveness of the European Convention on the Suppression of Terrorism of 27 January 1977, with the necessary amendments or additional protocols".

6.   The growing number of terrorist acts committed throughout Europe in the past few years and the difficulty of dealing with this highly complex phenomenon now make it imperative to reflect together on ways of

---

[1] Assembly debate on 23 September 1997 (27th Sitting) (see Doc. 7876, report of the Committee on Legal Affairs and Human Rights, rapporteur: Mr López Henares; and Doc. 7904, opinion of the Political Affairs Committee, rapporteur: Mr Galanos).

Text adopted by the Assembly on 23 September 1997 (27th Sitting).

strengthening action against terrorism, while respecting the rights and freedoms secured in the European Convention on Human Rights.

7.   Holding a parliamentary conference on the subject should be a means of moving forward. Such a conference would be the appropriate frame for conducting fruitful discussions, identifying the problems posed by terrorism, studying measures for prevention, protection and surveillance, and measures to reinforce international co-operation, and making practical proposals for more effective action against terrorism, which would include revising the European Convention on the Suppression of Terrorism.

8.   Consequently:

   i.   the Parliamentary Assembly reiterates its forceful and unreserved condemnation of acts of terrorism and welcomes the French initiative to include the fight against terrorism, corruption and organised crime on the agenda of the 2nd Summit of Heads of State and Government of the Council of Europe;

   ii.   in this connection, it decides to hold a parliamentary conference to study, with the assistance of experts, the current phenomenon of terrorism in the democratic system, devise measures for prevention, protection and surveillance or suppression, and measures for strengthening international co-operation, and to analyse the requisite amendments to the European Convention on the Suppression of Terrorism;

   iii.   it instructs its Committee on Legal Affairs and Human Rights to organise this conference, with the assistance of other committees as necessary.

Recommendation 1426 (1999)[1]
on European democracies facing up to terrorism

1.   In its Resolution 1132 (1997) the Assembly decided to invite parliamentarians and experts to a conference aimed at strengthening democratic systems in Europe and co-operation in the fight against terrorism. In October 1997 this initiative received the support of the 2nd Summit of Heads of State and Government of the Council of Europe.

2.   The parliamentary conference on European Democracies Facing Up to Terrorism, which the Committee on Legal Affairs and Human Rights was responsible for organising, took place in Strasbourg from 14 to 16 October 1998.

3.   Terrorism in Council of Europe member states assumes a variety of forms, but its invariable aim is to undermine democracy, parliamentary institutions and the territorial integrity of states. Terrorism represents a serious threat to democratic society, whose moral and social fibre is affected by it. It attacks the most fundamental human right, the right to life, and for that reason must be totally condemned.

4.   The Assembly strongly and unequivocally condemns recent explosions of apartment buildings in various cities of the Russian Federation and reiterates its position that terrorist acts cannot have any justification whatsoever. The Assembly expresses sympathy to families of the victims of these barbaric acts and hopes that the Russian Federation will be able to overcome the terrorist menace without deviation from the democratic process and bring the criminals responsible for these attacks to justice.

5.   The Assembly considers an act of terrorism to be "any offence committed by individuals or groups resorting to violence or threatening to use violence against a country, its institutions, its population in general or specific individuals which, being motivated by separatist aspirations, extremist ideological conceptions, fanaticism or irrational and subjective factors, is intended to create a climate of terror among official authorities, certain individuals or groups in society, or the general public".

6.   The Council of Europe and its member states should take concrete steps to facilitate co-operation in combating terrorism. Anti-terrorist measures should include, inter alia, exchanges of information, detention and extradition of persons accused of terrorist crimes, and uncovering and cutting off the channels through which terrorists are provided with weapons, explosives and financial means.

---

[1]   Assembly debate on 20 September 1999 (25th Sitting) (see Doc. 8507, report of the Committee on Legal Affairs and Human Rights, rapporteur: Mr López Henares; and Doc. 8513, opinion of the Political Affairs Committee, rapporteur: Mrs Stanoiu).

Text adopted by the Assembly on 23 September 1999 (30th Sitting).

7.   To prevent the ethnic or religious tensions that are liable to give rise to terrorist phenomena, democratic states should respect social and political pluralism by taking into account the legitimate aspirations of minorities and respecting cultural characteristics.

8.   However, the Assembly considers that no support, even of a moral kind, should be given to any organisation advocating or encouraging violence as a method of settling political, economic and social conflicts.

9.   The prevention of terrorism also depends on education in democratic values and tolerance, with the eradication of the teaching of negative or hateful attitudes towards others and the development of a culture of peace in all individuals and social groups.

10. The Assembly, recognising the vital importance of free media in a pluralistic democracy, acknowledges that the media too have a responsible role to play by reporting terrorist actions and by firmly refusing to allow themselves to be exploited by terrorism.

11. The Assembly believes that the fight against terrorism should be conducted on the basis of respect for the rule of law and the fundamental rights and freedoms of individuals, and it therefore regards recourse to special legislation as inadvisable.

12. Recognising the importance of respect for the rule of law, effective judicial and police co-operation on a continental scale is necessary to combat terrorism. The Assembly therefore welcomes the creation of Europol, even though it is confined to the fifteen member countries of the European Union. Furthermore, since terrorism is not restricted to Europe, it is important to co-ordinate European initiatives with other international initiatives.

13. The conventions of the Council of Europe, whether they be the 1977 European Convention on the Suppression of Terrorism or the 1957 European Convention on Extradition, should be reviewed in the light of experience to make them more effective in the fight against terrorism.

14. The European Convention on the Suppression of Terrorism, by failing to cover all criminal offences capable of being considered terrorist actions or collaboration with these actions, does not enable terrorism to be combated as effectively as would be desirable.

15. The European Convention on Extradition, by enabling extradition to be refused if the offence is a political one, should be modified to prevent abuses of the right to asylum for terrorists.

16. The Assembly recommends that the Committee of Ministers:

   i.   revise the European Convention on the Suppression of Terrorism, of 27 January 1977, by broadening the definition of criminal offences of a terrorist nature to include preparatory acts, the membership of associations and the funding and setting up of logistics to perpetrate these kinds of offences;

ii. consider as terrorist acts not only attacks against persons but also attacks against property and material resources;

iii. delete Article 13 of the European Convention on the Suppression of Terrorism;

iv. amend the European Convention on Extradition, of 13 December 1957, by defining the concept of a political offence and proposing a simplified extradition procedure, with measures to avoid abuse of the right of asylum;

v. consider the possibility of setting up a European criminal court to try terrorist crimes in certain cases;

vi. consider the establishment of a procedure whereby, in certain cases, a person accused of committing a terrorist offence could be charged and tried for such an offence in a country other than the one in which the offence was committed;

vii. initiate co-operation with the United Nations' Special Committee on Terrorism to consolidate the general legal framework of conventions on international terrorism;

viii. encourage member states to co-operate together more closely within Interpol, and examine, in conjunction with the European Union, the possibility of extending the Europol convention to all Council of Europe member states and establishing a Europol judicial control system;

ix. envisage the preparation of a civic education textbook for all schools in Europe so as to combat the spread of extremist ideas and advocate tolerance and respect for others as an essential basis of community life;

x. consider the incorporation of the principle of fuller protection for victims of terrorist acts at both national and international level;

xi. invite Council of Europe member states to incorporate the principle *aut dedere aut iudicare*[2] in their criminal legislation;

xii. invite member states to strengthen bilateral co-operation in respect of their judicial authorities, police forces and intelligence services.

---

[2] That is, "either extradite or try".

Order No. 555 (1999)[1]
on European democracies facing up to terrorism

1. The Assembly, having regard to its Recommendation 1426 (1999), instructs its Committee on Legal Affairs and Human Rights to make a study of the anti-terrorist laws of Council of Europe member states and, in particular, of statutory texts enabling the principle *aut dedere aut iudicare* ("either extradite or try") to be applied.

2. It instructs its President to transmit the above-mentioned recommendation to the Council of the European Union, the European Commission and the European Parliament.

---

[1] Assembly debate on 20 September 1999 (25th Sitting) (see Doc. 8507, report of the Committee on Legal Affairs and Human Rights, rapporteur: Mr López Henares, and Doc. 8513, opinion of the Political Affairs Committee, rapporteur: Mrs Stanoiu).

Text adopted by the Assembly on 23 September 1999 (30th Sitting).

Recommendation 1534 (2001)[1]
on democracies facing terrorism

1.   The Parliamentary Assembly refers to its Resolution 1258 (2001) on democracies facing terrorism.

2.   It strongly condemns all forms of terrorism as a violation of the most fundamental human right: the right to life.

3.   It takes note of the declaration by the Committee of Ministers of 12 September 2001 and welcomes its decision of 21 September 2001 to include the fight against terrorism in the agenda for the 109th Session of the Committee of Ministers (7 and 8 November 2001).

4.   The Assembly regards the new International Criminal Court as the appropriate institution to consider international acts of terrorism.

5.   The Assembly urges the Committee of Ministers to:

   i.   ask those member states who have not yet done so to sign and ratify the existing relevant anti-terrorist conventions, especially the International Convention for the Suppression of the Financing of Terrorism;

   ii.   invite member states to lift their reservations to anti-terrorist conventions, which hinder international co-operation;

   iii. ensure the full implementation of all existing Council of Europe conventions in the penal field;

   iv.   request those member and Observer states that have not done so to sign and ratify, as rapidly as possible, the Treaty of Rome, which provides for the establishment of the International Criminal Court;

   v.   make it possible for Observer and non-member states to accede to the European Convention on the Suppression of Terrorism at its 109th Ministerial Session, and invite them, as well as those member states who have not yet signed and/or ratified this convention, to do so at this session;

   vi.   establish immediate, concrete and formal co-operation with the European Union, the OSCE and the Commonwealth of Independent States (CIS) on the basis of the Council of Europe's values and legal

---

[1] Assembly debate on 25 and 26 September 2001 (27th and 28th Sittings) (see Doc. 9228, report of the Political Affairs Committee, rapporteur: Mr Davis; and Doc. 9232, opinion of the Committee on Legal Affairs and Human Rights, rapporteur: Mr Jansson).

Text adopted by the Assembly on 26 September 2001 (28th Sitting).

instruments, in order to guarantee coherence and efficiency in Europe's action against terrorism;

vii. ask member states to review their education programmes in order to enhance the role of democratic values, as children and the younger generation are often used by the terrorists to achieve their aims;

viii. reconsider the basis of international co-operation in criminal matters in Europe, in order to find new and more effective means of co-operation which take account of present-day realities and needs;

ix. extend the terms of reference of the Committee of Experts on the Criminalisation of Acts of a Racist or Xenophobic Nature Committed Through Computer Networks (PC-RX) to terrorist messages and the decoding thereof;

x. as regards the European Convention on the Suppression of Terrorism, remove as a matter of urgency Article 13, which grants contracting states the right to make reservations which can defeat the purpose of the convention by enabling the states to refuse extradition for offences otherwise extraditable;

xi. give urgent consideration to amending and widening the Rome Statute to allow the remit of the International Criminal Court to include acts of international terrorism;

xii. review the relevant existing conventions in the light of the recent events and declare terrorism and all forms of support for it to be crimes against humanity.

6. The Assembly recommends that the Committee of Ministers examine, in co-operation with the European Union bodies, the modalities for extending the European Union arrest warrant to all Council of Europe member states in the field of the fight against terrorism.

7. It reiterates its Recommendation 1426 (1999) on European democracies facing up to terrorism and calls on the Committee of Ministers to provide a more substantial reply to it as a matter of urgency.

Resolution 1258 (2001)[1]
on democracies facing terrorism

1.   The members of the Parliamentary Assembly of the Council of Europe and the 800 million Europeans whom it represents were horrified by the recent terrorist attacks against the United States of America.

2.   The Assembly conveys its deepest sympathies to the people of the United States and to the families of the victims, including citizens of other countries.

3.   The Assembly condemns in the strongest possible terms these barbaric terrorist acts. It considers these attacks as a crime that violates the most fundamental human right: the right to life.

4.   The Assembly calls on the international community to give all necessary support to the Government of the United States of America in dealing with the consequences of these attacks and in bringing the perpetrators to justice, in line with existing international anti-terrorist conventions and United Nations Security Council resolutions.

5.   The Assembly regards the new International Criminal Court as the appropriate institution to consider terrorist acts.

6.   The Assembly welcomes, supports and shares the solidarity shown by members of the international community, which has not only condemned these attacks, but also offered to co-operate in an appropriate response.

7.   These attacks have shown clearly the real face of terrorism and the need for a new kind of response. This terrorism does not recognise borders. It is an international problem to which international solutions must be found based on a global political approach. The world community must show that it will not capitulate to terrorism, but that it will stand more strongly than before for democratic values, the rule of law and the defence of human rights and fundamental freedoms.

8.   There can be no justification for terrorism. The Assembly considers these terrorist actions to be crimes rather than acts of war. Any actions, either by the United States acting alone or as a part of a broader international coalition, must be in line with existing United Nations anti-terrorist conventions and Security Council resolutions and must focus on bringing the perpetrators, organisers and sponsors of these crimes to justice, instead of inflicting a hasty revenge.

---

[1] Assembly debate on 25 and 26 September 2001 (27th and 28th Sittings) (see Doc. 9228, report of the Political Affairs Committee, rapporteur: Mr Davis; and Doc. 9232, opinion of the Committee on Legal Affairs and Human Rights, rapporteur: Mr Jansson).

Text adopted by the Assembly on 26 September 2001 (28th Sitting).

9.   At the same time, the Assembly believes that long-term prevention of terrorism must include a proper understanding of its social, economic, political and religious roots and of the individual's capacity for hatred. If these issues are properly addressed, it will be possible to seriously undermine the grass roots support for terrorists and their recruitment networks.

10.   The Assembly supports the idea of elaborating and signing at the highest level an international convention on combating terrorism, which should contain a comprehensive definition of international terrorism as well as specific obligations for participating states to prevent acts of terrorism on a national and global scale and to punish their organisers and executors.

11.   The recent terrorist acts appear to have been undertaken by extremists who have used violence with a view to provoking a serious clash between the West and the Islamic world. Therefore, the Assembly emphasises that any action to prevent or punish terrorist acts must not discriminate on ethnic or religious grounds and must not be directed against any religious or ethnic community.

12.   If military action is part of a response to terrorism, the international community must clearly define its objectives and should avoid targeting civilians. Any action should be taken in conformity with international law and with the agreement of the United Nations Security Council. The Assembly therefore welcomes Security Council Resolution 1368 (2001), which expresses the Council's readiness to take all necessary steps to respond to the attacks of 11 September 2001 and to combat all forms of terrorism in accordance with its responsibilities under the United Nations Charter.

13.   The Assembly expresses its conviction that introducing additional restrictions on freedom of movement, including more hurdles for migration and for access to asylum, would be an absolutely inappropriate response to the rise of terrorism, and calls upon all member states to refrain from introducing such restrictive measures.

14.   The Assembly believes that international action against terrorism can only be effective if it is carried out with the broadest possible support. It calls for close co-operation at a pan-European level, especially with the European Parliament, as part of a global effort and calls on the European Union, the Commonwealth of Independent States (CIS) and the OSCE to co-operate closely with the Council of Europe in this regard.

15.   The Assembly expresses support for the proposal to establish an international anti-terrorist mechanism within the United Nations to co-ordinate and promote co-operation between states in dealing with terrorism.

16.   The Assembly recalls its report on terrorism of 1984, as well as Recommendation 1426 (1999) on European democracies facing up to terrorism. It reiterates the proposals made in this recommendation, including

the principle of *aut dedere aut judicare* (either extradite or try), and instructs its relevant committees to update them if necessary.

17. The Assembly calls on the Council of Europe member states to:

    i.   stand firmly united against all acts of terrorism, whether they are state sponsored or perpetrated by isolated groups or organisations, and show a clear will and readiness to fight against them;

    ii.   introduce economic and other appropriate measures against countries offering safe havens to terrorists or providing financial and moral support to them;

    iii.   concentrate their efforts on improving judicial co-operation and police co-operation and on the identifying and seizing of funds used for terrorist purposes in the spirit of the International Convention for the Suppression of the Financing of Terrorism;

    iv.   review the scope of the existing national legal provisions on the prevention and suppression of terrorism;

    v.   take the necessary steps to ensure that appropriate domestic measures exist to prevent and counteract the financing of terrorists and terrorist organisations;

    vi.   lift their reservations to all existing conventions dealing with terrorism;

    vii.   provide access to bank accounts for the authorities responsible for investigating international crime and terrorist networks in particular;

    viii.   renew and generously resource their commitment to pursue economic, social and political policies designed to secure democracy, justice, human rights and well-being for all people throughout the world;

    ix.   give urgent consideration to amending and widening the Rome Statute to allow the remit of the International Criminal Court to include acts of international terrorism;

    x.   reaffirm their commitment to the status of the United Nations Security Council as the ultimate authority for approving international military action.

18. The Assembly invites the member states of the United Nations to amend their Charter so that it may also address crises other than those arising between states.

19. The Assembly requests that the present resolution be transmitted to the Congress and to the President of the United States and to the Secretary General of the United Nations.

20. The Assembly furthermore instructs its Bureau to ensure that, in the follow-up to this resolution, there is appropriate co-operation and co-ordination between the Parliamentary Assembly and the European Parliament, involving also the respective competent committees of each institution.

Recommendation 1550 (2002)[1]
on combating terrorism and respect for human rights

1.   The Parliamentary Assembly refers to its Resolution 1271 (2002) on combating terrorism and respect for human rights, in which it advocates a number of measures member states should take to combat terrorism while ensuring respect for human rights.

2.   It has noted the possible contradiction between, on the one hand, the desire to open for ratification by Observer states and other non-member states of the Council of Europe the European Convention on the Suppression of Terrorism, which contains no explicit provision for refusing extradition in cases where there is a risk the death penalty may be applied, and on the other hand, the refusal to extradite suspected terrorists to countries applying the death penalty. The Assembly considers that this matter ought to be settled in the context of the work to update the European Convention on the Suppression of Terrorism.

3.   The Assembly welcomes the decision taken by the Committee of Ministers to set up a Multidisciplinary Group on International Action against Terrorism (GMT) with the tasks of updating Council of Europe instruments in this field and identifying new and better ways in which the Council of Europe could combat this dangerous form of crime within the limits of its scope. Steps should also be taken to accelerate international co-operation in combating the laundering of the proceeds from crime, in particular with respect to financial investigations, and to step up action to prevent the financing of terrorism.

4.   Furthermore, the Assembly notes the ten new recommendations on the financing of terrorism adopted in December 2001 by the Financial Action Task Force on Money Laundering (FATF) and welcomes the decision taken by the Council of Europe's Select Committee of Experts on the Evaluation of Anti-Money-Laundering Measures (PC-R-EV) to extend the scope of the FATF's new recommendations to the whole of Europe by incorporating them in its own programme of activities.

5.   Lastly, the Assembly considers that when working to promote better pan-European co-operation against terrorism, the GMT should consider using the definition of terrorism adopted by the European Union.

6.   Improvements to the European judicial area are a precondition for effective European co-operation: the definition, creation and prosecution of indictable offences need to be harmonised.

7.   The Assembly recommends that the Committee of Ministers:

---

[1] *Assembly debate* on 24 January 2002 (6th Sitting) (see Doc. 9331, report of the Committee on Legal Affairs and Human Rights, rapporteur: Mr Hunault).

Text adopted by the Assembly on 24 January 2002 (6th Sitting).

i.   amend the European Convention on the Suppression of Terrorism to include a provision according to which extradition may be refused in cases where there are no guarantees that the death penalty will not be sought for the accused person;

ii.   step up international co-operation in combating the laundering of the proceeds from crime, in particular with respect to financial investigations, as well as efforts to combat the financing of terrorism;

iii.   request that the Multidisciplinary Group on International Action against Terrorism (GMT) consider using the definition of terrorism adopted by the European Union (see Appendix).

European Council Common Position of 27 December 2001 on the application of specific measures to combat terrorism
(2001/931/CFSP)
Article 1

...

3. For the purposes of this Common Position, "terrorist act" shall mean one of the following intentional acts, which, given its nature or its context, may seriously damage a country or an international organisation, as defined as an offence under national law, where committed with the aims of:

i. seriously intimidating a population, or

ii. unduly compelling a government or an international organisation to perform or abstain from performing any act, or

iii. seriously destabilising or destroying the fundamental political, constitutional, economic or social structures of a country or an international organisation:

a. attacks upon a person's life which may cause death;

b. attacks upon the physical integrity of a person;

c. kidnapping or hostage-taking;

d. causing extensive destruction to a government or public facility, a transport system, an infrastructure facility, including an information system, a fixed platform located on the continental shelf, a public place or private property, likely to endanger human life or result in major economic loss;

e. seizure of aircraft, ships or other means of public or goods transport;

f. manufacture, possession, acquisition, transport, supply or use of weapons, explosives or of nuclear, biological or chemical weapons, as well as research into, and development of, biological and chemical weapons;

g. release of dangerous substances, or causing fires, explosions or floods the effect of which is to endanger human life;

h. interfering with or disrupting the supply of water, power or any other fundamental natural resource, the effect of which is to endanger human life;

i. threatening to commit any of the acts listed under *a* to *h*;

j.   directing a terrorist group;

k.   participating in the activities of a terrorist group, including by supplying information or material resources, or by funding its activities in any way, which knowledge of the fact that such participation will contribute to the criminal activities of the group.

For the purposes of this paragraph, "terrorist group" shall mean a structured group of more than two persons, established over a period of time and acting in concert to commit terrorist acts. "Structured group" means a group that is not randomly formed for the immediate commission of a terrorist act and that does not need to have formally defined roles for its members, continuity of its membership or a developed structure.

Resolution 1271 (2002)[1]
on combating terrorism and respect for human rights

1.   Recalling its Recommendation 1426 (1999), its Resolution 1258 (2001) and its Recommendation 1534 (2001) on democracies facing terrorism, the Parliamentary Assembly considers it necessary to take stock of the means used to combat terrorism.

2.   First of all, the Assembly would like to draw attention to the new nature of the conflict that arose as a result of the terrorist acts of 11 September, which cannot be classed as a "war" in the traditional sense according to international law in so far as there was no declaration of war, nor has it been proved that the terrorist acts were carried out on the orders of a particular country. The military intervention carried out in Afghanistan as a result of the attacks was directed not against a country but against a terrorist organisation and against the former regime in Afghanistan, suspected of supporting such organisations.

3.   The Assembly considers there is a need to study the causes of terrorism in order to find better ways of combating and, above all, of preventing them. It reiterates, however, that there can never be any justification for resorting to terrorism.

4.   Eliminating support for terrorism and depriving it of all sources of funding are essential ways of preventing this form of crime.

5.   The combat against terrorism must be carried out in compliance with national and international law and respecting human rights.

6.   The Assembly considers that higher levels of education, access to decent living conditions and respect for human dignity are the best instruments for reducing the support currently given to terrorism in certain countries.

7.   The Assembly, which has declared itself to be strongly opposed to capital punishment and which has succeeded in ridding Europe of the death penalty, tolerates no exceptions to this principle. Therefore, prior to the extradition of suspected terrorists to countries that still apply the death penalty, assurances must be obtained that this penalty will not be sought.

8.   The Assembly also insists on the fact that member states should under no circumstances extradite persons who risk being subjected to ill-treatment in violation of Article 3 of the European Convention on Human Rights or being subjected to a trial which does not respect the fundamental principles of a fair trial, or, in a period of conflict, to standards which fall below those enshrined in the Geneva Convention.

---

[1] *Assembly debate* on 24 January 2002 (6th Sitting) (see Doc. 9331, report of the Committee on Legal Affairs and Human Rights, rapporteur: Mr Hunault).

Text adopted by the Assembly on 24 January 2002 (6th Sitting).

9.   In their fight against terrorism, Council of Europe member states should not provide for any derogations to the European Convention on Human Rights.

10.   The Assembly hopes that the statute of the International Criminal Court will be rapidly ratified and its remit extended to acts of terrorism.

11.   Concerning judicial co-operation, the Assembly considers that the European arrest warrant to be introduced by the European Union, in so far as it applies to crimes related to terrorism, should be extended to include all member states of the Council of Europe, in full respect of the fundamental rights guaranteed by the European Convention on Human Rights.

12.   The Assembly therefore calls upon all Council of Europe member states to:

    i.   ratify without delay, if they have not already done so:

        – the International Convention for the Suppression of the Financing of Terrorism;

        – the European Convention on the Suppression of Terrorism;

        – the European Convention on Extradition and its two additional protocols;

        – the European Convention on Mutual Assistance in Criminal Matters and its two additional protocols;

        – the European Convention on the Transfer of Proceedings in Criminal Matters;

        – the Convention on Laundering, Search, Seizure, and Confiscation of the Proceeds from Crime;

        – the Convention on Cybercrime;

    ii.   ratify as soon as possible, if they have not already done so, the statute of the International Criminal Court;

    iii.   set up networks for co-operation between Financial Intelligence Units (FIUs) and ensure the necessary means of co-operation are put in place;

    iv.   refuse to extradite suspected terrorists to countries that continue to apply the death sentence, in accordance with the decision of the European Court of Human Rights in the Soering case and with

Article 11 of the European Convention on Extradition, unless assurances are given that the death penalty will not be sought;

v.　refrain from using Article 15 of the European Convention on Human Rights (derogation in time of emergency) to limit the rights and liberties guaranteed under its Article 5 (right to liberty and security).

13. The Assembly supports the proposal to convene an international conference on the combating of terrorism in St Petersburg, to be held in co-operation with the Interparliamentary Assembly of the Commonwealth of Independent States as well as other international parliamentary organisations, and believes that this conference should pay special attention to legal issues related to the suppression of terrorism.

Recommendation 1549 (2002)[1]
on air transport and terrorism: how to enhance security?

1. The hijacking of four US airliners in the United States on 11 September 2001, resulting in the killing of nearly 3 500 people in New York and Washington, highlights the need for reinforced security measures in air transport.

2. The Assembly acknowledges the long-standing work against air terrorism pursued by the European Civil Aviation Conference (Ecac) on behalf of its thirty-eight member states and recalls its own steadfast support for this work, as expressed in its Recommendation 1099 (1989) on aviation security.

3. The Assembly welcomes the close co-operation established since the events of 11 September between Ecac and the European Union, and the latter's subsequent draft legislation, largely based on Ecac's aviation security measures (Avsec).

4. The Assembly takes note of the considerable impact the adopted measures have already had on reinforcing security in air transport, but reinforcement of the security should be permanently accompanied by appropriate activities to inform the public about the progress achieved.

5. The Assembly recalls the importance of the following guiding principles underlying the new security level required:

On the ground

i.   "100% reconciliation" between checked-in luggage and passengers to ensure that no luggage travels unaccompanied;

ii.   reinforced security control of passengers and their hand luggage, as well as of all those with access to restricted areas (for example, catering, duty free and in-flight service items);

iii. 100% screening of checked-in luggage introduced as early as possible, at the latest by the end of 2002;

iv.   pre-flight checks of the interior and exterior of aircraft;

v.   implementation of the special security regime developed by Ecac for cargo, mail and express parcels;

---

[1] *Assembly debate* on 23 January 2002 (5th Sitting) (see Doc. 9296, report of the Committee on Economic Affairs and Development, rapporteur: Mr Billing).
Text adopted by the Assembly on 23 January 2002 (5th Sitting).

In the air

vi.   prevention of any attempt by an unauthorised person to gain access to the cockpit, for example by the instalment of doors equipped with bars and locks capable of withstanding bullets and explosives, while at the same time permitting crew members to access and control the rest of the aircraft, and to escape in the event of an emergency;

vii.   maintenance of contact at all times between the ground and the aircraft through vocal communication; transponder communication giving the aircraft's location, under the authority of Eurocontrol as the "European regional focal point" for civilian and military air traffic management information; and a press-button alarm function at the start of terrorist attacks;

viii. presence, at each country's discretion, of armed in-flight security personnel, and the international acceptance of such presence through international agreements;

Implementation

ix.   the implementation and continued enforcement of the new security level should be ensured by European and global audit (inspection) teams, preferably through the development of the Ecac Aviation Security Airport Audit programme already in operation.

6.   In view of the fact that air terrorism knows no national frontiers, the Assembly calls on the Committee of Ministers of the Council of Europe, which includes all European Union, Ecac and Eurocontrol member states as well as five additional countries, to ensure that the totality of the above measures, as called for in Ecac's Avsec recommendations and in the forthcoming European Union legislation, are introduced as a matter of urgency in the territory of all the forty-three member states of the Council of Europe.

7.   The Assembly furthermore calls for the rapid development of further means to identify passengers, such as computer recognition of facial and eye (iris) characteristics and handprints.

8.   Finally, in recognition of the global impact of terrorist attacks in the air, the Assembly calls on the Committee of Ministers, Ecac, Eurocontrol and the European Union to work towards the earliest possible worldwide introduction of the above measures, through the International Civil Aviation Organisation.

Recommendation 1584 (2002)[1]
on the need for intensified international co-operation to neutralise funds for terrorist purposes

1.   The terrorist attacks against the United States of America on 11 September 2001 demonstrated in the most dramatic and tragic fashion the vulnerability of civilisation vis-à-vis those seeking to destroy it, and the resulting need to take every measure to prevent terrorist acts and apprehend the perpetrators, organisers and sponsors, along the principles set out in Parliamentary Assembly Recommendation 1534 (2001) on democracies facing terrorism.

2.   The Assembly, referring in particular to its Recommendation 1550 (2002) on combating terrorism and respect for human rights, underlines the importance in this struggle of identifying and neutralising funds destined for terrorist purposes – an undertaking which is possible only if the world community, and notably Europe, reach a new degree of co-operation at the normative, operative and implementation levels. While such an effort may not ensure the prevention of all terrorist acts, it can contribute significantly to weakening terrorist infrastructure. This is so especially if measures can neutralise terrorism's legal sources of financing, which in certain cases operate under the cover of humanitarian, non-profit or even charitable organisations. It is also necessary to prevent general criminal activities that often serve to finance terrorism, such as trafficking in human beings, drugs and weapons. The systems and measures developed over the last few years to prevent the laundering of proceeds from crime can, if conscientiously applied, play a significant role in the detection, freezing and confiscation of terrorist funds.

3.   The Assembly, with the above in mind, recommends strongly that the Committee of Ministers of the Council of Europe undertake the following measures:

At the normative level

i.   to work in favour of the ratification, by all Council of Europe member states and others, of the totality of international legal instruments concerned with the fight against terrorism and its financing, and in particular the 1999 United Nations International Convention for the Suppression of the Financing of Terrorism;

ii.   to reach immediately an agreement on a definition of terrorism, preferably based on that adopted in December 2001 by the European Council of the European Union in a common position;

---

[1]   *Text adopted by the Standing Committee,* acting on behalf of the Assembly, on 18 November 2002 (see Doc. 9520, report of the Committee on Economic Affairs and Development, rapporteur: Mr Marty).

iii.   to render any financial activity in support of terrorism thus defined a criminal offence;

iv.   further to strengthen domestic legislation and any international convention in need thereof, by adapting them to new technological and other developments as well as to the growing sophistication of terrorists, for the purpose of successfully tracing the origin – whether legal or illegal – as well as the routing of funds intended for terrorist ends, with a view to their seizure or confiscation. The Assembly in this connection welcomes the Committee of Ministers' decision taken in May 2002 that an additional protocol should be drawn up to the 1997European Convention on the Suppression of Terrorism (ETS No. 90), and asks the Committee of Ministers also to envisage the possibility of adapting the Council of Europe Convention on Laundering, Search, Seizure and Confiscation of the Proceeds from Crime (ETS No. 141), for instance through an additional protocol;

At the operative level

v.   to intensify co-operation between national administration, police forces, courts, financial institutions, regulatory and other authorities in order to uncover suspicious international transactions and thereby reach the organisations and individuals behind them. The Assembly in this context welcomes the creation in 2001 of EuroJust and supports decisions taken to widen the mandates of the Financial Action Task Force (FATF) and the Council of Europe's Select Committee of Experts on the Evaluation of Anti-Money Laundering Measures (PC-R-EV), to include also the detection of terrorism financing and welcomes in addition the establishment within Europol of an international terrorism task force dealing also with its financial aspects;

At the level of monitoring implementation

vi.   to ensure that international conventions and other agreements against terrorism financing are effectively implemented in Council of Europe member states and other participating states – notably by strengthening the mandates and increasing the resources of the FATF and other competent bodies such as the PC-R-EV, and by rendering public any national shortcoming so as to increase pressure for remedial action;

vii.   finally, the Assembly reiterates its belief, as expressed notably in its Resolution 1271 (2002) on combating terrorism and respect for human rights, that the fight against terrorism must never be allowed to harm the Council of Europe's fundamental values of democracy, the rule of law and human rights – including the provisions of the European Convention on Human Rights and the prohibition of the death penalty it upholds.

Recommendation 1644 (2004)[1]
on terrorism: a threat to democracies

1.   The Parliamentary Assembly refers to its previous texts, in particular Recommendations 1534 (2001) on democracies facing terrorism and 1550 (2002) on combating terrorism and respect for human rights, and replies of the Committee of Ministers thereon, which were on the whole positive. The Assembly welcomes the Guidelines on Human Rights and the Fight against Terrorism, adopted by the Committee of Ministers on 11 July 2002, which formulate criteria for safeguarding human rights in the fight against terrorism.

2.   It observes that terrorist attacks of particular ferocity have been carried out in different parts of the world since the attacks of 11 September 2001, and the existence of a global terrorist threat is now a well established fact.

3.   The Assembly conveys its deepest sympathies to the families of the victims and to all those affected or injured by the recent terrorist bombings in the Russian Federation and in Turkey and, in general, by any terrorist attack.

4.   Whereas the improvement of international co-operation, the stepping up of national security measures and the increase in the number of ratifications of various international legal instruments are positive signs in the fight against terrorism, loopholes still exist in legislation, cross-border controls, prosecution and extradition arrangements, and these are exploited by terrorists.

5.   In this connection, the Assembly welcomes the setting up of the Counter-Terrorism Committee in the United Nations, established pursuant to Security Council Resolution 1373 (2001), the adoption of the Common Position and the Framework Decisions by the Council of the European Union, which is a rather significant attempt to a structured approach in the fight against terrorism, and the setting up of the Committee of Experts on Terrorism (Codexter) in the Council of Europe, with the aim of reinforcing and co-ordinating the Organisation's action in this field.

6.   The Assembly is convinced, however, that a new impetus is necessary in order to give a clear signal to the public about the importance of multilateral efforts. The incorporation, therefore, of fragmented legal texts together with the necessary additions in one comprehensive convention would present considerable added value to the fight against terrorism, as first expressed in its Opinion No. 242 (2003) on the draft protocol amending the European Convention on the Suppression of Terrorism.

---

[1] *Assembly debate* on 29 January 2004 (6th Sitting) (see Doc. 10056, report of the Political Affairs Committee, rapporteur: Mr Mercan).

Text adopted by the Assembly on 29 January 2004 (6th Sitting).

7.   Despite the progress so far reached in this regard, the possibility of achieving this in the framework of the United Nations is almost non-existent due to difficulties in defining terrorism. A more homogenous group of states, such as the Council of Europe member states, should be able to overcome this obstacle.

8.   The Assembly is convinced that the motive behind an act of terrorism does not change the nature of that act. Terrorism has no justification and it must be considered illegal, abhorrent, unacceptable and a crime against humanity.

9.   As the Assembly has consistently stated in the past, action against terrorism must at all times be consistent with the fundamental freedoms and human rights which it is designed to protect. This is particularly so in the member states of the Council of Europe which should also be sensitive to the deep-rooted reasons of the changing nature of terrorism and promote dialogue between cultures and religions.

10.   The Assembly is convinced that the root causes – poverty, exclusion, disparity and desperation – which provide a fertile ground for the emergence and spread of terrorism should be addressed.

11.   The Assembly asks the Committee of Ministers:

i.   to begin work without delay on the elaboration of a comprehensive Council of Europe convention on terrorism, based on the normative acquis of the United Nations', Council of Europe's and European Union's legal instruments and other texts, and develop them as much as necessary;

ii.   to invite, in the meantime, the member states:

a.   to ratify existing conventions, or inform the Committee of Ministers and the Assembly about the grounds for not doing so, in particular: the European Convention on the Suppression of Terrorism (1977) in conjunction with its Protocol (2003), the European Convention on Extradition (1957) and its Additional Protocols (1975 and 1978), the European Convention on the Transfer of Proceedings in Criminal Matters (1972), and the Convention on Laundering, Search, Seizure and Confiscation of the Proceeds from Crime (1990);

b.   to condemn strongly countries encouraging, helping, providing financial support, or offering safe haven to terrorists and introduce economic and other appropriate measures against them;

  c. to promote democracy and human rights in their foreign relations and refrain from complacency towards despotic and obscurantist regimes for reasons of strategic and economic interests;

iii. to study, in consultation with the European Union, the possibility of transforming Europol into an effective pan-European agency, with sufficient means to challenge international terrorism;

iv. to repeat the appeal to the member states, as stipulated in Parliamentary Assembly Recommendation 1534, to "give urgent consideration to amending and widening the Rome Statute to allow the remit of the International Criminal Court to include acts of international terrorism".

Resolution 1367 (2004)[1]
on bioterrorism: a serious threat for citizens' health

1. Since 11 September 2001 the threat of large-scale terrorism against the public is no longer in the realms of the unthinkable. Some believe that the risk of nuclear, biological or chemical attack by a terrorist organisation is imminent; for others the probability remains low. However, everyone agrees that such an eventuality would have disastrous consequences for the public and wonders about the ability of most states to cope with them.

2. n a globalised and economically interdependent world, the recent Sars (severe acute respiratory syndrome) epidemic originating from China gave a particularly clear illustration of the difficulties and challenges faced by states in the event of the spread of an infectious disease as well as the devastating economic impact this could have. The Sars threat helped to increase awareness of what a bioterrorist attack could mean for the public.

3. The Parliamentary Assembly stresses that bioterrorism could also cause environmental damage, which could be dangerous for people living in the area concerned.

4. The Assembly therefore believes that, given the possible consequences of the bioterrorist threat to the public, it would be unwise to underestimate it; states should thus prepare for the worst.

5. The Assembly reiterates that there can be no justification for terrorism. The international community, without exception, must rally to the common aim of combating this global scourge. International co-operation must be pursued unremittingly if political decision makers are not to stand accused of an irresponsible attitude towards the populations to whom they are accountable.

6. The nature of the potential risks and the need for effective public protection make it necessary to rise above national interests and call for strengthened co-operation, particularly at European level. The creation of a two-speed Europe in the area of public health and safety must be refused. However, public safety has a high cost which presupposes, at national and European level, budgetary priorities and financial solidarity between states.

7. The Assembly invites member states:

    i.   to inform and educate the public about the inherent dangers of bioterrorism;

---

[1] *Text adopted by the Standing Committee*, acting on behalf of the Assembly, on 2 March 2004 (see Doc. 10067, report of the Social, Health and Family Affairs Committee, rapporteur: Mr Jacquat; and Doc. 10095, opinion of the Committee on the Environment, Agriculture and Local and Regional Affairs, rapporteur: Mr Toshev).

ii.   to draw up an objective assessment of the potential sources of bioterrorist danger and an inventory of dangerous and sensitive sites with the aim of securing them and acquiring efficient and effective surveillance and warning systems;

iii.   to devise emergency intervention and public-health relief plans in case of bioterrorist attacks and to test them on a regular basis;

iv.   to provide the professionals required to work in intervention teams with training in the special characteristics of the bioterrorist threat, particularly health care staff;

v.   to introduce or step up teaching concerning transmissible, infectious native and tropical diseases in medical studies;

vi.   to frame a suitable public vaccination policy, compile adequate stocks of vaccines and consider the necessity of vaccinating animals;

vii.   to introduce strict procedures for controlling the purchase and movement of dangerous substances;

viii. to establish strict control over activities based on the use of modern biotechnologies in order to avoid their misuse for bioterrorism.

8.   The Assembly welcomes in particular the recent setting up by the European Union of the European Centre for Disease Prevention and Control, which should be operational by 2005, and wishes for further measures to strengthen European solidarity.

9.   Finally, it invites member states to accede to the existing international instruments aimed at combating terrorism, to reinforce them through appropriate supervision procedures and to establish binding instruments to protect against potential threats that are not well – or not at all – covered.

10.   It also invites states to accede to and implement, in particular, two relevant conventions of the United Nations: the Convention on the Prohibition of the Development, Production, Stockpiling and use of Chemical Weapons and their Destruction and the Convention on the Prohibition of the Development, Production and Stockpiling of Bacteriological (Biological) and Toxin Weapons and on their Destruction.

Resolution 1400 (2004)[1]
on the challenge of terrorism in Council of Europe member states

1.   The Parliamentary Assembly is outraged by the recent wave of acts of terrorism which have plunged several Council of Europe member states into mourning, killing and injuring hundreds of innocent people. It extends its deepest sympathy to the victims' families and all who have suffered from these odious crimes.

2.   In spite of the international community's efforts, the scourge of terrorism continues to spread throughout the world, assuming ever more terrible and murderous forms. The resurgence of acts of terrorism of an extreme brutality shows that the international community, including the countries of Europe, have not been sufficiently alert to the gravity of the danger and have failed to take effective action to counter a new-style terrorism which stops at nothing.

3.   Through its barbaric methods, terrorism attacks the fundamental values of society and challenges the very existence of democracy.

4.   The protection of human rights plays a key role in the fight against terrorism. These rights are central to our credibility. Any violation of these rights weakens the international coalition in the fight against terrorism and drives new supporters into the hands of the terrorists.

5.   The Assembly refers in particular to Recommendation 1426 (1999) on European democracies facing up to terrorism where it considered an act of terrorism to be "any offence committed by individuals or groups resorting to violence or threatening to use violence against a country, its institutions, its population in general or specific individuals which, being motivated by separatist aspirations, extremist ideological conceptions, fanaticism or irrational and subjective factors, is intended to create a climate of terror among official authorities, certain individuals or groups in society or the general public".

6.   All attempts to provide terrorists with political, material, financial and other forms of support should be resolutely condemned.

7.   Terrorism heeds neither law nor morality and must not be allowed to exploit the freedoms and advantages of modern democratic societies.

8.   The Assembly considers that no cause can justify terrorism. Public expressions of support for terrorist actions may amount to incitement to violence and as such be the subject of restrictive measures in conformity with the European Convention on Human Rights.

---

[1] *Assembly debate* on 6 October 2004 (28th Sitting) (see Doc. 10312, report of the Political Affairs Committee, rapporteur: Mr Kosachev).

Text adopted by the Assembly on 6 October 2004 (29th Sitting).

9.   The Assembly firmly reiterates its condemnation and utter rejection of terror as a means of achieving political ends. Every act of terrorism, regardless of the reasons given, aims pursued, methods used or demands made by the terrorists, is a challenge to democracy and must be considered a crime against humanity. It is unacceptable and dangerous to apply double standards to terrorists, depending on their alleged motives. There are no "good" or "bad" terrorists.

10.   Democracy cannot compromise over terrorism. For terrorists, human life, which is the supreme value in a democratic society, is a bargaining counter.

11.   The Assembly is concerned about the fact that the threat or effects of terrorism can profoundly alarm and unsettle the community and affect the institutions and machinery of democracy. It believes that action must be taken to ensure that terror can exert no direct influence on democratic choices.

12.   In accordance with the principles recorded in paragraph 5, the Assembly reaffirms its position of principle that the fight against terrorism must always be compatible with the fundamental freedoms and human rights which it has the task of protecting, taking as its basis the absolute primacy of the fundamental and inalienable right to life, which implies the right to protection from terrorism and all other attacks on human life and health. There should be no exceptions to the human rights standards of the Council of Europe, as well as to the legitimate right to resist oppression. Obligations under the United Nations Convention relating to the Status of Refugees must likewise be fully respected. All the member states of the Council of Europe must avoid any erosion of these standards and ensure that the action they take against terrorism respects the principles on which democratic states are founded, their international commitments and the standards of their internal legislation. In this connection, it welcomes the adoption by the Committee of Ministers of the Council of Europe of guidelines on human rights in the fight against terrorism.

13.   The Assembly reiterates that the fight against terrorism does not justify the introduction of new and/or additional restrictions on freedom of expression, which is one of the fundamental pillars of democracy that terrorists want to destroy. The Assembly welcomes the drafting of a declaration on freedom of expression and information in the media in the context of the fight against terrorism by the end of the year.

14.   The Assembly remains convinced that the deep-rooted causes – poverty, exclusion, inequality, despair, widespread disorder, impunity for serious human rights violations and crimes, and blatant disregard for the rights of national minorities – which provide fertile soil for terrorism, must be carefully analysed and systematic action taken to remove them. This work

must be undertaken in parallel with necessary urgent lawful measures to prevent further acts of terrorism.

15. The Assembly accordingly calls on national parliaments:

    i.   to adopt an integrated and co-ordinated approach to countering terrorism at all its stages, including drawing up a legislative framework aimed at:

        a.   removing the factors contributing to the development of a favourable environment for terrorism;

        b.   suppressing the sources and channels of finance, recruitment and propaganda;

        c.   organising operational co-operation between special services, police and justice systems as part of anti-terrorist and preventive action;

        d.   protecting, rehabilitating and compensating victims of terrorist acts;

        e.   developing mechanisms and a legal basis for protecting witnesses, collaborators of justice and reformed criminals;

    ii.   to pass laws for reinforcing public security, consistent with human rights and fundamental freedoms, and obligations under international law and conventions;

    iii.   to make full use of their powers in promoting intensified international co-operation in the fight against terrorism, with paramount emphasis on harmonising Council of Europe member states' anti-terrorism law so as to create a unified European legal area in anti-terrorism matters;

    iv.   to ratify, using the accelerated procedure, the protocol amending the European Convention on the Suppression of Terrorism (ETS No. 190), so that it can take effect as soon as possible;

    v.   to ensure that their states, if they have not already done so, sign, ratify and effectively implement the Council of Europe instruments concerned with action against terrorism and particularly:
- the European Convention on the Suppression of Terrorism (1977);
- the European Convention on Extradition (1957) and its protocols (1975 and 1978);
- the European Convention on Mutual Assistance in Criminal Matters (1959) and its Protocols (1978 and 2001);

- the European Convention on the Transfer of Proceedings in Criminal Matters (1972);
- the European Convention on the Compensation of Victims of Violent Crimes (1983);
- the Convention on Laundering, Search, Seizure and Confiscation of the Proceeds from Crime (1990);
- the Convention on Cybercrime (2001) and its protocol (2003).

16. The Assembly calls on all the political forces in member states:

    i.   to resolutely condemn all terrorist action, regardless of the country in which it takes place, as well as all activity whose purpose is to organise, finance or incite to acts of terrorism or harbour terrorists;

    ii.   to prevent manifestations of ethnic hatred, racism and xenophobia and also the justification of terrorism;

    iii. to consolidate democratic institutions and interaction with civil society in order to ensure maximum support for national and international anti-terrorism measures;

    iv.   to rally society around the principles of total rejection of and opposition to terror and that any form of psychologically pressurising the population is unacceptable;

    v.   to support measures to prevent persons implicated in terrorism from abusing any kind of institution or organisation, governmental or non-governmental, for the purpose of planning or preparing terrorist acts;

    vi.   to promote social cohesion and intercultural and inter-confessional dialogue for the purpose of removing factors contributing to the development of fertile breeding grounds for terrorism and preventing the spread of extremist theories seeking to justify acts of terrorism.

17. Moreover, the Assembly deems it necessary:

    i.   to elaborate a comprehensive Council of Europe convention against terrorism;

    ii.   to analyse the effectiveness of Council of Europe conventions and other international instruments on combating terrorism and, on the basis of that analysis, draw up protocols to render those instruments capable of responding to the new terrorist threats;

    iii. to instigate the extension of the list of offences in the 1998 Rome Statute of the International Criminal Court (ICC) so as to include certain offences of a terrorist nature, thereby widening ICC jurisdiction to encompass such offences;

iv. to review European Union experience with the European arrest warrant and to look into creating a legal basis for extending its applicability to Council of Europe member states;

v. to intensify work on drawing up a Council of Europe convention on reinforcing the protection of witnesses and reformed criminals in the context of acts of terrorism, the protocol to the 1990 Convention on Laundering, Search, Seizure and Confiscation of the Proceeds from Crime, and a recommendation on special investigation techniques in relation to acts of terrorism;

vi. to begin the groundwork for setting up a European register of national and international standards so as to provide a system for computer access to the law of member states of the Council of Europe and other European organisations and for exchange of legal information;

vii. to establish a partnership between the Council of Europe and the European Union, and create, in addition to the EU's own anti-terrorism co-ordination work, a joint framework for practical co-operation and information sharing which involves all Council of Europe member states and develop enhanced co-operation with the United Nations, the Organization for Security and Co-operation in Europe and other international organisations;

viii. to initiate a special programme, enabling exchanges of experience and best practice, for persons with operational responsibilities in the member states for handling concrete crisis situations, in order to ensure that they are highly professional and adequately trained so as to minimise risks to human lives;

ix. to finalise as soon as possible the elaboration of guidelines on the rights of victims and the corresponding duties of member states to provide all necessary assistance and to create a forum for the exchange of good practice and training experiences between member states.

18. A serious study should be undertaken by the Council of Europe on the acceptable limits of freedom of expression and the possible abuse of that freedom by terrorists.

19. The Assembly decides to follow closely, through its relevant committees, international developments concerning terrorism, action by member governments and by national parliaments and the activities of the Council of Europe's Committee of Ministers in this field.

Recommendation 1677 (2004)[1]
on the challenge of terrorism in Council of Europe member states

1. The Parliamentary Assembly refers to Resolution 1400 (2004) on the challenge of terrorism in Council of Europe member states, to the many resolutions, recommendations and orders which it has adopted on terrorism since 1972 and to the action taken by the Committee of Ministers for the purpose of introducing, within the Council of Europe, co-ordinated measures to counter terrorism.

2. The Assembly refers in particular to Recommendation 1426 (1999) on European democracies facing up to terrorism, where it considered an act of terrorism to be "any offence committed by individuals or groups resorting to violence or threatening to use violence against a country, its institutions, its population in general or specific individuals which, being motivated by separatist aspirations, extremist ideological conceptions, fanaticism or irrational and subjective factors, is intended to create a climate of terror among official authorities, certain individuals or groups in society, or the general public".

3. In spite of undeniable progress with the introduction of convention-based European co-operation on action against terrorism, the Council of Europe's collective response to the growing threat of terrorism remains insufficient.

4. Failings in national and European legislation on the suppression and prevention of terrorism still leave the way open for trafficking in arms, munitions and funds for international terrorism and for movement of persons associated with terrorism in Council of Europe member states.

5. The global nature of the terrorist threat makes total cohesion and solidarity within the international community, unwavering political determination and full and effective co-operation between Council of Europe member states, essential. The security of Europeans in the face of terrorism is indivisible.

6. The Assembly notes that, following the terrorist attacks of 11 September 2001, the Committee of Ministers attempted to intensify co-operation between Council of Europe member states, and particularly within the Committee of Experts on Terrorism (Codexter), on the subject of the repression of terrorism.

---

[1] *Assembly debate* on 6 October 2004 (28th Sitting) (see Doc.10312, report of the Political Affairs Committee, rapporteur: Mr Kosachev).
Text adopted by the Assembly on 6 October 2004 (29th Sitting).

7.   The Assembly nonetheless considers that a more sustained commitment on the part of member states is needed to ensure an adequate response to the challenge of terrorism.

8.   The Assembly asks the Committee of Ministers:

i.   to intensify its efforts to establish a common legal area for action against terrorism in Europe, based on human rights and the fundamental values of the Council of Europe and, for this purpose:

    a.   to start the preparation of a comprehensive Council of Europe convention against terrorism, as was requested by Assembly Opinion No. 242 (2003) on the draft protocol amending the European Convention on the Suppression of Terrorism and Recommendation 1644 (2004) on terrorism: a threat to democracies;

    b.   in the meantime, to conclude, without delay, its work on remedying existing omissions in international law or in action taken against terrorism, by adopting instruments on which member states can reach a consensus;

    c.   to analyse the effectiveness of Council of Europe conventions and other international instruments on combating terrorism and, on the basis of that analysis, draw up protocols to render those instruments capable of responding to the new terrorist threats;

    d.   to review European Union experience with the European arrest warrant and to look into creating a legal basis for extending its applicability to Council of Europe member states;

    e.   to promote a homogeneous definition of the crime of terrorism in the laws of member states and at international level, along the lines of the aforementioned Recommendation 1426 (1999);

    f.   to intensify work on drawing up a Council of Europe convention on reinforcing the protection of witnesses and reformed criminals in the context of acts of terrorism, the protocol to the 1990 Convention on Laundering, Search, Seizure and Confiscation of the Proceeds from Crime and a recommendation on special investigation techniques in relation to acts of terrorism;

    g.   to begin the groundwork for setting up a European register of national and international standards so as to provide a system for computer access to the law of member states of the

Council of Europe and other European organisations and for the exchange of legal information;

h. to establish a partnership between the Council of Europe and the European Union, and create, in addition to the European Union's own anti-terrorism co-ordination work, a joint framework for practical co-operation and information-sharing which involves all Council of Europe member states, and develop enhanced co-operation with the United Nations, the Organization for Security and Co-operation in Europe and other international organisations;

i. to initiate a special programme, enabling exchanges of experience and best practice, for persons with operational responsibilities in the member states for handling concrete crisis situations, in order to ensure that they are highly professional and adequately trained so as to minimise risks to human lives;

j. to finalise as soon as possible the elaboration of guidelines on the rights of victims and the corresponding duties of member states to provide all necessary assistance and to create a forum for the exchange of good practice and training experiences between member states;

k. to undertake a study on the acceptable limits of freedom of expression and the possible abuse of that freedom by terrorists;

ii. ask the member states:

a. to increase multilateral co-operation and reciprocal assistance concerning the prevention and punishment of acts of terrorism;

b. to bring the Protocol amending the European Convention on the Suppression of Terrorism (2003) into force as soon as possible;

c. to sign and/or ratify, if they have not yet done so, the Council of Europe's conventions on action against terrorism;

iii. repeat the appeal to member states, made in Assembly Recommendations 1534 (2001) on democracies facing terrorism and 1644 (2004), to "give urgent consideration to amending and widening the Rome Statute to allow the remit of the International Criminal Court to include acts of international terrorism";

iv. turn its attention once again to the relevant parts of the earlier Assembly recommendations, and particularly Recommendation 1644 (2004), in which the Assembly asked the Committee of Ministers, in paragraph 11, *inter alia*:

" ii. to invite [, in the meantime,] the member states:

(…)

b. to condemn strongly countries encouraging, helping, providing financial support, or offering safe haven to terrorists and introduce economic and other appropriate measures against them;

c. to promote democracy and human rights in their foreign relations and refrain from complacency towards despotic and obscurantist regimes for reasons of strategic and economic interests; (…)

iii. to study, in consultation with the European Union, the possibility of transforming Europol into an effective pan-European agency, with sufficient means to challenge international terrorism".

9. The Assembly wishes to be fully informed about work on action against terrorism done by the Committee of Ministers and by committees and working parties which it establishes.

10. The Assembly recommends that the Committee of Ministers include the question of European co-operation in the fight against terrorism on the agenda for the 3rd Summit of Heads of State and Government of the Council of Europe.

Recommendation 1687 (2004)[1]
on combating terrorism through culture

1. Faced with the growing terrorist threat in the world, the Parliamentary Assembly stresses the need for an overall approach to combating terrorism, combining cultural with political, economic, legal and social methods. It is not a matter here of confusing blind terrorism and its innocent victims with what are sometimes acts of resistance to oppression and violation of human rights.

2. Culture in all its aspects – the arts, heritage, religion, the media, science, education, youth and sport – can play an important role in preventing the development of a terrorist mentality, in dissuading would-be terrorists and in cutting them off from wider support. Its importance in this respect is, however, often underestimated.

3. The basis for any cultural action against terrorism lies in understanding the complex and delicate relationship between terrorism and its cultural context.

4. The Assembly stands resolutely against attempts to qualify any specific world, national, regional or local culture as terrorist. At the same time, under certain conditions, any society is capable of producing terrorism. Extremist interpretation of elements of a particular culture or religion, such as heroic martyrdom, sacrifice, apocalypse or holy war, as well as secular ideologies (nationalist and revolutionary), can also be invoked to justify terrorist acts.

5. Culture is, however, also becoming increasingly a target of terrorism. Beyond the physical damage or destruction of monuments, temples or symbols of a given culture and way of life, such terrorist acts target the very cultural identity of a people or a population. They also harm a cultural heritage that is common to all peoples of the world.

6. Globalisation and the information society allow unprecedented contact and interaction between peoples, ideas and cultures. Some aspects of it, however, can potentially foster terrorism and the ideologies that encourage it in several ways:

   i.   the gap is increasing between rich and poor nations and populations. Poverty, oppression, disrespect for human rights, a sense of injustice and the lack of brighter prospects provide a breeding ground for all kinds of violence;

   ii. the world dominance of western culture in its most commercial forms, based on violence, money and sex, is perceived by more

---

[1] *Text adopted by the Standing Committee,* acting on behalf of the Assembly, on 23 November 2004 (see Doc.10341, report of the Committee on Culture, Science and Education, rapporteur: Mr Sudarenkov).

traditional societies as deeply offensive and in sharp contradiction with the high democratic standards which it is supposed to reflect;

iii.   the global village created by the modern media and the Internet means that never before have terrorist acts gained such public prominence. Terrorist acts thus appear to extremists as the most efficient and "cost-effective" means of getting a message through;

iv.   modern information technologies have also allowed far better communication and networking of terrorist groups, leading to a new form of international terrorism with an "a-territorial" and "a-cultural dimension", even if affiliation is claimed with a particular territory or culture;

v.   dependence on information technologies has led to the appearance of cyberterrorism, threatening the functioning of modern life through manipulation of computer systems.

7.   The Assembly welcomes responsible media portrayal of terrorist acts and handling of the public debate on terrorism, and encourages further discussion between media professionals on the relevant professional ethics.

8.   Greater acceptance of terrorism is linked to the acceptability of violence as a means of conflict resolution in society in general, which the Assembly deplores.

9.   It is becoming vital to consider education not purely in quantitative but in qualitative terms, as a means of transmitting not only knowledge but also values, and as a means of developing a critical mind. Education should also offer individuals the possibility of participating fully in the development of a democratic, just and equitable society in which terrorism has no place.

10. A further challenge of education is to improve mutual understanding between different groups and cultures. The main aim of any cultural action aimed at combating terrorism should be to create a culture of tolerance, dialogue, understanding, respect and pluralism. This, in turn, would reduce the heroic aura surrounding terrorists and help eradicate public acceptance of terrorist acts.

11. The Assembly notes that several Council of Europe projects have promoted such goals, for instance projects on education for democratic citizenship, on history teaching, on combating violence or on intercultural dialogue and conflict prevention. It also welcomes the Declaration on Intercultural Dialogue and Conflict Prevention adopted by the European Ministers of Culture in Opatija on 22 October 2003, the Declaration on Intercultural Education in the New European Context adopted by the European Ministers of Education in Athens on 12 November 2003 and the ongoing work on a declaration on freedom of expression and information in the context of the fight against terrorism. There is, however, a need for

further and more concerted action by the different sectors of the Organisation.

12. The Assembly therefore recommends that the Committee of Ministers:

   i.   include relevant provisions on the role of culture in a future comprehensive Council of Europe convention against terrorism, as already recommended by the Assembly;

   ii. ensure co-ordinated action between the Council of Europe bodies involved in the fight against terrorism and in culture;

   iii. organise a European conference on combating terrorism through culture with the involvement of other European and international bodies;

   iv. make intercultural and interreligious dialogue and conflict prevention one of the main areas of activity of the Council of Europe and provide for this in the action plan and in the final declaration to be adopted by the 3rd Summit of Heads of State and Government of the Council of Europe;

   v.   develop, or further strengthen, projects aimed at:

       a. encouraging reflection and research on terrorism and culture, in order to understand better and monitor the causes and development of terrorism;

       b. developing educational programmes aimed at promoting better knowledge of different cultures and religions, ensuring that this extends beyond the European dimension;

       c. continuing its work on history teaching and the revision of school books, extending it to the countries neighbouring Europe, in order to reduce prejudice and stereotypes and remove incitements to terrorism;

       d. encouraging discussion on terrorism among the younger generation; supporting international youth work as a way of giving concrete expression to intercultural dialogue; further developing youth projects on conflict prevention and the promotion of a culture of peace;

       e. developing human rights education and education for citizenship, thereby creating better understanding of human rights and of the ways of protecting them;

f. ensuring that states, in their policy towards the media and the Internet, strike the right balance between protection of human rights and the fight against terrorism;

g. guaranteeing in all member states an appropriate legal and political framework for free expression and true representation of all opinions, political views, religious beliefs and cultural minorities;

h. developing intercommunal cultural activities as a way of relieving tension between communities;

i. promoting understanding and tolerance by encouraging the distribution of cultural and audiovisual works from other parts of the world and supporting mobility and exchanges of artists, performers, scholars and scientists;

vi. design cultural projects targeting specific critical areas of tension and potential terrorism in Europe;

vii. support and actively contribute to the creation of international instruments on cultural diversity, co-operation and dialogue;

viii. enhance dialogue and cultural co-operation between European and neighbouring countries, along the lines of Assembly Resolution 1313 (2003) and Recommendation 1590 (2003) on cultural co-operation between Europe and the south Mediterranean countries.

European Ministers of Justice

24th Conference, Moscow, 4-5 October 2001
Resolution No. 1 on combating international terrorism

THE MINISTERS participating in the 24th Conference of European Ministers of Justice (Moscow, October 2001),

Condemning the heinous terrorist attacks in the United States of America on 11 September 2001;

Deploring the loss of life and the injuries suffered by thousands of innocent people as a result of these attacks as well as those in other regions of the world;

Expressing their deeply felt sympathy with the victims and their families;

Reaffirming their determination to combat all forms of terrorism;

Welcoming the declarations and decisions of international organisations condemning terrorism, in particular the Declaration adopted by the Committee of Ministers on 12 September 2001 and the Decision taken on 21 September 2001, and expressing their full support for the measures envisaged in this Decision;

Bearing in mind Parliamentary Assembly Recommendation 1534 (2001) on democracies facing terrorism;

Convinced of the need for a multidisciplinary approach to the problem of terrorism, involving all relevant legal aspects;

Resolved to play their part in States' efforts to reinforce the fight against terrorism and to increase the security of citizens, in a spirit of solidarity and on the basis of the common values to which the Council of Europe is firmly committed: Rule of Law, human rights and pluralist democracy;

Recognising the need to involve and motivate the public in this fight, including relevant organisational, social and educational measures;

Convinced of the urgent need for increased international co-operation,

CALL UPON member and observer States of the Council of Europe

a.   to become Parties as soon as possible to the relevant international treaties relating to terrorism, in particular the International Convention for the Suppression of the Financing of Terrorism of 9 December 1999;

b.   to participate actively in the elaboration of the draft United Nations comprehensive Convention on International Terrorism; and

c.   to become Parties as soon as possible to the Statute of the International Criminal Court;

INVITE the Committee of Ministers urgently to adopt all normative measures considered necessary for assisting States to prevent, detect, prosecute and punish acts of terrorism, such as:

a.   viewing existing international instruments - conventions and recommendations, in particular the European Convention on the Suppression of Terrorism - and domestic law, with a view to improving and facilitating co-operation in the prosecution and punishment of acts of terrorism so that the perpetrators of such acts can speedily be brought to justice;

b.   drafting model laws in this field, and codes of conduct in particular for law enforcement agencies;

c.   reviewing existing or, where necessary, adopting new rules concerning:

   i.   the prosecution and trial of crimes of an international character, with a view to avoiding and solving conflicts of jurisdiction and, in this context, facilitating States' co-operation with international criminal courts and tribunals;

   ii.   the improvement and reinforcement of exchanges of information between law enforcement agencies;

   iii. the improvement of the protection of witnesses and other persons participating in proceedings involving persons accused of terrorist crimes;

   iv.   the improvement of the protection, support and compensation of victims of terrorist acts and their families;

   v.   the reinforcement of the prevention and punishment of acts of terrorism committed against or by means of computer and telecommunication systems ("cyber-terrorism");

d.   depriving terrorists of any financial resources which would allow them to commit acts of terrorism, including amendments to the law, in conformity with Security Council Resolution 1373 (2001);

e.   reinforcing, through adequate financial appropriation, the work of Council of Europe bodies involved in the fight against money laundering, in particular the Committee evaluating States' anti-money laundering measures (PC-R-EV);

f.   facilitating the identification of persons by means of appropriate identity, civil status and other documents, as well as by other means, including the possibility of using genetic prints (DNA);

g.   ensuring the safety and control of dangerous or potentially dangerous substances;

DECIDE to remain in close contact on these matters, in particular in order to review the steps taken to give effect to this Resolution, at the latest on the occasion of their next Conference.

25th Conference, Sofia, 9-10 October 2003
Resolution No. 1 on combating terrorism

1.   THE MINISTERS participating in the 25th Conference of European Ministers of Justice (Sofia, October 2003);

2.   Deploring the loss of life and the injuries suffered by thousands of innocent people as a result of terrorism;

3.   Condemning all terrorist attacks and reaffirming their determination to combat all forms of terrorism while fully respecting human rights;

4.   Aware that concerted international action is vital to success in the fight against the scourge of terrorism, including action aiming, where appropriate, at preventing or remedying situations which may foster terrorism;

5.   Welcoming the efforts of international organisations and institutions to fight against terrorism under the aegis of the UN and, in particular, the creation of the Counter-Terrorism Committee (CTC) by the Security Council of the UN and, in this respect:

6.   Welcoming the co-operation between the Council of Europe and these organisations and institutions, in particular the EU, the OSCE and the UN;

7.   Welcoming the decisions taken by the Committee of Ministers of the Council of Europe, in particular its Declaration of 12 September 2001, its Decision of 21 September 2001 and the outcome of the 109th, 110th and 111th Ministerial sessions and ;

8.   Welcoming the adoption the Guidelines on Human Rights and the Fight against Terrorism on 11 July 2002;

9.   Welcoming the setting up of the European Commission for Efficiency of Justice (CEPEJ) by the Council of Europe on 18 September 2002;

10. Considering the relevant texts adopted by the Parliamentary Assembly[1];

11. Bearing in mind Resolution No. 1 adopted at their 24th Conference (Moscow, October 2001);

12. Resolved to pursue their efforts to reinforce the fight against terrorism and to increase the security of citizens, in a spirit of solidarity and on the

---

[1] In particular, Recommendation REC 1534 (2001) Democracies facing terrorism; Recommendation REC 1550 (2002) and Resolution RES 1271 (2002) - Combating terrorism and respect for human rights; Recommendation REC 1549 (2002) - Air transport and terrorism: how to enhance security ? and Recommendation REC 1584 (2002) - The need for intensified international co-operation to neutralise funds for terrorist purposes.

basis of the common values to which the Council of Europe is firmly committed: the rule of law, human rights and pluralist democracy;

13. Recognising the need to raise public awareness, through education and information, about the dangers of terrorism and encourage the public to co-operate with authorities against this form of criminality;

14. Convinced of the need to continue to strengthen international co-operation;

15. WELCOME the results achieved by the Multidisciplinary Group on International Action against Terrorism (GMT) of the Council of Europe, in particular the drafting of the Protocol Amending the European Convention on the Suppression of Terrorism of 15 May 2003 (European Treaty Series, ETS No. 190);

16. CALL UPON the member States of the Council of Europe to become Parties to this Protocol to ensure its entry into force as soon as possible; and INVITE observer States to become Parties to the European Convention on the Suppression of Terrorism, as revised by its amending Protocol;

17. WELCOME the large number of member States of the Council of Europe which have become Parties to international treaties on terrorism, in particular, those concluded in the framework of the United Nations, as well as to the Rome Statute of the International Criminal Court; and INVITE those which have not yet done so to become Parties as soon as possible to these instruments and also to other international treaties concerning co-operation which are most relevant in the field of the fight against terrorism;

18. SUPPORT the priority counter-terrorism activities launched by the Council of Europe in response to Resolution No. 1 adopted at their 24th Conference (Moscow, October 2001); and in this respect:

19. WELCOME the setting up by the Committee of Ministers of the Committee of Experts on Terrorism (CODEXTER), responsible for coordinating the work of the Council of Europe in the field of the fight against terrorism;

20. INVITE the Committee of Ministers, on the one hand, to pursue without delay the work with a view to adopting relevant international instruments on the protection of witnesses and *pentiti* and on the use of special investigation techniques relating to acts of terrorism and, on the other hand, to review the European Convention on the Compensation of Victims of Violent Crimes of 24 November 1983 (ETS No. 116) or, where necessary, adopt new rules concerning the improvement of the protection, support and compensation of victims of terrorist acts and their families;

21. CALL upon all member States to contribute to discussions in the United Nations with the intention to resolve the outstanding issues in negotiations

on the draft UN Comprehensive Convention against terrorism and on the draft UN Convention for the suppression of acts of nuclear terrorism;

22. INVITE the Committee of Ministers to launch work with a view to examining, in the light of the opinion of the CODEXTER, the added value of a comprehensive European Convention against terrorism, open to observer States, or some elements of such a convention, which could be elaborated within the Council of Europe, and to contributing significantly to the UN efforts in this field;

23. INVITE the Committee of Ministers to entrust the CEPEJ with the task of ensuring the preparation of an assessment report on the effectiveness of national judicial systems in their responses to terrorism;

24. INVITE the Committee of Ministers, in the framework of the co-operation programmes with member States of the Council of Europe, to provide support for States in upgrading their counter-terrorism legislative and institutional capacities and to pursue effective co-ordination with other international bodies;

25. INVITE the Committee of Ministers to consider the feasibility of setting up a European register of national and international standards, starting as a matter of priority with standards in the field of the fight against terrorism;

26. ASK the Secretary General of the Council of Europe to report on the steps taken to give effect to this Resolution, on the occasion of their next Conference.

THE MINISTERS participating in the 26th Conference of European Ministers of Justice (Helsinki, 7 and 8 April 2005);

1. Concerned by the threats posed by terrorism to the core values on which Europe is based, namely pluralist democracy, the rule of law and the protection of fundamental rights and freedoms;

2. Deploring the loss of life and the injuries suffered by thousands of innocent people as a result of terrorism;

3. Condemning all terrorist attacks and reaffirming their determination to combat all forms of terrorism while fully respecting human rights;

4. Aware that concerted international action is vital to success in the fight against the scourge of terrorism, including action aiming, where appropriate, at preventing or remedying situations which may foster terrorism;

5. Recalling the importance of the international instruments against terrorism and, in this respect, welcoming the finalisation within the United Nations at expert level of the draft International Convention for the suppression of acts of nuclear terrorism;

6. Welcoming the efforts of international organisations and institutions to fight against terrorism under the aegis of the United Nations Security Council Counter-Terrorism Committee (CTC);

7. Welcoming the co-operation between the Council of Europe and these organisations and institutions, in particular the European Union, the OSCE and the United Nations;

8. Recalling the relevant texts adopted by the Parliamentary Assembly;

9. Bearing in mind Resolution No. 1 adopted at their 24th Conference (Moscow, 4-5 October 2001) and Resolution No. 1 adopted at their 25th Conference (Sofia, 9-10 October 2003) as well as the report of the Secretary General concerning the follow-up given to this Resolution;

10. Bearing in mind the Resolution adopted at the Third High Level multilateral meeting of Ministries of Interior on the theme of the "Fight against terrorism and organised crime to improve security in Europe" (Warsaw, 17-18 March 2005);

11. Bearing in mind the report prepared under the aegis of the European Commission for the Efficiency of Justice (CEPEJ) on the effectiveness of national judicial systems in their responses to terrorism;

12. Resolved to pursue their efforts to reinforce the fight against terrorism and to increase the security of citizens, in a spirit of solidarity and on the basis of the core values to which the Council of Europe is firmly committed: the rule of law, human rights and pluralist democracy;

13. Recalling the Guidelines on Human Rights and the Fight against Terrorism adopted by the Committee of Ministers in July 2002;

14. Convinced of the need to continue to strengthen international co-operation;

15. Noting the importance in this regard of the Third Summit of the Heads of States and Governments of the Council of Europe, which will be held in Warsaw in May 2005, and of the impetus which it will add to the future work of the Council of Europe in the fight against terrorism;

16. WELCOME the progress achieved by the Council of Europe in the implementation of the priority activities against terrorism, in particular the elaboration of two new conventions respectively on the Prevention of Terrorism, and on Laundering, Search, Seizure and Confiscation of Proceeds from Crime and on the Financing of Terrorism, as well as three new Recommendations of the Committee of Ministers to member states on Special Investigative Techniques, Protection of Witnesses and Collaborators of Justice, and on Identity and Travel Documents and Terrorism, and in this connection;

17. WELCOME the adoption by the Committee of Ministers of the Recommendation on Identity and Travel Documents and the Fight against Terrorism and CALL UPON the Committee of Ministers to adopt, at an early date, the two above-mentioned Conventions, in order to allow as far as possible their opening for signature at the Third Summit of the Heads of States and Governments of the Council of Europe, as well as to adopt, as soon as possible, the remaining Recommendations ;

18. WELCOME the adoption by the Committee of Ministers of the Guidelines on the Protection of Victims of Terrorist Acts and the Declaration on Media and Terrorism in March 2005;

19. WELCOME the work of the Committee of Experts on Terrorism (CODEXTER) in coordinating the work of the Council of Europe against terrorism in the legal field;

20. WELCOME the contribution of the European Committee on Crime Problems (CDPC) and its subordinated committees the Committee of Experts on the protection of witnesses and collaborators of justice (PC-PW), the Committee of Experts on special investigation techniques (PC-TI) and the Committee of Experts on the revision of the Convention on Laundering, Search, Seizure and Confiscation of the proceeds from crime laundering (PC-RM), as well as of the European Committee on Legal Co-operation

(CDCJ) to the implementation of the priority activities of the Council of Europe against terrorism in their respective fields of competence;

21. WELCOME the number of signatures and ratifications to the Protocol Amending the European Convention on the Suppression of Terrorism (ETS No. 190) whilst regretting that this new instrument has not yet entered into force, and therefore,

22. CALL UPON the member States of the Council of Europe to become Parties to this Protocol so as to ensure its entry into force as soon as possible, and INVITE observer States to become Parties to the European Convention on the Suppression of Terrorism, as revised by its amending Protocol, as soon as possible thereafter;

23. INVITE those States which have not yet done so to become Parties to other instruments of the Council of Europe which facilitate measures against terrorism, in particular the Convention on Cybercrime (ETS No. 185), the Conventions on Corruption (ETS No. 173 and ETS No. 174) and the 2nd Additional Protocol to the European Convention on Mutual Assistance in Criminal Matters (ETS No. 182);

24. WELCOME the large number of member states of the Council of Europe which have become Parties to international treaties on terrorism, in particular, those concluded in the framework of the United Nations, as well as to the Rome Statute of the International Criminal Court;

25. INVITE those States which have not yet done so to become Parties as soon as possible to these instruments and to ensure their effective implementation in pursuance of United Nations Security Council Resolution 1373 (2001);

26. CALL upon all member states to contribute to resolving the outstanding issues in negotiations within the United Nations on the draft Comprehensive Convention against terrorism;

27. WELCOME the work of MONEYVAL regarding the evaluation of member states compliance with the Special Recommendation on Terrorist Financing of the Financial Action Task Force (FATF);

28. CALL upon the Council of Europe to continue its work against terrorism, including the development of country-profiles on counter-terrorism capacities, activities concerning victims of terrorism and international co-operation;

29. INVITE the Committee of Ministers:

    a.   to instruct the CODEXTER to identify additional priority activities against terrorism particularly in the light of the report of the Multidisciplinary Group on International Action against Terrorism

(GMT) and the report prepared for the CODEXTER on gaps regarding international law and action;

b. to instruct, in particular, the CDPC and the CDCJ, in the framework of their specific terms of reference and as regards the implementation of the activities identified to ensure the coherence of the action of the Council of Europe in their respective fields of competence;

30. INVITE the Committee of Ministers, in the framework of the co-operation programmes with member states of the Council of Europe, to provide support for States in upgrading their counter-terrorism legislative and institutional capacities and to pursue effective co-ordination with other international bodies;

31. EXPRESS THE WISH that the Third Summit of Heads of State and Government of the Council of Europe to support and strengthen the role of the Council of Europe in the prevention and suppression of terrorism, through standard setting, monitoring and technical co-operation, and to give impetus to the early signature and ratification of the new Council of Europe conventions relating to terrorism;

32. INVITE the Secretary General of the Council of Europe to report on the steps taken to give effect to this Resolution on the occasion of their next Conference.

European Ministers responsible for Cultural Affairs

**Declaration on Intercultural
Dialogue and Conflict Prevention
Opatija (Croatia), 22 October 2003**

Introduction

The general objective of this text is to specify, in the area which it covers, the roles and responsibilities of the Ministers responsible for Cultural Affairs by defining a European framework of co-operation creating on one side the conditions allowing for the promotion and construction of a society based on intercultural dialogue and respect of cultural diversity, and on the other, contributing to the creation of conditions favouring the prevention of violent conflicts, the management and control of conflicts and post-conflict reconciliation. This objective should be reached through the implementation of cultural action programmes involving all generations and aiming at bringing cultures closer, through constructive dialogue and cultural exchanges in all their tangible and intangible components, e.g.: archaeological, architectural, artistic, economic, ethnic, historical, linguistic, religious and social.

The present text builds on a number of texts adopted by the Council of Europe or by other international organisations, including:

- the Convention for the Protection of Human Rights and Fundamental Freedoms (particularly Articles 9, 10, 11 and 14) (Rome, 4 November 1950), hereafter European Convention on Human Rights,

- the Council of Europe's European Cultural Convention (Paris, 19 December 1954),

- the European Charter for Regional or Minority Languages (Strasbourg, 29 June 1992),

- the Framework Convention for the Protection of National Minorities (Strasbourg, 1 February 1995),

- the European Social Charter (Turin, 18 October 1961, revised 3 May 1996),

- the Council of Europe Declaration on Cultural Diversity (adopted by the Committee of Ministers on 7 December 2000),

- the Final Declaration of the 3rd Ministerial Conference on the Culture of Francophonie (Cotonou, 15 June 2001),

- the Olympia Charter, adopted at the International Symposium "Re-thinking Culture" at the opening ceremony of the Cultural Olympiad (Athens, 23 September 2001),

- the UNESCO Universal Declaration on Cultural Diversity (Paris, 2 November 2001).

To familiarise readers with the thinking behind the Declaration, the terms "conflict", "intercultural dialogue" and "cultural diversity", as used in the text, are defined in an appendix. The principles and approaches which underlie the concepts of "cultural diversity", "intercultural dialogue", "good governance in cultural policy" and "inter-sectoral co-operation and exemplary conflict prevention practices" are also explained.

The Ministers responsible for Cultural Affairs of the member states of the Council of Europe,

Aware of the vital importance of culture as a primary vehicle of meaning and tool for understanding, a democratic agent and instrument of individual and collective human development, and as a forum for rapprochement and dialogue between all men and women,

Concerned that new forms of conflict, increasing the difficulties of dialogue between cultures, may be used by certain groups with the avowed or unstated aim of fuelling hatred, xenophobia and confrontation between different communities,

Emphasising the fact that nobody should be harassed on account of his or her lawful opinions, and that every individual therefore enjoys an inalienable right to define and choose his or her cultural and/or religious affiliation and identity,

Aware that cultural "impoverishment" and marginalisation, on the one hand, and prejudice and ignorance, on the other, are among the prime causes of increasing violence and stereotypes of others, thus altering the nature of peaceful and constructive relations between different cultural communities,

Taking the view that it is appropriate to ensure that rapprochement between cultures and intercultural dialogue become a means of conflict prevention at every level and in all its contexts and components,

In line with the European Convention on Human Rights, and respectful of the principles of cultural diversity and freedom of expression,

Sharing a single body of cultural values as a result of their state's accession to the European Convention on Human Rights and to the European Cultural Convention, and agreement to all the ideals and principles which are the Council of Europe's common heritage,

Bearing in mind that there can be no exceptions to the human rights principles defended by the Council of Europe, given that human rights are not a constraint but constitute the primary source of the principles and action of the Council of Europe and of the States that have ratified the European Cultural Convention of the Council of Europe,

Taking into account the fact that the Council of Europe is engaged in initiatives aiming to create cooperation networks between regions and cities, and to formulate action plans on the intercultural dimension in the arts, culture or institutional training and mutual cooperation (museums, libraries, archives), between European countries and beyond,

Considering that public authorities may draw, as appropriate, on existing examples of good practices enabling intercultural dialogue when devising public and democratic cultural policies in the national context or in that of inter-state cooperation,

Aware that the present Declaration is based not only on the conventions, recommendations, resolutions and declarations adopted by the Council of Europe within the framework of cultural co-operation activities, but that it also has its source in other international instruments and in numerous countries' domestic legislation,

Having agreed to base their actions on a set of principles and shared values listed below:

i.   respect for the concept of cultural democracy and cultural citizenship that implies rights and obligations;

ii.   respect for cultural identities and practices, as well as for expressions of their heritage provided that these comply with the principles upheld by the Council of Europe;

iii. the safeguard and protection of tangible and intangible heritage;

iv. fair treatment for all cultures and beliefs or convictions which respect the principles of the Council of Europe;

v.   mutual respect through the recognition of diversity in terms of education on culture, in all its components;

vi. equality in access, participation and creativity of every sector of society so as to take into account the totality of the cultural dimension and promote cultural diversity in the spirit of cultural democracy;

Are determined to implement, in their fields of responsibility, and while respecting where necessary the rules of subsidiarity and national priorities, ways of cooperation with a view to achieving the objectives of the present text, namely the promotion of the respect of diversity, intercultural dialogue and the prevention of conflict;

In so doing, do not intend to supersede, but to co-operate with the responsible authorities at all levels (local, regional, and national) in the other sectors of governmental policy, as well as with civil society;

Express their willingness to work in a co-ordinated manner in the following fields:

A.   Diversity and dialogue

The European Ministers responsible for Cultural Affairs intend to preserve the balance which must exist between the safeguarding of cultural diversity and the necessary social cohesion within the various states. The aim is to create and maintain harmonious relations between all groups in society, in the interests of all its members, independently of their culture, ways of life and cultural practices. Respect for cultural diversity and intercultural dialogue as well as of equal opportunity are vital elements of conflict prevention within the framework of a democratic cultural policy.

Aware of the rich nature of cultural diversity in Europe both within and between Member States, the Ministers responsible for Cultural Affairs intend to concentrate on encouraging dialogue as one of the bases for conflict prevention. Accordingly, they agree to seek inspiration in the values upheld by the Council of Europe that offer scope for a range of converging measures capable of generating strong synergies.

1.   Cultural diversity

The European Ministers responsible for Cultural Affairs, with respect for the rules of subsidiarity and national priorities, and encouraging their other Ministerial colleagues to develop intercultural dialogue within the exercise of their competences, express their commitment to:

1.1. ensure the free expression of different forms of artistic, cultural, social, religious and philosophical practice adopted by individuals or specific cultural groups, provided that these individuals or groups abide by the fundamental principles upheld by the Council of Europe, in accordance with the introduction to the present Declaration;

1.2. support cultural and intercultural policies and practices allowing cultural identities to flourish and reach out to other communities;

1.3. protect, according to the means at their disposal, tangible and intangible heritage in all its components;

1.4. condemn all forms of violent and forced assimilation and encourage in all States the creation of the conditions necessary for the development of societies open to cultural diversity

2.   Intercultural dialogue

The European Ministers responsible for Cultural Affairs, with respect for the rules of subsidiarity and national priorities, and encouraging their other Ministerial colleagues to develop intercultural dialogue within the exercise of their competences, concur to:

2.1. contribute, in full respect of human rights and with particular focus on the local and regional level, to the creation or development of tolerant and equitable relations between States as well as amongst culturally diverse groups settled in the territory of their state;

2.2. endeavour to set up or develop, in their states, actions conducive to intercultural dialogue;

2.3. encourage, at local and regional level, participation in intercultural dialogue in the spirit of cultural citizenship and leading up to cultural democracy;

2.4 create a public space for dialogue and cultural citizenship, allowing for the expression of disagreement, which is not only part of the democratic process but also its guarantee.

B.   Governance and intersectoral co-operation

The European Ministers responsible for Cultural Affairs consider that it is necessary to promote the cultural dimension of democratic citizenship and to foster good governance in cultural policy in association with all actors, relying on intersectoral co-operation and on the dissemination of conflict preventing exemplary practices.

3.   Good governance in cultural policy

The European Ministers responsible for Cultural Affairs, with respect for the rules of subsidiarity and national priorities, and encouraging their other Ministerial colleagues to develop intercultural dialogue within the exercise of their competences, are united in their common goal to:

3.1 consider cultural diversity as a contributor to individual and collective human capital, in the light of sustainable development;

3.2 consider the possibilities of enhancing the intercultural dimension of societies through co-operation, between governmental institutions, the private sector and civil society in order to achieve an interactive reflection;

3.3 acknowledge the importance of the principle of subsidiarity in the framework of the cultural governance of diversity as a principle fostering the empowerment of actors of civil society;

4.   Intersectoral co-operation and exemplary conflict prevention practices

The European Ministers responsible for Cultural Affairs, with respect for the rules of subsidiarity and national priorities, and encouraging their other Ministerial colleagues to develop intercultural dialogue within the exercise of their competences, express their determination to:

4.1. promote, with their ministerial colleagues responsible for other public policies, the setting up of intersectoral public policies which foster intercultural dialogue;

4.2. consider the development of knowledge of history, cultures, arts and religions from school age onwards to be of central importance;

4.3. encourage, through cooperation with the ministerial authorities directly competent for matters of education in the different States, the inclusion in school curricula of teaching on historical and contemporary mutual influence between cultures and civilisations, phenomena of cultural cross-fertilisation, in collaboration with representatives of the different components of cultural diversity, including religious diversity, when appropriate and possible;

4.4. contribute to the development of intercultural dialogue by encouraging, whenever possible, actions intended to bring together the different cultural groups through intercultural events and practices, aimed at all age groups and all socio-cultural groups, within programmes implemented by cultural institutions responsible for fine arts, theatre, literary expressions, etc.

*
* *

In conclusion, the European Ministers responsible for Cultural Affairs agree to share their experience in relation to policies and programmes favouring intercultural dialogue or conflict prevention, particularly in the form of an exchange of good practices.

Appendix
Definitions, principles and methods

For the purpose of the present Declaration, the following definitions are applicable:

- Conflict: for the purpose of this text, the term "conflict" covers forms of - real or masked- disagreement giving rise to resentment and violent behaviour or even injustice which may culminate, at their most exacerbated stage, in destructive and uncontrolled violence. Conflict may be the result of discrimination due to non-recognition of cultural diversity and democratic openness. Conflicts arise for complex and multiple reasons, and their cultural dimension may be the consequence of various causes, including political, economic and social ones. The text proposes actions to promote the management and control of conflicts within European societies characterised by cultural diversity (in all the components mentioned in the Introduction to the Declaration) and post-conflict reconciliation;

- intercultural dialogue: this term defines tools used to promote and protect the concept of cultural democracy, and encompasses the tangible and intangible elements likely to foster all forms of cultural diversity, manifesting themselves in multiple identities whether individual or collective, in transformations and in new forms of cultural expression. Intercultural dialogue must extend to every possible component of culture, without exception, whether these be cultural in the strict sense or political, economic, social, philosophical, or religious. In this context, for instance, inter-faith and interreligious dialogue must be viewed in terms of its cultural and social implications versus the public sphere;

- cultural diversity: "cultural diversity is expressed in the co-existence and exchange of culturally different practices and in the provision and consumption of culturally different services and products", hence the need to pay attention to differences between and within cultural groups.[1] Cultural diversity should go beyond the "majority/minority" dichotomy and integrate the complementarity between the "universal" and the "singular" so that intercultural dialogue is experienced in a flexible, dynamic and open way. In all its dimensions, cultural diversity gives rise to the enrichment of individuals and groups, and produces not only new forms of social relationships, fuelled by migration and strengthened by exchange processes, but also new forms of multicultural identity. Hence, cultural differences should neither result in a retreat into identity or community, nor justify a policy of forced assimilation, due to a will of domination, as both processes may lead to conflicts. On the contrary, cultural diversity can bring about a

---

1 This definition comes from the Council of Europe Declaration on Cultural Diversity adopted by the Committee of Ministers on 7 December 2000.

strengthening of peace through knowledge, recognition and development of all cultures, including those originating in or existing in Europe, or arriving from geographical areas outside Europe.

* * *

To familiarise readers with the thinking behind the Declaration, the principles and methods on which the concepts are built are explained as follows:

1. Cultural diversity

Principle: It is necessary to distinguish two dimensions within cultural diversity: intra-state diversity which refers to the respect of cultural rights, tolerance, political and cultural pluralism and the ability to accept otherness, and the inter-state dimension of diversity which identifies itself with the principle of equivalence between cultures. The model of an intercultural society is based on the principle of equality between cultures, the value of cultural heterogeneity as well as the constructive dimension of dialogue and of peace. Hence, elements of difference and division must not be viewed as harmful and inimical to the creation of a collective plan requiring differences to be taken into account and otherness to be respected. Cultural diversity is synonymous with exchange and makes it possible to combat the autarky which leads to isolation and xenophobia.

Method: this principle cannot be applied exclusively in terms of "majority" or "minority", for this pattern singles out cultures and communities, and categorises and stigmatises them in a static position, to the point at which social behaviour and cultural stereotypes are assumed on the basis of groups' respective status. In contrast, an effort should be made to seek multiple ways of expressing diversity, and to raise citizens' awareness of the richness of diversity, the more so that globalisation of exchanges can only be conceived of with due respect for diversity.

2. Intercultural dialogue

Principle: intercultural dialogue must be encouraged and fostered. It necessarily comes within the framework of the principles of freedom of thought, of conscience, of religion, of expression, of assembly and of association defined in Articles 9, 10, 11 and 14 of the Convention for the Protection of Human Rights and Fundamental Freedoms, and contributes to the fundamental objective of social cohesion.

Method: the application of this principle cannot be limited to dialogue about convergence; it should include dialogue about what separates cultures and populations. The two aspects of "similarities" and "differences" must not be regarded as alternatives, but more as the two sides of a single coin which should be explored in order to start a true dialogue and to identify solutions so as to transcend apparent or real antagonisms. Communication, information and media must foster intercultural dialogue and mutual respect.

3. Good governance in cultural policy

Principle: while public cultural policy is an essential means of developing democracy in Europe, it is vital that it should create close links with the private sector, and with the civil society sector (associations, NGOs, etc), which are both involved in and also produce culture. The principle of cultural governance is based on the fact that the political, economic and social spheres have a cultural dimension which must never be ignored or neglected. Nonetheless, it is a role of the Ministers of Cultural Affairs to strike a balance between the public sector, private sector and civil society in the cultural sphere. In this field cooperation at European level is highly advisable.

Method: this principle must be applied with a view to including culture among the factors of good governance, enabling intercultural conflicts to be prevented and cultural diversity to be promoted.

4. Intersectoral co-operation and exemplary conflict prevention practices

Principle: the more cultural diversity is promoted by European government officials, social actors, non-governmental organisations and religious communities promoting intercultural dialogue, in addition to the Ministers responsible for Cultural Affairs, the more effective intersectoral co-operation on conflict prevention will be.

Method: this principle should be applied to encourage the numerous players to commit themselves to interministerial and intersectoral activities and to collect exemplary "good practices", reproducible in multicultural sites and areas.

Recommendations

The European Ministers responsible for Cultural Affairs,

meeting in Opatija (Croatia), from 20–22 October 2003,

aware of the necessity of fully taking into account their new role and new responsibilities to contribute to the creation of conditions favouring the prevention of violent conflict, the management and control of conflicts, and post-conflict reconciliation, while encouraging both cultural diversity and intercultural dialogue,

decide to ensure the follow-up and the evaluation of the concrete forms of implementation of the Declaration on Intercultural Dialogue and Conflict Prevention that they have adopted.

In order to guarantee the implementation of the Declaration on Intercultural Dialogue and Conflict Prevention, the European Ministers responsible for Cultural Affairs, encouraging their other Ministerial colleagues to develop intercultural dialogue within the exercise of their competences,

recommend to the Committee of Ministers of the Council of Europe that the proposals mentioned below be included, as much as possible, in the annual Programme of Activities of the Organisation;

express the wish that these actions be implemented in coordination with those that may be proposed by the Steering Committees responsible for sectors working in conflict prevention and by the Committee of Ministers' "Working Party with the task of examining proposals of the Secretary General on multicultural and inter-religious dialogue" (hereafter GT-Dialogue);

consider particularly that it is necessary to:

1.   request the Steering Committee for Culture (CDCULT) to entrust the follow-up and application of the Declaration on Intercultural Dialogue and Conflict Prevention to a project group, in cooperation, as much as possible, with other Steering Committees and GT-Dialogue as well as with the Parliamentary Assembly and the Congress of Local and Regional Authorities of Europe, and in harmony with the follow-up to the relevant decisions on 'intercultural education' to be adopted by the 21st Session of the Standing Conference of the European Ministers of Education (Athens, 10 to 12 November 2003);

2.   encourage the CDCULT to:

-    pursue, even to prolong or develop, the implementation of the Intercultural Dialogue and Conflict Prevention Project Action Plan 2002-2004, and

-      organise, in a city symbolic of cultural diversity and democracy, an annual Intercultural Forum bringing together researchers, experts, representatives of different forms of cultural diversity, representatives of civil society, cultural players, Culture Ministry officials, in order to closely follow and encourage the different developments of intercultural dialogue;

3.   request that the CDCULT:

a.   examine the possibilities of implementing a flexible system of inventory and evaluation of good practices, within each member State, destined to encourage and facilitate intercultural dialogue, whether they be implemented at the political-administrative level, or by civil society, in Europe or in cooperation with other regions, more specifically with the south of the Mediterranean;

b.   study the means of dissemination of these practices, notably by means of Forums organised within the framework of the Action Plan and the "Compendium" («Cultural policies in Europe: a compendium of basic facts and trends», an on-line information service available at: http://www.culturalpolicies.net.).

High-level meetings of Ministries of the Interior

Third High-level multilateral meeting of the Ministries of the Interior
Warsaw (Poland), 17-18 March 2005
Resolution

1.   Ministers and Heads of Delegations participating in the Third high-level multilateral meeting of the Ministries of the Interior on the fight against terrorism and organised crime to improve security in Europe (Warsaw, Poland, 17-18 March 2005);

2.   Concerned by the threats posed by terrorism and organised crime to the core values on which Europe is based, namely pluralist democracy, the rule of law and the protection of fundamental rights and freedoms;

3.   Appreciating the efforts undertaken by the Council of Europe to fill gaps in the international legal framework against terrorism, and noting that several conventions and recommendations are about to be completed;

4.   Recalling the successful work carried out by the Council of Europe within the field of crime problems, including organised crime, money laundering, cybercrime, corruption and trafficking in human beings;

5.   Underlining the need to fight terrorism and organised crime while ensuring the protection of human rights, and recalling the Guidelines on Human Rights and the Fight against Terrorism (adopted in 2002), the Guidelines on the Protection of Victims in Terrorist Acts (adopted in March 2005) and the Declaration on "Media and Terrorism" (adopted in March 2005);

6.   Noting the importance of the 3rd Summit of the Heads of States and Governments of the Council of Europe, which will be held in Warsaw in May 2005, also in view of the impetus which it will add to the future work of the Council of Europe in the fight against terrorism and organised crime;

7   APPRECIATE the pro-active response of the Council of Europe towards increasing threats and their impact on European societies, such as terrorism, financing of terrorism, money laundering, trafficking in human beings, cybercrime, and corruption;

8.   PLEDGE to co-operate fully with the Council of Europe in a coherent and systematic approach, consisting of the setting of European standards through treaties and recommendations, monitoring compliance by countries with these standards, and building capacities through technical co-operation programmes;

9.   CALL UPON the Committee of Ministers to adopt the following instruments as soon as possible:
   •   the draft Convention on the Prevention of Terrorism

- the draft Convention on laundering, search, seizure and confiscation of proceeds from crime and on the financing of terrorism
- the draft Convention on trafficking in human beings
- the draft Recommendations on Special Investigative Techniques, the Protection of Witnesses and Collaborators of Justice, and on Identity and Travel Documents and Terrorism;

10. PLEDGE to make every effort in their countries to ensure signature, ratification and implementation of these new treaties;

11. REMIND member States of the need to ratify and implement existing United Nations instruments on terrorism;

12. INVITE those States which have not yet done so to become Parties to instruments of the Council of Europe which facilitate measures against terrorism and organised crime, in particular the Amending Protocol to the Convention on the Suppression of Terrorism (ETS 190), the Convention on Cybercrime (ETS 185 and its Protocol), the Conventions on Corruption (ETS 173 and ETS 174) and the 2nd Additional Protocol to the European Convention on Mutual Legal Assistance in Criminal Matters (ETS 182), and CALL UPON member States to implement fully treaties of the Council of Europe which are already in force;

13. CALL for widest possible geographical adherence to the Convention on Cybercrime, given that information and communication technologies are exploited by organised crime and terrorism globally;

14. REQUEST the Council of Europe to continue its work in the field of terrorism, including the development by CODEXTER of country-profiles on counter-terrorism capacities, the follow-up to activities concerning victims of terrorism, monitoring compliance with the treaties, and to strengthen its co-operation with other organisations and institutions active in the field of the fight against terrorism and organised crime, notably the United Nations, OSCE, the European Union and INTERPOL;

15. REQUEST the Council of Europe to ensure that its different bodies contribute as much as possible to the prevention and control of terrorism;

16. SUPPORT the continued preparation of the organised crime situation reports by the Council of Europe, and APPRECIATE that it intends to pay particular attention to the issue of economic crime, also in view of the inadequacy of existing European standards with regard to a rapidly changing phenomenon;

17. UNDERLINE the need for continued monitoring of compliance by Parties with the requirements of treaties related to terrorism, organised crime, corruption, money laundering and other forms of serious crime, in order to enhance the effectiveness of these treaties;

18. INVITE all Parties to fully co-operate with existing monitoring mechanisms on corruption (GRECO) and money laundering (MONEYVAL) and to support the creation of the monitoring mechanisms foreseen under the conventions on trafficking in human beings and terrorism;

19. UNDERLINE the need for comprehensive and integrated training of law enforcement officials involved in measures against organised crime and terrorism, preferably on the basis of common European training standards, and ENCOURAGE Ministries of Interior to develop specific proposals to this effect;

20. CALL UPON the Council of Europe to support the widest possible implementation of relevant European and other international standards through capacity building programmes, in particular in the fields of financing of terrorism, money laundering, trafficking in human beings, corruption and cybercrime;

21. COUNT on the 3rd summit of Heads of State and Government:

-      to support the strengthening of the role of the Council of Europe in the prevention and control of terrorism, organised and other forms of serious crime through standard setting, monitoringand technical co-operation, and

-      to give impetus to the early signature and ratification of the new Council of Europe conventions on terrorism, trafficking in human beings, money laundering and financing of terrorism.

Congress of Local and Regional Authorities of Europe

Resolution 159 (2003)[1]
on tackling terrorism – the role and responsibilities of local authorities

The Congress, bearing in mind the proposal of the Chamber of Local Authorities,

1.   Expresses its satisfaction at the successful organisation by the CLRAE of the Conference on "Tackling terrorism – the role and responsibilities of local authorities", held in Luxembourg, on 20 and 21 September 2002, during the Grand Duchy of Luxembourg's presidency of the Committee of Ministers of the Council of Europe;

2.   Notes that the conference was attended by 250 participants from twenty-seven countries;

3.   Wishes to acknowledge the full support, in the organisation and conduct of the Conference, of the Luxembourg Ministry of Foreign Affairs and the Union of Luxembourg Towns and Municipalities (Syvicol);

4.   Recalling that the general theme on "Tackling terrorism – the role and responsibilities of local authorities", was subdivided into four further specific themes, namely:

   a.   local authorities, organised crime and terrorism;

   b.   protection of industrial plants and public places;

   c.   the role of local authorities in promoting dialogue between cultures, ethnic groups and religions;

   d.   civil defence and crisis management; all of which were illustrated by case studies from a wide range of the forty-four member countries of the Council of Europe;

5.   Wishes to thank the Luxembourg authorities and the CLRAE for having designed and organised the conference;

6.   Reiterates its horror at the loss of life caused by the terrorist attacks of 11 September 2001, and its belief that terrorist threats are now a global problem requiring concerted and determined international action and responses;

7.   Considers that local and regional authorities, alongside national governments and international organisations and agencies, have a clear

---

[1]   Debated and approved by the Chamber of Local Authorities on 21 May 2003 and adopted by the Standing Committee of the Congress on 22 May 2003 (see Document CPL (10) 5, draft resolution presented by Mrs L. Laurelli and Mr V. Rogov, rapporteurs).

responsibility to protect their citizens against terrorist attacks and threats to a democratic way of life;

8. Deplores the high number of victims of terrorist crime in recent years, and the fact that local authorities in Europe have been faced with atrocities such as attacks on – and even the murder of – local councillors;

9. Convinced that terrorism as a mechanism for change has not always been as universally condemned in Europe as it should have been;

10. Convinced that while terrorism did not begin on 11 September 2001, it is now more dangerous and unpredictable than beforehand, bringing in its wake the threat of disorder and instability;

11. Draws attention, in a wider setting, to the changes in the pattern and type of crime arising from political and economic change in Europe – the smuggling of people, arms and raw materials, the organisation of clandestine immigration, an extensive and pervasive drug trade and political corruption – all of which may be considered as a breeding ground for acts of violence and terror;

12. Recalls the series of annual conferences organised by the CLRAE on different aspects of local authorities' work in preventing and dealing with crime, the results of which have now been drawn together into the Council of Europe publication *Urban Crime Prevention – A guide for local authorities*, and notes that the next conference on this subject will be held in Prague from 13 to 15 November 2003;

13. Condemns radical religious fanaticism and the perversion of cultural and regional identities and religious beliefs and structures for the purposes of terrorism and subversion, resulting in death, violence, injury and intimidation, bringing about in the public a sense of insecurity, apprehension and fear;

14. Notes, furthermore, that recent armed conflict, in addition to the death and destruction in the area concerned, and violent images in the media have contributed to the generation of a culture of violence and given rise to the emergence of aggressive male role models;

15. Believes also that the downward spiral of multiple deprivation, often in urban areas – poor housing, a barren monotonous environment, social exclusion, unsatisfactory employment prospects and poor education – is a factor in alienation, a sense of rejection, lack of respect for human dignity and civic unrest;

16. Considers that the absence of cultural dialogue and solidarity between different communities and creeds helps to fuel conditions for violence and conflict;

17. Believes strongly, as a result, that the fight against terrorism has strong public support; that it requires courage, determination and commitment on the part of those holding public office; and that it is a political and public priority requiring constant and extensive vigilance, co-ordination between a range of partners, effective legislation against violence and a determined and proactive judicial and political approach to racial and religious intolerance and extremism;

18. Wishes for the affirmation of autonomous and unitary European policies on the world scene in order to strengthen the combating of terrorism and to overcome current differences between European states;

19. Believes that, despite continuing threats from terrorist networks, it is important to maintain a sense of perspective and proportion, and that most people live in peace with their neighbours, follow their religion without restriction, respect the law of the land in which they live and have no desire to overthrow its governments;

20. Consequently, considers that the protection of human rights and civic liberties should be seen as an integral part of the struggle against terrorism, not as an obstacle to it; that the fundamental values of human rights and dignity must not be sacrificed in the combat against terrorism; and that anti-terrorism measures should be reasonable, proportionate and non-discriminatory; that the Council of Europe *Guidelines on human rights and the fight against terrorism* be used as a benchmark in this respect;

21. It is therefore essential that care be taken to avoid discriminatory legislation; arbitrary prolonged detention sometimes without trial; the definition of certain peaceful activities as terrorism; unnecessary increased surveillance powers; and erosion of rights at trials;

22. Welcomes the recent work of the Council of Europe on combating terrorism, such as the amendments to the European Convention on the Suppression of Terrorism, the publication of the *Guidelines on human rights and the fight against terrorism* and the constant review of measures taken by the Multi-Disciplinary Group on Terrorism;

23. As a consequence of the above, asks local authorities in Europe to:

    a.   devise strong and clear policies to:

        i.   foster social cohesion and eradicate social exclusion;

        ii.   promote tolerance through educational and cultural programmes;

        iii. ensure respect for cultural diversity and the peaceful coexistence of different cultures, minorities and communities; and

iv.   prevent residential or educational segregation;

b.   seek to address in an equitable manner social, political and economic problems in their populations and ensure fair and equal access to public utilities and educational and employment opportunities;

c.   encourage and promote regular dialogue between different religious faiths, in other words between their leaders, institutions and communities, ensuring that equal conditions exist for the practice of each faith, and recall in this context the debates of the hearing on intercultural and interfaith dialogue held during the spring session of the Chamber of Local Authorities;

d.   remain vigilant and, in particular, take all necessary steps to protect people in places where they gather and in partnership with specialised agencies and governments, to protect major civil and industrial and nuclear installations;

e.   fully inform the public about all threats and risks, planned contingency measures and subsequent crisis management, using up-to-date information technology, including the Internet;

f.   take all necessary steps to ensure the co-ordination of emergency services, ensuring that:

   i.   the chain of command, accountability and responsibilities are clearly defined;

   ii.   there is a back-up supply of basic services, communications and infrastructure which can be used in the event of a crisis; and

   iii.   that adequate training exercises and response simulations are organised in advance;

24. In respect of the CLRAE itself, to:

a.   ensure that the CLRAE continues to be fully involved with the Council of Europe's Integrated Project on responses to violence in everyday life in a democratic society, and that the results of the Conference on "Tackling terrorism – the role and responsibilities of local authorities", held in Luxembourg, are incorporated into the work of the project;

b.   identify particular aspects of the Luxembourg Conference and the current debate which may be further developed at future CLRAE conferences, particularly that on Local Authorities and Crime Prevention, to be held in Prague in 2003;

c. give maximum publicity to the recent publication *Urban Crime Prevention – A guide for local authorities* and organise its translation into a wide range of languages of Council of Europe member countries;

d. co-operate fully with the work of the Parliamentary Assembly of the Council of Europe towards the establishment of a European observatory for urban safety;

e. consider the preparation of a manual or guide to help local authorities confront terrorism;

f. encourage the strengthening of international co-operation between networks of local authorities in confronting terrorism.

European Commission against Racism and Intolerance (ECRI)

European Commission against Racism and Intolerance General Policy Recommendation No. 8 on combating racism while fighting terrorism (2004)

Adopted by ECRI on 17 March 2004

The European Commission against Racism and Intolerance:

Having regard to the European Convention on Human Rights, and in particular to its Article 14;

Having regard to Protocol N° 12 to the European Convention on Human Rights;

Having regard to the International Covenant on Civil and Political Rights, and in particular to its Articles 2, 4 (1), 20 (2) and 26;

Having regard to the Convention relating to the Status of Refugees and the Protocol relating to the Status of Refugees;

Having regard to the Guidelines of the Committee of Ministers of the Council of Europe on human rights and the fight against terrorism;

Recalling the Declaration adopted by ECRI at its 26th plenary meeting (Strasbourg 11-14 December 2001);

Recalling ECRI General Policy Recommendation No. 7 on national legislation to combat racism and racial discrimination and ECRI General Policy Recommendation No. 5 on combating intolerance and discrimination against Muslims;

Recalling the Convention on cybercrime and its additional Protocol concerning the criminalisation of acts of a racist and xenophobic nature committed through computer systems as well as ECRI General Policy Recommendation N° 6 on combating the dissemination of racist, xenophobic and antisemitic material via the Internet;

Recalling the European Convention on the Suppression of Terrorism, the Protocol amending the European Convention on the Suppression of Terrorism and other international instruments against terrorism, notably those adopted in the framework of the United Nations;

Firmly condemning terrorism, which is an extreme form of intolerance;

Stressing that terrorism is incompatible with and threatens the values of freedom, democracy, justice, the rule of law and human rights, particularly the right to life;

Considering that it is therefore the duty of the State to fight against terrorism;

Stressing that the response to the threat of terrorism should not itself encroach upon the very values of freedom, democracy, justice, the rule of law, human rights and humanitarian law that it aims to safeguard, nor should it in any way weaken the protection and promotion of these values;

Stressing in particular that the fight against terrorism should not become a pretext under which racism, racial discrimination and intolerance are allowed to flourish;

Stressing in this respect the responsibility of the State not only to abstain from actions directly or indirectly conducive to racism, racial discrimination and intolerance, but also to ensure a firm reaction of public institutions, including both preventive and repressive measures, to cases where racism, racial discrimination and intolerance result from the actions of individuals and organisations;

Noting that the fight against terrorism engaged by the member States of the Council of Europe since the events of 11 September 2001 has in some cases resulted in the adoption of directly or indirectly discriminatory legislation or regulations, notably on grounds of nationality, national or ethnic origin and religion and, more often, in discriminatory practices by public authorities;

Noting that terrorist acts, and, in some cases, the fight against terrorism have also resulted in increased levels of racist prejudice and racial discrimination by individuals and organisations;

Stressing in this context the particular responsibility of political parties, opinion leaders and the media not to resort to racist or racially discriminatory activities or expressions;

Noting that, as a result of the fight against terrorism engaged since the events of 11 September 2001, certain groups of persons, notably Arabs, Jews, Muslims, certain asylum seekers, refugees and immigrants, certain visible minorities and persons perceived as belonging to such groups, have become particularly vulnerable to racism and/or to racial discrimination across many fields of public life including education, employment, housing, access to goods and services, access to public places and freedom of movement;

Noting the increasing difficulties experienced by asylum seekers in accessing the asylum procedures of the member States of the Council of Europe and the progressive erosion of refugee protection as a result of restrictive legal measures and practices connected with the fight against terrorism;

Stressing the responsibility of the member States of the Council of Europe to ensure that the fight against terrorism does not have a negative impact on any minority group;

Recalling the pressing need for States to favour integration of their diverse populations as a mutual process that can help to prevent the racist or racially discriminatory response of society to the climate generated by the fight against terrorism;

Convinced that dialogue, including on culture and religion, between the different segments of society, as well as education in diversity contribute to combating racism while fighting terrorism;

Convinced that thorough respect of human rights, including the right to be free from racism and racial discrimination, can prevent situations in which terrorism may gain ground;

Recommends to the governments of member States:

-    to take all adequate measures, especially through international co-operation, to fight against terrorism as an extreme form of intolerance in full conformity with international human rights law, and to support the victims of terrorism and to show solidarity towards the States that are targets of terrorism;

-    to review legislation and regulations adopted in connection with the fight against terrorism to ensure that these do not discriminate directly or indirectly against persons or groups of persons, notably on grounds of "race", colour, language, religion, nationality or national or ethnic origin, and to abrogate any such discriminatory legislation;

-    to refrain from adopting new legislation and regulations in connection with the fight against terrorism that discriminate directly or indirectly against persons or groups of persons, notably on grounds of "race", colour, language, religion, nationality or national or ethnic origin;

-    to ensure that legislation and regulations, including legislation and regulations adopted in connection with the fight against terrorism, are implemented at national and local levels in a manner that does not discriminate against persons or groups of persons, notably on grounds of actual or supposed "race", colour, language, religion, nationality, national or ethnic origin;

-    to pay particular attention to guaranteeing in a non discriminatory way the freedoms of association, expression, religion and movement and to ensuring that no discrimination ensues from legislation and regulations - or their implementation - notably governing the following areas:

- checks carried out by law enforcement officials within the countries and by border control personnel
- administrative and pre-trial detention
- conditions of detention
- fair trial, criminal procedure
- protection of personal data
- protection of private and family life
- expulsion, extradition, deportation and the principle of *non-refoulement*
- issuing of visas
- residence and work permits and family reunification
- acquisition and revocation of citizenship;

-       to ensure that their national legislation expressly includes the right not to be subject to racial discrimination among the rights from which no derogation may be made even in time of emergency;

-       to ensure that the right to seek asylum and the principle of *non-refoulement* are thoroughly respected in all cases and without discrimination, notably on grounds of country of origin;

-       to pay particular attention in this respect to the need to ensure access to the asylum procedure and a fair mechanism for the examination of the claims that safeguards basic procedural rights;

-       to ensure that adequate national legislation is in force to combat racism and racial discrimination and that it is effectively implemented, especially in the fields of education, employment, housing, access to goods and services, access to public places and freedom of movement;

-       to ensure that adequate national legislation is in force to combat racially motivated crimes, racist expression and racist organisations and that it is effectively implemented;

-       to draw inspiration, in the context of ensuring that legislation in the areas mentioned above is adequate, from ECRI General Policy Recommendation No.7 on national legislation to combat racism and racial discrimination;

-       to ensure that relevant national legislation applies also to racist offences committed via the Internet and to prosecute those responsible for these kinds of offences;

-       to ensure the existence and functioning of an independent specialised body to combat racism and racial discrimination competent, *inter alia*, in assisting victims in bringing complaints of racism and racial discrimination that may arise as a result of the fight against terrorism;

-      to encourage debate within the media profession on the image that they convey of minority groups in connection with the fight against terrorism and on the particular responsibility of the media professions, in this connection, to avoid perpetuating prejudices and spreading biased information;

-      to support the positive role the media can play in promoting mutual respect and countering racist stereotypes and prejudices;

-      to encourage integration of their diverse populations as a mutual process and ensure equal rights and opportunities for all individuals;

-      to introduce into the school curricula, at all levels, education in diversity and on the need to combat intolerance, racist stereotypes and prejudices, and raise the awareness of public officials and the general public on these subjects;

-      to support dialogue and promote joint activities, including on culture and religion, among the different segments of society on the local and national levels in order to counter racist stereotypes and prejudices.

Intergovernmental Committees

Extortion under Terrorist Threats: Report prepared by the European Committee on Crime Problems (1986)

This report was prepared by a select committee of experts under the authority of the European Committee on Crime Problems who adopted it at its 34th plenary session.

The Committee of Ministers of the Council of Europe authorised its publication.

I. TERMS OF REFERENCE

The committee's terms of reference are to:

"Examine the problems relating to extortion under terrorist threats."

a. Interpretation

The committee had to interpret its terms of reference. It considered that extortion should be given a wider scope than was usually the case in national legislation, since it does not comprise only offences against property. In the present context, securing something by extortion is the criminals' immediate objective and may take the form either of money being handed over or of a given act being performed-whether actively for example/freeing prisoners) or passively (for example, the authorities do not hinder the free passage of the criminals' accomplices)-or again, of a promise to perform a certain act (for example, improve the conditions in which certain prisoners are held or to refrain from prosecuting a certain person).

The expression *extorsions obtenues* (which in fact appears only in the French version of the terms of reference) is not to be taken in a narrow sense. In the committee's opinion, the problems arising before the planned result is secured, in particular during the phase of "negotiations" should also be considered.

A threat consists in announcing future unlawful harm in the event of the extortion not being secured. It is therefore the means whereby the criminals propose to succeed in their purpose. It may take various forms. It may, for instance, take the form of an act of violence foreshadowing the possibility of other, more serious violence. It may also be implicit and stem from the intimidatory power of the group making the threat. This is the case, for example, where organised groups ask certain categories of people for payment of a fee in exchange for "protection" or of a "revolutionary tax" to further the organisation's particular aims.

It should be pointed out that the person who suffers or may suffer from the carrying out of the threat is not necessarily the one to whom the threat is made. In other words, in this kind of manoeuvre the criminals commonly threaten to inflict a form of harm principally affecting X if they do not succeed in extorting what they want from Y. This is the case where a person is subjected to threats for the sole purpose of extorting something from the state.

The terms of reference define the type of threat on which the committee's views are sought: they must be terrorist threats. The committee noted that the term "terrorist" was somewhat ambiguous. It is often used in connection with acts whose aim, in the minds of those who commit them, is political. Reference to the political nature of the motive, however, introduces a number of subjective elements, on the definition of which lawyers have hitherto been unable to reach agreement.

The committee accordingly dropped this subjective concept in favour of a more objective interpretation. It took the view that threats are to be regarded as terrorist threats if they are made by an organised group and if the threatened harm is particularly serious, especially where:

-    it is to the life, physical integrity or freedom of individuals, particularly individuals unconnected with the motives prompting it; or

-    it is against property and creates a collective danger for persons; or

-    its carrying out involves the use of cruel or treacherous means.

The committee based this interpretation notably on Recommendation No. R (82) 1 of the Committee of Ministers to member states concerning international co-operation in the prosecution and punishment of acts of terrorism. It also considered that the acts referred to by Articles 1 and 2 of the European Convention on the Suppression of Terrorism are covered by this report.

b.   Purpose

The situations covered by the terms of reference as interpreted by the committee raise countless problems. It is impossible to give a single uniformly applicable reply to the problems, because each situation has its own special features and the problems consequently arise in their own particular way. The committee also noted that some of the measures envisaged in Recommendation No. R (82) 14 on measures to be taken in cases of kidnappings followed by a ransom demand are also applicable in cases of extortion. In the time available to it the committee was accordingly not able to produce a sufficient number of consistent proposals to warrant a recommendation.

This report merely contains general guidelines which may be useful to governments when they are framing their crime policies in this area.

II. THE BASIC PROBLEM: THE STATE'S RESPONSE

When threats such as those that have been described are made, the state-or, more specifically, those who are required in such circumstances to act on behalf of and with the powers of the state-is faced with an exceptional situation which challenges the authority of the state, the rule of law or the normal functioning of institutions in a democratic society.

Those who find themselves in such an exceptional situation are faced with a dilemma, either to ensure strict enforcement of the law or to disregard it in order to safeguard other interests, such as the lives of threatened persons.

In a democratic state in which by definition the rule of law prevails, the state or its agents cannot in principle give in to such threats or even be a party on any preliminary negotiations which may lead to its giving in. Where it does give in, the law prevails no longer but is governed by circumstances. It has to be acknowledged, however, that there are no fixed rules in this sphere. Every situation needs to be assessed in the light of the circumstances.

Accordingly it seems vain to attempt to sketch a legal framework in which such circumstances ought to be assessed. Suffice it to say that their assessment is a matter, first, for the conscience of the person or persons who may be called upon to decide and, secondly, of balancing the various interests at stake, particularly those to which the law attaches a special value, such as life, freedom, dignity and physical integrity of the person.

In this balancing exercise account must be taken not only of the interests that are immediately threatened but also of those which may be threatened if the objective of the extortion is achieved.

For example, when the authorities of one of the member states had to free prisoners so as to prevent serious terrorist threats from being carried out, the prisoners, once freed, killed other persons.

Another relevant example is that of the "revolutionary tax". It is tempting to think that the state might not have to intervene, since the money involved is but little compared with the lives threatened in order to obtain it. Once the money is in the hands of the terrorists, however, it will be used to finance further terrorist acts, possibly leading to the death of other victims.

It is necessary, lastly, to recall that when the state gives way to terrorist threats, its concerns being confined to the interests that are under immediate threat, it is in danger of weakening its power or even destroying it totally, and so spreading among the population a feeling of unsafely which extremists may exploit in order to come to power.

III. REFERENCES

The Council of Europe has already laid the legal foundations for international co-operation between member states with regard to terrorism in the strict sense. Relevant here are both the European Convention on the Suppression of Terrorism and Recommendation No. R (82) 1 concerning international co-operation in the prosecution and punishment of acts of terrorism.[1,2]

The committee also noted (see above) that some of the measures envisaged in Recommendation No. R (82) 14 would apply equally to extortions under terrorist threats, for example when it is recommended that the governments of member states:

1. set up or reinforce the international machinery needed to co-ordinate the action of the various police authorities and to provide information for the judicial authorities to which cases of terrorist threats are referred;

2. be prepared to deal with such threats, in particular:

    a. by ensuring that the emergency arrangements necessary to safeguard the lives of the victims and so help to resolve the affair can be made by a permanent or ad hoc group comprising representatives of the various authorities concerned;

    b. by providing suitable professional and technical training for the police officers responsible for combating such crimes and the prosecutors and judges to whom such cases are referred;

---

[1] Other Council of Europe initiatives in this field include:

- European Convention on Extradition (1957), with two additional protocols (1975 and 1978);

- European Convention on Mutual Assistance in Criminal Matters (1959), with additional protocol (1978);

- Resolution (74) 3 on international terrorism, adopted by the Committee of Ministers at its 53rd Session (January 1974);

- Declaration on Terrorism, adopted by the Committee of Ministers at its 63rd Session (November 1978),

- Statements by the Committee of Ministers at its 67th (October 1980), 68th (May 1981) and 69th

(November 1981) Sessions;

and, in the case of the Parliamentary Assembly:

- Assembly Recommendations 684 (1972), 703 (1973), 852 (1979) and 916 (1981); and

- Conference on "Defence of democracy against terrorism in Europe-Tasks and problems" (November 1980).

[2] Reference should also be made in this context to Recommendation No. R (80) 10 on measures against the transfer and the safekeeping of funds of criminal origin.

c.	by drawing up operational plans to ensure that the authorities are not caught off their guard by such actions;

d.	by ensuring that the family and relatives of the victims can be advised and assisted by qualified persons;

3.	ensure that their legislation allows the competent judicial authorities before which a case is brought to take account in their decisions of any action by the criminal having caused the crime to miscarry or the victims to be freed.

Lastly, the New York Conventions, one on the Prevention and Punishment of Crimes against Internationally Protected Persons, including Diplomatic Agents (14 December 1973) and the other against the Taking of Hostages (18 December 1979), should in the view of some experts be mentioned as being useful instruments in the fight against terrorist threats.

Three points deserve, however, special mention, although they are general ones:

-	legislation,

-	the role of the media,

-	international co-operation.

## IV.	LEGISLATION

a.	Threats as well as extortions in general-and more particularly, those being discussed in this report-ought to be covered by specific legislation and should be made special offences. Their seriousness and special nature justify a legal framework specific to them. This must take account of the various ways in which threats can be made and transmitted, in particular the various technical means used (writing, tape recording, published message or any other means that technology provides or will provide).

In particular it must be ensured that legislation covers, first, not merely extortion of money but also the other forms of extortion mentioned above, and, secondly, threats made to the state or its agents as such.

b.	The committee acknowledged that eavesdropping on electronically transmitted messages is a particularly effective means of defeating threats and preventing threatened harm from occurring[3]. Nevertheless, it considers it to be indispensable that such eavesdropping be strictly governed by law in a

---

[3]	On telephone tapping and the recording of telecommunications in some Council of Europe member states, see the Legislative Dossier, No. 2, published by the Directorate of Legal Affairs of the Council of Europe.

manner compatible with the provisions of the Convention for the Protection of Human Rights and Fundamental Freedoms, particularly Article 8 thereof.[4]

In this connection it is also important to dispose of the problems raised by international letters of request to carry out such eavesdropping. The committee will not be required to study these problems, as the PC-R-OC Committee has already done so.

V. MEDIA

The mass media often have an important part to play in this kind of affair, either as an intermediary between the terrorists and those against whom they are trying to bring pressure to bear or as a means whereby the terrorists hope to gain publicity for what they are doing or for their ultimate goals, or again because the media are themselves the victims of extortion in that they are being compelled to publish - or not to publish - a prepared communiqué or other information.

---

[4] It is appropriate here to recall certain passages from the relevant case-law of the European Court of Human Rights, in particular from the Klass and the Malone cases.

In its judgment in the Klass case, the Court ruled that:

"Democratic societies nowadays find themselves threatened by highly sophisticated forms of espionage and by terrorism, with the result that the state must be able, in order effectively to counter such threats, to undertake the secret surveillance of subversive elements operating within its jurisdiction. The Court has therefore to accept that the existence of some legislation granting powers of secret surveillance

over the mail, post and telecommunications is, under exceptional conditions, necessary in a democratic society in the interests of national security and/or for the prevention of disorder or crime" (paragraph 48).

"Nevertheless, the Court stresses that this does not mean that the Contracting States enjoy an unlimited discretion to subject persons within their jurisdiction to secret surveillance. The Court, being aware of the danger such a law poses of undermining or even destroying democracy on the ground of defending it, affirms that the Contracting States may not, in the name of the struggle against espionage and terrorism, adopt whatever measures they deem appropriate" (paragraph 49).

In the Malone case, the Court ruled similarly, adding that:

"Since the implementation in practice of measures of secret surveillance of communications is not open to scrutiny by the individuals concerned or the public at large, it would be contrary to the rule of law for the legal discretion granted to the executive to be expressed in terms of an unfettered power. Consequently, the law must indicate the scope of any such discretion conferred on the competent authorities and the manner of its exercise with sufficient clarity, having regard to the legitimate aim of the measure in question, to give the individual adequate protection against arbitrary interference" (paragraph 68).

"However, the exercise of such powers, because of its inherent secrecy, carries with it a danger of abuse of a kind that is potentially easy in individual cases and could have harmful consequences for democratic society as a whole. This being so, the resultant interference can only be regarded as 'necessary in a democratic society' if the particular system of secret surveillance adopted contains adequate guarantees against abuse" (paragraph 81).

Freedom of expression is a fundamental right in our democratic societies. Even the most serious crimes cannot justify restrictions other than those provided for in the Convention for the Protection of Human Rights and Fundamental Freedoms. It is mainly exercised through the mass media, whose decision-makers normally agree to abide voluntarily by the rules of professional ethics.

Any intervention by the public authorities might upset an often fragile equilibrium. For this reason the committee considers that in relations between the authorities and the media, even in cases as serious as those discussed in this report, any attempt to formalise relations or to bring them within a legal framework is likely to be damaging. Such relations must be established in a climate of trust, particularly during the period of crisis which occurs in such situations. Obviously such a climate has to be fostered and permanently maintained so that benefit may be had from it as soon as a crisis breaks out.[5]

Two limits on the freedom of the media should be pointed out here, however.

The first is that the media must not hamper or harm the authorities' actions. The hostage-taking at the Iranian Embassy in London is a good example of that. While the security forces were preparing to storm the building to free the hostages, television cameras transmitted live pictures so that the terrorists inside the embassy had only to watch the transmission on their television screen to be fully informed about everything that was going on outside and were therefore in a position to prepare their response.

The second limit forbids the media to go further than the right to information demands-for example, by propagating views which the average reader would interpret as an apology for, or incitement to, criminal violence, cruel or inhuman acts, racial discrimination or threats creating alarm in the public (such as threats of murder, looting, fire, etc.).

It has to be acknowledged that it is in certain instances difficult to draw a line between carrying out the duty to inform, on the one hand, and vindication, incitement or even complicity, on the other. It appears that this line should be drawn both by the law and by professional ethics. But, it is better to rely in the first place on informal relations of mutual trust between the authorities and the media, based on welt-established professional ethics, to ensure in each individual case that the mark is not overstepped.

It should be stressed too that the media can take positive steps in this connection. Thus in Italy, at the time of the kidnapping of Judge D'Urso by terrorists, most of the media not only refused to accede to the terrorists' request to publish certain statements, but on their own initiative also suspended the diffusion of any information about the affair.

---

[5] See item 5 in Recommendation No. R (82) 14 mentioned above.

VI. INTERNATIONAL CO-OPERATION

Terrorist threats often have an international dimension, either because they are directed at a state or a state's interests or nationals and are made on the territory of another state or because acts are carried out in different states. In such cases, the problems mentioned above arise in respect of two or more states.

In order that these situations may be dealt with more effectively, it is desirable that there should be the closest and most frequent contacts possible between the authorities of member states. Some experts think that these contacts might be envisaged as part of arrangements for the rapid setting up, in the event of a crisis, of an ad hoc International team of representatives of the authorities concerned in each of the states involved with the task of preparing the decisions to be taken in each state with a view to helping to resolve the affair.

Further publications

"*Apologie du terrorisme*" and "Incitement to terrorism" (2004)
English edition only

The fight against terrorism must never lead to a curtailing of the values and freedoms terrorists intend to destroy: the rule of law and freedom of thought and expression must never be sacrificed in this struggle.

This report analyses the situation in member and observer States of the Council of Europe and their different legal approaches to the phenomenon of the public expression of praise, justification and other forms of support for terrorism and terrorists, referred to in this publication as "apologie du terrorisme" and "incitement to terrorism".

ISBN: 92-871-5468-6, € 19 / US$ 29

Terrorism: special investigation techniques (2005)
English edition only

In order to combat terrorism and serious crime, law enforcement authorities have had to adapt their investigative means and develop special investigation techniques. Since there is a risk that they may infringe individual rights, special investigation techniques must be subject to control.

This publication contains an analytical report, which examines special investigation techniques in relation to law enforcement and prosecution, the control of their implementation, human rights and international co-operation and also contains a survey of national practice.

ISBN: 92-871-5655-7, € 39 / US$ 59

Human rights and the fight against terrorism –
The Council of Europe Guidelines (2005)

The Council of Europe believes that an effective fight against terrorism fully respecting human rights is possible.

This publication contains the Guidelines on Human Rights and the fight against terrorism, the first international instrument in this area, and the Guidelines on the protection of victims of terrorist acts, together with the reference and supporting texts and relevant case-law of the European Court of Human Rights.

ISBN:92-871-5694-8, € 8 / US$ 12

Order from http://book.coe.int or from specialised bookshops

Sales agents for publications of the Council of Europe
Agents de vente des publications du Conseil de l'Europe

BELGIUM/BELGIQUE
La Librairie européenne SA
50, avenue A. Jonnart
B-1200 BRUXELLES 20
Tel.: (32) 2 734 0281
Fax: (32) 2 735 0860
E-mail: info@libeurop.be
http://www.libeurop.be

Jean de Lannoy
202, avenue du Roi
B-1190 BRUXELLES
Tel.: (32) 2 538 4308
Fax: (32) 2 538 0841
E-mail: jean.de.lannoy@euronet.be
http://www.jean-de-lannoy.be

CANADA
Renouf Publishing Company Limited
5369 Chemin Canotek Road
CDN-OTTAWA, Ontario, K1J 9J3
Tel.: (1) 613 745 2665
Fax: (1) 613 745 7660
E-mail: order.dept@renoufbooks.com
http://www.renoufbooks.com

CZECH REP./RÉP. TCHÈQUE
Suweco Cz Dovoz Tisku Praha
Ceskomoravska 21
CZ-18021 PRAHA 9
Tel.: (420) 2 660 35 364
Fax: (420) 2 683 30 42
E-mail: import@suweco.cz

DENMARK/DANEMARK
GAD Direct
Fiolstaede 31-33
DK-1171 KOBENHAVN K
Tel.: (45) 33 13 72 33
Fax: (45) 33 12 54 94
E-mail: info@gaddirect.dk

FINLAND/FINLANDE
Akateeminen Kirjakauppa
Keskuskatu 1, PO Box 218
FIN-00381 HELSINKI
Tel.: (358) 9 121 41
Fax: (358) 9 121 4450
E-mail: akatilaus@stockmann.fi
http://www.akatilaus.akateeminen.com

GERMANY/ALLEMAGNE
AUSTRIA/AUTRICHE
UNO Verlag
August Bebel Allee 6
D-53175 BONN
Tel.: (49) 2 28 94 90 20
Fax: (49) 2 28 94 90 222
E-mail: bestellung@uno-verlag.de
http://www.uno-verlag.de

GREECE/GRÈCE
Librairie Kauffmann
Mavrokordatou 9
GR-ATHINAI 106 78
Tel.: (30) 1 38 29 283
Fax: (30) 1 38 33 967
E-mail: ord@otenet.gr

HUNGARY/HONGRIE
Euro Info Service
Hungexpo Europa Kozpont ter 1
H-1101 BUDAPEST
Tel.: (361) 264 8270
Fax: (361) 264 8271
E-mail: euroinfo@euroinfo.hu
http://www.euroinfo.hu

ITALY/ITALIE
Libreria Commissionaria Sansoni
Via Duca di Calabria 1/1, CP 552
I-50125 FIRENZE
Tel.: (39) 556 4831
Fax: (39) 556 41257
E-mail: licosa@licosa.com
http://www.licosa.com

NETHERLANDS/PAYS-BAS
De Lindeboom Internationale
Publikaties
PO Box 202, MA de Ruyterstraat 20 A
NL-7480 AE HAAKSBERGEN
Tel.: (31) 53 574 0004
Fax: (31) 53 572 9296
E-mail: lindeboo@worldonline.nl
http://home-1-orldonline.nl/~lindeboo/

NORWAY/NORVÈGE
Akademika, A/S Universitetsbokhandel
PO Box 84, Blindern
N-0314 OSLO
Tel.: (47) 22 85 30 30
Fax: (47) 23 12 24 20

POLAND/POLOGNE
Głowna Księgarnia Naukowa
im. B. Prusa
Krakowskie Przedmiescie 7
PL-00-068 WARSZAWA
Tel.: (48) 29 22 66
Fax: (48) 22 26 64 49
E-mail: inter@internews.com.pl
http://www.internews.com.pl

PORTUGAL
Livraria Portugal
Rua do Carmo, 70
P-1200 LISBOA
Tel.: (351) 13 47 49 82
Fax: (351) 13 47 02 64
E-mail: liv.portugal@mail.telepac.pt

SPAIN/ESPAGNE
Mundi-Prensa Libros SA
Castelló 37
E-28001 MADRID
Tel.: (34) 914 36 37 00
Fax: (34) 915 75 39 98
E-mail: libreria@mundiprensa.es
http://www.mundiprensa.com

SWITZERLAND/SUISSE
Adeco – Van Diermen
Chemin du Lacuez 41
CH-1807 BLONAY
Tel.: (41) 21 943 26 73
Fax: (41) 21 943 36 05

E-mail: info@adeco.org

UNITED KINGDOM/
ROYAUME-UNI
TSO (formerly HMSO)
51 Nine Elms Lane
GB-LONDON SW8 5DR
Tel.: (44) 207 873 8372
Fax: (44) 207 873 8200
E-mail: customer.services@theso.co.uk
http://www.the-stationery-office.co.uk
http://www.itsofficial.net

UNITED STATES and CANADA/
ÉTATS-UNIS et CANADA
Manhattan Publishing Company
468 Albany Post Road, PO Box 850
CROTON-ON-HUDSON,
NY 10520, USA
Tel.: (1) 914 271 5194
Fax: (1) 914 271 5856
E-mail: Info@manhattanpublishing.com
http://www.manhattanpublishing.com

FRANCE
La Documentation française
(Diffusion/Vente France entière)
124 rue H. Barbusse
93308 Aubervilliers Cedex
Tel.: (33) 01 40 15 70 00
Fax: (33) 01 40 15 68 00
E-mail: vel@ladocfrancaise.gouv.fr
http://www.ladocfrancaise.gouv.fr

Librairie Kléber (Vente Strasbourg)
Palais de l'Europe
F-67075 Strasbourg Cedex
Fax: (33) 03 88 52 91 21
E-mail: librairie.kleber@coe.int

Council of Europe Publishing/Editions du Conseil de l'Europe
F-67075 Strasbourg Cedex
Tel.: (33) 03 88 41 25 81 – Fax: (33) 03 88 41 39 10 – E-mail: publishing@coe.int – Website: http://book.coe.int